GARRINCHA

Ruy Castro is the author of several biographies and collections of quotations. His most recent works include *Bossa Nova: The Story of the Brazilian Music that Seduced the World* and *Rio de Janeiro: Carnival under Fire*. He is currently working on a biography of Carmen Miranda. He lives in Rio de Janeiro.

Also by

*Bossa Nova: The Story of the Brazilian
Music that Seduced the World*

Rio de Janeiro: Carnival under Fire

GARRINCHA

The Triumph and Tragedy of Brazil's Forgotten Footballing Hero

Ruy Castro

Translated from the Portuguese by
Andrew Downie

YELLOW JERSEY PRESS
LONDON

Published by Yellow Jersey Press 2005

2 4 6 8 10 9 7 5 3 1

Copyright © Ruy Castro 1995
Translation copyright © Yellow Jersey Press 2004

First published in Great Britain in 2004 by
Yellow Jersey Press

Yellow Jersey Press
Random House, 20 Vauxhall Bridge Road,
London SW1V 2SA

Random House Australia (Pty) Limited
20 Alfred Street, Milsons Point, Sydney,
New South Wales 2061, Australia

Random House New Zealand Limited
18 Poland Road, Glenfield,
Auckland 10, New Zealand

Random House South Africa (Pty) Limited
Endulini, 5A Jubilee Road, Parktown 2193,
South Africa

The Random House Group Limited Reg. No. 954009
www.randomhouse.co.uk

A CIP catalogue record for this book
is available from the British Library

ISBN 0-224-06433-9

Papers used by Random House are natural, recyclable products made from wood grown
in sustainable forests. The manufacturing processes conform to the environmental
regulations of the country of origin

Printed and bound in Great Britain by
Cox & Wyman Ltd, Reading, Berkshire

Contents

Picture Credits

Note on the Currency

PROVIDING AN ACCURATE PICTURE OF CURRENCY IS DIFFICULT. IN THE past sixty years, Brazil's unit of currency has changed nine times. When Garrincha was first contracted to Botafogo football club in 1953 the currency was the reis. By the time he played his last game in 1982 the currency was the cruzeiro. Today it is the real. It's hard therefore to give a comparable account of Garrincha's earnings in pounds sterling. Throughout the book, Ruy Castro has used the real (the currency at the time the book was originally published in Brazil), with equivalent terms in contemporary US dollars.

Introduction

AT THE START OF 2000, JUST A FEW MONTHS AFTER ARRIVING IN BRAZIL, I went to a party at the British vice-consul's house. Like many parties that take place in Rio de Janeiro it was both a chic and a laid-back affair, much of which took place on a terrace that boasted stunning views of Christ the Redeemer and the lagoon at his feet. It was one of the first real parties I had been to in my new home town and I still had that dazed look of someone who can't quite believe they are living in a city where everything revolves around beer, football and sex.

Halfway through the night I turned around and saw a woman sitting quietly in the corner of the terrace. It was a startling moment. She looked twice the age of anyone else at the party and almost half the size. But it was her face that most surprised me. It looked as if it had been pulled back and stapled to her skull.

When I asked the Brazilians who she was, they all said the same thing, 'That's Elza Soares, Garrincha's lover.'

That description did Soares, famed as a classic beauty, one of the best Brazilian singers of all time and a remarkable character in a country filled with people who are larger than life, a great disservice. But it made it abundantly clear to me where Garrincha stood in the pantheon of Brazilian legends.

I had heard of Garrincha before coming to Brazil but I never knew much about him, largely because he played at a time before the marriage of football and television. I resolved there and then to find out more about the man who could relegate a woman as talented as Soares to his mere consort.

All my Brazilian friends knew of Garrincha and all of them had an amazing anecdote about him but detailed information was hard to find and footage even harder. And then a few months later I was in a bar when I saw someone who could only be Garrincha appear on the screen. He stood by the touchline dressed in the familiar black and white stripes of Botafogo football club with the ball at his feet, his opponent standing opposite him. In a flash he bolted to his right and with the defender in hot pursuit he started to sprint down the wing. Two or three steps later he ran back. He had jumped over the ball and left it behind.

Garrincha stood dead still over the ball for a few seconds and then bolted down the wing again. Once more the defender followed him and once more Garrincha had left the ball exactly where it was. He took two or three quick paces towards the byline and then jauntily jogged back to the ball. He was obviously enjoying himself and the defender was just as obviously bemused and embarrassed.

Garrincha stood with the ball at his feet for a second or two and then darted off down the wing once again, this time with the ball. The defender didn't move a muscle.

I roared with laughter. It was the funniest thing I had seen on a football field since George Best took a slug from a beer can thrown at him by a Rangers fan at Easter Road. I began to understand why Brazilians loved Garrincha so much. Why they called him 'Joy of the People'.

It is no coincidence that Garrincha reminded me of Best, although if I had been born in another continent or another era, the opposite would have been true. When Brits ask me who Garrincha was I usually tell them he was an exaggerated version of Bestie, more Best than Best ever was. They look at me as if I am being ridiculous. How can that be? they ask. Both on and off the field Best's exploits were legendary and he remains perhaps the greatest footballer ever to come from these isles.

The answer is easy. No disrespect to Best, who even when I saw him playing for Hibs in the twilight of his career, was head and shoulders above everyone else on the pitch. But next to Garrincha, his achievements, if that is the word, are strictly second division.

Let me spell it out. Best never played in the World Cup finals, Garrincha went there three times, and twice came home with a winner's medal (the second of which, in Chile in 1962, he is to said have won almost single-handedly). Best may have dated some of the most beautiful women on the planet, but when it comes to womanising he could not compare with Garrincha who fathered 14 children by five different women (and those are just the ones we know about). Sadly, even when it came to drinking, he outdid the great Irishman. Garrincha drank himself into an early grave at the age of 49.

Like Best, Garrincha was beloved not only for his genius with a football but for his frailties without it. Garrincha was the kind of free spirit that people are instinctively drawn to. In a country like Brazil, where at least a third of the people live in poverty, people admire and respect Pelé, an impoverished black man who turned his unparalleled talent with a football into great riches off it, but they identify with Garrincha. As Pelé became more and more famous the gap between who he had been, or at least the perception of who he had been, and who he had become, widened to the point where he ceased to be a mere mortal. Pelé became not only 'the king' but also a deity, at one point even good-naturedly joking that he was better known than God because his fame reached across Asia, where they worshipped Buddha.

Garrincha, on the other hand, rarely went on business trips, he seldom donned a suit and tie and he had neither the inclination nor the aptitude for schmoozing with politicians or captains of industry. He didn't hide out behind the gates of a palatial home and he never lost touch with the friends he had had since childhood.

Moreover, he played football like Brazilians were meant to play football. People who saw Garrincha play at his peak say his exploits often had them doubled over with laughter. He was talented and inspiring but most of all he was fun. Football was a game to him and not much else. As Ruy Castro puts it, perfectly, he was 'the most amateur footballer professional football ever produced'. Garrincha played for the love of the game and if he brought joy to others in doing so – and he won his famous nickname for a very good reason – then great. Anyone who has seen that footage of him bamboozling the defender can see a man in his element.

If that was not enough to endear him to his countrymen and women, then there was also the string of tragedies that seemed to throw themselves at him with all the wrath of a malevolent full-back. Garrincha was born half crippled, he was taken advantage of by club directors, he suffered from alcoholism, he attempted suicide on several occasions, and he killed his mother-in-law in a car crash. And that was only when he was alive. Even after he died, the curse continued. His two Brazilians sons both died in car crashes: Garrinchinha, the boy he had with Soares, perished when he was nine on the same road as his grandmother had decades earlier; and Neném, his son with an earlier girlfriend, died in an accident in Switzerland at the age of 28. Two of the eight daughters he had with his wife Nair were dead from cancer before they were 50.

Such tragedies do not happen to superstars, they happen to ordinary people and when Brazilians saw someone as gifted as Garrincha suffer it was one more reason to see him as one of them. Perversely, the lows were as crucial in creating his legend as were the highs.

Nowhere was that more poignantly evident than when he passed away in 1983. Garrincha died in a Rio hospital but he had demanded to be buried in his home village of Pau Grande and from the moment the fire engine carrying his body left the Maracanã, where thousands of fans, friends, and former players had gathered to pay their respects, it was swept along by a wave of emotion. So many people wanted to go to Pau Grande to attend the funeral that traffic on the Avenida Brasil, the main road leading out of the city, came to a standstill. All along the sides of the bleak, grey highway and on the pedestrian bridges crossing it, weeping fans gathered to watch the cortege go by. The bottleneck was so concentrated on the edge of Pau Grande that some people abandoned their cars and walked into town. It took the fire engine two hours to travel 65 kilometres.

At the funeral itself the scenes were every bit as dramatic. More than 3,000 people fought for one of the 500 seats inside the town's church, forcing hundreds to wait outside. The tension was such that the priest thought it too dangerous to say mass and instead merely blessed the body and let the mourners take it to the town's cemetery, where another 8,000 people had been waiting for hours. Botafogo fans surrounded the plot in a bid to keep fans from other teams out and Garrincha's family never made it to the graveside to see him buried. Even when the coffin finally did make it through the throngs of people it was too big for the grave and more chaos ensued while mourners tried to fit the deluxe coffin into the undersize plot. In short, it was a death entirely in keeping with his life. Colourful, chaotic and perversely entertaining.

Ruy Castro brings alive the incredible events of the life that led so many people to grieve that day. His studious reporting and obvious love for his subject enables him to capture the essence of the man they gathered to honour. Reading it in Portuguese, I at last began to understand the reverence I had sensed in those Brazilians at the party that February night. Without it, I would always have wondered who Garrincha really was. Thanks to this book I know. With this translation you will too.

Andrew Downie, March 2004, Rio de Janeiro

for Heloisa Seixas

CHAPTER 1

1865–1933: The Fulniô Arrow

IT WASN'T EVEN NECESSARY TO TIE THEM UP – AND THIS WAS 1865. They just needed a bit of coaxing. The small group of Indians came out of their hiding place in the forest of the Barriga mountains in Alagoas, a state in north-eastern Brazil, and approached the white men who were waving to them. The Fulniôs knew they should advance with caution. Three hundred years of history had taught them that white men were crooks, liars and more treacherous than snakes. Since arriving in Brazil in 1500, the Portuguese had decimated the Indian population. But some temptations were impossible to resist. And sure enough, when the Indians' curiosity got the better of them, the white men pounced. There and then they were bound to one another, whipped across the back and ordered to march towards civilisation.

In more heroic times, their captors would have chased them through the forest of brazilwood trees, risking the disgrace of being left behind by the Indians' quick-footedness. But by the middle of the nineteenth century it seemed as if the art of the mazy dribble – that jinking run that humiliates the pursuer and leaves him beaten and dejected – had already been lost by Garrincha's great-grandparents. Had it not, they wouldn't have let the region's ranchers and sugar-cane producers tie them by the neck and take them so easily.

1

Theoretically, enslaving Indians was a *démodé* practice in Brazil by 1865. Not to mention forbidden by law: Indians were forced to stay in the government-appointed areas or reservations where they were free to paint their bodies without having to worry about scaring anyone. However, no one was naive enough to believe that the ban on enslaving them was totally respected, especially not by the oligarchs of the country's impoverished north-east. Still, one of the reasons the colonisers preferred black slaves to those seized locally – in addition to the easy profits made in the slave trade – was the belief that the natives were layabouts who were interested only in drinking and sex.

They were right about the drinking and sex. The first Portuguese to arrive in Brazil at the dawn of the sixteenth century were shocked at the naked barbarians who happily indulged in all the sexual deviations then known to man: polygamy, incest, sodomy and homosexuality. And they did indeed produce a highly alcoholic fizzy drink fermented from fruit and the roots of the cassava plant that the men of the tribes drank during the days and nights of festivals.

But when it came to work the Indians were not in the least bit lazy or incompetent. They might not have aced the psychometric tests – had they existed back then – but they were good at what they did. Had the first explores taken advantage of their specialist skills – hunting, fishing, exploring forests, cutting trails, acting as guides and building huts – the young Brazil would have been a tropical picnic and a lot of bloodshed would have been avoided. But the colonisers tried to force them to work the land, a pursuit the Indian warriors understandably found boring. And if that were not enough, the Jesuits insisted on clothing them, teaching them how to read and write, and saving their souls, without first asking their souls if they wanted to be saved. Naturally, there were uprisings, massacres and wars, and the Indians came off worse.

A few hundred years later, at the start of the nineteenth century, there were more Indians in a Pedro Américo painting than in the whole of Brazil. Only a few tribes were available for the census and almost all of them were confined to reservations, close to the cities and the ranches of the white people and far from their homes in the forest. But even in the reservations the Indians got no peace. All they had to do was take a step outside the boundary, to catch a deer or kill a *tatupeba* for lunch, and the white men would move in to slaughter or banish them. Some of the Indians fled to escape the massacre. But as soon as they were spotted wandering in the forest they were captured again. Some were forced to join the circus as freaks, and the young females were sold to randy men or, more or less as today, straight into prostitution.

During the 49 years under Dom Pedro II that led to Brazil's transition to a republic in 1889, the end of slavery from Africa began to seem inevitable and the price of Indians rose. They were rounded up again. In the north-east they were put to work cutting sugar cane, preparing firewood on the plantations and herding animals on ranches. It was nothing like the old days, when they had spent their time hunting bears or fighting bloody wars with their neighbours. But they had no choice. This was the nineteenth century, and that was what happened to Garrincha's great-grandparents in the state of Pernambuco. Expelled from their land, the Fulniôs went in search of something new.

Since the eighteenth century, the Fulniôs had lived on a reserve in Águas Belas in the backwoods of Pernambuco, a few miles from the state border with Alagoas. They were one of the last tribes in the region. There was not one member of the Caeté tribe left in either state to tell of how their predecessors had eaten Bishop Sardinha in 1556; nor one wild Tupinambá to recount how they had decimated and eaten the Caetés before they themselves were exterminated even more ferociously by the Portuguese. The life of a Brazilian Indian was often worth little more than an animal. It was a miracle that any of them lived long enough to see the nineteenth century.

The Fulniôs were among those that did, although under the permanently vigilant eye of the white man they lost many of their old customs.

3

One of them was endocannibalism – the practice whereby the first-born child was killed, flavoured with honey caught by the father, grilled over an open fire, and eaten by the grandparents. The Fulniôs believed that this would strengthen the race. Some other customs survived, including one that said when they ran into a stone they must take revenge by biting into it. And the children never lost their extra-ordinary ability to hunt. They were brilliant at throwing stones – they hunted without slings or catapults or any other weapons – and when they got small animals such as monkeys or birds in their sights, they were dead meat.

In 1860 there were close to 700 Fulniôs living in Águas Belas on land the white men had long coveted. In that year, with the collusion of the authorities, the invasions began. The white men came early in the morning and set fire to the Indians' humble homes. Whole villages were burned to the ground; if the local families wanted to live they either had to flee or succumb to their new masters. There was no way to fight back or resist. To add insult to injury, more than a hundred Fulniôs were recruited to fight in the War of the Triple Alliance against Solano Lopez, a Paraguayan they had never heard of. The first ones were 'volunteers for the motherland'; the others had to be dragged away in chains. When the women in the tribe heard that military recruiters were on their way, they dressed their boys in women's jewellery so they would not be taken from them. But many of them were, and few returned. As a result, almost 500 of the 700-strong Fulniô population had been forced from their land by the end of the decade. Many of them were taken so far from Águas Belas that they would never find their way back. But it hardly mattered as they would have had nowhere to go back to: in 1870 the reserve was closed down.

The Fulniô diaspora spread their mestizo roots across Brazil. Garrincha's great-grandparents, who were probably among the first to leave Águas Belas in around 1865, followed the Ipanema river for 28 miles and tried to set up home in Santana do Ipanema, just across the state border in Alagoas. They managed to set up a village but, perhaps because they were forced to run again, many moved on, took a left turn and ended up in the Barriga mountains on the outskirts of a town called União dos Palmares. It was there they were finally captured, strung together and taken to a nearby town called Quebrangulo and the plantations and ranches from which they never left.

The running wouldn't end until nearly half a century later, in 1914, when the Pernambuco state government gave the last remaining Fulniôs part of their land in Águas Belas. However, most of the area's original inhabitants had died by then. And their children – one of whom, José Francisco dos Santos, would become Garrincha's grandfather – were middle-aged, born on ranches, far from their origins. And in the case of José Francisco dos Santos and his children, much further than the mere 100 kilometres that separated Quebrangulo from Águas Belas.

José was probably born sometime between 1865 and 1875, perhaps even in Quebrangulo, the son of the first batch of Fulniôs chased from the Barriga mountains. There is no birth certificate, and the names of his parents are unknown. The custom of the time was to give the Indians the name of their captor, for easy identification if they went missing, and those Fulniôs took the name of the man who had seized them, Francisco dos Santos. That he bore a white man's name was just one of the factors that would make José forget he was an Indian.

José would have been between 18 and 28 years old in 1893, when he married Antonia, the daughter of a black slave and an Indian woman. It was not a good time to marry and start a family. The years following the fall of the monarchy and the declaration of the republic in 1889 were particularly hard for the north-east. Its three main sources of wealth – slavery, monarchy and sugar – had suddenly disappeared. Brazil, or rather southern Brazil, had become a country of

5

immigrants, republicans and coffee. In Alagoas, the refineries and ranches were going bankrupt one after another and their owners, who had recently been so powerful, were selling their pianos in order to keep their horse-drawn carriages on the road.

Until then, José and Antonia, like millions of other poor north-easterners, had been the servants of rich men; the changes meant they were now the servants of poor men. While the children of ranchers and plantation owners went to the capital to become doctors, lawyers and even writers, the former slaves, without any prospects, stayed right where they had grown up, struggling to keep their heads above water at the abandoned refineries around Quebrangulo. If they were lucky, the rancher gave them a plot of land on the condition they shared their harvest with him. What was left would not have filled a saucepan.

And so it was for José and Antonia. On the eve of the twentieth century, as they looked towards the horizon from the top of Quebrangulo's hills, the future did not appear to hold much in store.

Quebrangulo was a district of Palmeira dos Índios between the sea and the backwoods of rural Alagoas. Back then it was almost deserted; José and Antonia were among fewer than 5,000 inhabitants spread out across more than 300 square kilometres. In 1889, with the clamour for a republic growing, gangs of bandits took advantage of the political crisis and turned the region into their own little fiefdom. They looted the ranches, stole cattle and horses, broke into homes and shops, started riots, and generally made life a nightmare for all and sundry.

José and Antonia, like everyone else in Quebrangulo, lived in permanent fear. But they were determined to start a family, and the presence of bandits and an uncertain future did not stop them. Their first child was Manuel, born in 1894. Three years later came Amaro, then Maria, José, Isabel and João – all baptised with the surname Francisco dos Santos. None of them would call themselves Fulniôs, or even Indians. Their own mother was a *cafuza*, half Indian and half black, and they were *cafuzos* too. In truth, though, they were simply dark-skinned Brazilians born during tough times, and therefore obvious candidates to be illiterate, ignorant and backward. Brazil did not let them down.

That was until Manuel, the oldest and cleverest child, began to look for ways to invent a future. In 1909, aged around 15, he left home and went to work as an odd-job man in the city. Quebrangulo had nothing to offer, but Manuel did anything and everything he could. He learned to read, discovered he was good with numbers and, smarter than most ambitious young men, began to cultivate friendships. One of them was with José Peixoto da Silva, a Pernambucan who fancied himself as a poet and a journalist, and his daughter Adelaide, who was pretty and of marrying age. In 1915 or 1916, Peixoto and his daughter moved from the north-east to Rio de Janeiro, bringing Manuel with them as their lodger.

With a hand from Peixoto, Manuel got a job as a cook in the São Sebastião tuberculosis hospital in Caju, a small neighbourhood near Rio's docks. He did his job the best he could, but he soon saw that his future lay elsewhere. He studied at night and got as far as primary-school level. At the same time, Manuel was secretly courting Peixoto's daughter. Adelaide's father, a descendant of Dutch settlers, liked Manuel but he did not see him as a potential son-in-law – he was too dark-skinned for a start. Manuel was not allowed to get too close to Adelaide, to touch her hand, or to address her by anything but the formal term *senhorita*. But when Peixoto travelled north on a trip, Manuel and Adelaide took advantage and secretly tied the knot.

Arriving back in Rio to the sound of wedding bells, Peixoto almost turned his house upside down. He disowned his daughter, new husband and all. Manuel was shocked at his reaction. He had not counted on such a radical response. The bright future he had sought to build for himself appeared to be fading fast. Then he heard about a place a few miles away called Magé. The English had built textile factories there and Manuel was confident that a creative and hardworking man would

7

have no trouble finding a job in such a place. So he and his new wife set off for Raiz da Serra and Pau Grande, two small towns in the municipality of Magé.

Manuel was a natural leader, and as soon as he arrived he rolled up his sleeves and got to work. He was a focal point for the other immigrants in the region, and he organised them into shifts. One of the shifts cleaned the rivers and fields for América Fabril, the enormous textile factory based in Pau Grande, while the other chopped wood to feed the factory's huge boilers. If he caught one of the men shirking his responsibilities, Manuel rolled up his sleeves, got hold of the axe, and without any further ado set about turning the tree into a pile of logs himself. Then he set about the slacker. No one dared say a word.

At 5'11" and almost 20 stone, Manuel stood out from the crowd. Some people hated him for being harsh and arrogant, and he might have unwittingly stood on a few toes, even if it was only because he was so big. The Englishmen who ran América Fabril, however, liked him. Mr Smith, the mill director, Mr Hall, the manager, and Mr Lindsay, the industrial director, all trusted him, and they adopted him as their man.

In Pau Grande, Manuel set up a pottery firm alongside the textile factory and became América Fabril's principal supplier of tiles. Because of the pottery concern, everyone forgot the name Manuel and started calling him Mané Caieira, after the oven where the tiles were baked. But he didn't stop there. He soon diversified, becoming first the man in charge of keeping Pau Grande's streets clean, and then assuming responsibility for maintaining the railway lines built by the English. In fewer than four years he had an army of men working under him and had become indispensable to América Fabril – without ever being an employee. When he felt he had established himself, and at around the same time he found out that his parents had died in Alagoas, Manuel decided it was time to fetch his brothers and sisters to come and work for him. All of them came except Amaro.

Amaro was not in Quebrangulo when Manuel put the rest of the family on the steam train to Rio. In 1923, at the age of 26, he had gone to try his luck as a cobbler in Olinda, one of Pernambuco's most beautiful colonial towns. Amaro was said to be a good cobbler, but history has tended not to smile on people who mend shoes. Unlike Manuel, Amaro had never learned how to read or write or even to do simple arithmetic; he therefore didn't have many career options available to him. The best thing he did in Olinda was to get married in 1924 to Maria Carolina, a thin, light-skinned Pernambucan girl. When he received Manuel's telegram in December that same year asking him to come and join the family in Rio, Amaro had to ask the Western telegram official to read it to him. He responded, saying he wanted to come but that his wife was about to have a baby. Manuel wrote back, telling him to have the baby and then to travel down afterwards.

Twenty days after their daughter was born, with Rosa stuck firmly to her mother's breast, Amaro and Maria Carolina boarded the train south. Manuel met them at the station in Rio and took them to Pau Grande where he gave them a place to stay at the back of his tile workshop. At first, Amaro worked as a cobbler in a small workshop Manuel set up for him in the neighbouring town of Raiz da Serra. Later, he helped Manuel in the workshop making tiles. Finally, he found his true vocation: as the man whose eagle eye and gruff voice kept workers on their toes.

With Maria Carolina also earning money by cooking for the contractors they soon had enough to move into their own house on rua Chiqueiro. At the edge of a river and close to a waterfall, it was a pleasant enough place to live. Maria Carolina raised goats, pigs and chickens in the yard at the back of the house, and it was in that relatively happy home that she added to her brood: José, Cicero, Maria de Lourdes and, in 1933, another son, this one baptised Manuel after her brother-in-law and protector.

Or Garrincha, as everyone in Pau Grande would soon be calling him.

*   *   *

9

In the 1930s, if you'd asked anyone from Pau Grande where they wanted to go when they died, there was a good chance they would have answered Pau Grande. Mother Nature had been exceptionally generous. There was honey flowing in abundance, the villagers lived and worked in peace and freedom. Heaven was at hand, and the people of Pau Grande didn't even have to die to get there. That is, as long as they didn't mind giving their body and soul to a higher power: the English. Or to be more precise, the América Fabril company.

In 1871, when the English first arrived in Magé, a lush green region cut by rivers and waterfalls snuggled in at the foot of the Órgão hills north-east of Rio, much of the area was still untouched by human hands. They built roads, constructed dams and installed textile factories in the small towns of Andorinhas, Santo Aleixo and Estrela, as well as in Magé, the seat of the municipality itself. The factories all made money but the most successful of them was built in Pau Grande, despite the fact that the English had got off to an inauspicious start in the town, cutting down a tree that had grown there for centuries. The tree was gigantic: 50 metres high and so wide that 30 men could not join their hands around it. This was the Pau Grande, or big stick, that gave the town its name. The English used its wood to build the workshops that manufactured the fan belts that were indispensable to the workings of the big factory.

Everything in Pau Grande belonged to the factory – in truth, everything in Pau Grande *was* the factory. The factory built houses and gave them rent-free to the 1,200 workers and their families who had come from all over Rio and the north-east to work there. It laid roads and put in place water, electricity and sewage systems; it built schools and health centres. Medicine was free at the purpose-built chemist, as was the milk, the school dinners and the students' books. Once a week the factory gave each house a pile of wood for their fires. If an employee's daughter was to be married, the factory would be informed and a team would set off immediately to get their house ready for its new arrivals – it was automatically assumed the new couple would move in with the bride's family. Their children would enjoy the same benefits as their parents, their destinies would be mapped out for them: when they reached seven they would go to school, and when they got to 14 they would get a job at América Fabril. At 44 they could retire.

Football came to the town in 1908 when the first English visitors brought balls, taught the locals how to play, and founded the Sport Club Pau Grande. It was a sport for everyone; there was no fence around the pitch, and no one had to pay to watch the matches. The players were amateurs and would continue to be long after professional football was introduced to Brazil in 1933.

Any leisure time not filled by football, carnival or the town's one picture house was spent enjoying the area's natural beauty. Adults and children alike swam, or went fishing and hunting in the rivers and forests that surrounded the town. Because everything belonged to the factory there were no barbed-wire fences and no Keep Out signs. Until at least 1940 the rivers were awash with fish, the skies were filled with birds, and one could hardly take a step without tripping over armadillos, monkeys and other exotic animals.

The influence of the English extended far beyond the factory. The people of Pau Grande were imbued with a sense of traditional British superiority; they were made to feel as if they were a class above their colleagues in the company's other factories. Although the other employees went on strike – textile workers seemed to find it extraordinarily easy to learn the words to 'The Internationale' – no serious stoppages ever hit the Pau Grande factory. The strikes that did take place were always short-lived.

The townspeople lived together like a family. Life was trouble-free; muggings, robberies and violence were only read about in newspapers. Perhaps once a year someone's chicken went missing. Had it not been for the insects no one would have bothered closing their doors and windows at night. Which, conveniently, helped the English bosses keep control. The guards who patrolled the town at night kept their superiors up to date with all the important gossip. They monitored things so closely that the patrician Englishmen had no qualms about telling off the locals, even on matters such as basic hygiene. Mothers were called to be given lectures in Oxford-accented Portuguese: 'You must wipe your child's bottom! We will not have children with dirty bottoms running about here!' If a couple had an argument, the factory manager invited them to drop by his office the next morning to patch things up. If it was discovered that an employee was beating his wife, he was sanctioned; if he was caught doing it again the most lenient punishment he could expect to face was suspension. The English managers even caned repeat offenders. Grown men extended their hands to receive corporal punishment as if they were at an English public school – and in many ways that is exactly how it was in Pau Grande. Or at América Fabril. Where the boss was the judge and the jury.

Mané Caieira knew how to make his presence felt in the little town. He was one of the first people in Pau Grande to own a car, a radio and all sorts of other mod cons that were then coming into vogue. But no matter how hard he tried, he was unable to give his brothers the push they needed to take the same steps forward. They were content to reproduce the life they had had in Alagoas, perhaps because the setting was so similar: in Quebrangulo, the Barriga hills were on the horizon; in Pau Grande, it was the Órgãos. The bags they brought from the north-east might have held only leather sandals and a few old shirts, but they also brought the undying customs of the region: superstitions, competitions between guitarists, hammocks to sleep in, the unquestioned ease with which they produced children outside marriage, and bottles of *cachimbo*, a mixture of *cachaça* (fermented sugar cane), honey and sticks of cinnamon that was given medicinally to everyone from pregnant mothers to children with colds. Amaro had been brought up in Alagoas drinking *cachimbo* and his offspring, including Garrincha, would grow up the same way.

Amaro was small and strong. His skin was as tough as the bark on a tree, and he had a squashed nose and thick, wavy hair. He loved making and setting off fireworks and singing his own verses to the tunes he played on his little guitar. He was talented at killing goats and he would regularly slaughter up to 30 in a weekend for his neighbours, each animal sent crashing to the floor with a well-aimed blow to the forehead. As payment he kept the tripe, which he cooked and shared with his friends.

In spite of appearances he was a religious man, and he had a special devotion to St George, perhaps because of their common love of horses. Amaro had his own horse, named Champion after Gene Autry's famous steed, but when he went out he didn't hunt down dragons. Amaro's target was altogether different: he went after women.

Married or single, to Amaro they were all *comadres*, a Portuguese word that literally means 'godmother' or 'mother of one's godchild', but which back then also meant a bit on the side. That may just have been Amaro's way of referring to the occasional objects of his affection, but it could also have been because many of them asked him to serve as godfather to their children – children who in some cases were actually his. Amaro is believed to have fathered at least 25 children in and around Pau Grande, not including the nine he had with Maria Carolina.

His performance with the ladies had to be short and sweet. He would ride off on his horse, neckerchief at his throat and knife on his belt, and make his way out into the country. He would stop at the house of a married couple and clap his hands. When the lady of the house appeared he would ask if her husband was around. If he was, they exchanged greetings and he rode on. But if he wasn't, Amaro accepted her invitation to come inside and have a coffee, and – nine times out of ten, according to the legend – he gave her something extra special in return. It was always quick. They didn't even have to take their clothes off, she just lifted her skirt and he unbuckled his trousers. Even a bed was a luxury; they did it standing up, against the stove or on the kitchen floor. For those friends who asked him if he wasn't ashamed to be screwing *comadres*, he had an answer prepared: 'A *comadre* is only a *comadre* from the waist up.'

Many husbands feared that Amaro was carrying on with their wives but no one acted on their suspicions. When he got a new job at the factory at the end of the 1930s the possibility of retribution became even more unlikely. For, as a guard at América Fabril, Amaro had a position that gave him almost military power. Dressed in a yellow uniform, he patrolled the city making sure everything was in order. His tasks included breaking up arguments in bars and houses and pulling apart those couples getting amorous at the back of the S.C. Pau Grande.

There was nothing hypocritical about his behaviour. Amaro was a moral man, and had one of his sons got a girl into trouble he would have forced him to marry her. Adults, though, were old enough to know what they were doing, and he was not going to be the one to castigate them. In addition, Amaro did not use his new position as a way to woo the ladies. In his own primitive way he would have been considered a bit of a charmer; in his deep voice, he complimented them on their hair, waist or backside, especially if it was nice and round, the way he liked it. He flirted in such a way that if he was rejected he could claim he was merely joking around. If the husbands were afraid of him because he was Mané Caieira's brother (and, later, Garrincha's father), then it was hardly his fault.

Even though the impunity he enjoyed allowed him the pick of the women of Pau Grande, Amaro was not in the slightest bit choosy and he made no distinction because of colour, looks or age. 'As long as they are breathing' was his motto, and he might even have dispensed with that formality: at more than one wake he was heard to ask, half seriously, 'Is the *comadre* cold yet?'

Women were not his only vice. Like all his brothers (except Mané Caieira), Amaro was an alcoholic. Having been raised on *cachimbo*, he had a high tolerance to alcohol and plenty of opportunities to show that no matter how many *cachaças* he had, he never seemed to get drunk. He was philosophical about it: *cachaça* was there to cheer people up, not to degrade them. He had no respect for those who drank in local bars or who threw back so much they could hardly stand. The place to drink was at home or at friends' houses, and he took his own advice – all day, every day.

Amaro drank *cachaça* straight, or mixed it with gooseberry juice. He would tie the bottle to a string and lower it into the cistern or the river to keep it cool. He used any excuse to take it out and have a slug, but it was rare to see him drunk at any time other than at local feasts or during singalongs – occasions when anything was acceptable. And he never complained about hangovers the morning after.

When Garrincha was born in 1933, Amaro was 36 years old and at his sexual and alcoholic prime. But the massive quantities of alcohol he kept sticking away eventually took their toll, and there are stories of how by the end of the 1940s he was being carried home. Other tales told of his walking the streets naked without the slightest idea what he was doing. It is almost certain he was impotent by the time he was 60. The once formidable Amaro, a man whose sexual exploits shocked and delighted the people of Pau Grande, had withered almost visibly.

Bit by bit, he disappeared. But in his place came someone who would surpass him in everything he had been good at, and whose star contained its own brilliance.

CHAPTER 2

1933–1952: Childhood in Shangri-la

WHEN MANUEL WAS BORN, THE MIDWIFE WAS THE FIRST PERSON TO notice that his legs were crooked. The left leg bent out and the right leg bent in, as if a gust of wind had blown them out of position. Manuel inherited his legs not from Amaro but from Maria Carolina, his mother, although hers were not as badly distorted as her son's. A calliper would have put them right in no time, but no one thought of that in Pau Grande in 1933.

It took Amaro a while to get round to completing his son's birth certificate, and when he did he made a mess of it. He finally made it to the registrar's office in Raiz da Serra in the first week of November, and then he mixed up the dates, giving Garrincha's birthday as 18 October when it should have been 28 October. The registrar, a local bigwig who was always three sheets to the wind, wasn't much of a stickler for detail either. When Amaro gave his son's name as Manuel, he simply wrote down Manuel.

Such mistakes were not uncommon. In Brazil, where people use both their mother's and their father's last names, Garrincha should have been given the surnames Francisco and dos Santos, Francisco being the surname of his father and dos Santos the surname of his mother. But because Francisco was also a first name it was mistakenly left off

17

the certificate, and in all future official documents Garrincha's full name was recorded as Manuel dos Santos.

Manuel was Amaro's fifth child, or rather the fifth child he had with Maria Carolina. After Manuel he would have four more: Josefa, Antônia, Teresinha and Jorge. It would be several years before Amaro was taken on at the América Fabril factory and his child-rearing methods were not yet subject to the scrutiny of his bosses. Manuel, therefore, grew up without any strict supervision from his parents. He rarely cleaned his teeth or clipped his nails, and no one told him to blow his nose or brush his hair. He had his hair cut at home every six months. He went everywhere barefoot and was capable of disappearing for hours into the woods and forests without anyone even noticing he was gone. He learned to ride a horse before he was even old enough to mount it himself, and far from his family's protective gaze he would jump into the Inhomirim river and paddle his way out among the teeming fish. The only Indians he ever saw were the ones printed on packets of soap powder, but he didn't need to rub away the dirt to see he was one of them.

All of young Manuel's friends said he was a sweet child who didn't talk back to his elders or even to those children his own age. He said little and never raised his voice. But he was also hard to control. When he got a telling-off for stealing sweets or biscuits from the kitchen he just smiled – and then did it again, first chance he got. He might have been given a belting now and then, but perhaps less often than he should have thanks to his size. He was smaller than the other kids his age and people were inclined to feel sorry for him.

As small as a little bird. The first one to notice the similarity was his eldest sister Rosa, and it wasn't long before she started calling him *garrincha*, the north-eastern name for the wren, a little brown bird with a black-striped back that lived on insects and spiders. It had a beautiful song but did not adapt well to captivity. Pau Grande was full of them. The name stuck, and by the time he was four years old Manuel was known as Garrincha to his parents, his brothers and sisters, and his friends.

18

Just like the bird that gave him his name, young Garrincha did not take well to confinement. Until he was seven years old his life revolved around swimming in the river, kicking a football about and hunting birds. The romantic association with a little bird would play a fundamental role in his life, but back then his attitude towards them was anything but benevolent or poetic. All he wanted to do was kill them. One after another, like ducks at the fair, he knocked doves, finches, parrots and even *garrinchas* (the fact they had given him his nickname was no reason for pity) out of the sky with a well-aimed throw or a shot from his catapult. One day he came home with 48 dead birds in a sack, every one of them having been picked from above courtesy of his deadly aim.

Unlike the other children of the town, who lived by the old dictum that you eat what you kill, Garrincha didn't eat the animals he took home. He killed for the pleasure of hitting the target, and besides, his favourite meal was rice, beans and spaghetti – and it always would be. He enjoyed hunting so much that when he got a job at the factory he bought a rifle, which only increased the number of animals vulnerable to his predatory instincts. For it wasn't just birds that were under siege; to Garrincha, all manner of creatures were fair game. He and his friends caught rabbits, possums and any number of the myriad rodent-like animals that lived in the nearby forest, either by lassooing them or by beating them with sticks. He went after fish with nets or with a spear, and some people even said that Garrincha tried to catch snakes.

Garrincha swam while he was at the river, but the most fun came not from diving off the rocks – he was a courageous child who would climb to the highest point and throw himself into the pools below – but from standing naked alongside his friends and seeing who could pee furthest. A few years later the peeing competitons turned into masturbation contests as the boys raced to see who could ejaculate first. This might even have developed further as they got older – but when they looked at him, his friends, even the older ones,

19

surely decided that sex with Garrincha was perhaps not a good idea after all.

Because, according even to impartial witnesses, by the time he was ten Garrincha had the penis of a man twice his age, the size of which was frightening.

Unlike many of his peers, Garrincha didn't have a scooter, a bike with stabilisers or a water pistol. But he did have the freedom to kick a ball around whenever he wanted. In the 1940s, when playing soccer was second nature to everyone in Brazil, every young boy's survival kit included a football. Only rich children had proper leather footballs, however; the poorer ones had to improvise, and the first ball Garrincha ever kicked was made from paper stuffed into his aunt's old stockings. Later he used one made from an inflated goat's bladder, secured by tying the guts in a knot.

The first real ball he ever owned was a red rubber one that Rosa bought at the local corner shop for his seventh birthday. But Garrincha didn't need his own ball to make sure he was picked when the kids lined up for a kickabout – he was already better than anyone else in Pau Grande. Having his own ball simply meant that he didn't need anyone else to play with. Now he could play alone, dribbling his ball around trees and kicking it against walls.

In spite of all the risks he took by the river and in the forest, the only accident Garrincha ever suffered took place in the back yard of his home. One day, when he'd just returned home after playing football with his friends, Garrincha was bitten by Leão, one of Amaro's dogs. Until then Leão had been a mongrel whose specialities were sleeping and scratching, but that day he went for Garrincha, almost tearing his neck off. When his parents tried to pull him off and the dog bit Garrincha again, this time in the arm, Amaro took him outside and shot him.

The attack served as a wake-up call to Amaro and Maria Carolina. They suddenly saw that their son was wild and out of control, and they decided to try to calm him down. They bought him his first pair of shoes for his confirmation ceremony, which he took off immediately afterwards. And they also sent him to school at the start of the term in 1941. No one could accuse Amaro of not trying.

The Santana School was owned and run by the factory, and Garrincha's first teachers were Olinda and Maria das Dores. They were saints who made it their policy never to fail a student. No matter how many times Garrincha skipped school to hunt, fish or play football, he always passed the year. But in 1942 he came face to face with Santinha, a rigorous teacher whom many pupils from Pau Grande had already had the dubious pleasure of knowing. Santinha passed only the children who studied. Garrincha suffered under her, but she helped him learn enough so that he could read comics and film subtitles – if they stayed on the screen long enough. And it was Santinha he had to thank for the scrawled signature he would place at the bottom of contracts for the rest of his life.

However, his command of the alphabet was not good enough to get him the marks that would allow him to move on to the third year of primary school, so Garrincha decided to call a halt to his education there and then – much to the disgust of Amaro, who warned his child about the future with the saying, 'Idiots don't get anywhere.'

At the same time as Amaro and Maria's attempts to provide their son with some formal education were failing, their efforts to instil in him a sense of responsibility were also proving less than successful. Garrincha's father put him in charge of feeding his horse at the end of the day, but every time Garrincha went to get the hay he came across a group of children playing football and he couldn't resist getting involved. By the time night fell, the horse would be starving. Amaro punished him with a beating, but it never did any good. Garrincha subconsciously even tried to discipline himself – again, without any effect. He asked Gloria, the local sweet-shop owner, for a job selling sweets outside the factory. But at the end of the day the money taken never did tally with the number of sweets that had been eaten and he always ended up owing her his wages. Gloria said he had no head for business.

But he did have a head for some things. Having spent most of their young lives watching chickens and goats and horses copulating freely, the youth of Pau Grande learned early on that the myth about babies coming from storks was nonsense. They knew the story, and they were permanently in heat. And Garrincha was no exception. At the age of about 11, with puberty gushing from every pore, his sex drive was raging. Worse, no matter how close that sex drive came to bursting his trousers, Garrincha was a romantic and had high hopes of meeting a nice girl. Unfortunately for him, the girls of the town didn't pay him the slightest bit of attention.

That was why in 1945, aged 12, when Garrincha had sex for the first time, it wasn't exactly the experience he had dreamt of. Because it was with a goat.

Ninety-nine per cent of the other youngsters outside the big cities in Brazil in the 1940s and 1950s had the same experience. Garrincha was simply doing what he had seen older men do. He would rather have gone to a prostitute, but there was no red-light district in Pau Grande and he did not have the time, the money or the resourcefulness to go to the one in Petrópolis, the nearest big town, on his own. Had he had the choice, he would have lost his virginity to Maria Montez, the brunette he saw in the films of the time. Or Maureen O'Sullivan, who played Jane in the Tarzan films. But he was desperate, and the only way he was going to have sex was with a goat. Or several goats.

Money, at least that destined for sex or *mariolas*, the popular banana-flavoured sweets, ceased to be a problem in 1947 when Garrincha was hired to work at the textile factory. In keeping with local tradition, he was taken on a month and a day after his fourteenth birthday, on 19 November. His shift ran from seven in the morning to 4.40 p.m., Monday to Friday, with an hour for lunch, and from seven to 11.40 a.m. on Saturdays. It was a 48-hour week at 1.2 cruzeiros an hour.

Garrincha started off in the cotton section. It was not easy work. Conditions in the English factories for long periods of the twentieth century were not much better than those at the start of the Industrial Revolution, and the cotton section was exclusively for boys, perhaps because they were the only ones who would allow themselves to be put to work in hell's annexe. Their work took place in the basement, where the big machines that removed the seeds from the cotton were housed. It is not known what was more maddening, the deafening noise of the machines, the 40-degree heat, or the incredibly high levels of cotton dust that filled the air. Whatever it was, the residue had to be swept up and sifted in order to separate the reusable material from the waste. Garrincha did the sweeping.

The machines were dangerous, and sometimes there were accidents as a result of which workers lost fingers or hands. But there was little chance of that happening to Garrincha. He spent half his life skipping work, and when he was there his favourite place was inside the enormous boxes of cotton, where he would hide out and nap. At first, his bosses thought he was absent when he was just sleeping – they couldn't conceive that anyone could sleep with that din going on. But no one spent much time in any one section (especially the cotton section), and Garrincha was soon promoted to the mill section, the area where they transformed the cotton into thread. Compared to the noise in the basement, the machines there sounded like a flute concerto.

Anyone else behaving like Garrincha would have been handed his pink slip within weeks of setting foot on the factory floor. In those first few weeks when he should have got his head down and applied himself, he was caught napping on the job, arriving late and not turning up. They were not serious offences on their own, but one after another they amounted to misconduct. But even though he continued to treat the job as a joke – he failed to turn up on average once a week – he was never fired, because Boboco, one of the section heads, was also the president of S.C. Pau Grande, the local football team with whom Garrincha was a promising player. Once a good player himself, Boboco protected Garrincha and turned a blind eye to his misdemeanours as long as he was turning out for his side.

In 1948, however, Garrincha's luck ran out and he was shown the door. The factory could no longer continue to employ someone who set such a bad example, and Garrincha was one of the worst workers ever to have set foot in América Fabril. Amaro almost died of shame. As if to wash his hands of his son, he told him to pack his bags and get out.

Without a job or a place to stay, Garrincha took a look around and saw nowhere to go. His horizons extended no further than Pau Grande and the towns around it. But if he had learned anything so far in life, a life spent out of doors, it was that he did not need a roof over his head. The church bandstand had a roof but no walls, and it was there that he chose to spend the night, using a bundle of clothes as a pillow, until the next day, when he hoped his father would take him back. But Amaro chased him away at his first and only attempt to apologise. So Garrincha adopted the bandstand as his new home and spent two weeks of exile under its draughty cover.

He never went hungry. During the day he ate at friends' houses. At night, Nair, a girl from school who, like many of her classmates, had taken a shine to him, secretly brought him a steak sandwich or a leg of chicken left over from her dinner. For dessert, he got a slice of guava jelly. She watched him eat and then bolted for home when he tried to repay her with kisses.

Two weeks later, Boboco convinced his bosses at the factory to take Garrincha back again. Without a job he couldn't play for Pau Grande, and his bosses agreed with certain conditions: he would return to work in the cotton section and make an extra effort to turn up on time. The factory was content with demoting him and Pau Grande got their player back.

Amaro was happy too, and he let Garrincha come home. His son was stubborn but he believed that the fright would help him come to his senses. It didn't happen. The factory gave Boboco permission to pay him even when he didn't turn up, and before long the only reason Garrincha went to work was to catch up on some sleep in the cotton boxes.

Among Garrincha's new colleagues were the brothers Pincel and Swing. From the nearby town of Raiz da Serra, they were both black, the same age as Garrincha and poor enough (they had no rich uncles like Mané Caieira) to make Garrincha look as if he were well off. Pincel was the less serious of the two, the one most inclined to be mischievous, while Swing was quieter and more lugubrious. The brothers had a lot in common with Garrincha. Neither of them liked to study, work or be tied down by timetables, bosses or anything else. And like Garrincha, they enjoyed a drink. In those days there were no restrictions on drinking or smoking in rural Brazil. From a young age Garrincha was allowed to drink at the barbecues Amaro held at home and he was smoking regularly by the time he started work at América Fabril.

The factory provided a lunch of milk and bread for the youngsters who didn't go home to eat, and Garrincha's mother sometimes treated him with a banana sandwich. But these home comforts didn't last long because in June 1949 Maria Carolina died after giving birth to another son, Jorge. She was 48.

Like any boy, Garrincha, who was not yet 16, was devastated by his mother's death. She had shielded him from his father when he got too tough. His grief was compounded when, less than a month after his mother died, Amaro brought another woman home. A widow who would also help Amaro raise the children, Cecília was a good woman but she took Amaro's decision to give her carte blanche over the running of the house too seriously. She tried to instil a discipline none of the children was used to after years of growing up under the auspices of their easy-going mother. Garrincha felt abandoned.

This feeling of desertion didn't last long. Boboco intervened at the factory and managed to transfer Garrincha to the cloth section where life was much easier. There he got what he wanted, in more ways than one. The cloth section was staffed predominantly by women, dozens of them, in all ages, shapes, sizes and colours. They doted on Garrincha and brought him snacks from home. Garrincha was 16 going on 17 and his hormones were running wild. Some of the women were the same. One was Nair, the girl who had looked after him when he was homeless and who would come to play an increasingly prominent role in his life.

The expression 'natural genius' couldn't have been much bandied about in the Serra dos Órgãos in the 1940s. But it was the only way to explain how Garrincha played football. Like a *curupira*, the demon of rural folklore whose feet were back to front, he was crafty, mischievous and impossible to catch. Where could he have learned to run, dribble and shoot like that? There were no football players in the family. Amaro wasn't a big fan and his uncle Mané Caieira cared even less. The only one to have any affinity with the leather ball was an uncle who was proud to say he had trained with a long-defunct team called Andaraí. Of Garrincha's brothers, only José, known to everyone as Zé Baleia, played football – and he was a goalkeeper.

In 1945, at the age of 12, Garrincha already spent more time playing football than anything else. He kicked a ball about with his friends at least two or three times a day. The clay field he played on measured about 50 yards by 30 yards and was filled with holes and perched on the edge of an embankment. Just dribbling the ball barefoot on that rutted and uneven surface was a skill in itself. Taking it along the side of the embankment without letting the ball roll over the edge was an even greater feat. Garrincha managed to do both with ease. He got round the problem of the holes by dribbling past them as if they were opponents, and he hated having to scale down the embankment to look for the ball so he took extra care when out on the wing. Usually, Garrincha and a couple of his friends played against seven or eight others. It was fairer that way.

Garrincha wasn't the only good player around but he was the best, even if he was the smallest. Diquinho, França, Arlindo and Tovar could play a bit too, and Garrincha's brother Zé Baleia saw the constellation of promising youngsters and came up with the idea of getting them together to play for a team that would serve as a stepping stone to S.C. Pau Grande. Baleia named his team Palmeiras FC and he insisted they take themselves seriously; they had shirts, they trained regularly, and Garrincha was an ever-present, in left midfield. Brazilian sides didn't wear numbers on their shirts in those days, but had they done Garrincha would have worn the number 10.

No one knows why he chose to play in a position that demanded at least some ability to kick a ball with his left foot. Garrincha couldn't do anything with his left foot. According to his cousin Renato Peixoto dos Santos, Garrincha didn't even know which foot was his left foot. Baleia taught him the difference and, it seems, more than just that, because in 1947 and 1948 almost all the kids with Palmeiras went on to play first for Pau Grande's youth team and then, in 1949, the senior side.

The managers of other teams had their eyes on the boys of Pau Grande. The factory team was not affiliated to the Mageense Football League, the regional league whose catchment area included Pau Grande, so the league clubs felt free to go to the town and cherry-pick the young talent. One of the clubs was Cruzeiro do Sul from Petrópolis. In one fell swoop, Cruzeiro lured away Garrincha, Diquinho and França to play for their youth team. For two years, the three youngsters went every Sunday morning to Cruzeiro, albeit without turning their backs on Pau Grande. One of Garrincha's fans, a taxi driver named Cabinho, took it upon himself to pick them up in Pau Grande, drive them to play for Cruzeiro and then bring them home again afterwards, to play for Pau Grande.

When he reached the age for military service, Garrincha reported

27

to the First Cavalry Regiment in Petrópolis. He was wearing only his shorts, and the sergeant took one look at him before deciding that he didn't even need to bother sending him to the battalion doctor. The sergeant thought him skinny for his age and pronounced him 'physically handicapped'. Garrincha was discharged and given a number way down the draft.

He might not have been in any fit shape to serve his country, but he was fit enough to do a shift for the Petrópolis clubs starting to fight for his signature. By now he had moved to right midfield, and it was there that he turned out for Serrano, the club that lured him away from Cruzeiro. Serrano were savvier than Cruzeiro and in 1951 they signed Garrincha to a contract, registered him with the league and even paid him a symbolic wage, 30 cruzeiros per game plus lunch. The money was worth about a dollar.

Until then, Garrincha had never thought about football in monetary terms. Or in any other terms. He didn't like to talk about football, he never went to Rio to watch matches and he never listened to games on the radio. If he supported any team it was Flamengo, and only then because when he was six years old in 1939 everyone raved about the Flamengo side that won the Carioca Championship – the state league and still the big prize for Rio's clubs – with players such as Domingos da Guia, Leônidas and Zizinho. Brazil lost the World Cup in 1950 at the Maracanã in a famous game against Uruguay, but Garrincha was so uninterested that he didn't even listen to the match on the loudspeakers set up in the town's main square. He went fishing instead, and when he came back to find the whole town in tears he thought they were all idiots. The best thing about football was playing it.

But now Serrano were paying him to play, and when his uncles did the maths they discovered the salary was a lot more than symbolic. For an hour and a half's work he received 25 times the 1.2 cruzeiros he got per hour at the factory.

Still, it didn't seem to mean much to Garrincha. After playing professionally for three months he grew tired of travelling up and down the road every Sunday to Petrópolis. He forgot he had signed a contract with Serrano and never went back. His team was Pau Grande, where he played for free. If he was going to leave Pau Grande it would be for a team in Rio, and only then because they kept insisting.

Garrincha had tried his luck in Rio a few times before. A year earlier, in 1950, on the eve of his seventeenth birthday, one of the factory directors had insisted on taking him to Vasco da Gama to train. Or at least to try to train. The big teams set aside a day or two each week for youngsters who wanted to try out for the youth team. The trials could be dramatic: almost all of the kids were poor and football was their sole chance to make something of their lives. They could also be comical: no matter how outstanding they were in their villages, when they walked out on to the pitch of a big club, the youngsters were overawed. The man in charge of the trials might be a recently retired player, or someone else associated with the club, someone with an eye for which kids had the most to offer, and not necessarily just on the pitch. The boys got a corned-beef sandwich (and some of them desperately needed it) and then went out and played a trial match. Every one of them saw it as his big chance. A bit of skill that caught the trainer's eye could be enough to mean a contract, a place in the team and, in the future, maybe even a call-up to the national side – the holy grail for players in the 1950s.

The Vasco side of the 1950s was known as the 'Victory Express'. The team had won the Carioca Championship unbeaten in 1945, 1947 and 1949 and provided the backbone of the national side. The dream for any talented Brazilian youngster was to turn out for a team that boasted Ademir, Ely, Danilo, Jorge, Ipojucan, Barbosa and Augusto. The day Garrincha went there it felt as if they were all present.

At Vasco, the man in charge of the trials was Volante, an Argentine who used to play for the club. When he saw Garrincha wearing just his socks in the middle of a group of kids, he asked him why he hadn't put his boots on. Garrincha answered timidly that he had left them at home; he didn't tell Volante that he was ashamed of the old, beat-up boots he wore in Petrópolis. He thought Vasco would lend him a pair. Volante sent him packing with the words, 'You can't play without boots.'

A few months later Garrincha tried his luck with São Cristovão at the insistence of Mané Caieira. São Cristovão was the only one of the small teams ever to be champions of Rio (in 1926) and they had a loyal following, including Garrincha's uncle. This time Garrincha did not go alone. Diquinho and Arlindo accompanied him, each with his old boots wrapped up in brown paper. They were brought on with 10 minutes of the game remaining but didn't get a kick of the ball. The trainer dispensed with them without even offering them a sandwich.

Mané Caieira was not discouraged. Later that year he ordered Garrincha to go to Fluminense and ask for Gradim, the youth team coach. Gradim was a friend who owed him a favour; when he heard Mané Caieira's name he would listen to what he had to say. Garrincha invited Diquinho and Arlindo to go with him again, but Diquinho was having none of it so Garrincha and Arlindo set off with their newly polished boots – after all, this was Fluminense, the grandest of Rio's football teams, they were going to. They walked into the sumptuous stadium at Laranjeiras and Garrincha told Gradim he was 'Mané Caieira's nephew'. Unfortunately for Garrincha the name must not have rung any bells with the coach because they spent hours leaning against the fence at the side of the pitch watching other boys run on and off. By 6.30 it was getting dark. Garrincha was afraid he'd miss the last train home and Gradim asked them to come back another day. Garrincha said yes sir, but in truth he had no intention of returning.

Every time he tried out with a team in Rio it cost him a day's wage at the factory, three hours there and back on the train – and, because he always got lost, innumerable bus rides around Rio's complicated streets. Worse than that, when he got there he had to endure the humiliation of watching a bunch of kids younger than he was playing football while he waited for a chance that never came. In Pau Grande, things were different.

In the eyes of Pau Grande manager Carlos Duarte Pinto, the best player in the side was not Garrincha but a player named Vu. Because Vu played right midfield, Duarte Pinto moved Garrincha out to the right wing. The idea of forcing Garrincha out wide because of another player might seem comical today, but Duarte Pinto had his reasons: he thought that Vu was a better midfielder, or more cerebral at least, than Garrincha. With Vu's footballing brain in midfield and Garrincha out wide on the right, Pau Grande went unbeaten for two years. They played against the best sides in the region in 1951 and 1952 and never lost once. It was a great team: Gido Cabuqueiro, João Birruga and Nonô; Jorge, Zé Pires and Sílvio; Garrincha, Vu, Diquinho, Arlindo and Hélio.

If the majority of them didn't get their faces on the football stickers of the time, part of the reason was the Pau Grande club which, because it refused to put a fence around its pitch, was forbidden from joining the local league. But the team nevertheless managed to carve out a niche for itself. Its reputation spread down the road to Rio, and some of the city sides got hold of a few ringers and went to Pau Grande to take them on. But they all came back beaten. Some, bad losers that they were, blamed the food and beer given to them by their hosts before the match.

On those Sunday afternoons, Garrincha shone. He took on whoever appeared in front of him. He would leave two or three defenders on the seat of their pants and then, with a jink or a feint, send another over the touchline. He would then move into the box and, with just the keeper to beat, there was nothing to do but dribble the ball around him and into the empty net.

Roughly speaking, that was also what he was doing with the girls of Pau Grande. At the back of the stadium there was a narrow strip of ground about four feet wide with a cosy patch of grass that separated the church from the stand. At night, the only people who went there were the couples who wanted to get up to more than they could on the benches in the main square. 'Get up to more' in the early 1950s meant that the girl performed oral sex on the boy, or perhaps even let him go as far as anal penetration. Full penetration implied the loss of virginity and the risk of pregnancy, something that was rewarded with the worst of all punishments: marriage. Only the most irresponsible youngsters would go all the way.

Youngsters such as Garrincha and Nair. Or Garrincha and Iraci. Or Garrincha and any one of a cast of thousands.

CHAPTER 3

1952–1953: *Curupira* in the City

NAIR MET GARRINCHA IN 1948 WHEN SHE WAS 12 YEARS OLD. SHE WAS an ordinary woman, of average height, slimmish, neither beautiful nor ugly. She was down to earth, and like Garrincha she had a natural aversion to school books. She dropped out of primary school after just three years and never learned more than how to spell her name, Nair Marques, which the registrar incorrectly recorded as Noir. Nair's parents Geraldina and Alexandre Marques were well-respected members of the Pau Grande community. Alexandre worked as a guard at the factory, but unlike Amaro he did not drink, chase women, massacre goats or sing *repentes*, the north-eastern folk music in which two people joust lyrically to the accompaniment of guitars. When he warned lovers to stop their canoodling in the back row of the cinema or on the lawn behind the club, they took him seriously and put away their hands or whatever else they had out.

Like all the other youngsters who lived in Pau Grande, Nair went to work at the América Fabril factory when she turned 14. She started out in the cloth section in 1950 before moving on to work behind the counter, delivering packages of material to the salesgirls. She earned slightly more than Garrincha and had eyes only for him – although in that respect she was only one of many.

Forming relationships while working at América Fabril was not easy. With guards patrolling the factory floor to break up conversations that were not quick or work-related, bonds had to be formed through glances, winks and smiles. Garrincha, like everyone else, spent his days flirting. The factory had nothing against couples arriving and leaving together, or against groups forming at lunchtime and when shifts ended; they just didn't want it to affect productivity. Outside working hours, they helped organise Sunday-night parties held at the S.C. Pau Grande's headquarters or at the América Fabril Employees Association, the factory's social club. The dances were, inexplicably, known as 'pig's heads', and were kept alive by music from small orchestras that played foxtrots, boleros and sambas. They were staunchly family affairs. The mothers prepared home-made fruit juices or coconut milk; not even Coca-Cola was available, never mind alcohol. Factory guards kept their eyes on the dance floor and so, not surprisingly, what happened outside on the grass behind the club was more daring than anything that happened inside the hall. While the orchestra played the hits of the day, couples would sneak out and return half an hour later. Garrincha disappeared more often than most.

One night, Garrincha and Nair crept out the back door and finally did what he had been trying to do ever since Nair looked after him during his exile under the bandstand. Until then, their romance had been platonic. But Nair was 16 now and she had her own desires burning away inside her.

A few weeks later, when Nair told him she had been feeling sick and strange inside, Garrincha was scared. He was old enough to know what such symptoms meant. But he was not old enough to be a father; he was barely old enough to be a son. Garrincha's brother Zé Baleia was living in Petrópolis at the time and he went there to ask him for advice. Baleia said there was only one thing for it: go to his father and tell him everything. He would go nuts and tell Garrincha that he had to marry the girl, but they had no other choice. The fact that

Amaro had fathered kids in towns and hamlets across the region was never mentioned, much less the word abortion. He returned to Pau Grande and told Amaro everything. He went nuts, and told Garrincha that he had to marry the girl.

The wedding took place on 20 October 1952, two days after Garrincha's nineteenth birthday. The bride appeared not in a wedding gown but in an ordinary dress made by a friend's mother, and the groom wore a brown suit, which was hurriedly made by a tailor and paid for with money raised by a whip-round among the players and officials of Pau Grande. The ceremony was held at the registrar's office in Raiz da Serra, and when it was over the newly-weds packed their bags and went not on honeymoon but to Nair's parents' house on rua Centenario, where in keeping with tradition they made their home. Seven months and two weeks later, Terezinha was born.

Of course, Nair was not the only damsel Garrincha had his way with at the back of the club. There was Iraci, a pretty *mulata* who, like Nair, he had first met at school and then bumped into again at the factory. Iraci and Nair were the same age, they both loved Garrincha and both were prepared to give up anything for him, from their supper to their virtue. Iraci, however, was more careful than Nair and was not about to get pregnant. When Garrincha told her he was going to marry Nair and have a child, she burst into tears and asked what was going to happen to her. 'Don't worry, *amor*,' Garrincha replied. 'You are young. When you grow up you'll be as good as new.' Iraci wasn't stupid enough to believe him but she knew she had no alternative. She was even poorer than Nair and her father didn't work as a guard at the factory or enjoy his local connections. She understood that if Garrincha was going to get married then he would marry Nair. After all, she got there first. But she was not about to let him go. She loved him, and the fact that he had a ring on his finger did not prevent her from meeting and sleeping with him, which she continued to do throughout his marriage to Nair.

Neither his new marital status nor his wife's increasingly swollen

35

stomach prompted Garrincha to change his ways. He still went to the factory only when he felt like it, he still delighted the fans every Sunday, and when he had time off, or even when he didn't, he kicked a ball around with his mates or disappeared into the forest for a spot of hunting or fishing. When he wasn't playing, he was sitting in Dódi's bar with Pincel and Swing, demolishing the stock of beer.

Life couldn't have been more perfect for Garrincha in Pau Grande. He didn't have a lot of money and he hardly lived a life of luxury, but he had comfort, women and credit at the local bar. In other words, leisure, pleasure and freedom – everything he needed. Pau Grande *was* paradise. So when a man named Araty asked Garrincha to come and have a trial with Botafogo, it took him more than a year to say yes.

One Sunday in March 1952, Botafogo right-back Araty Vianna was invited to go to Pau Grande by his good friend Paulo Olegário, the manager of the Bonsucesso branch of the Boavista bank. The bank side was considered one of the best amateur teams on the whole of Rio's North Side (the North Side being the rougher, more working-class part of the city, the South Side the moneyed Rio of Sugarloaf, Copacabana and Christ the Redeemer) and was scheduled to play the team from the local factory after a *feijoada*, a traditional meal of rice, beans and pork leftovers. Araty was asked to referee the match. He had received more exciting invitations in his time but Botafogo were not playing that weekend so he decided to go.

The home side's number 7 wreaked havoc on the bankers. He had a funny pair of legs but he made a mockery of the opposition with his mesmerising dribbles, scoring three goals in the first half an hour and another two before the final whistle went. Araty didn't know whether to referee the game or run to the side of the pitch and scream, 'This guy is a hundred times better than the wingers at Botafogo!' When the whistle went, he approached Garrincha over by the corner flag. 'Listen,' he said. 'Your place is in Rio, with Botafogo. There's no one there as good as you.' He gave him a business card with the words

ARATY VIANNA – BOTAFOGO FOOTBALL AND ROWING CLUB printed on it and told him to come and look for him at the club's ground on rua General Severiano in the Botafogo district. Garrincha thanked him and promised him he would.

Fifteen months later, he went looking for Araty.

It was perhaps just as well that Garrincha took his time in going to Botafogo because had he gone there straight away Araty would not have been there to welcome him. A week after seeing Garrincha play in Pau Grande, Araty was called into the Brazil squad to take part in the Pan-American Championship in Chile. Nevertheless, before leaving he had raved about the young player he saw in Pau Grande and told people at the club to keep an eye out for him. His reports were so glowing that they sounded as though they came from someone with an overactive imagination. According to him, out there in the hills was a winger with bent legs who dribbled like the devil and was totally unmarkable. It was unbelievable. If the guy was so good then why had no one heard of him before? And what was the story with the legs? The players and directors didn't have much faith in Araty's reports.

However, one person did put enough credence in Araty's stories to go and take a look for himself. Several months later, when he found the time, Botafogo fanatic Eurico Salgado went to Pau Grande to watch Garrincha play. At the end of 1952, Pau Grande played two matches against Ana Nery, a team that had won one of Rio's principal amateur leagues three years in a row. Pau Grande won both games 5–0 and Garrincha was outstanding in both matches, delighting the watching Salgado. Unaccustomed to losing, Ana Nery demanded an opportunity for revenge, this time on their own pitch. In the third match, on 7 June 1953, Pau Grande lost five goals in the second half and went down 5–3. Even so, when the match was over Salgado approached Garrincha on the sidelines and told him, 'You are coming with me to Botafogo.'

Garrincha had never seen the man before, and although he listened politely he tried to turn down the offer. He had been to other clubs, missing a day's work in the process, and none of them had given him a chance to show what he could do. 'It'll be different this time,' said Salgado. 'If I take you, you'll get a chance.' Franklyn Leocornyl, the president of Pau Grande, and Duarte Pinto, the club's manager, were listening to the conversation. Salgado gave Leocornyl his card and put 100 cruzeiros in Garrincha's hand and told him he'd be waiting at midday on Tuesday at the Rio train station to take him to Botafogo. Leocornyl gave Garrincha the day off work and Duarte Pinto promised Salgado that he'd put him on the train that morning.

The following Tuesday, Salgado met Garrincha at the train station and took him to Botafogo in a taxi. There, he introduced him to Newton Cardoso, the youth-team coach and the son of team manager Gentil Cardoso. Salgado identified Garrincha as the star Araty had raved about and asked Newton to give him a run-out with the youngsters. Garrincha asked for Araty, who had trained in the morning and already left, and was instead told to go and prepare for a training session with the youths.

It was a while before Garrincha got his first touch of the ball, but when he did he was sensational. He set off into space to receive a pass but the ball arrived about three feet behind him. On the run, Garrincha flicked it with his heel over the oncoming defender, brought it down and then hammered the ball against the bar. Newton and the other 21 players on the park were amazed. Their jaws dropped. No one had ever seen anyone do anything like that before.

After 30 minutes, Newton Cardoso brought the first half to a close and asked Garrincha his age and real name. Garrincha said his name was Manuel and that he was 19. Newton was disappointed: he was too old for the youth team. Although, frankly, with skills like those he should be in the first team anyway. Newton didn't even bother to play him in the second half of the training match. He said he would talk to Gentil, and asked Garrincha if he could return the next morning and work out with the professionals. Eurico Salgado answered on Garrincha's behalf – yes, he'd come back – and then took him to get his train back to Pau Grande.

When he had gone, Newton Cardoso bumped into some reserve-team players who were in the gym. 'Look,' he said. 'Tomorrow you are going to train with a guy Araty discovered. When you see his bent legs you won't believe he can play football. But he is spectacular. He's going to be a star.'

The next morning Garrincha left Pau Grande at six a.m. and was at Botafogo by nine. Trainer Gentil Cardoso was expecting him, his son Newton having spent the previous night raving about the right-winger who had trained with the youth team. When Garrincha walked in, Cardoso couldn't resist asking him sarcastically, 'Are you Araty's star?' Garrincha didn't know what to say, so Gentil sent him to see coach Paulo Amaral. 'This is Araty's star,' he announced. 'Put him up against Nílton Santos.'

Amaral took Garrincha into the dressing room, where he met Araty. He embraced Garrincha, and, when he saw how apprehensive he was, assured him, 'Just play your normal game. Everyone is the same here.'

Garrincha took off his tatty shirt while he chatted with Araty. When he took off his even scruffier trousers, all eyes turned to his legs. The players had been warned his legs were crooked, but they hadn't thought they'd be that bad. Garrincha didn't so much walk as sway. There was no doubt about it: Araty and Newton Cardoso must be out of their minds if they thought this guy could play football.

Not that Botafogo were in a position to pass up any potential stars. It had been five years since the club had won the Carioca Championship and some of the veterans from that side were still first-team regulars. They were good players, but their careers were coming to an end. There were a few decent players who were still young enough to form the basis of a new side, including the 28-year-old Nílton Santos, who could have given speeches at the UN on the art of being a left-back and who had still not reached his prime. But most of the squad, though not quite bad enough to embarrass Donald Duck, the club's symbol, were far from being world-class.

Paulo Amaral blew the whistle to start the game. Soon after that Garrincha got the ball and found himself face to face with a tall and powerful defender. Nílton Santos had not yet won the nickname 'The Encyclopedia of Football', a moniker given to him during the 1958 World Cup, but he was already known to some as 'the new da Guia' – a reference to Domingos da Guia, then considered the most complete defender the world had ever seen. That morning, however, Nílton Santos wasn't feeling on top form. He was to be married on 1 July to Abigail Batalha, and with the wedding just 20 days away he was enjoying every last minute of the single life. Although he wasn't much of a drinker, he had gone out the night before to a Copacabana nightclub with his journalist friend Armando Nogueira. He had downed a few whiskies, and now he was paying the price.

Not that that was any excuse. Ten minutes had passed by the time Nílton Santos saw Garrincha coming towards him with the ball, more than enough time for him to have taken the measure of his opponent. When Garrincha stopped before him with the ball, Nílton moved slowly forwards to take him on. Far too slowly, because by the time he realised what was going on, Garrincha was past him. He spun around and chased back, and a few seconds later they were face to face again. This time he tried to register his presence with a tough tackle, but once again Garrincha was too fast for him and he was left standing. A few minutes later, Garrincha had the temerity to put the ball through his legs. No one had ever nutmegged Nílton Santos before.

But it was not all Garrincha. Time has served to exaggerate what happened, and the stories of that day make it seem as if there was an almighty battle between the two of them. Garrincha did skin Nílton Santos, and he did put the ball through his legs, but Nílton Santos also managed easily to disarm his young adversary and dribble past him on other occasions. Overall, it was a fairly even tussle. Which was what made it so amazing. On one side was full-back Nílton Santos, capped 16 times by Brazil, and on the other was an unknown player with bent legs who preferred to play football barefoot.

By half-time, Gentil Cardoso had seen enough. He took Garrincha off and sent him to speak with the club's directors.

When the training session was over, the reporters ran to interview Garrincha. Nílton Santos, still exhausted from his efforts on the pitch and in the bar the night before, told Gentil Cardoso, 'The boy's a monster. I think you should sign him. It's better to have him playing for us than against us.' Veteran team captain Geninho told the club's treasurer, Júlio de Azevedo, 'If I was a director, I wouldn't let that boy go home. Botafogo should sign him right now.' Sandro Moreyra, a reporter with the newspaper *Diário da Noite*, was another who ran off to phone the club's acting chairman Paulo Azeredo. But Azeredo already knew about Garrincha: Alexandre Madureira, director of the club's technical department, had beaten Moreyra to it.

With no time to draw up a proper contract, they wanted Garrincha to sign a blank one that the club would fill in later. But they had to agree on a salary, and they had to do it quickly. Botafogo knew they had to get his signature before the other clubs got word of the prospect they had on their hands.

That feeling was reinforced when Madureira got off the phone and was told that a spy from another club had watched the training session from the stands. The spy was Edgar Freitas, Madureira's counterpart at Vasco da Gama. The clubs routinely watched each other's training sessions and stole each other's players. Two years before, winger Joel had come through the ranks of Botafogo's youth teams only to be pinched from under their noses by Flamengo. Today, Joel was one of Flamengo's main strikers and a furious Alexandre Madureira was determined not to let the same thing happen with Garrincha. He knew that Freitas would not be so cheeky as to try to poach Garrincha from right under their noses, but it would not be difficult to find out that he lived in Pau Grande and there was every chance he might dash up there to try to sign him. The answer was to keep Garrincha at the club, or take him somewhere else, and not let him go home until he had signed a contract – any contract.

Madureira told Garrincha that they could discuss wages only with Paulo Azeredo. The problem was that Azeredo would not arrive at the club until later that night. They would have to wait.

'If he takes long, I'll miss the train to Raiz da Serra,' Garrincha protested.

'That doesn't matter. You can sleep at the club.'

'Fine. My wife is already used to me not coming home.'

'What wife?' asked a worried Madureira.

'Nair. I'm married and about to have a baby.'

When Madureira heard that, he was over the moon. Garrincha's slight frame and boyish ways had given Madureira the impression he was still not even 18 and would have to be treated as an amateur. Gentil Cardoso informed him that Garrincha was almost 20. He could be signed on professional terms. Even better, the fact that he was married meant that they would not have to go to Pau Grande to get permission from his father.

In order to register Garrincha the club needed photos, so to save time Madureira took him into town to have his picture taken. Half a dozen passport-sized shots were taken, and while they waited for them to be developed Madureira took Garrincha for lunch at a Portuguese restaurant called Timpanas. Madureira knew the owner, Lino Soares de Almeida, and it was he who waited on them personally.

Garrincha pretended to read the menu, then ordered, 'Rice, beans and spaghetti.'

Lino tried to convince him to try the squid or dried cod, the specialities of the house. 'You don't want to try our cod?'

Garrincha was sure. 'No, sir. Just give me rice, beans and spaghetti.'

Garrincha's simplicity was one of the things that most shocked the people at Botafogo. His accent was strange, and he didn't even know the right words for some of the most basic footballing jargon. What Brazilians called a half, from half-back, he mispronounced 'harf', and instead of saying penalty, he said 'penaty'. But before anyone could accuse him of being stupid, the directors were quick to point out that entire teams were made up of players who spoke like him and yet couldn't do half of what he could with a ball.

Alexandre Madureira and Garrincha returned to Botafogo at the end of the afternoon, and when Paulo Azeredo arrived at around nine p.m., they, together with Júlio de Azevedo and the club's director of football, Estanislau Pamplona, hammered out an agreement. Garrincha signed the blank contract, the first of many, which gave him just 300 cruzeiros more than he was earning at the factory. He was also spending his first night in the city. Not in a fancy hotel or a flat with a view overlooking Copacabana beach, but in a cheap and cheerful dorm room under the stands at General Severiano.

Meanwhile, the readers of the evening newspapers *O Globo* and *Diário da Noite* were discovering that Botafogo had found a 'spectacular winger'. Both reports were enthusiastic about the new player. *O Globo* got Garrincha's age wrong (it said he was 18), but it got his name right: Garrincha. The article in the *Diário da Noite* was accompanied by a photo but simply said that the player had been brought to Botafogo's attention by Araty and had gone straight to train with the first team. It gave his name as Manuel dos Santos and said that 'at Botafogo he was given the nickname Gualicho'.

'At Botafogo' actually meant 'by Sandro Moreyra', the journalist who wrote the piece. Moreyra was a Botafogo fanatic and a close friend of some of the club's directors. Like the other reporters who saw Garrincha's trial, Moreyra clearly heard the new boy say his name was Garrincha. But he didn't think much of it, especially when he heard him say that Garrincha was the name of a bird. It didn't do justice to the young man who galloped down the wing like a thoroughbred, hurdling over and weaving in and out of anyone who tried to stop him. When he got back to the newsroom to write his story, Sandro raved about Garrincha to Fernando Bruce, the sports editor whose real passion was horse racing. And, like all horse-racing aficionados in 1953, he was a fan of Gualicho, the horse that had run away with the previous year's Brazilian Grand Prix, the local equivalent of the Derby, and who was the favourite to repeat that performance on 4 August. Sandro and Bruce agreed that Garrincha should change his name to Gualicho. It would be better for the player, who would be identified with an unbeatable horse, and better for the paper, which could run football and horse-racing stories side by side.

On that first day after he appeared at Botafogo it was impossible to prevent the other papers calling him Garrincha, but the *Diário da Noite* insisted on Gualicho, and after a while the name stuck. By the time Garrincha made his debut for Botafogo a few weeks later, radio commentators had taken to calling him by the unwelcome nickname. And when Gualicho romped home in the Brazilian Grand Prix, winning by nine lengths, it seemed as if the fate of Garrincha's name was sealed.

The decision, of course, had had nothing to do with him. He did not want to share his name with a racehorse, and in pitch-side interviews he timidly hinted that he preferred the name Garrincha. But with editors and reporters failing to reach any consensus, the confusion spread, and during his first few months as a professional he was variously called Gualicho, Garribo, Garrico, Carricho, Garricho, Garricha, Garrinha, Garrincho and Garrincha. It eventually fell to *O Globo*, the paper that had called him by his preferred name, to draw a line under the issue with a story headlined MY NAME IS MANUEL AND MY NICKNAME IS GARRINCHA.

'Garrincha has exceptional skill. He has only one weakness, an easily correctable one, which is the tendency to dribble too much.'

Had those been Paulo Amaral's last words, his reputation would have been compromised for ever. Because that was how Amaral summed up Garrincha's first two performances for Botafogo during a short tour of Rio state at the end of June.

In his first match, on 21 June, a Garrincha goal gave Botafogo a 1–0 victory over Avelo. In his second, a week later, they defeated Cantagalo 5–1; for one of the goals Garrincha dribbled past the entire Cantagalo defence and then turned in front of the open goal and passed the ball to Ariosto to score. Ariosto couldn't understand why Garrincha hadn't just put it in the net himself.

That would be just the first of the questions Botafogo would ask about Garrincha. Another would be why, after beating the defender, did he wait for him to get back so he could beat him again? And why did he insist on dribbling even after he had beaten the whole team?

People hadn't yet realised that Garrincha was the most amateur footballer professional football would ever produce. Or that for him, the joy of playing didn't come with scoring goals, or winning games or even making money. Goals, victories, win bonuses – they were all just the inevitable products of the business of football. For Garrincha, the fun was in dribbling. Just dribbling.

CHAPTER 4

1953–1954: The Vital Fluids

IN MARCH 1950, BANGU HAD BOUGHT ZIZINHO FROM FLAMENGO FOR 600,000 cruzeiros, or about $33,000. At the time it was the highest transfer fee in Brazilian history. Three years later, in June 1953, Botafogo bought Garrincha from Serrano de Petrópolis, the club that held his registration, for 500 cruzeiros, or about $27. No one had ever paid so little for such a great player.

On 25 June Garrincha sat down with the directors to sign the back-dated contract. With some difficulty, he managed to scribble his name on a piece of paper that guaranteed him 1,500 cruzeiros per month (and another 500 under the table). The one-year contract was co-signed by Paulo Azeredo for Botafogo and gave Garrincha the option of living in the club dorm under the stand. He politely turned down the offer, saying that his first child had just been born and his family might need him at home to change nappies.

Signing a contract to play professional football did not alter Garrincha's status in Pau Grande. The new manager of the América Fabril factory gave Garrincha a year's leave of absence and made it clear that he could have his job back at the end of the year if he needed it. It was not that they wanted him to fail. It was just that they knew all too well what he was like.

Botafogo, however, didn't, least of all medically. Brazilian sportsmen of the time were in no better condition than the average man on the street. Football players, especially those from the countryside, arrived at the big city clubs in a shocking state. They looked healthy enough, but they were awash with parasites. Many were undernourished and anaemic. It was not unheard of for players to have syphilis or tuberculosis. The majority had what Nelson Rodrigues, one of Brazil's best-known playwrights and a football fanatic, called 'an anthology of dental disasters'. Such disasters brought on circulatory and muscular problems, which made the players more susceptible to aches and strains. Those weaknesses meant that injuries took longer to heal. With their teeth a mess, players were unable to chew properly, and that brought on digestive problems. Their weakened bodies were also susceptible to sexually transmitted diseases. Gonorrhoea was common and, although it could be treated with antibiotics, it put players out of action for three or four days. Away from the club, the players didn't always move in the most salubrious social circles. There were players who, as soon as they picked up their pay packets, waved the cash in the air and announced they were off to spend it on whores. Quite a few of them smoked, even at half-time, and so many of them drank that inebriation was tolerated as long as they didn't turn up at the club half-cut.

Garrincha was no exception to the unhealthy rule. Before arriving at Botafogo he had been to the gym fewer than ten times in his whole life. He was 5'6½" tall and weighed 10½ stone. His right knee bent inwards, his left knee bent outwards and he had a dislocated hip. According to the club doctors, his left leg was more than two inches shorter than his right, and, depending on the angle of vision, one could see he was slightly cross-eyed. Doctors at professional football clubs liked to give players a medical before signing them, but it was not a priority and sometimes, as in the case of Garrincha, there was no time. If they had a trial and the manager liked what he saw, they dispensed with the formalities and rushed to get a signature on the dotted line.

It was just as well they didn't have a chance to give Garrincha the once-over because Botafogo were in desperate need of a decent right-winger. Veteran Paraguaio was about to go to Fluminense, and although Gentil Cardoso had tried out a series of youngsters in his place none of them was good enough. The best was Mangaratiba, a quick young lad who had come through the ranks, and it was he who Gentil named in the side for Botafogo's first Carioca Championship match against São Cristovão on 12 July. Botafogo struggled to a 1–0 win and Mangaratiba, who played poorly, was the target of the crowd's abuse. The anger was not personal; the problem was that the fans had seen the alternative. Before the main match, Botafogo's reserves had demolished São Cristovão's reserves 5–0, with a young debutant on the wing called Garrincha scoring one and playing a part in the other four.

Gentil Cardoso had seen the match too and he regretted not having given Garrincha his full debut in the first team. It was not because he hadn't wanted to. In the week leading up to the opener, Garrincha disappeared. When he didn't turn up for gym work on the Tuesday or to take part in ball work on the Wednesday, Gentil started to get worried. At first he thought something might have happened to him, but he discounted that possibility and convinced himself that Garrincha was taking advantage. When someone from Pau Grande called the club to say that Garrincha had had a tooth out, he was not happy. It was an old excuse, a Brazilian equivalent of 'I was at my grandmother's funeral.' Gentil calmed down only when Garrincha turned up on Thursday with his face swollen and a hole in the upper left-hand side of his jaw where his molar used to be. He ordered him to rest and called Mangaratiba into the squad for the weekend match.

A week later, on 19 July, Botafogo were at home to Bonsucesso and 2–1 down with 14 minutes of the second half gone. In the 1950s, when big teams such as Botafogo lost to the smaller clubs it was as if the sky had fallen in, and it was even worse if they were playing at home. Vasco fans ripped up their season tickets, Fluminense fans threw oranges, and Flamengo fans waited outside the club to abuse the players. At Botafogo that afternoon, with the sky black and the rain falling, it really did seem as though the heavens were about to collapse. And then Botafogo were awarded a penalty.

The question was, who was going to take it? The eldest and most experienced players weren't interested. Geninho, Araty, Juvenal, Nílton Santos and striker Dino all made sure they were nowhere near the penalty area. Botafogo had not played well against São Cristovão and they were not playing well against Bonsucesso. The player who missed the penalty would not be popular. Then Geninho looked up and saw Garrincha placing the ball on the spot.

Garrincha was the regular penalty-taker at Pau Grande, and when no one wanted to take this one he wasn't afraid to assume responsibility. He hadn't started well, but he had come into the game as the match wore on and Botafogo's goal had come from his corner kick. Ary, the Bonsucesso keeper, knew Garrincha was making his debut and tried to wind him up: 'Take your time, son. Make sure you stick it right in the corner. Gentil Cardoso won't forgive you if you miss.'

He didn't have to worry. Garrincha slammed the ball into the corner of the net, giving Ary the honour of being the first keeper to be beaten by Garrincha in an official match. The goal inspired Garrincha and he went on to play a blinder: dribbling, attempting bicycle kicks, being upended in the box and scoring the fourth and sixth goals in Botafogo's 6–3 victory, the second of which came in the last minute off the outside of his right foot from an impossible angle. The terraces went wild and Garrincha ran to the rowdiest section to celebrate his goals. When the final whistle blew he was hoisted into the air by two black men who were celebrating as if Botafogo had won the World Cup.

The two men who carried Garrincha on their shoulders were Pincel and Swing. They and 30 others had come to the city from Pau Grande to see their friend make his debut and throughout the game they had chanted his name. When the match was finished they carried him triumphantly through the streets around the stadium, and when they were done Garrincha jumped on the back of the truck with his mates and they drank *cachaça* and let off fireworks all the way home.

Their arrival in Pau Grande sparked another massive celebration. Few people in town had a radio so Pau Grande president Roberto Leite Rodrigues had installed a loudspeaker in the main square in front of the church, just as he had done during the 1950 World Cup finals. The live game that day, however, was Flamengo–Olaria at the Maracanã, so those who had gathered to hear about Garrincha had had to be content with score flashes coming across from the stadium at rua General Severiano. It was only when the truck rolled into town that they got to hear the details of Garrincha's performance.

The lack of live commentary was the main reason why in the following weeks more and more people joined the convoy that left Pau Grande and headed to the city to watch Garrincha play. Flamengo and Vasco were the two biggest clubs in Rio at the time and they were invariably the focus of the day's live commentary match. Those who wanted to know about Botafogo had to go to the stadium. And they did. In his first months at Botafogo, after every game, Garrincha and his friends could be seen leaving the ground and heading home on the back of a truck winding its way up the road to Pau Grande. It was not always a happy journey. Botafogo finished in third place in the Carioca Championship that year, though Garrincha was the second top goalscorer with 20 goals in 26 games, just two behind Flamengo's Paraguayan striker Benitez. Flamengo won the title.

The Pau Grande delegation did not limit themselves to watching official matches. Pincel and Swing often skipped work to go and watch Garrincha train, and they would sometimes even go to Rio straight from work and wait for Garrincha at the train station, just to accompany him back home. Everyone at the club came to know them and they were treated with respect. Friends of Garrincha were friends of Botafogo.

The journey from Pau Grande to Botafogo was a complicated one, and Garrincha's days were long. When he trained in the morning he had to get up at five in order to be at General Severiano by eight. He left the house in darkness and watched the sun come up from the window of the train. When he trained in the afternoon, the return was even worse. The last train was the famous 'eight twelve', the Raiz da Serra train that left Rio at 20:12. The journey took between an hour and 40 minutes and two and a half hours, depending on how many of the 30 possible stops it made on the way. There was no train station in Pau Grande, so Garrincha had to catch the old wooden bus home from the train station at Raiz da Serra. If he missed the last one he had to walk almost three miles along the unlit dirt road that connected the two towns. When he was a child, his father had told him of the headless mules that haunted the highway, and even though the 20-year-old Garrincha no longer believed in ghost stories the slightest noise coming from the forest sent shivers down his spine.

The train drivers got to know him as Garrincha from Botafogo – to his relief no one called him Gualicho any more – and on the nights when he was too tired to walk from Raiz da Serra to Pau Grande he asked them to slow the train down a little so that he could jump off closer to home. One night he jumped off the train, safely as usual, but stumbled when he hit the ground. The train driver happened to look round and see him fall, and shortly afterwards the news that Garrincha had fallen from a train near Pau Grande was being broadcast on Radio Nacional. Gentil Cardoso and Alexandre Madureira jumped in a taxi and sped off to Pau Grande to check out the damage to their prize asset, only to find him sprawled out in the back seat of a car with a bottle of *cachaça* and a woman. They pulled him out of the car, hustled him into their taxi and took him straight back to the dorm underneath the Botafogo stand.

Even with the hassle of going back and forth every day, Garrincha preferred to remain in Pau Grande. And not only because his wife and daughter were there. Pau Grande was where his friends lived and he had a lot more freedom there than he did in the city, where Gentil,

Madureira and the other directors could keep a close eye on him. The club had no idea, for example, that when he returned to Pau Grande after a match on Sunday he didn't head straight to his home sweet home.

His first stop was Osmar Abraão's bar, right there in the train station at Raiz da Serra, where he filled up on *batidas*, cocktails of rum, sugar and fruit juice. From there he would go to the house Pincel and Swing shared with friends. There, they would throw drinks back all Sunday night and well into Monday. It was a miracle they made it to Tuesday alive.

Garrincha's appearances at General Severiano on a Tuesday morning were rare, and Botafogo got used to hearing his excuses when he finally made it in on Wednesdays. 'My father fell off a horse', 'My aunt died', and 'I had to take my wife to the doctor' were just some that he came up with. After a while no one at Botafogo believed him, but they had no idea what he was really up to; they thought he was at home playing with his children. However, his appearances at home with Nair were equally rare. After leaving Pincel and Swing in Raiz da Serra, Garrincha would go home just long enough to shower and change. For waiting for him in Pau Grande were his mates Valtinho, Arlindo, Fumaça ('Smoke'), Malvino, Albino, Ary, Carlito, Didico, Nelson and Pinico. They hardly amounted to local royalty but they had known Garrincha since they were children and they had a special place in his heart. Together they hung out at Dódi's bar or Constâncio's bar, where Garrincha would pay one of the old regulars to sing, or they would find the energy to get up and kick a ball about on the local pitch.

It took Botafogo a while before they realised the risks they were running of losing an important player on the eve of a derby or league decider. In the days before big matches, Garrincha twisted and turned over the holes and bumps of the Pau Grande pitch and jumped over the tackles of his adversaries, many of whom played in shoes as football boots were still a luxury.

Of course, the main reason Garrincha wanted to stay in Pau Grande was his girlfriends, of whom Iraci continued to be the most important. She saw him every week, and every week he made the same promise: 'Look, sweetheart, I owe you a marriage. It's just that I am already spoken for. But don't worry, I am going to take you to Rio. I am going to set you up in a house and we'll live together for ever.' It would take a while to happen – Garrincha didn't get round to making good on his promise until 1957 – but Iraci didn't seem to mind. She was in love, and she was faithful. Garrincha slipped into her house through the back door and she would give him home-made *mariolas* before making love as loudly as if the walls were three feet thick.

Nair's brothers knew about Garrincha's antics, but there was nothing they could do. Garrincha played for Botafogo and he was on his way to being rich, so why fight with him? As long as he did not publicly embarrass Nair or let her go without, there was nothing to make a fuss about. They believed that no matter how many girlfriends he had in Pau Grande, Nair was a kind of First Lady. In newspaper interviews he always referred to her as 'my lady', or 'the boss'.

But those terms by definition imply the existence of others, and in addition to Iraci there was Alcina, a tall and vain factory worker who was one of the stars of a samba school. Alcina could have been another Iraci, but when she gave birth to Garrincha's daughter Rosângela in 1954, Garrincha kept his distance. Alcina didn't make a big deal of it, and never asked for a penny to help her raise the child. Had she done so Garrincha could have been in trouble, for his baby-making factory was now up and running. That same year he would father his second little girl with Nair.

The birth of Edenir in September made the house they were sharing with Nair's father seem crowded, so they moved to rua Demócrito Seabra 7, to a house that was to become the most famous address in Pau Grande. It had three bedrooms, a living room, a kitchen, a bathroom and a yard with a veranda at the front. It was the smallest possible place for the size of family he would eventually have with Nair – eight girls.

Sex was Garrincha's main method of keeping fit. The alternative, working out, was not a priority for him or for the clubs. In 1953, football coaches did not specialise in physical education and their main exercise routine was 'Rule No. 7', a programme created by the French Army during the First World War that comprised running, stretching and doing star jumps to the trainer's count of one – two – three – four. It was easy, and players used the time to gossip about what they did the night before or to arrange what they planned to do when training was over. It was the same story at all the clubs.

If the regime was tougher at Botafogo it was thanks to the presence of Paulo Amaral, the 30-year-old trainer who was bigger, stronger and braver than all the players put together. A student boxer and the 1951 Carioca weightlifting champion, Amaral taught physical education to the feared special police squad. He was the man charged with knocking Garrincha into shape.

Garrincha arrived at Botafogo at an age when he was about to stop growing. However, exercises would help him to build himself up, and although he never grew an inch he did add four and a half pounds of muscle to his legs during his first two years at Botafogo. Before long, club doctor Nova Monteiro would say he had a muscle mass 'comparable to a horse'. That strength was one of the secrets behind Garrincha's balance – legs like tree trunks allowed him to stay upright even after the most vicious assaults. It took lunges or scything tackles to knock him down, and even when he was felled he got up quickly.

Garrincha was able to put on some weight not because he enjoyed training but because he couldn't avoid it. Although he rarely turned up for Tuesday's training session, he could not escape the one on Thursday because he was being held prisoner at the team's *concentração*.

And the players really were prisoners. Under the *concentração* system players were taken to a hotel where they were sequestered until the match. If the game was on a Saturday, the *concentração* started on a Wednesday: if the game was on a Sunday, it started on a Thursday. The system was designed to stop the players doing one thing: having sex. According to the thinking of the time – it was a theory supported by doctors and coaches – sex tired out the players. The vital fluids that were indispensable if they were to win football matches would be wasted on women, and the only way to ensure they behaved themselves was to lock them up for three days.

Their despair was bad enough on Thursday, but it blackened further after Friday's training session because the players were ordered to take it easy – as if their bodies were batteries they could recharge by doing nothing. By Saturday afternoon they couldn't stand the sight of one another and were sick to death of playing cards, snooker or table tennis. There was no television and the players were not big readers. Books were almost unheard of, and most, including Garrincha, never got further than scanning the sports pages of the newspapers. A few couldn't even read or write and signed their names on the team sheet by inking over the pencil signature drawn in by one of the directors.

The *concentração* was often home to the high jinks and practical jokes usually reserved for the playground. The established players quickly realised that Garrincha wasn't as naive as some of the other newcomers so he was spared the worst of the ritual humiliations. He was, however, capable of getting involved in the most childish pranks, such as walking past another player and passing wind in his face, or sneaking up behind his team-mates and grabbing their backsides. On one occasion during a meal at the team hotel he got hold of the waiter's tray and took over as the *garçon*. He stopped a few feet away from the table and asked team-mate Paulo Valentim, 'Chicken or beef, Paulinho?'

'Beef,' Valentim replied.

Garrincha speared the meat with his fork, shouted, 'There you go. Air mail!' and threw it at Valentim's plate.

No one got angry with him when he pulled such stunts because Garrincha wasn't perceived as malicious. In fact he disguised what malice he did have, and he was also clever enough to know who to pick on and who to leave alone. And there was no denying he was funny. Even the way he looked, with his baggy trousers hanging from his hips like the Mexican comedian and film star Cantinflas, could make people laugh. Without him, the *concentração* would have been worse than it was.

The clubs that did not have their own base to use as a *concentração* stayed in hotels or rented homes. The players preferred hotels because it was easier to sneak out without getting caught. Often, as soon as they found out which hotel they'd be staying in, one of the squad would secretly book a room which they could all use to drink, play cards or entertain women. They stocked up on cognac and laid aside decks of cards, and when the night was over more often than not one of the players had gambled away the next day's win bonus. The directors knew what the players were up to but they didn't know where and could hardly go from door to door looking for them.

Garrincha was not a card player and neither did he play dice; he thought betting was a mug's game. At first, when he found out about the spare room, he didn't get involved, principally because he had his own way of escaping. When Zezé Moreira took over from Gentil Cardoso as manager, Garrincha used to claim he had to return to Pau Grande for family reasons. Zezé was a liberal man who saw no reason to prevent Garrincha from leaving, on the condition that he returned right away. At first he really believed that Garrincha needed to go home. But one day he gave Garrincha permission to go to Pau Grande to get a set of keys he claimed to have left in his bag. A short while after he left, Zezé went for a walk and saw Garrincha in the back seat of a taxi with two women who left him in no doubt as to their profession. Hours later, when Garrincha returned to the hotel, Zezé was waiting.

'Did you find your keys, Garrincha?'

57

Garrincha took them out of his pocket and smiled triumphantly. 'Yes, I did, Zezé.'

'Were they by any chance in one of those girls' handbags?'

Garrincha was punished, and from that moment on he added his name to the list of those using the spare room.

CHAPTER 5

1954–1956: Changes

IN A CAREER THAT BEGAN AT BOTAFOGO IN THE 1920S, CARLITO ROCHA had served as player, manager, director, chairman, chaplain, nutritionist, spiritual guide and every other position there was to fill. His principal role at Botafogo was to unify the club's two greatest characteristics: those of faith and superstition. With him, it was impossible to say where one ended and the other began. During his first year as president in 1948 Botafogo were crowned Carioca champions, something he attributed to the fact that the players had eaten the mangoes he personally handed out before each game. As long as the players sucked on mangoes, they were unbeatable. On his orders, the curtains at the club's headquarters were tied during matches (to tie the legs of the opposing team's players); he made the players take baths of arruda, a plant that was supposed to bring luck; he forced each of them to lie on the floor and eat three apples; and when the club won the title after signing Flamengo's centre-forward Pirilo in 1948 he recommended the club sign a Flamengo player every close season. His main talisman, however, was not a man, or a flower, or even a fruit. It was a dog.

Biriba was a friendly black and white mongrel that reserve-team player Macaé had found one day on the street outside the club.

Botafogo won the following weekend with Biriba on the bench, and from that moment on Carlito adopted him as the club's mascot. In fact, the little dog soon became much more than a mascot. When Botafogo were under pressure, Carlito had Macaé put Biriba on the pitch. He went after the ball, and the Botafogo players had been told not to stop him. While the referee and the opposition tried to catch him, Botafogo took the opportunity to compose themselves. Biriba became almost as good as a substitute. Other teams soon cottoned on to Carlito's ploy and someone tried to kidnap the dog, prompting Carlito to order Macaé to sleep alongside it. On hearing rumours someone was going to poison the animal he even had Macaé test his food first. When Botafogo beat Vasco to win the championship, Biriba took his place in the team photo. He was given a gold collar decorated with the Botafogo badge and was served champagne in a silver-plated dish. On one occasion, Carlito kicked a player off the team bus so that there was enough room for Biriba to take his place.

By 1949, however, Botafogo were so poor that not even the talismanic effects of a wonder dog could help them. They needed another lucky charm. The one that ended the era of superstition in the 1950s – with dribbles, goals and titles that had nothing to do with the supernatural – was a little bird.

Brazil's campaign in the 1954 World Cup in Switzerland was going well until they were drawn against the invincible Hungarians. The Brazilian delegation in Berne was overcome with panic when they heard the news. Even though the only Hungarian magic they had seen was at the end of newsreels, they knew they were the best team in the world.

The Hungarian team that won the Olympic gold in 1952 had gone 30 games unbeaten and just a few months earlier they had hammered England 6–3 to become the first foreign side ever to win at Wembley. In the rematch in Budapest their superiority was even more pronounced: Hungary won 7–1. In the World Cup they beat South

Korea 9–0 and West Germany 8–3. It was a wonder team, a side with names like Puskas, Czibor, Kocsis, Boszik, Budai and Hidegkuti. All of them were Hungarian army officers and ten of them played for Honved, then considered the best club side in the world. Their manager Giula Mandi was a genius. The team went 2–0 up within the first ten minutes of every game they played and then started taking it seriously and banging home the goals. On the eve of the match, such statistics struck fear into Brazilian hearts.

According to all reports, when Brazil walked out to face Hungary in Berne on 27 June 1954, the players were shaking with fear. The senior members of the Brazilian delegation had exhorted them to kiss the flag, avenge Brazilian deaths in the Second World War and even – in the words of João Lyra Filho, the chief of the Brazilian delegation – 'go out there and perform miracles', but the appeals had served only to demoralise the already terrified squad. As usual, Hungary scored two goals in the first seven minutes – without Puskas, who was injured. Some of the Brazilians were so overawed that they could hardly stand up; the only way to stop the Hungarians was by kicking them off the park. The game, which could have been a classic, turned into a battle in which the ball was forced to take second billing. The English referee Arthur Ellis gave each side a penalty and sent off Brazilians Nílton Santos and Humberto and Hungary's Boszik. Hungary won 4–2, and when the final whistle went the fighting started up again.

As the players walked off Czibor offered his hand to left-winger Maurinho, but when Maurinho went to shake it Czibor pulled it away. Maurinho slapped him on the stomach and the Hungarians attacked him. Manager Zezé Moreira pulled his player off but the Hungarians spat on the ground in front of him. Zezé was holding one of Didi's boots in his hand, and he threw it at them, hitting the country's assistant sports minister. Puskas then hit centre-half Pinheiro over the head with a bottle. Mayhem ensued. The Swiss police intervened and journalist Paulo Planet Buarque hit one of them, flattening him. Brazilian referee Mario Vianna went on Brazilian radio and

61

accused Ellis of participating in a Communist plot to help Hungary into the next round. To compound the embarrassment Lyra Filho sent a formal protest to FIFA accusing Ellis of being a Kremlin operative. When the Brazil team arrived home they were greeted as heroes. At least they had proved they were men.

Before the team had taken off for Switzerland, a few people, albeit most of them Botafogo supporters, had lobbied for Garrincha's inclusion in the squad. But Brazil was not exactly suffering from a shortage of right-wingers. The first choice was Julinho, the Portuguesa de Desportos player who, in spite of the team's poor showing, was voted the tournament's best right-wing. His understudy was São Paulo's Maurinho, who was also no slouch. Counting against Garrincha was the fact that he was only 20 and had been a professional for less than a year. It could also be argued that he was immature and, as the famous Flamengo fan Ary Barroso said, 'a one-trick pony'. A few people were disappointed that Garrincha hadn't made it into the squad, but no one was indignant.

In fact, Garrincha's name had been on the list of 40 the Confederação Brasileira de Desportos (the Brazilian Sports Confederation, or CBD, the forerunner to the Brazilian Football Confederation) had sent to FIFA before the cup. The 22 players who went to Switzerland were chosen from that list and Garrincha was one of the unlucky 18 who didn't make the cut.

In 1954, many would never have given Garrincha a chance in the national side. Every Sunday he committed the worst sin a winger could commit: he was greedy. He would beat one or two men with ease and then lose the ball to a third or fourth when he could easily have laid it off to a team-mate. One regular criticism heard around Botafogo at the time was: 'Yet another pointless demonstration of his undeniable talents as a dribbler.' His team-mates started to get annoyed and the fans swung between rapture and despair. When Botafogo won, he was the man whose dribbles brought them victory; when they lost, it was because he dribbled too much.

That year Botafogo lost a lot more games than they won. They finished in sixth place in the Carioca Championship, the last of the big teams and behind even América and Bangu. Flamengo won the title amid huge celebrations at the Maracanã. Ginger Rogers was there to give them their title sash and help them celebrate.

Botafogo decided to rebuild in time for the new season, bringing in new faces and hiring Zezé Moreira to take over from Gentil Cardoso. The new manager's first task was to teach Garrincha not to dribble. Zezé got a chair from the side of the field, placed it on the edge of the 18-yard box and called Garrincha over.

'Pretend that chair is a defender,' he said. 'As you can see, there's only one chair there, it's like that chair is the last man. From now on, when you are playing in a match and you go past the man marking you on the edge of the box, I want you to pretend that there's no one else ahead of you to beat. Cross the ball into the middle, do you understand?'

Trying not to laugh, Garrincha answered, 'I understand.'

'OK then, let's give it a go. Get the ball, come past the chair and cross it into the middle.'

Garrincha dribbled the ball, stuck it through the chair's legs and crossed it into the middle. Zezé could hardly believe it. He had intended to follow that lesson with one showing Garrincha how to chase back and defend, but he could see he was wasting his time. Garrincha, he decided, was impervious to instruction.

In May 1955, Portuguese businessman José da Gama arranged for Botafogo to go on a long European tour. Because transatlantic travel was so much more difficult back then, Brazilian teams had to be guaranteed 15 or 20 games to make the tour worthwhile. Such a lengthy trip lasted almost three months and involved close to 40 flights. The club brought with them not only strips, boots, balls and other training materials but enough supplies of beans, coffee and cigarettes to ensure that the players did not feel homesick. And because their initial flight

63

went Rio–Recife–Dakar–Lisbon–Madrid, they set off a full week before their first match.

The trip was not Garrincha's first outside Brazil. A year before, in July 1954, he had spent a month in Colombia and Ecuador with Botafogo. They played seven matches, winning all of them, and Garrincha didn't find Bogotá or Guayaquil that much different from Belém, the Amazonian city where he had played in February. In fact, the football in Belém was better. That flight north marked the first time Garrincha had ever been on an aeroplane. The Rio–Belém flight involved spending ten hours on a small twin-engine plane that stopped numerous times the length and breadth of the country. He felt a tiny bit sick when they took off, just as he had done when he went up in his first lift not long before, but within minutes he was right at home and soon unveiling what would become one of his classic airline pranks: pouring water into the open mouth of a sleeping colleague.

On that first trip to Europe in 1955, Garrincha was aware that everyone would be speaking languages that were foreign to him. On the club's first stop in Recife, he saw a parrot for sale in the airport and wanted to buy it and take it with him. When he was told he wasn't allowed, he asked, 'Who else am I going to speak Portuguese with if he doesn't go with me?'

The trips to the Old World were like voyages to Mars. If something happened to the club no one would know unless someone survived to tell the tale. The games were not transmitted by radio, let alone on television. Nothing was filmed, and newspapers did not send reporters or photographers. The CBD obliged clubs to include one reporter in the official delegation but, as a club representative who got bonuses and was treated almost like one of the players, he could not be counted on to report everything. He was usually so pleased to be there that had he caught the goalkeeper and the coach in a romantic clinch at the top of the Eiffel Tower he would have pretended not to see.

In Europe there were no points at stake and no Botafogo fans to shout at Garrincha to pass the ball. In addition, the accredited journalist was Sandro Moreyra, and Sandro had already decided that his reports were going to wax lyrical about Botafogo's spectacular displays. Garrincha was free to play however he wanted, and since his opponents had never seen him play he destroyed them in every game. The big, blond, Aryan defenders who laughed at his bandy legs got the shock of their lives.

In a game against Reims in Paris on 2 June, Garrincha was a one-man sensation. Botafogo were winning 5–1 with just over five minutes to go. Zezé shouted to Nílton Santos to keep possession and not to waste energy chasing a sixth. When the message reached Garrincha, however, he took it literally. 'So we're not to give the ball away, eh?' He started dribbling, sticking it between defenders' legs, going round others and refusing to pass the ball to anyone. He kept possession for so long that no one dared try to take the ball from him. Maybe because it was a friendly it never occurred to the French to go after him and try to break his legs. So Garrincha went after them, dribbling around them once more and even, when he had gone far enough one way, turning around and dribbling back towards his own goal. The whole stadium rose to give him a standing ovation and the match ended with the ball still at his feet.

Although Brazilians tell Portuguese jokes as the English tell Irish jokes, da Gama, the Portuguese businessman who had organised the tour, was no fool. When he saw how much of an attraction Botafogo were turning out to be he scheduled more matches. The additional dates were difficult to arrange in any orderly fashion, so Botafogo would go south from Paris to Rome and back north again a day later to play in Copenhagen. On one occasion they spent eight days in Amsterdam waiting for a game to be arranged in Zurich.

There, the team's hotel was on a street that ran parallel to the red-light district. In the absence of any matches, Garrincha practically moved in. He walked up and down the streets joking with the scantily clad women who passed time between clients knitting. Garrincha

65

thought it was hilarious that the prostitutes should knit; to him, knitting was something for grandmothers, and these girls were no grandmothers. Garrincha spent the days diving in and out of their ample bosoms.

In general, though, the players preferred not to have to leave the hotel in order to have sex. Instead they ordered a sandwich from room service and then jumped into bed. If the food was brought by a female, one of the players whipped off the sheet to reveal his team-mate lying there with an erection and a dollar. If she was up for it, great; if she wasn't, they ate the sandwich. They soon realised there was little risk of causing a fuss. Even if they turned down the offer the European waitresses were rarely offended. At worst they laughed and excused themselves. But they could not fail to be impressed by Garrincha's manhood.

It was while he was in Europe that Garrincha got himself a radio, and with it a reputation as naive and backward. The story about how he bought a radio in Europe and sold it to a colleague when someone told him he wouldn't understand the broadcasts back in Brazil became the stuff of legend. There are different versions of where he bought it (Berlin, Stockholm, Oslo, Helsinki, Reykjavik) and to whom he later sold it (Nílton Santos, Didi, João Saldanha, Quarentinha, Manga). The real story, however, is quite different.

Transistor radios were all the rage in 1955, even in Europe. The Brazilian players bought several each to take home to friends and families. Garrincha had more friends and family than most, and he always was a big fan of the radio. He had even given a big Grünfeld valve-powered wireless to Dódi to put behind the bar so that customers could hear live commentary of his matches.

The Botafogo side had one especially naive player, their reserve left-winger Hélio. It was Hélio who bought the radio in Copenhagen, and when he got back to the hotel and switched it on, Garrincha said to him, 'Does your family speak that language, Hélio?' Hélio didn't understand, so Garrincha, putting on his most serious voice, explained,

'If you don't change the valves when you get to Brazil no one will understand what the announcer is saying. And you can't get those valves back home.'

A disappointed Hélio resolved to take the radio back to the shop. No one knows if he actually did, but Garrincha certainly didn't buy it or sell his own. Furthermore, no one can remember how Garrincha came to be the butt of the story, especially since he took home radios for Nair, Iraci and several of the other girls he was seeing at the time.

Botafogo's successful showing in Europe was rewarded with a return to Rio aboard the ship *Conte Grande*. Botafogo had played 18 games, winning 11, drawing five and losing only two, both of which had come at the start of the trip when they were still jetlagged. They beat some excellent teams, their victories including a 6–0 drubbing of the Dutch national side and a 6–2 thrashing of Grasshoppers in Switzerland. The Europeans were keen to play them again and had already arranged ten more games to take place the following year. And da Gama had other reasons to feel pleased with himself. The goal sprees had enabled him to sell two Botafogo players and take a fat commission: Vinícius went to Napoli for five million cruzeiros, or $50,000, and Dino went to Juventus for the same sum. Part of the cut should really have gone to Garrincha, whose brilliance had turned Vinícius and Dino into such saleable assets.

The return trip was scheduled to take ten days – by the time they berthed at the Praça Mauá in Rio's docklands they would have been on the road for 80 days. The Carioca Championship opener against São Cristovão was due to take place soon after they hit dry land and Zezé Moreira was worried that the players would be short of fitness after their inactivity on board the ship. So he got permission for the players to run on board and kick a ball about, hoping that these work-outs would keep them in shape and away from the bar. But even then, Zezé knew he had to keep an eye on them.

He had noticed that Garrincha was drinking a lot of tonic water, and one day he decided to go to his table and investigate.

'Drinking tonic water, Garrincha?'

'Yes indeed, Zezé.'

'Give me a little drink, I'm thirsty,' the manager asked.

'But I've already taken a drink from the bottle, Zezé.'

'That's all right, Garrincha. You don't have tuberculosis.'

And with that he reached out and took the bottle from Garrincha's trembling hand. The tonic water burned his mouth and he spat it out. It was straight gin.

Before the *Conte Grande* even docked in Brazil, the players knew that Dino and Vinícius had been sold to Italian clubs. Instead of taking the boat, the Europe-bound duo had flown home in order to pack their bags and say their goodbyes. Around the same time, word went around that Juventus were after Garrincha.

Although there is no official record of a bid, da Gama had asked the Botafogo directors how much they wanted for their star winger and the club had responded by citing a fee of 15 million cruzeiros – equivalent to $150,000. Had the deal been done, it would have set a Brazilian record. That same month Portuguesa de Desportos sold Julinho to Fiorentina for nine million cruzeiros, or about $90,000 – and Julinho was the best winger in the world. Juventus tried to negotiate a deal that would take Garrincha to Turin, but when Botafogo insisted on 15 million the Italians dropped their interest – for a few years at least.

Garrincha was at sea when he heard of Juventus's interest and Botafogo's response. He hadn't the slightest notion of money or value but he knew that the transfer talk meant he was important. He wasn't angry that the deal never got off the ground. If Botafogo didn't want to sell him that was fine by him, he didn't want to leave Brazil anyway. Moreover, his contract was about to end and Sandro Moreyra, who was operating as his unofficial agent, had advised him to ask for a big pay rise.

When Moreyra saw Garrincha for the first time that June day in 1953, his life changed for ever. He was 35 at the time and had spent half his life at Botafogo. He was a confidant of Nílton Santos and a close friend of all the club's directors, most of whom treated him as a director without portfolio. He had been a sportswriter since 1946 but he never really considered himself a sports journalist per se. He was, to be more exact, a Botafogo journalist.

Garrincha's appearance at Botafogo was like an epiphany for Moreyra. Until that moment the person he had most looked up to was Nílton Santos. But Nílton Santos was as grave, adult and ministerial in real life as he was on a football pitch. He was like a serious older brother. Garrincha was different; Moreyra thought he was Chaplinesque. He could have been his son or his youngest brother. When Moreyra convinced himself that Garrincha should keep his own nickname, he was the first to see in him the soul of a bird. He couldn't believe that someone as talented as Garrincha could be so humble. Moreyra felt that he had to protect him from the cut-throat world of football he had seen only too often.

That meant advising him when it came to negotiating a contract and preventing people from taking advantage of him – without, if possible, harming Botafogo's interests. It also meant covering up anything that could bring him or the club into disrepute. He was the first and for a long time the only person to see Garrincha in his natural habitat of Pau Grande. So when the *Diário da Noite* published a story saying that Garrincha hadn't turned up at training because he was 'resting in Pau Grande' Moreyra was the only one who knew that the real reason for his absence was that he was probably recovering from an almighty drinking session with Pincel and Swing.

When he had renewed his contract for the first time in August 1954, Garrincha's monthly salary went from 2,000 cruzeiros to 10,000 cruzeiros – a 500 per cent rise, but a 500 per cent rise on next to nothing. Botafogo had also given him a 40,000-cruzeiro signing-on bonus, perhaps out of embarrassment. Now, fresh from the success in Europe, he asked for 20,000 cruzeiros a month. Botafogo offered him 16,000 cruzeiros, saying they were not going to break their wage scale to accommodate his demands. Garrincha knew they were lying because he knew the club's highest-paid player, Nílton Santos, was getting 22,000 cruzeiros. Even centre-half Gérson was getting more than they were offering him: 17,000 cruzeiros a month. And Gérson had been around so long that he still used rolled-up newspapers as shin pads.

Essentially, Botafogo were trying to avoid paying 4,000 cruzeiros to a player they valued at 15 million. Garrincha once again told them he wanted 20,000 cruzeiros. The club stood their ground and told reporters that if Garrincha continued with his intransigence he would be suspended. It was the first time anyone had treated him so harshly in public. Garrincha was hurt, and he reacted the only way he knew how: he spent the whole opening week of the Carioca Championship in Pau Grande, missing Botafogo's first match against São Cristovão. Someone, though, must have convinced him to give in, for the following Monday he turned up at General Severiano and signed a new contract – as usual a blank one that would have the numbers filled in later: 16,000 cruzeiros.

It was not a bad salary for 1955. The best-paid player in Brazil was Zizinho, who got 30,000 cruzeiros a month from Bangu. A senator got 36,000, a doctor or a lawyer 20,000. And the players got their bonuses on top of that, which, when they won, gave them enough to live the good life. But, as usual, the majority weren't paid nearly as handsomely and even the big names were light years from getting the multi-million-pound contracts, big cars and social success that today's stars enjoy.

Most players lived on Rio's North Side, on the working-class Ilha do Governador, or in Niterói, the city across the bay from Rio. The most valuable objects in their homes, aside from the blender and the floor polisher, were their trophies and medals. More often than not the walls were covered in Miss World-style champions' sashes and pennants presented to them when they played small sides from the provinces.

Few players thought to make any preparations for life after football. They didn't study, they didn't save, and hardly any of them gave a thought to what they would do when they retired. Only a handful had bank accounts; they were paid in cash and spent what they had and what they didn't.

The 16,000 cruzeiros Botafogo paid Garrincha was enough to sustain a family with two children. But now he was responsible for two or three of his brothers and sisters, several more of Nair's, uncles and aunt, cousins, nieces and nephews on both sides, and a whole army of friends and acquaintances from Pau Grande. All of them survived on what he got from the club. They made his home a meeting point (whether he was there or not), asked him for loans, and even ate and drank at Dódi's and Constâncio's and put the bill on his tab. When Moreyra asked him if they weren't taking advantage, he simply replied, 'Everything's fine, everything's great.' His wallet was as big as his heart.

Things weren't fine or great at Botafogo. The club seemed to have left its football in Europe. Dino and Vinícius weren't there to score goals any more and Garrincha, obliged to pass to João Carlos and Mario so that they could squander their chances, hit the net just three times in 21 games. They managed to do even worse than the year before, finishing seventh, behind even Bonsucesso. Flamengo took the title.

While Botafogo were dropping down the league table, Brazil were back in business again, one year and three months after their World Cup defeat by Hungary. They had arranged to play two matches against Chile in September 1955, first at the Maracanã and then at the Pacaembu stadium in São Paulo. In the backward thinking of the federation's top men, there were to be two teams, one comprising players from Rio and another comprising players from São Paulo.

71

Even the managers were different: Zezé Moreira would lead the team in Rio and Vicente Feola would take charge in São Paulo. Zezé called up Garrincha for the Maracanã.

Although it was his first time in a Brazil squad, Garrincha behaved exactly as if he was with Botafogo. And why not? The team was being managed by his club manager; his team-mate Nílton Santos was alongside him; and the *concentração* was at the hotel Botafogo always used. Two days before the game, with the team safely ensconced in the Paysandú Hotel, Garrincha invited Nílton Santos's understudy, Flamengo full-back Jordan, to go with him for a drink of water. When they got to the bar on the corner, the waiters greeted him as if he was there every day.

'Give me two waters, mate,' Garrincha said.

The waiter filled two glasses with *cachaça*. Jordan, who was himself no innocent, was horrified.

'That's *cachaça*, Garrincha!'

Garrincha just laughed. 'What did you think it was?'

'Water. I don't like *cachaça*.'

'Well, I love it. I'll drink yours. Give me a glass of water for my friend Jordan here.'

Jordan was impressed. He knew that every team had a player who enjoyed a drink but he had never seen anyone down as much *cachaça* as Garrincha and still walk straight.

It didn't seem to affect Garrincha when he made his debut in a 1–1 draw on 18 September. It wasn't a bad result for a team that had never played together before. Garrincha dribbled past the Chileans with every chance he got; one cross rolled along the top of the bar, and in the second half he galloped down the wing and fired in a shot that the surprised keeper did well to stop. The next day the newspapers complained, as usual, that he hadn't passed the ball enough.

With Flamengo winning the title again Botafogo knew they had to take action if they were not to finish even further down the table the following season. And in February 1956 they did, by signing Didi from Fluminense for 1.8 million cruzeiros, or about $15,000. Didi asked for, and got, a monthly salary of 70,000 cruzeiros – close to $650. It was a huge sum.

No one believed that Didi deserved less, but there was no denying he could be problematic. In 1952, a year after winning the league title with Fluminense, he had left his wife and son to marry a curvaceous Bahian singer called Guimoar. He had refused to pay his ex-wife alimony, and though he might have been a great football player, as well as being tall, charming and handsome, Fluminense did not take kindly to such scandal at their esteemed old headquarters in the Rio neighbourhood of Laranjeiras.

The Fluminense fans admired Didi, but Castilho, Telê, Carlyle and Orlando were all more popular and, although he scored the goals that won them the Carioca Championship in 1951, they never took Didi to their hearts. In a club that was overwhelmingly white and elitist, the black Didi was always an outsider. He angered the club by insisting on walking through their front door instead of the side entrance reserved for players; he fought with them over his ex-wife's pension, which the club was legally obliged to deduct from his wage; and he was disgusted by their refusal to allow players to make telephone calls from the *concentração*. When club officials tried to prevent him from calling his pregnant wife on the eve of a match, he walked out and never returned.

A thoughtful man who was an exponent of what might be called cerebral football, he was equally unique on the field. He treated the ball as if it were a precious object – he called it 'my girl' – and was proud to say he did not stand on her with his studs. He never headed the ball, saying that his head was for thinking with, and while he was a great dribbler, he only did so if he had no other choice. He would much rather pass the ball. The technique and skill that characterised his defence-splitting 40-yard passes were also at the heart of his speciality: *folhas secas*, free kicks that looked as if they were going straight to

73

the goalkeeper but then fell away at the last minute like a *folha seca* or dry leaf.

But for all his undoubted talent he was not able to turn things around at Botafogo overnight. The 1956 title was won by Vasco, who denied Flamengo a fourth championship in a row. Botafogo finished third, which was an improvement on the previous years' displays. They would use the close season to start building a side that, from 1957, would form the basis of the Brazil squad.

The most immediate consequence of Didi's arrival, however, was that next to his 70,000-cruzeiro salary Nílton Santos and Garrincha looked as though they were on peanuts. Botafogo had to give them a rise. And they did. Nílton Santos's monthly salary jumped to almost 30,000. And Garrincha went from receiving 16,000 to 18,000 a month.

CHAPTER 6

1956–1957: The Chrysalis

WITHIN MINUTES OF CHECKING INTO HIS ANTWERP HOTEL ROOM AT the start of Botafogo's European tour in 1956, Garrincha plugged in his record player, put on the samba records he had brought with him and lowered himself slowly into the bath. Before he was fully under the water, he heard a crackling noise and smelled smoke. Without thinking, he jumped out of the bath, pulled the record player from the socket and dumped it straight in the water, records and all. No one had told him the voltage was different in Belgium. For that trip at least, his sambas and mambos were history.

The 1956 tour was Botafogo's second consecutive long excursion to Europe and took in 22 games against teams from Belgium, England, France, Spain, Holland and Hungary. They won 16, drew three and lost three – an excellent record considering they were playing clubs such as Racing de Paris, Honved (to whom they lost) and Barcelona, teams among the best on the continent at the time. The most remarkable thing about the tour, however, was its length. Between the beginning of March and the end of June, the club packed and unpacked their bags in 45 cities, including four or five times in places such as Paris, Madrid and Barcelona.

These trips to Europe in the 1950s were decisive in helping the

Brazilian players broaden their horizons. Many of them knew little about the world outside Brazil and little about the football played there, and they laughed when they saw pictures of Russians or Czechs kissing each other when they scored goals. Telling them that was simply the way they did things in Europe made no difference. Whenever they saw the big, hairy foreigners celebrating with kisses and hugs their response was always the same: 'Poofs!' Years later, when they came face to face with the 'poofs' on their home turf, they were surprised to see they were every bit as rugged and masculine as themselves. Perhaps even more so, for these men played in the dead of winter, on pitches covered with freezing mud and snow, and with referees who, unlike their Brazilian counterparts, were willing to turn a blind eye to sliding tackles and shoulder charges.

The Brazilian ignorance of European football was complete. Few European teams, and certainly not top sides such as Real Madrid, Fiorentina or Manchester United, came to Brazil to take on the top Brazilian clubs, and when the Brazilians travelled it was in their own backyard of Latin America. Even the national side had never been to Europe other than to play in the World Cup finals. That changed in April 1956 when the national side undertook their first European tour, coincidentally at the same time as Botafogo. It was almost a complete disaster. Flávio Costa's team played poorly. They beat Portugal, Austria and Turkey, but drew with Czechoslovakia and Switzerland and were demolished 3–0 by Italy and 4–2 by England. In the game against England at Wembley, Gilmar saved two penalties and a 31-year-old Nílton Santos was turned inside out by Stanley Matthews, who was 41. When the side came home there were people who would have bet their homes on Brazil not winning the 1958 World Cup. The trusty old excuse trotted out after every World Cup finals – 'we went there to learn' – was no longer convincing. Brazil would never learn. They were mongrels who were scared of the Europeans, and even of the Argentines and Uruguayans.

Garrincha did not make the squad for that European trip. For the right-wing berth Flávio Costa preferred Vasco's Sabará and Flamengo's Paulinho, who could also play through the middle. Sabará, however, fell from grace halfway through the tour. In London on the eve of the England game the players were returning from a training session at Wembley when they were ordered to get off the bus to attend a memorial service with Brazilian and British diplomats at the tomb of the unknown soldier. Like his team-mates, Sabará was dirty, sweaty and dressed in a tracksuit, but unlike the others he was wearing flip-flops, and when he got off the bus the British officials were clearly offended at his footwear. The Brazilians noticed the gaffe but it was too late for Sabará, who was blamed for the incident and left out of the side for the England game.

Botafogo were in Europe when the national side's tour ended, and when the rest of the Brazil squad went home Didi and Nílton Santos flew to Spain to join their club. Didi had, of course, only just signed for Botafogo, and although he had played a few friendlies in Brazil, Europe was his first real introduction to the advantages and disadvantages of having Garrincha as a team-mate.

In his first game, against Rot Weiss Essen of West Germany, Didi sent a lovely through-ball down the outside-right channel for Garrincha to run on to. There was no one near him and he had all the time in the world; all he had to do was cross the ball or run in on goal himself. But Garrincha put his foot on the ball and waited for the defender to get back – he wanted the pleasure of beating a man. By the time he had done so, the penalty box was like a bunker with more Germans per square foot than Berlin's Alexanderplatz. Didi knew Garrincha had a habit of toying with defenders because he had played against him for Fluminense, but he didn't know how much of an obsession it was. Several times during the game he shouted for Garrincha to release the ball – or 'the girl' – but Garrincha pretended he couldn't hear and kept dribbling. Only when he was satisfied that he had beaten enough men would he lay the ball off, then turn to Didi and ask, 'What was that you were saying?'

Off the pitch, Garrincha took liberties with Didi he would never have taken with Nílton Santos. He grabbed his cheeks and wiggled them, or tried to grab his penis. An irritated Didi jumped back and screamed at his team-mate, 'Stop that, Mané! I am not a little boy.' Garrincha apologised, but when Didi looked away he moved in again. Didi eventually gave in and laughed. Other players didn't know what to say. When Didi signed for the club he was held in such high esteem that some players even addressed him as sir, and here was Garrincha treating him as just another *crioulo* (a once affectionate slang name with racial undertones, now highly offensive in Brazil and punishable by a prison term).

Didi quickly learned how to deal with his mischievous new friend and before long he had mastered the psychology needed to get the best out of him. Didi noticed that Garrincha was erratic: sometimes he would take on the opposition single-handed yet other times he would stand there staring into space as though his legs were a million miles from his head. Didi realised that he could predict whether or not Garrincha was up for it by watching him in the dressing room before the game. If he was running about and warming up it was a sign that he was ready to turn it on; but if he sat on the bench and changed very slowly into his strip, it was a sure sign he wasn't interested. When it looked as if he was somewhere else, Didi wound him up.

'Have you heard what they're saying about you, Mané?'

'No, Crioulo. What?'

'That you used to be hot but now you're burned out. And that if Botafogo hadn't signed Waldir Perreira to supply the ball, none of the forwards would get a kick of the ball.'

'Really? They're saying that? Who says that?'

'It doesn't matter. If I were you, I'd shut them up.'

'Leave it to me. I'll show them.'

And with that, Garrincha got changed and sprinted up and down the tunnel, ready to be true to his word.

* * *

On 7 February 1957, with 21 minutes gone in the first half of a match against Honved, Garrincha took a pass from Evaristo out on the left wing. He left two Hungarian defenders in his wake, moved into the Honved penalty area, shifted the ball on to his right foot and fired a shot into the net. As the fans celebrated the goal, the lights went out at the Maracanã.

Garrincha's goal was the first in a 6–2 win for a Botafogo–Flamengo select eleven chosen at the last minute to play what was at that time one of the three best club sides in the world (Real Madrid and River Plate were the other two). The short-circuit of the Maracanã's electrics marked the end of an era. That match, Honved's last on a short tour of Brazil, was the last time Honved would be Honved. Or at least the Honved of Puskás, Boszik, Kocsis, Czibor, Budai and Sandor, the greatest Hungarian players of all time. Hungarian football would never be the same again.

For in 1957 Honved was a football team in the midst of a tumultuous political drama. They were on tour in Europe in November 1956 when the USSR invaded Hungary to put down the uprising against the Communist regime. The day the Russians crossed the border, they were playing a Spanish side in Switzerland. Honved were the best team in the world, but because, nominally at least, they were Hungary's military team, they were treated as amateurs. While the team itself could command $10,000 per game, each player got a miserable eight dollars per performance. The major European clubs were constantly trying to lure the players away with big-money offers and the Russian invasion gave them the perfect excuse to take advantage. The night the tanks rolled into Budapest, the squad told the man running the tour that they would not be returning home. They were refugees. Honved would be a travelling side that played its home matches on the pitches of Western Europe.

The crisis at home jeopardised Honved's tour to Brazil. The Hungarian Football Association asked FIFA to ban them from playing any matches against affiliated clubs and to punish clubs that insisted on taking them on. The Hungarians had already signed a contract to play Flamengo, however, and neither side wanted to rip it up. The head of FIFA, Englishman Arthur Drewry, warned the CBD that if Flamengo played Honved they would be banned and Brazil would be tossed out of the 1958 World Cup. The CBD first tried to get Flamengo to withdraw from the match, but when Flamengo refused the CBD argued that they were not responsible for decisions made by their individual members and that the contracts had been signed before the crisis began. Nevertheless, in a bid to share responsibility, Flamengo asked other Brazilian sides to play them too. Botafogo was the only one to accept.

FIFA reconsidered their position and allowed the games to go ahead. The matches proved to be a feast of football. Thirty-nine goals were scored in the five games at an average of 7.8 goals per game. In the first match Flamengo won 6–4; in the second the visitors beat Botafogo 4–2; and in the third at the Pacaembu, Honved beat Flamengo by the same scoreline as in the opener. Honved won the fourth match 3–2 against Flamengo and lost the final match 6–2 against the Botafogo–Flamengo select. It was proof, if proof were needed, that the best players in Brazil were capable of taking on and beating the best in the world.

The man who led the Botafogo–Flamengo select that day was Geninho, a former Botafogo player who had taken over from Zezé Moreira as Botafogo manager in the middle of the 1956 Carioca Championship. A midfielder who had hung up his boots less than two years before, Geninho had seen first-hand the tricks Garrincha used to skip training or sneak out of the *concentração*. He knew that when he missed the last train to Pau Grande he would drink in the bar at the station until a taxi driver named Cabrita picked him up and drove him home. And he knew that when Cabrita wasn't available Garrincha would spend the night in Rio, often at the home of Neivaldo, another of Botafogo's right-wingers.

Until then, Garrincha had rarely brought Nair to Rio. He didn't

From the moment he was born, Garrincha's father struggled with his new born son, recording both his birthday and name incorrectly. But the confusion did not end there. At the start of his career some newspapers christened him 'Gaulicho' and he had to make a statement confirming what everyone in Pau Grande already knew: 'My name is Manuel and my nickname is Garrincha'.

Manuel signed for Botafogo aged 19 and did not take long to make his presence felt; at his first training session he stuck the ball through his opponent's legs.
With Araty (left), who first saw him play for Pau Grande and Gentil Cardoso at Botafogo.

Giving a new
dimension to
Botafogo: Above,
against Bangu, and
left and below
against Flamengo.

Before even arriving in Sweden in 1958, Garrincha had bent the new rules prohibiting players from wearing hats or carrying umbrellas. This natty headpiece, along with the rakish umbrella, made comparisons with Mexican comedian Cantiflas inevitable.

It hits the post!
Garrincha leads Brazil against the
USSR in 'the greatest three
minutes of footballing history.'

Family joy: holding
the Jules Rimet
with Mane Caieira.

The simple life: Pau Grande had enough adventures to keep any young man occupied.

When he wasn't kicking a ball around its dirt roads, Garrincha was hunting birds and animals or fishing and swimming in the rivers than ran by the little town. But he always made time for the fairer sex.

Fun in Mexico, above. An inveterate ladies man, Garrincha had more than his fair share of conquests first as a boy and later as a man. The romance with showgirl Angelita Martinez (left), was nothing more than a quick affair, but others were longer lasting. With Elza Soares (below), the true love of his life. They were together on and off for 20 tumultuous years.

know what do with her or where to take her, and besides, he preferred to spend his spare time in Pau Grande. In 1957, however, things began to change. The train journey up the hill every night was becoming more and more of an ordeal.

Garrincha tried to drag Nair down to the city with him so that Neivaldo's mother and sisters could take her shopping. On more than one occasion he told Neivaldo that, had it been up to him, he would have Nair and the girls come and live with him in a flat in Rio, somewhere close to Botafogo and a good school where the girls could get a decent education. Girls plural, because now there were four of them: Marinete was born in 1956 and Juraciara came along the following year. Nair had resigned from the factory and was now a full-time mother.

Garrincha's plans weren't pipe dreams. His last contract gave him only 30,000 cruzeiros a month but the bonuses he made on top of that meant he earned more than enough to live well in Rio. Nair, though, wasn't interested. She hated the hustle and bustle of Rio and felt uncomfortable away from her country home. Cars, lifts and brightly lit shops scared her and she resisted Garrincha's move to the big city. So he brought with him another of the women in his life. His childhood sweetheart, Iraci.

Garrincha was making good on a promise he had made to Iraci five years earlier when he told her that he would find a way for them to be together even if they could not be married. He had continued to see Iraci even after marrying Nair, and although she never complained, it was hard to hide such goings-on in a small town and people were starting to look down on her as the 'other woman'. So at the end of 1957 Garrincha had her give up her job at the factory and move to Rio.

Once there, he set her up in a two-bedroom flat in Ipanema and paid for everything she needed. He assured her she would want for nothing, and he was as good as his word. He fitted out the flat with a telephone, an oven, a fridge, a record player and all the furniture she needed. When he got home from training he would toss money on the table and ask her, 'Do you think that will be enough?'

Iraci took what she needed to pay for the rent, gas, electricity, water and telephone bills but not much more, against the advice of her neighbour, the singer Linda Batista, a former girlfriend of Orson Welles and Ali Khan, who told her to take what she could get. Iraci, though, did not want to take advantage. Garrincha visited her two or three times a week and always left her money. When he knew he'd be away on tour he left her more cash and told her that if she was ever ill or needed to speak to someone urgently she should go to Botafogo and ask for one of the club doctors, Renê Mendonça. When he came back from overseas trips he brought her perfumes, French if he'd been to Europe and Argentine if he'd been in Latin America.

Iraci was a million times more organised than Nair but Garrincha still thought she could do with some polishing. He introduced her to cigarettes, arguing, 'For a woman to be charming, she needs to smoke.' He would not let her cook, and when they went out after training it was to the darkest restaurant in the tiny neighbourhood of Arpoador or far away in Barra de Tijuca where there was less chance they'd be seen together – he was worried about the press picking up on the story. Iraci's role was to run errands, chat with Linda Batista and have a sexy negligé on when Garrincha came home at night.

Nair knew what was going on. When she heard that his ex-girlfriend was leaving Pau Grande to go and live in Rio at the same time as Garrincha stopped coming home every night it wasn't difficult to work it out. Nair questioned him and he confirmed her suspicions. 'You didn't want to go with me,' he said. 'So get used to it.' He calmed her with a promise that he'd never leave her, or Pau Grande. If she didn't give him any grief, everything would be fine, he assured her. Nair had no option but to agree.

In May 1957, when Botafogo announced that their new manager was a man called João Saldanha, some people asked, 'Who's João

Saldanha?' A Gaúcho (as those from the southern state of Rio Grande do Sul are known) who came to Rio with his family in 1931, Saldanha was known only at the Osmar bar on rua Miguel Lemos, where he and his friends talked football and made up political jokes that were later heard across the country; on the sands of Copacabana where he was one of the first stars of beach soccer; and inside Botafogo, where he had been a member since first arriving in Rio at the age of 13.

Tall, thin, charming and with never a hair out of place, Saldanha was a man about town. His father's wealth meant that João never needed to work. His time was instead devoted to hanging out at the Osmar spinning apocryphal stories of how he had fought alongside Mao Tse-tung in the Chinese Revolution or taken on the Germans on D-Day.

When he wasn't in Manchuria marching with Mao, or storming the beaches at Normandy, Saldanha was either at the Osmar or at Botafogo. His old friend Renato Estelita was director of football there, and in 1956 he gave Saldanha a job on the coaching staff even though he had never previously been involved in the game. When Geninho replaced Zezé Moreira in 1956, Saldanha remained. When Geninho himself left after a pay dispute, Estelita had run out of options so he asked Saldanha to take over as interim manager. It was a revolutionary idea: people like Saldanha, who had no experience as either a player or a manager, were not appointed to run football teams, especially not big ones like Botafogo.

On 1 June 1957, Saldanha led Botafogo to the Pacaembu where his new charges drew 2–2 with Palmeiras in the Rio-SP tournament, the annual competition played out between the best sides from the two most important states. From there, they went on a 12-match tour of the north-east and Venezuela, winning six, drawing five and losing one. The record was a good one, but the other clubs didn't see any reason to take Saldanha seriously. His first dozen games as manager had taken place outside Rio so they didn't count. He would only really be tested when the Carioca Championship got under way.

Saldanha was not in the slightest bit worried about the sceptics. He might not have been a football player, but the things that happened on and around a football pitch were not new to him. He had, after all, spent his life on the touchlines. During his time at Botafogo he had seen some of the great coaches in action – the Hungarian Dori Kruschner, the Uruguayan Ondino Viera and the Brazilians Zezé Moreira and Gentil Cardoso – and he had concluded that there was nothing mysterious about football. All you had to do was understand the players. And Saldanha spoke the language of the players and the language of the streets. He couldn't fail.

To create a team capable of winning the title, Saldanha and Estelita went back to the drawing board and built an almost totally new side. They already had Amaury in goal, but they went to Santos to sign ex-Fluminense keeper Adalberto as back-up. In central defence they signed Beto from Vasco, Servílio from Flamengo and promoted Tomé from the reserves. Midfielder Edson was also brought in from the second eleven, while up front they re-signed former players Quarentinha and Paulo Valentim. The other regulars had been at the club a while. And what regulars: Garrincha, Didi, Nílton Santos and Pampollini, the holding man in midfield. Even the strikers they had on the bench were strong: Neivaldo, Rossi, Amoroso, China and Othon Valentim.

The new Botafogo were not Honved, though, and Saldanha knew it. But for the first time in years they were ready to compete for silverware. The problem was that all the teams in Rio were just as competitive. A glance at the forward lines of their rivals said it all. Flamengo had Joel, Moacir, Henrique, Dida and Zagalo; Fluminense had Telê, Léo, Valdo, Robson and Escurinho; Vasco had Sabará, Almir, Vavá, Ruben and Pinga; and América had Canário, Romeiro, Leônidas, Alarcón and Ferreira.

Botafogo spent almost the whole of the 1957 tournament in second or third place, always a point or two behind Fluminense or Flamengo, who were vying for the top spot. But the championship began to take shape after the halfway stage and with only one game to go Vasco and Flamengo had fallen away to leave Fluminense and Botafogo as the only two clubs still in with a chance of taking the title. Fluminense were leading their rivals by a point and needed only to draw their final match – against Botafogo.

Everything suggested that Fluminense would be champions. They had been the most consistent side during the season and only needed a point to win the title. Businessman Cacildo Osés had arranged for them to go on a lengthy tour of South America, Mexico and Central America straight after the game. All the players had to do was go home, pick up their bags and wipe the celebratory rice powder off their faces (Fluminense's first black players had put rice powder on their faces to make them appear paler, and the fans still brought the substance to the stadiums). Botafogo, however, had not read the script.

Fans of both clubs would never forget that December day in 1957. Paulo Valentim put Botafogo ahead in the third minute and he had scored two more by the fortieth minute. Fluminense felt as though they were not in the Maracanã but stuck in a black, white and grey nightmare. Every time he got the ball, Garrincha first went round his marker Altair and then past Clóvis when the centre-half moved over to cover. After he'd opened the Fluminense defence like a can, Garrincha's crosses were met by Paulo Valentim with headers, shots and overhead kicks. Valentim could do no wrong; some of the balls seemed to be guided by the spirits. One goal went in off his knee.

With eight minutes of the second half gone, just after Valentim had made it 4–1, Telê said to Didi, 'You're champions. Tell Garrincha to stop embarrassing Clóvis and Altair. Enough is enough.' Telê was worried Fluminense would score seven or eight, and the way things were going it looked highly likely that they would. Twelve minutes into the second half Garrincha made it five after beating half the Fluminense team. When he saw that Botafogo weren't going to ease up, Telê started kicking lumps out of his friend Didi. The only reason

Botafogo didn't score more was because they missed a series of sitters. They didn't humiliate their opponents, but they tried. As he bore down on Castilho to knock in the sixth, Paulo Valentim shouted to the keeper, 'Which corner do you want it in, donkey?'

Before the game started Tomé and Nílton Santos had agreed that every time Botafogo scored a goal they would tear their shirts open at the collar. But when the fourth goal went in Tomé was so excited he ripped his shirt almost wide open, and when Nílton Santos saw him he did the same. Such attitudes would not be permitted by referees today, but in 1957 it was not seen as an affront. It was, however, enough to make some Fluminense players cast doubt on the legitimacy of Botafogo's 6–2 win. Rumours were rife that some players had competed under the influence of drugs.

The stimulants used in the 1950s were Exedrin, Pervitin, Preludin, Estelamina and Dexamil. They were called 'little balls' and were sold openly by chemists, often to students who needed to stay awake to cram on the eve of university entrance exams. Zizinho, when he played for Flamengo, accused his coach at the time, Dr Newton Paes Barreto, of giving players stimulants before matches. Paes Barreto, who was now doctor at Fluminense, claimed he had only given the players salt tablets. His counterpart at Botafogo, Dr Carlos Carvalho Leite, admitted to doing the same. And no wonder: the temperature that afternoon was pushing 40 degrees centigrade. It was not illegal.

But although the doctors denied giving their players the so-called little balls, there was nothing to prevent the players themselves taking drugs to improve their performance. Anti-doping tests were still a thing of the future, and although Saldanha would insinuate in a book six years later that both Botafogo and Fluminense players had indeed taken stimulants that day, the charges went uninvestigated and nothing more was said.

In truth, the real stimulant that day was Garrincha. Fluminense coach Silvio Pirilo had told Altair to stick close to Garrincha so that he would not have time to control the ball when he got it. But Pirilo had not counted on Didi passing the ball behind him for Garrincha to run on to. And Saldanha had warned the Botafogo players, 'Get out of Manés way. The right-wing channel should be left open exclusively for him. When he heads towards the byline I want to see the rest of you running into the box.' Castilho, the last line of defence against the hordes of Botafogo attackers that invaded his penalty area, later said that not even five Altairs could have shut down Garrincha that day.

The World Cup was just six months away. If anyone had any doubts about whether Garrincha should be in the team that went to Sweden they were dispelled that afternoon. And, with Botafogo champions instead of the favourites, Cacildo Osés apologised to Fluminense, prepared 22 new passports for the Botafogo players and three days later, late on Christmas Day, they set off to see the rest of Latin America.

It was at Botafogo that Garrincha got the nickname Mané. In Pau Grande everyone called him Garrincha, except for Nair, who called him Manuel. At the club, some people used Manel, the Portuguese version of Manuel, while others referred to him as 'Torto', which which means crooked, or squint. But in 1957 the press adopted him as 'Mané Garrincha' and it stuck. Suddenly the name took on a life of its own, and in bars, headlines and on the radio, Mané Garrincha was the man.

It was also during the 1957 Carioca Championship that the first magazine reporters made the trek to Pau Grande, a town with a name that so embarrassed the locals they preferred to say they were from Raiz da Serra (Pau Grande, literally 'big stick', was also slang for an erection). The photographers took pictures documenting Garrincha's simple life and time after time he posed shooting rabbits, riding horses, playing with his four daughters, chatting with Nair and playing football with the local children. All the stories compared the hero who delighted packed stadiums with the down-to-earth country boy for whom the bright lights of Rio de Janeiro held no appeal.

To highlight his uncomplicated approach to life, Sandro Moreyra made up the story that Garrincha called his markers 'João', or John, the implication being that to Garrincha all defenders were the same, he could beat anyone. Mario Filho, the most influential sports journalist of the era, loved the story so much that he went round repeating it and before long everyone believed that Garrincha really did call all his markers João. Garrincha didn't like the stories. He didn't want to hear that he was invincible. He looked in the mirror and saw a simple, ordinary man.

In fact, Garrincha was both ordinary and extraordinary. During a game in Venezuela in July another pitch battle had confirmed Garrincha's easy-going reputation. Botafogo were playing Spanish side Seville in Caracas and were winning 2–0 when an incident involving Quarentinha and a Spaniard spiralled out of control. Within seconds, 50 players and officials from both sides were going at it, and they were soon followed by the Spanish and Portuguese fans watching from the stands. Apart from the local police, who let the two sides fight it out, the only two men who did not get involved were Garrincha and Seville player Pepillo. When the fighting started the two of them walked to the corner flag, sat down on the turf and chatted away.

When it came to fights, Saldanha's Botafogo had a few heavyweights in their ranks: trainer Paulo Amaral, centre-half Tomé, goalkeeper Amaury and Saldanha himself. On another foreign tour, the unscheduled trip that followed the 1957 Carioca Championship win, Botafogo took on Costa Rican side Saprisa. Saldanha surpassed himself by slapping the referee after he had chalked off a Botafogo goal. As if that wasn't enough, when the officers tried to calm him down he hit the chief of police. Saldanha took a punch on the nose and was arrested along with Paulo Amaral, who was loaded into the police car only after laying out half a dozen Costa Ricans. Once again, Garrincha was one of the few players, if not the only one, to keep his distance from the mêlée. When Edson tried to escape two Costa Rican opponents, he ran past Garrincha sitting quietly minding his own business and asked him, 'Aren't you going to fight?'

Garrincha, with a Zen-like calm, replied, 'Who with? No one has hit me.'

Botafogo knew not to count on Garrincha whenever there was a battle going on, but no one ever accused him of not getting involved because he was scared. Garrincha simply had other things to do. And on that same tour one of the things he did set the tone for supporters all over Latin America. According to Saldanha, Garrincha inspired the first *olé*.

It happened during the Botafogo–River Plate match in Mexico City on 20 February 1958. River had ten men in the Argentina team and were considered one of the best club sides in the world, a team that could command $10,000 for each friendly match – five times what Botafogo could charge. The difference was not apparent during the game that day, however; with Garrincha, Didi and Nílton Santos, Botafogo were as good as or even better than River. It was a hard-fought contest that ended 1–1, but it was not the scoreline that was relevant, rather the footballing lesson that Garrincha gave to River full-back Vairo.

Almost from the kick-off, whenever Garrincha dribbled the ball past the Argentine or stuck it through his legs, the supporters in the Estadio Universitario roared '*Olé!*' as if they were at a bullfight. To them, the jinks and feints that sent Vairo one way and another were worthy of Ordonez or Dominguín, the great Spanish matadors of the era. Time after time Garrincha teased Vairo, and when he 'forgot' the ball and sprinted away with Vairo running after him the thousands of voices chanting '*Olé!*' changed to peals of laughter.

River manager Minella decided the best thing to do was to substitute the poor defender. If Garrincha kept it up he would have Vairo on his knees awaiting the final sacrifice. Vairo was delighted when he was taken off. When he got to the bench, Saldanha heard him say, 'There's nothing you can do. It's impossible.'

Soon the echoes of the *olé* arrived in Rio and were heard to ring around the Maracanã. Before long, fans across the country were doing it.

But in the stadiums where a few months later Garrincha most deserved to be celebrated, the supporters were blond, aloof and happy to applaud politely as if they were at a classical-music concert. The World Cup in Sweden was just around the corner. And it was an orchestral performance conducted by Didi, a truly extraordinary maestro. All eyes, however, would be on the soloist.

CHAPTER 7

1958: An Ice Lolly in the Sun

IN THE 1950S, IF YOU SAW A FOOTBALLER SWAGGERING ALONG THE street, his chest puffed out and his hips and arms swinging, you could bet that he had just been called into the Brazil squad. Or that he had a big head. Or sometimes both.

Getting called up to the national side was the dream of every Brazilian player. Just like today, it meant that they were part of an elite, and back then the national side played fewer matches. Amassing even 50 caps was a significant achievement. Zizinho, who made his international debut in 1942 at 20, wouldn't reach that mark until 1957. Getting called up more than once really was something to tell your grandchildren about.

In professional terms, getting a cap gave the players a higher profile at their club, but it did not mean they would automatically get a pay rise. Playing in the World Cup might attract the interest of Spanish or Italian clubs, but some players were so afraid of leaving home they might have hidden under the bed had agents knocked on their doors. They did not dream of playing for Brazil because they lusted after dollars. They dreamt of playing for Brazil because it was Brazil.

For Garrincha, not even that mattered. Whether he was called up or not, he was the same man. His complete lack of interest in the rewards football could bring him was phenomenal. Prior to the 1958 World Cup there is no record of his ever having said whether or not he thought he was worthy of a place in the team. And neither had anyone heard him say a word on the string of players who had worn the number 7 jersey since Julinho was sold to Italy in 1955.

In the three years since their regular right-winger had gone abroad, Brazil had done everything bar tie right-backs to the corner flags to see if they would adapt to the role. Maurinho, Sabará, Canário, Paulinho, Joel and Garrincha himself had all been tested out on the right wing. They were all great players with their clubs, but none of them, not even Garrincha, had stood out when wearing the yellow jersey. There was a distinct nostalgia for Julinho, and for good reason. He was the best right-winger the country had ever produced: devastating in the dribble, on the run, and with the accuracy of his shots. He was one of the few players to emerge from the 1954 World Cup disaster with his reputation intact. He was exactly what Brazil needed in Sweden.

But Julinho was in Italy. The Italians had given him everything: a house, a car, money galore, even love. He could not set foot in a piazza without being mobbed by adoring fans. Thanks to him, Fiorentina were crowned Italian champions for the first time. The Italians offered him fortunes to become a naturalised citizen and play for the *squadra azzurra* but the boy from São Paulo would not give up his Brazilian passport for all the riches in Florence. He invested the money he made in land in Penha, the neighbourhood where he had grown up. He owned half the region, and his plan ever since arriving in Italy was to come home when his contract was up. He missed his mother.

At the beginning of 1958, João Havelange wrote to Julinho asking him when his contract ended and if he would consider playing for Brazil in the World Cup in June. He would not even have to come home, Havelange said: Brazil were playing a friendly against Fiorentina on 29 May and he could join the squad there. Julinho wrote back to say that his contract ended the day after the game on 30 May; that he was ready both mentally and physically; and that nothing would make him happier than playing for his country – but that he did not think it fair he should replace the players who had stayed in Brazil and had been fighting to take his place for three years.

The letter was greeted with shock when it arrived at the CBD's headquarters in Rio. The CBD did not usually call up players who plied their trade outside the country but they had made an exception for the brilliant Julinho. However, if the invitation was unusual, the refusal was even more so. Julinho's decision changed the course of footballing history. Had he accepted the offer, he would have walked back into the team. Joel, the player who was then the first choice, would probably have been picked as cover.

And Garrincha would never have gone to the World Cup.

The prophets of doom were predicting failure once again. No one had forgotten Brazil's inability to produce results when it mattered both in Europe in 1956 and, more recently, in the South American Championship (the forerunner to the Copa America) in Lima in March 1957. There, Brazil hammered the continent's whipping boys Ecuador 7–1 and Colombia 9–0, but when they came up against the big sides they lost – 3–2 to Uruguay and 3–0 to Argentina. In the World Cup qualifiers a month later, Brazil faced Peru for a spot in the finals and managed only to squeak past: they drew 1–1 in Lima and won 1–0 in Rio with a second-half *folha seca* from Didi.

The national mood was low and made worse by the apparent lack of direction. With four months to go to the start of the tournament, the team was without a manager. When they did finally appoint someone to the job in March it did not set the nation's pulse racing. Vicente Feola, 48 years old and over 16 stone, was respected in football circles, having won several titles with São Paulo and the state select, but he was virtually retired because of heart trouble. At São Paulo he had assumed a less hands-on position as technical director alongside Hungarian coach Bela Gutman. São Paulo won the Paulista Championship (the São Paulo equivalent of the Carioca Championship) in 1957 with a great side that included Zizinho, De Sordi, Mauro, Dino Sani, Maurinho, Gino and Canhoteiro. With Gutman unable to speak Portuguese, Feola had played a key role. But could a man who wasn't even fit enough to run his own team be expected to run the national side?

In fact, the selectors at the CBD wanted a coach exactly like Feola, someone talented and respected but not too independent or outspoken. They wanted a team player who could fit into a group comprising a supervisor (Carlos Nascimento of Bangu), a trainer (Paulo Amaral of Botafogo), a doctor (Hilton Gosling of Bangu), an administrator (José de Almeida of Fluminense) and a treasurer (Adolpho Marques, also of Fluminense). The manager had to be flexible and diplomatic, capable of listening to and accepting the majority opinion. In return, he would be freed from the responsibility of booking the players into hotlels, checking on them every now and again to see if they had sneaked out, verifying that they were getting enough beans, picking up kit bags at the airport, blowing up balls at training, or taking the training sessions like managers at club sides did. There were other people to do all that. Feola would only have to worry about technical and tactical affairs. He would not even pick the team himself.

For the first time Brazil would go to the World Cup finals with an almost neurotically detailed plan of action. The team had scheduled everything from the moment the squad was to meet (on 7 April) to the day of the final (29 June). The planning covered transport and training in both Brazil and Sweden and even the weight and calorie count of each steak. Officials at the CBD had been preparing for months.

In the middle of 1957, for example, team doctor Hilton Gosling visited the host cities to look for the best hotel – one that was comfortable, close to a training pitch and not too far from the stadiums where the games would take place. It was a novel move for the Brazilians:

in past tournaments they had got off the plane and checked into whatever hotel the FIFA officials had assigned them. Gosling had even investigated what the probable temperature would be in each of the cities that were hosting matches.

Reservations had been made for three return flights: on 16 June if Brazil were knocked out at the group stage; on 20 June if they were eliminated at the quarter-final stage; and – there was no harm in dreaming – on 1 July in case Brazil got to the final. For once, the CBD was leaving nothing to chance.

The men responsible for the organisation were João Havelange, the recently elected president of the CBD (he beat Carlito Rocha by 185 votes to 19), and his vice president Paulo Machado de Carvalho. The powerful 'Dr Paulo', patron of São Paulo and the former president of the Paulista Federation, held a big advantage over the majority of directors: he was not in football to get rich (he was already rich) or as a stepping stone into politics. He was the owner of TV Record, of São Paulo radio stations Record and Panamericana, and of a big chain of other stations across the state. He accepted the invitation to lead the delegation to Sweden but he had already warned that he was not one for adventures. Football tended to be chaotic, but he wanted to see everything run like clockwork, just like his businesses. At 57 years old 'Dr Paulo' was jovial, open and easy to get along with.

Carlos Nascimento, the man chosen by Havelange and Paulo de Carvalho to be the team's supervisor, was quite the opposite: he kept the world at arm's length. The world for its part was quite happy for him to remain there. Nascimento, then with Bangu, was linked to Havelange through Fluminense, the team he had once played for and trained. He was 54 and his fanaticism for efficiency was matched only by his fanaticism for football itself. The plan of action was a reflection of the man himself: rigid and inflexible in every way.

The team was to prepare by training for 40 days in Poços de Caldas, Araxá and Rio, and by playing two friendlies against Paraguay and two against Bulgaria at the Maracanã and the Pacaembu. The friendlies

95

were arranged not only to help the manager prepare his side but also to make enough money to keep the side in Sweden until FIFA coughed up their advance. Expenses were covered by Brazil's government, headed by President Juscelino Kubitschek, who gave them 12 million cruzeiros (or $80,000), and by the CBD itself. This included the players' salaries: while on duty with the national side they got the same as they did at their clubs, which meant, for example, that Didi cost the CBD the same as he cost Botafogo, 120,000 cruzeiros a month. Pelé cost them what he cost Santos, 6,000 cruzeiros.

The 'technical commission' – comprising Feola, Nascimento, Gosling and Amaral, those directly responsible for the team – called up 33 players, 11 of whom would be cut before the team flew to Europe. They arrived, as scheduled, on 7 April, but instead of taking them to the training ground the CBD sent them to Rio's Santa Casa de Misericórdia hospital for what was then an unprecedented series of examinations by doctors, neurologists, cardiologists, ophthalmic surgeons, chiropodists, dentists and ear, nose and throat specialists. Worried about what would happen if players fell ill far from home they wanted to do everything possible to ensure they were physically prepared for the rigours of a World Cup campaign.

When Garrincha appeared the hospital came to a standstill. Doctors arrived from all over to admire his famous legs. 'I feel like Lollobrigida,' he said, referring to the Italian film star Gina Lollobrigida, the owner of the finest set of pins in Hollywood. The tests revealed that in spite of being grotesquely off centre, Garrincha had the poise of an angel. Gosling took plaster casts of all the players' feet, but no one's toes, arch and instep were as neatly aligned as Garrincha's. In compensation, he had a squint in his right eye. But what most grabbed the doctors' attention were the scars on his legs, signatures carved into the skin by the studs (wooden ones hammered in with nails) of over-zealous defenders. Doctor Pedro Cunha pointed to Garrincha's scars and turned to Vasco defender Bellini, who was next in line. 'How many of these are yours, Bellini?' Garrincha thought it was funny. Bellini didn't.

A mountain of material was sent to the labs for analysis and the results shocked the top men at the CBD. Here was the crème de la crème of Brazilian football, the best players with the biggest salaries, and physically they looked as if they'd just walked out of the woods with a bundle of clothes slung over their shoulder and a blade of grass between their teeth. The majority had intestinal parasites to spare; several were anaemic; one player even had syphilis. There were precarious bladders, tonsils begging to be removed and players with chronic digestive and circulatory problems. Worst of all, though, was the state of their teeth. Corinthians left-back Oreco had to have seven teeth, or what remained of them, taken out; handsome Corinthians goalkeeper Gilmar lost four; and Santos left-winger Pepe said goodbye to three, as well as having to have more widespread work carried out on his gums. Garrincha himself bade farewell to one more tooth – he had already lost almost half his upper set. In total, the 33 players had 470 bad teeth between them – an average of more than 15 each.

When the rest of the squad went to their first stop in the Minas Gerais town of Poços de Caldas, Garrincha and Vasco centre-half Orlando stayed behind to have their tonsils taken out. Garrincha's were the size of marbles and should have been removed by Botafogo two years earlier when current club doctor Santamaria first diagnosed the problem. But Garrincha had always managed to postpone it, and when the day had eventually come round he hadn't shown up. If it was out of fear, no one took him to task: removing tonsils in Brazil in the 1950s would not have produced any less blood had the operation been carried out by Jack the Ripper. And Botafogo, who needed him to be fit for leagues, friendlies and tours, did not force him to have the operation done.

Now, for the first time, Garrincha gave in to a higher authority and opened his mouth to take the fearsome anaesthetic injection. Surprisingly, he was not afraid. He took the anaesthetic without a whimper and when the blood flowed from his first strangled tonsil like water from a fountain on Praça Paris, he didn't even blink. It was

97

the same with the second tonsil. When it was all over he enjoyed an ice cream. Botafogo's doctors were irritated, and they had good reason to be: if he hadn't avoided having the operation because he was scared then why had he put up with the pain of those pus-filled balls in his throat for so long?

Garrincha lost a lot of blood during the surgery and came out of it nine pounds lighter. When he turned up at the Grande Hotel in Araxá he was as white as a sheet. Yet he was still smiling. 'I fulfilled a childhood dream,' he said. 'I got to eat ice cream after having my tonsils out.'

The short stay in Poços de Caldas and Araxá was designed to loosen the players' muscles, let the Carioca and the Paulista players get to know one another, and allow the physical preparations to get under way. The only attractions were the saunas and the carriages pulled by billy goats. The only horizontal exercise on offer was sleeping.

That changed when two local beauties, one dark, one blonde, checked into the hotel and found themselves rooms on the same floor as the players. At first glance they could have been mistaken for holi-daying schoolgirls were it not for the fact that it was April and it was still term time. Whatever their situation, when the dark one appeared in the hotel garden in a bathing suit and sexy sunglasses, she revealed a body like a mermaid. The blonde was also hot enough to stop traffic, but she was disappointed that her favourite player hadn't shown up yet and kept her distance from the 30 pairs of eyes running over her curves. The dark one's favourite was there, however, and she discreetly met with him in her room. The Carioca and Paulista journalists knew the players well – a couple of them sometimes even took part in the training sessions – and they had no intention of reporting such dalliances. The local reporters, however, were not on such intimate terms, and soon enough the scandal broke.

The story alone was bad enough. But because the player's name was not released, and the reports didn't state whether he was single or not, the shadow of suspicion fell on the entire side. When the news reached

Rio and São Paulo, wives and girlfriends, concerned about their partners' fidelity, bombarded Poços de Caldas with telephone calls.

The news broke just as the squad were packing their bags and getting ready to move to Araxá for the second stage of their preparations. It could have ended there, but the girls followed them to the Grande Hotel in Araxá, where they tried to get a visiting businessman to sign them in to the place as his secretaries. Carlos Nascimento heard what was going on and marched into the foyer to threaten the manager: if the two girls were given rooms, the squad would head back to Rio without even unpacking their bags. The hotel manager succumbed to Nascimento's ire and the girls were not allowed in. But no one could stop them from checking into the Colombo Hotel just down the road. Which was when the blonde got her hands on the man she was looking for.

The dark one was Gilmar's. The blonde, the recently arrived Garrincha's.

Until 1958, the general consensus was that when it came to World Cups the Brazilian players did not have what it took. The catastrophic defeats by Uruguay in 1950 and Hungary four years later seemed to bear that out: when it came to the crunch Brazil weren't up to it. When they travelled with their clubs the players were afraid of nothing, perhaps because the games were friendlies or perhaps because they took place so far from home that they were almost clandestine. But the World Cup was for real and the entire nation would be glued to the radio to listen to the action. Which was one reason why, when they put on the yellow jersey to face the Europeans, some of the Brazilian players melted faster than an ice lolly in the sun and others resorted to violence. A barely concealed racism attributed this lack of backbone to Brazil's racial cocktail, as if only the black and *mulato* players were nervous. To prevent the problem from recurring in Sweden, the CBD included an unusual figure for the first time: a psychologist.

99

Forty-year-old João Carvalhaes was a sociologist who studied psychology – more a psychomanager than anything else. His job was to put the players through a battery of tests to 'measure their intelligence and psychological balance', just as he did for those applying for jobs as bus drivers at his day job with a São Paulo transport company. In spite of his unusual background, it was not the first time he had been involved in football. In 1954, Paulo Machado de Carvalho had had him give the same tests to the players at São Paulo and then to the referees and linesmen at the Paulista Federation.

Nominally, the tests were designed to gauge the players' 'cultural awareness, tension levels, reflexes and motor skills' as well as measure their 'impulsiveness and levels of aggression'. In 1958, such statements were complex and had people running to consult their dictionaries. Psychologists were generally still seen as doctors for crazy people. But although the tests were supposed to serve only as a guide for the technical commission they had one simple aim: to identify which players might freeze on the big stage. They would not be decisive when it came to assembling the final squad.

The tests were carried out at the Santa Casa hospital in Rio, the same place where the players had had their medical exams shortly before, and at Carvalhaes's office at the São Paulo transport company. Some of the tests required the players to complete half-drawn figures or to sketch out the first thing that came into their heads and explain to Carvalhaes what they had drawn. Garrincha did terribly in them all. He even managed to get the form wrong: in the box for 'profession' he spelt athlete incorrectly, writing *atreta* instead of *atleta*. The tests classed him as having a primary-school education, below average intelligence and zero aggression. Out of a possible 123 points, he got 38, not even enough to get him a job driving a bus.

When rumours of Garrincha's less than brilliant results spread to the press, one journalist cheekily asked him if he thought of himself as stupid. Garrincha, ever the comic, replied, 'Well, I am no Rui Barbosa, but neither am I Mazzola.'

The young Palmeiras striker's score was never revealed and no one was ever going to mistake Garrincha for Rui Barbosa, the erudite Brazilian statesman. The results of another of the team's forwards were given however. Pelé had impressive motor skills, but Carvalhaes gave him just 68 points and described him thus: 'Pelé is obviously infantile. He lacks the necessary fighting spirit. He is too young to feel aggression and respond with appropriate force. In addition to that, he does not possess the sense of responsibility necessary for a team game.' Ignoring the fact that he was not to give direct recommendations, Carvalhaes summed up his report on Pelé with the following bold conclusion: 'I do not think it advisable that he be approved.' It was only natural that Carvalhaes had doubts about Pelé's maturity – he was only 17 years old. The technical commission, however, did not want to hear about doubts, they wanted to hear about certainties. And they seemed to have held one certainty since the squad was first named: who would fill the right-wing role.

For each of the other attacking positions, the commission had called up three players: midfielders Didi, Moacir and Roberto Belangero; centre-forwards Vavá, Massola and Gino; point men Pelé, Dida and Almir; and left-wingers Zagalo, Pepe and Canhoteiro. One man would be cut from each final list. But only two players had been called up for the right-wing berth, Joel and Garrincha. It was as if the technical commission all agreed: if they could not get Julinho, then these two were the unanimous choices to replace him. The question, if one existed, was which one of the two would end up as first choice. And there didn't seem to be much doubt: it would be Joel.

At the time there would have been a valid argument for picking Joel over Garrincha, even though he was not as spectacular a player. He was serious and didn't dribble the ball any more than he had to, yet he was capable of getting to the byline at speed and sending over a dozen precision crosses in each game. Flamengo had poached him from Botafogo's youths when he was 17 in 1951, angering Carlito Rocha so much that he had almost severed relations between the two clubs. It was worth the bad feeling though, because Joel's crosses produced hundreds of goals for Flamengo forwards Índio, Benitez, Evaristo and Dida, and he could score them as well. He had been capped 11 times since making his debut in the South American Championship in Lima the year before, including two appearances when he was shifted over to the left wing to make space for Garrincha on the right. Of all the candidates to fill Julinho's position, it was Joel who had had the most chances to shine. And it looked as though he would continue to get the opportunity.

French journalist Gabriel Hannot, who had come to Brazil to cover the team's preparations for his paper *L'Equipe*, thought differently. To Hannot, Garrincha would be first choice not only for Brazil but for any team in the world. When reporters asked him what he had discovered on his trip, he replied jokingly, '*Maracujá* and Garrincha.'

No one knows if the members of the technical commission liked passion fruit as much as Hannot, but when it came to picking the teams at training it was obvious they did not share his appetite for Garrincha. If the team with Nílton Santos was the first choice, Garrincha was picked for the reserves. The two of them tacitly agreed before the game started that, in order not to cancel each other out, when they came face to face they would take turns to beat each other. But as much as Garrincha wasn't bothered about being on the bench, Nílton Santos didn't want to risk losing his place in the side. At 33 he was the oldest player in the team, and everything suggested that this would be his last World Cup. Until recently he was the only player in the squad who could be considered a certainty. Even Didi's place was under threat thanks to a campaign the Flamengo journalists were waging in favour of the young Moacir. But Nílton Santos did not count on having one of the top officials rooting against him: the fabled president of the Paulista Federation João Mendonça Falcão.

In the modern era of João Havelange, Mendonça was the kind of official who was starting to look jurassic. He was a hick, barely literate, and when the team won he would walk fully dressed into the shower to hug the victorious players. In addition to all that he was anachronistically parochial: if he could, he would have picked a squad made up entirely of players from São Paulo. The simple sight of Sugarloaf was enough to give him indigestion, but he had a special dislike of Nílton Santos. Unable to reveal the real reason for his aversion (a woman he was after had eyes only for the Botafogo defender), he took the easy way out and made an issue of his age: Nílton Santos was too old for the first team and should be replaced by Corinthians full-back Oreco. And, sure enough, in the two friendlies Brazil played against Paraguay, Oreco got the nod.

With his World Cup spot under threat, Nílton Santos resolved to train seriously against Garrincha. Having played alongside him so often, he thought he had discovered the way to mark him. All he had to do was not take the bait when Garrincha appeared to offer him the ball. Because as soon as he went for it, he would be left on one foot, and in that split second Garrincha would put the ball past him. Therefore, the secret was to stay standing and wait for Garrincha to take the initiative. Nílton Santos tried out his strategy and Garrincha went past him anyway.

The third or fourth time it happened, Nílton Santos went to Didi to ask him for help. 'Didi, have a word with him and tell him to stop it.'

When the ball was on the other side of the pitch, Didi whispered to Garrincha, 'Damn, Mané, don't do that. Nílton is a Botafogo man and he's your mate.'

Garrincha realised that he was getting his team-mate in trouble and took it a bit easier. But a few minutes later he went past him again, prompting Nílton Santos to mark him more violently, jabbing him in the stomach when the referee wasn't looking. When the session was over, Garrincha lifted up his shirt and complained, 'What got into you? Look at my stomach, it's all red.'

'Either you calm down or I won't be playing in this World Cup,' Nílton told him. 'These guys want to leave me out. Let's take it easy.'

Nílton Santos got his place back, for good, in the two friendlies against Bulgaria at the Maracanã and Pacaembu. But Garrincha got his chance only in the second match after Feola gave a run-out to eight players, including Pelé, who had until then been considered reserves.

Brazil's 3–1 win over Bulgaria on 18 May at the Pacaembu was the first time that Garrincha and Pelé played together up front. No one could have guessed it then, but that Sunday afternoon was the start of a long and marvellous story. When those two were on the field together, Brazil would never lose a match.

Three days before Brazil set off for Europe, Corinthians defender Ari Clemente caught Pelé hard on the knee. He had been trying to nail him the whole game, and he finally hit his target. Pelé went down squirming in pain, clutching his right knee with both hands. Trainer Mário Américo, not even bothering to wait for the referee to wave him on to the pitch, ran to help his man. As he flew past Clemente, Américo, who had a stutter, shouted, 'Wh-why d-d-did y-y-you do that, you ssssson of a b-b-bitch?' When he saw Pelé being carried off in tears, Clemente wanted the ground to open up and swallow him. Carlos Nascimento was livid. The national side were at the Pacaembu playing a farewell match to make some easy money. The last thing they needed was to lose a player.

The Brazil–Corinthians match was arranged at the last minute and had not been part of Nascimento's plans. It was a reckless decision by the CBD who should have known that the fans would turn out against them: when it came to club versus country the fans always stuck with the club, especially if one of their favourites had been left out of the side, as had happened with Luizinho, Corinthians' most beloved player. Brazil, however, ignored the deafening boos and, with Orlando easily nullifying the threat from Luizinho, they won 5–0.

In the dressing room, Américo and the kit man Francisco de Assis placed hot towels on Pelé's knee. Gosling took a good look and pronounced the injury serious – Pelé might not recover in time for the finals. But when Nascimento asked him for the tenth time, Gosling admitted that because he was so young he might still have a chance. They called Feola and there and then decided that Pelé would not be left behind – at least not yet. They would wait a week until the thirtieth, the day the squad list had to be submitted to FIFA, before making a final decision. The squad would be about to leave Italy, where they were due to spend the first part of their acclimatisation period, to head for Sweden. If Pelé could not prove his fitness by then he would be dropped and Vasco's Almir would be called up to replace him.

Garrincha had been handed the number 7 shirt for the second consecutive time against Corinthians and had scored two goals in a performance that seemed to cement his claim as the first-choice right-winger. But nothing was certain; it might only have been another chance to impress. With two weeks to go to the start of the tournament, betting on either Garrincha or Joel would have been a gamble.

Whoever was picked, no one expected him to be chosen by Feola. The Brazilian fans, used to outspoken managers such as Flávio Costa and Zezé Moreira, found a discreet, serene and fat manager like Feola hard to take. When the story spread that he took naps on the bench during training, 60 million fans had no trouble believing it. For those who doubted it, they only needed to look at the photos of Feola sitting with his eyes closed while the players warmed up.

Feola's colleagues on the technical commission knew the criticisms were unfair. In fact, the big man suffered from coronary problems. Sometimes, during a meeting or a training session, he would be hit by a stabbing pain that started in the chest and ran down his left arm – angina. When he felt the pain he would lower his head, close his eyes and wait for it to pass. It could last up to 15 seconds. Not long, but enough time for him to be snapped 'sleeping'. An insinuating caption reinforced the impression and the readers' imaginations did the rest.

Curiously, Feola did not try to defend himself against the allegations. He didn't need to, for both Havelange and Paulo de Carvalho knew him very well. They, and Nascimento, Gosling and Paulo Amaral, all agreed that it was a fool who considered Feola a fool. And in reality it was better for the press and the fans to believe the national side had a manager who fell asleep than a manager who had heart attacks.

Brazil touched down in Rome on 25 May after a tiring 20-hour flight that stopped in Recife, Dakar and Lisbon. From there they took the train north to Florence, where two days later they beat a powerful Fiorentina side (including six members of Italy's first team) 4–0 in the famous game during which Garrincha beat half the Italian side before, with typical nonchalance, dribbling the ball into the net.

Julinho, Fiorentina's right-winger, was making his final appearance for the team. A proud Brazilian and a fierce patriot, he went to Paulo Machado de Carvalho before the match to ask his permission to face Brazil and played the game in tears, so troubling was the thought of dribbling past one of his own men. His fear gave Nílton Santos the freedom to attack down the left, while on the other side of the pitch Garrincha was making Italian full-back Robotti wish he had never been born.

It was that fourth goal from Garrincha in the seventy-fifth minute that dealt Fiorentina the killer blow. Garrincha transformed the Italian players into toy soldiers, knocking one down after another on his march towards the goal. First he went past Robotti, then Magnini, and lastly Cervato. Goalkeeper Sarti came off his line but Garrincha sold him a dummy and waltzed around him. With an open goal in front of him he could have shot, but Robotti had chased back. Garrincha threw his shoulders one way and went the other, leaving Robotti clinging to the goalpost, then walked the ball into the net. He flicked the ball up, stuck it under his arm and coolly started to walk back to the centre circle.

The goal was a stunner, and the terraces fell silent in awe. His team-mates, however, did not throw themselves on him to celebrate. They screamed at him. The Italians probably thought they were congratulating him, but had they understood Portuguese they would have heard the opposite. Almost the whole team was furious with him. Bellini, for example: 'This is the World Cup, for fuck's sake!' Garrincha looked at him in disbelief. Why was he so angry? It wasn't as if the World Cup had started yet; it was just a friendly against a club side. And they were 3–0 up with only 15 minutes to go.

The revolt was understandable. Garrincha's team-mates were afraid he would try similar moves during the real World Cup, and that Brazil would lose because of then. When they got to the dressing room after the game, Carlos Nascimento added to the chorus of criticism. 'It was childish,' he said. Garrincha just bowed his head.

The controversy was short-lived. Had it not been it would have been easy to cut Garrincha from the squad and call a substitute from Brazil. Which was almost what they did with Pelé.

With just hours to go before the Fiorentina game Pelé's place in the squad was hanging by a thread. He had failed a fitness test and José de Almeida suggested they send him home and draft in Almir, who was already in Europe with Vasco. Even Pelé himself was in favour of the idea and asked to go home. Gosling, however, guaranteed that with ten days of treatment Pelé would be fit to play in the tournament. He would not make the first two games against Austria and England, but he would miss the third against the USSR only if Feola chose not to pick him.

Garrincha was under no threat at all.

CHAPTER 8

1958: Sputnik Crashes to Earth

PAULO MACHADO DE CARVALHO WAS COUNTING ON THE MONEY FROM the games against Fiorentina and Internazionale (they were to get $15,000 for each game) to keep Brazil's Swedish operation up and running until FIFA paid their expenses. However, things got complicated when Fiorentina officials didn't turn up at the train station to hand over their appearance money, and by the time the team arrived in Milan, Carvalho was furious. It was only after he threatened not to let the team take the field against Inter that the Italian Federation coughed up. Brazil then went out and, with Joel on the right wing in place of Garrincha, hammered them 4–0.

Garrincha's absence from the side had nothing to do with his antics in the previous match. He was not the only one dropped. Castilho replaced Gilmar, Djalma Santos replaced De Sordi, Oreco replaced Nílton Santos, Vavá replaced Dida, and Zagalo replaced Pepe. Feola and Nascimento still hadn't decided on their first eleven even though the moment of truth was almost upon them.

On 2 June the squad left Milan on an SAS Convair destined for Gothenburg. In Brazil, 60 million people sweating with anticipation were getting ready to gather around eight million radios to listen to the action. Many of them predicted the worst as a way of insuring themselves against disappointment. And it was no wonder.

There was not a lot of hope under normal circumstances, but this year promised to be even more difficult because Brazil had been drawn in the strongest group of the tournament, alongside Austria, England and the USSR. Austria were no mugs; Brazil always feared England; and the USSR played the 'scientific football' that had captured the world's imagination. Defeat, elimination and embarrassment could come in any, or all, of the three games.

The players had been forbidden from boarding the plane with drums, tambourines or any other instruments. This was a football team, not a band of troubadors. The squad's new disciplinary regime was stricter than that imposed by the military. The players were given a list of 40 things they must not do and were forced to read and sign it by Carlos Nascimento so that no one could later claim they didn't know the rules. They were obliged to shave before breakfast and they weren't allowed to walk about the hotel in underpants, towels, pyjamas, sandals or clogs. They were not to smoke while wearing official clothing – which was particularly cruel given that the team doctor got through a pack an hour. The players were to wear their training gear or casual uniform at all times, in order to prevent them wandering around in flamboyant dark glasses or hats like Nat King Cole, and while training they were to tuck their shirts inside their shorts.

In Milan, Garrincha bought a hat for Pincel and an umbrella for Swing, and when he couldn't fit them in his suitcase he put the hat on his head and slung the umbrella over his arm. Nascimento complained, but Garrincha explained that there was nowhere else to put them and he got away with it. He was even photographed with his new purchases in a pose that looked like a perfect imitation of Cantinflas. In the future, the episode with the hat and umbrella would gain a relevance it never had: Garrincha's absence from the first two games of the tournament would be attributed to them, as though it were normal for a player to be left out of the side because of an umbrella.

There were more rules. The players were forbidden from speaking to the press about internal team affairs, or about anything at all outside the stipulated slots: between 11 a.m. and midday, and immediately after games and training sessions. Nascimento did not want to hear of gossiping between São Paulo players and São Paulo journalists or Carioca players and Carioca journalists – and there were more than 70 reporters, photographers and radio commentators following Brazil's progress. As for the presence of newspapers and magazines from home in the *concentração*, it was expressly forbidden.

The players could phone home only once a week for three minutes, and they were forbidden from sending messages back during radio interviews. It wasn't spelled out in so many words, but letters from home would be opened and read by the chief of the delegation before being passed on to the players. Officials wanted to make sure the players were not affected by small domestic blow-ups. The commission was particularly worried about Didi, the team's brain and backbone, who had the most jealous and most complicated wife of all. It had been difficult to stop him paying for his wife Guiomar and his daughter Rebecca to accompany him.

The *concentração* was at the Tourist Hotel in Hindas, a beautiful resort town between Gothenburg and Boras. Chosen the previous year by Gosling, the hotel had two training pitches: one in the hotel grounds and the other a little more than three miles away along a road that ran through glorious alpine forests. The front of the hotel had big bay windows that allowed the players to see the region's lakes and pine woods day and night. And there was further natural beauty to be seen in the form of the tall, freckle-faced blondes, some of them quite spectacular, who lived nearby.

Before the players arrived, Gosling had asked the hotel to replace its 28 female employees with men, and the hotel had agreed. There was also a nudist colony on an island on one of the nearby lakes. Gosling asked them to cover up for as long as Brazil were in Hindas, but they refused. The squad could see the nudist colony from the

111

hotel windows but it was some distance away, so on their first free day in Gothenburg some of the more enterprising players came back with binoculars. On their first day in Hindas, Paulo Amaral ordered the players to quick-march back to the hotel. All of them complained. On the second day, he gave them the same order and no one said a word. On the third day, Amaral found out why. The players had discovered a detour that would take them home via the edge of the nudist colony.

Everyone in the Brazil delegation had his part to play, from the most senior official right down to the lowly kit man. Carvalho was the head of the delegation, and before every game he gave a prayer-like recital in the dressing room. 'My World Cup brothers. We came here to win and we are going to win. I am with you come what may.' He crossed himself and the players did the same. But it was Nascimento who ran the squad's day-to-day affairs. All problems were brought to him first and he resolved them and then informed Carvalho. He was also the one who had the most influence on Feola when it came to picking the team. Gosling, meanwhile, did not limit himself to practising medicine. He spoke English and French fluently and was the one who dealt with the natives. When things got complicated he could call on the assistance of Swedes Gunnar Goransson and Sven Lindquist. Administrator José de Almeida looked after the accommodation, airports and customs, ensuring that strips were washed, balls were available for training, and other practical considerations. Treasurer Adolpho Marques took care of the financial dealings with FIFA, signed for the hotel bills and paid the players and the officials, each of whom got the same salary and bonuses as the players, even the two whose presence at the World Cup was unprecedented: Carvalhaes and dentist Mário Trigo.

None of the other 15 finalists included a psychologist or a dentist in their delegations; they assumed that their players had left home with healthy heads and teeth. Carvalhaes came to Sweden at Carvalho's insistence. His psychotests were worthless, but he might be needed if a player was overawed by the occasion – a weak argument, but one that won out anyway. As for Trigo, there was no doubt why he was there: he had been brought along to tell jokes. He had already taken out as many teeth as he could and he hadn't even bothered to pack his drill. Unlike Carvalhaes, the players loved him. Trigo was always laughing and he was up for anything, even running a gauntlet of players who lined up along the corridor to whip him with their T-shirts. In his own way, Trigo was doing what Carvalhaes was supposed to do: he was keeping the players calm.

Another important figure was not part of the delegation. He did not mix with the players or even watch Brazil play, because when Brazil were playing he was watching future opponents. With his white hair and his keen eye for the game, ex-Fluminense trainer Ernesto Santos fitted the bill perfectly as the team spy.

A year before the World Cup had even started, Santos was sent to Europe by the CBD. He watched the qualifiers, and when the draw was made he went to watch Austria, England and the USSR, the three teams Brazil would face in the first round. His folders were full of creased papers that detailed their formations, their tactics, their plays from dead-ball situations and where and how they were most danger-ous. In an era without videos, Santos's observations were vital to Feola and Nascimento.

On the eve of every Brazil game, Santos sat down in a locked room with Feola, Nascimento, Gosling and Paulo Amaral and told them all he knew. Sometimes he would use the blackboard to draw out their enemy's moves. The four would ask him questions, and when he had answered them he would leave the room and let them get down to picking the team. It was these four and no one else – not even Carvalho – who had the power to vote and veto.

The big fear for the technical commission was that Brazil would lose to Austria in the opening game. If Brazil went down then a whole year's worth of work could be lost. Not only would their chance of qualifying be dramatically reduced but the psychological effect on the players could be fatal; everyone knew that back home in Brazil no one had much faith in them. That was why Feola was contemplating putting three men in midfield: Dino Sani, Didi and Zagalo. In the 1950s, when football was more attacking, it was normal to have only two men in the middle of the park. But the information relayed by Ernesto Santos alarmed him, and although he didn't want to leave Garrincha out of the side he felt there was no other way.

Austria closed down the midfield with four men, Santos said, and it would be suicide to have only three men opposite them. Feola proposed telling Garrincha to drop back and cover on the right, just as he was going to have Zagalo do on the left. Nascimento agreed, and Gosling assured him Garrincha was physically prepared for the running involved. Only one voice objected: that of Paulo Amaral.

'It won't work,' he said. 'Garrincha won't follow your instructions. When we are discussing tactics at Botafogo we tell him to go and play table tennis or something. He's unpredictable out there. He's capable of passing the ball when he has an open goal. Or shooting from an impossible angle. He just does whatever is going through his head at the time.'

Feola and Nascimento pondered Amaral's words. They knew that as a Botafogo man he wanted Garrincha in the team – just not for that game. And so Joel, a player who was tactically disciplined and used to chasing back to help defend, got the nod to face Austria.

When the game kicked off it became clear that had they lined up without stringing four men across the middle Brazil would have struggled. They were all hyped up. They knew they were not going to waltz past Austria and they avoided falling behind thanks only to two good first-half saves from Gilmar. Brazil's eventual 3–0 win was not a true reflection of the game. Had it not been for Nílton Santos's goal things might have turned out differently.

The second half was only five minutes old and Brazil were winning 1–0 when Nílton Santos controlled the ball inside his own territory and set off. Midway into the Austrian half he laid it off for Mazzola and ran on for the one-two. Mazzola gave him it back on the edge of the area and with the keeper off his line, Nílton Santos put a classy lob over his head and into the net. The Brazil spectacle had started.

'You're under arrest! You're free! You're under arrest! You're free!'

During their first days in Hindas, Garrincha was one of the happiest players in the squad. He would run up behind team-mates and officials, grab their arms and shout, 'You're under arrest! You're free!' No one found it remotely as amusing as Garrincha did, but that didn't stop him doing it ten times a day to every one of them.

Garrincha lost his appetite for fooling around when he realised he was not going to be recalled for the England game. He got sick of mauling his team-mates. He wasn't eating properly and was the first to leave the table at meal times. He began to spend less and less time with the other players and more and more time in his room listening to records, or fishing alone on the lake. Being left on the bench depressed him, not because he felt the right-wing position was his but because he loved playing football. When he had convinced himself that he would be left out of the team for the second match he even asked Hilton Gosling, 'Doctor Hilton, wouldn't it be better to send me home?' Gosling told him to be patient and guaranteed him that his time would come. Garrincha was not convinced.

Joel, his rival from two doors down the corridor, rated Garrincha's chances more highly. On the eve of the Brazil–England match, he told his room-mate Zagalo, 'I need to get it just right. If Mané takes my place in the team I'll never get it back.'

Garrincha was not selected to play against England, and once again it was because of Ernesto Santos. Days before the match, Santos had warned the technical commission about the English left-back Banks, a man Santos said was the most perverse player he had ever seen play the game. He claimed Banks' game basically consisted of stamping on his rival's heel and pulling him to the ground.

Feola wanted to put out an attacking team against England. He

115

did not need four men in midfield because England were still playing football the same way they had done since the days of Charles Dickens: raining balls into the area for their forwards to get on the end of. If the Brazilian defence could handle the pressure, the forwards would be free to go at the English. The way was open for Garrincha to return, but Ernesto Santos's report made Feola think twice.

At the closed-door meeting to pick the team, the only one to vote to recall Garrincha was Carlos Nascimento. Nascimento argued that all they needed to do was to make sure he knew to pass the ball rather than try to beat Slater. But Feola and Paulo Amaral knew that Garrincha wouldn't listen and that the first time he went past him Slater would cripple him. Gosling agreed, saying that if he played against England Brazil risked losing him for the rest of the tournament. Joel got the nod again, with instructions either to play a one-two with Didi or to take the ball inside to avoid a confrontation with his rival.

Joel followed the instructions to the letter in the first half, playing through the middle, and even had a shot knocked off the line by Billy Wright. At the end of the second half he got over-keen and tried to take the ball past Slater, who put him up in the air.

The match finished 0–0, and although Brazil played better than they had in their opener against Austria the players were not satisfied. Hindas suddenly seemed to be inhabited by the ghost that had haunted Brazil throughout their previous World Cup campaigns – the fear of a decider. And the game against the USSR on the Sunday was more than a decider. Brazil either qualified for the next round or they went home with their tails between their legs and confirmed what everyone back home already believed – that Brazil was a country of mongrels.

For the past two years there had been a buzz about Soviet football, and it had increased after the USSR sent the first satellite into space – Sputnik, in 1957. Just like everything that came from the Soviet

Union, their football had about it a frightening aura of modernity and mystery. It was 'scientific football', and the players were fit enough to run for 180 minutes and then dance like victorious Cossacks over their rivals' spent bodies. It was said that Soviets did four hours of gym work on the morning of each game. It was also said that the KGB sent spies around the world to film matches, and that their computers – then called 'electronic brains' – had used them to produce a foolproof system to beat any team on earth. The Soviets were going to win the World Cup, and the Olympic title they won in Melbourne in 1956 served as proof to the Western world that they were to be taken seriously.

Many of the stories were typical Cold War propaganda. In real life, the team was not as good as *Pravda* and *Izvestia* made out. They had two great players: Lev Yashin, their nigh on unbeatable keeper, and Igor Netto, a midfielder who was a Soviet version of Didi. Little was known of their team-mates except that they were Communists and atheists who ate children with caviar and, like all Soviets, kissed each other on the mouth after scoring a goal.

The Brazil and USSR delegations were based 100 metres from each other in Hindas. Their hotels were side by side, with the Soviet hotel on top of a slight rise, which allowed them a privileged view of the Brazilian training sessions. When they looked up, all the Brazilians could see was silhouettes doing gymnastics. It was frightening. They seemed to work out day and night.

Nevertheless, for a team of supermen they hadn't shown themselves to be any better than Brazil: in their first two games they had drawn with England (2–2) and beaten Austria (although only 2–0). However, Igor Netto had missed both matches and he would finally make his World Cup debut against Brazil.

In addition to that, the game was all or nothing for both teams. To make matters even worse, the USSR's trainer Gavrin Katchalin had paid 'a courtesy visit' to the Brazilian camp in the week leading up to the game. When a reporter asked him to name Brazil's ideal forward line, Katchalin responded without hesitation: Garrincha, Didi, Mazzola, Pelé and Zagalo. Moscow seemed to be able to read the minds of the technical commission.

Many were clamouring for Garrincha's inclusion in the side. There were no more than 300 Brazilian fans in Sweden but a group of them had dedicated themselves to jeering Joel and cheering Garrincha. Although they were unaware of what the members of the technical commission were thinking, Didi and Nílton Santos were also unhappy with Garrincha's omission. On the day after the game against England, Nílton Santos wrote a letter to Sandro Moreyra in which he spoke of his 'disillusionment' with the Brazilian side and his disappointment at Garrincha's failure to find a place in it.

It was in this climate of unrest that one of the most fantastic stories of Brazilian football was created: that on the eve of the game against the USSR a commission formed by captain Bellini and senior players Didi and Nílton Santos pressured Feola and Carvalho into recalling Garrincha to the side.

The story has different versions. In one of them, Gosling fabricated an injury to Joel so that Feola would be forced to pick Garrincha. But Joel would have had to know about the ruse and agree to it, convinced by Carvalho that it was in his best interests. Another version has Carvalho asking Didi, 'Didi, we're from São Paulo. We don't really know Garrincha well. Can you vouch for him?' To which Didi responds emphatically, 'Pick the man, Doctor Paulo. Pick the man.' A third version claims that Joel, who was injured in the England game but would have been fit to face the Soviets had he missed training and rested, was deliberately ordered to work out so that his injury would not heal in time.

All these stories have been retold repeatedly in the Brazilian media. And they were all denied by the players who were interviewed for this book, including the protagonists, Bellini, Didi and Nílton Santos.

In fact, the 1958 Brazil squad was a model of organisation and discipline. The players' respect for hierarchy was absolute, their support for one another unrivalled. A campaign by three players in favour of one and to the detriment of another was inconceivable. As the two oldest and most experienced players, Didi and Nílton Santos were Feola and Nascimento's interlocutors with the rest of the squad. They never hid the fact that they wanted Brazil to play open, attacking football, which is why they wanted Garrincha in the team. But the opinion of the players was just one item on the technical commission's agenda – an agenda to which the players had no access (much less journalists). And as they had no access they could not know that Garrincha had been left out of the Austria and England matches for tactical reasons. Or that his presence against the USSR was certain, but secret.

Evidence of this came on the Thursday when the technical commission announced that they would hold a press conference at three o'clock the following afternoon. They asked for secrecy; the officials did not want foreign reporters, especially the Soviets, to find out and spy on their preparations. The following afternoon the Brazilian journalists, along with their foreign colleagues and Soviet spies, turned up at the training ground with their notebooks and cameras to see the players train. But they weren't there. The training session had been held that morning. Instead Carlos Nascimento was there, with a dirty look for the Brazilian hacks. He pointed to the foreign reporters and the Soviet spies and asked his fellow countrymen, 'Which one of you has the big mouth?'

No one said a word.

Earlier that morning Paulo Amaral had called the players together in the hotel foyer and told them, 'Grab your kit and get on the bus. We're getting out of here.' No one knew where they were going. Even the players had been kept in the dark about the location of the morning's workout, on a small pitch three miles from the hotel. When they got there, Feola started by putting Joel, Mazzola and Dida up front in team A and Garrincha, Vavá and Pelé up front in team B. Half an hour later, when he was satisfied they were not being watched,

119

he had the six switch shirts. None of them was told that Garrincha, Vavá and Pelé would start the match.

Vavá and Pelé's places in the side were confirmed at that training session; Mazzola and Dida had failed fitness tests. But Garrincha's place had been decided the night before. Dino Sani had suffered a groin strain against England and was out of the tournament. His replacement in midfield would be Zito, who was more of a marker than Dino Sani. With Zito protecting the defence, they would not need a fourth man in midfield.

In the end, the main reason Garrincha was called into the side was because the technical commission was afraid of the Soviets' superior fitness. If it was true that they were capable of running for 180 minutes then it was essential to scare them straight from the kick-off – if possible by scoring an early goal. To do that, Brazil had to go at them with all guns blazing.

On Saturday, Garrincha said to Nílton Santos, 'They're saying that I am going to play. But I'll only believe it if you say so. Is it true?'

'Seems like it,' he answered.

Didi geed him up. 'Tomorrow you're going to give the Russians the runaround, Mané.'

Garrincha said, 'Might these guys be good?'

A few minutes before the game started at the Nya Ullevi stadium in Gothenburg, while the players were getting a massage from Mário Américo, Nascimento decided to try to repay Katchalin's 'courtesy' visit of a few days earlier and went to nose around the Soviet dressing room. He grabbed some CBD pennants and went to offer them to his rival.

He came back a few minutes later with the same serious face – and eyes sparkling with glee.

'They're terrified!'

When the team gathered around Feola to hear his final team talk, everyone heard when he turned to Didi and said, 'Don't forget, Didi. The first ball goes to Garrincha.' And to Garrincha: 'Try to throw them off balance right from the start.'

'Monsieur Guigue, a gendarme in his spare time, blows his whistle to start the match. Didi quickly pushes the ball out to the right: 15 seconds of the game gone. Garrincha takes the ball with his instep: 20 seconds. Kuznetzov goes towards him. Garrincha feints left, but goes right. Kuznetzov falls to the ground to become the first João of the World Cup: 25 seconds. Garrincha takes the ball round Kuznetzov again: 27 seconds. And again: 30 seconds. And once more. The fans are on their feet. A startled Kuznetzov is on the ground: 32 seconds. Garrincha advances. Kuznetzov goes after him once more, this time supported by Voinov and Krijveski: 34 seconds. Garrincha pulls the ball this way, then that, and sets off with it down the right. The three Russians are scattered on the ground, Voinov with his backside in the air. The stadium explodes with laughter: 38 seconds. Garrincha fires in a powerful shot from a tight angle. The ball rockets off Yashin's left-hand post and goes out for a goal-kick: 40 seconds. The fans go mad. Garrincha returns to the middle of the park, as ungainly as ever. He is applauded.

'The fans are on their feet again. Garrincha moves forward with the ball. João Kuznetzov takes another tumble. Didi asks for the ball: 45 seconds. He sends a curved pass over Igor Netto and the ball falls at Pelé's feet. Pelé gives it to Vavá: 48 seconds. Vavá to Didi, to Garrincha, back to Pelé, Pelé shoots, the ball hits the bar and goes over: 55 seconds. The pace is mind-boggling. As is Garrincha's rhythm. Yashin's shirt is soaked in sweat, as if he's already been on the field for hours. The wave of attacks continues. Time after time Garrincha decimates the Russians. There is hysteria in the stadium. And an explosion when Vavá scores after exactly three minutes.'

That was how reporter Ney Bianchi, writing in the *Manchete Esportiva*, described the start of the game, as if he had one eye on the ball and another on the clock. Another journalist, the Frenchman Gabriel Hannot, would say later that they were the greatest three minutes in the history of football – and at more than 70 years old he had been a witness to much of it. The onslaught was so impressive that as soon as Brazil scored Yashin congratulated the first Brazilian to come near him – which happened to be Pelé.

And there were still 87 minutes to go. Had it gone on that way for the rest of the game the Soviets would have been looking at a season in Siberia. Their proud 'scientific football' had never before been so demoralised, and by the most improbable source: a poor Brazilian peasant – dark-skinned, small as a bird, cock-eyed and with ridiculously crooked legs. Garrincha was a perfect example of anti-science; he was anti-Sputnik, anti-electronic brain, anti-any brain. Kessarev, Krijveski, Voinov, Tsarev and especially Kuznetzov were all taken to the cleaners by the little man at some point during the game, either one at a time or in pairs or threes, or sometimes even one after another.

At the start of the game, after those ferocious opening three minutes, the Soviets still thought their problem was with marking, and they began to fight among themselves. But if they did tighten up it wasn't noticeable because Garrincha continued to run rings round them. Then the Soviets resorted to trying to bring him down, largely unsuccessfully. In one memorable incident, after leaving a defender on the ground Garrincha put his foot on the ball and with his back to the player offered his hand to help him up. He lifted the player up and then started running again as if it were the most natural thing in the world.

Brazil would score just once more, when Vavá doubled his tally 31 minutes into the second half. But it felt like the biggest hammering in World Cup history. At no time did the Soviets threaten to score; Gilmar had only one save to make. It was a different story at the other end, where only Yashin's brilliance had helped avoid a catastrophe. Brazil mounted 36 attacks, 18 of which were dangerous, and they hit the woodwork twice. Garrincha had arrived, and not just for those watching live but also for those listening in at home. From that day on there were no more Botafogo fans, Fluminense fans, Flamengo fans, Corinthians fans or Gremio fans. Everyone was now a Garrincha fan, even when he played against their own team.

In the dressing room after the game, Garrincha had no idea who had been marking him. And why would he? He hadn't been marked by one man but by many, and all their names ended in *ev* or *ov*. What did he care? The only thing he said, which summed up his performance perfectly, was, 'I was hungry for the ball today.'

CHAPTER 9

1958: Blue Victory

GARRINCHA DIDN'T KNOW THE WORDS TO BRAZIL'S NATIONAL ANTHEM. When the team lined up before that match against the Soviets he had stood hunched over, his hands in invisible back pockets, his feet splayed apart like a scarecrow. But when the whistle went a dancer emerged from the crooked body and, as the papers of the day put it, tore down the Iron Curtain. The European press ran out of words to describe Garrincha's performance. One Stockholm paper ran a story with the headline CONGRATULATIONS GOTHENBURG, ON THURSDAY YOU GET TO SEE GARRINCHA AGAIN!

They were referring to Brazil's quarter-final match against Wales, and they were not exaggerating. When they said Garrincha, they meant Garrincha – he was a one-man show. A French reporter called him 'the best substitute in the world' and an Englishman asked why he hadn't been picked from the start of the tournament. 'He would have beaten England single-handedly,' he said. A Swede, perhaps exaggerating, wrote that 'there was no club in Europe that could afford such a formidable player'. The day after the match Adolpho Marques handed Garrincha his win bonus: $50. In Brazil he was elected 'sportsman of the week' and given a bicycle.

On the Saturday before the USSR game, Carvalhaes had carried out more psychological examinations on the players in an attempt to ensure they were all in the correct mental state for such a crucial match. Of the 11 players tested, nine failed, Gilmar because he couldn't draw parallel lines – something Carvalhaes interpreted as nervousness. Didi, when asked to draw the first thing that came into his head, sketched a house with a chimney. When Carvalhaes asked him what it meant, he said it was 'the house I am going to buy with the money I intend on making during the cup'. Carvalhaes marked him down as a mercenary. When asked to perform the same task, Garrincha drew a circle with little lines coming from it. It could have been a ball, a sun, anything vaguely round. When asked what it was, he explained it was the head of Quarentinha, his colleague at Botafogo. Carvalhaes said he was mentally unfit. Of the 11 men marked down to start the match, only Pelé and Nílton Santos passed. Carvalhaes went to Feola with a sheet showing the results and Feola, faced with the choice between common sense and psychology, chose common sense. The days of Carvalhaes and his tests were over.

For the first time since 1950, when they almost won the tournament, Brazilians took to the streets to celebrate. In Rio, jubilant fans in cars and mopeds cruised along the beaches of Copacabana, Ipanema and Leblon waving banners and mixing with the samba schools that had come down from the nearby favelas to take part in the festivities. There was hope, a mood of genuine excitement. Garrincha had made winning the cup possible.

The winner of the match against Wales would move into the last four. For the Welsh it would be their third decisive match in five days: they fought out a 0–0 draw with Sweden on the Sunday, beat Hungary 2–1 on the Tuesday, and on Thursday they were preparing to face the team of the tournament. Brazil had had it somewhat easier: the players had been spending the same five days resting, shopping and going out with Swedish beauties. Still, they were not looking forward to the match. Wales represented their worst nightmare, a tough side that would quickly get 11 men behind the ball.

Didi would later say that he played the best game of his life that day against the Welsh. It was also a memorable day for Pelé, who chalked up one of the best of the more than 1,000 goals he would go on to score: he took a pass from Didi on the penalty spot and with his back to goal lifted the ball over Williams, turned, nipped around him and flicked it up with his left foot to volley past goalkeeper Kelsey with his right. He ran to the goal, picked the ball from the net and kissed it. It was the most important goal of his career: it guaranteed Brazil a 1–0 win and a place in the semi-finals.

Marked tightly by three Welsh defenders every time he got the ball, Garrincha was unable to produce the same magic he had shown in the previous match. He was still able to make a difference, though. The one-time left-back Hopkins was brave enough to face up to him alone, Garrincha beat him and laid the ball off to Didi – and it was from his pass to Pelé that Brazil got their goal.

While Brazil were hammering away at the Welsh defence, two hearts were beating fast at the Palacio de Catete, the home of Brazilian president Juscelino Kubitschek. On the morning of the game two members of Juscelino's staff went to Pau Grande with a special message for Garrincha's father Amaro. The president wanted Amaro to come to the presidential palace to listen to the game with him on the radio. He accepted, and persuaded his friend Nico Cozzolino to go with him. Together they put on their best clothes and went to Rio.

Sitting next to the president, Amaro had to control himself. In Pau Grande, whenever he heard defenders were getting stuck into his son he would bang his fist on the radio, sometimes hard enough to break it. But in the finely appointed rooms of the presidential palace, surrounded by people he didn't know, Amaro was too embarrassed even to speak, although inside his jacket his fists were rolled tightly into balls. When Pelé scored the winning goal he only just stopped himself from screaming an expletive. Juscelino smiled at him and swore himself! When the match was over, the president slapped Amaro on the back, handed him a 200-cruzeiro note, thanked him for all his son was doing for Brazil and ordered a car to take him back to Pau Grande.

Brazil were through to the semi-finals to face the French and were therefore at least the fourth-best team in the world. But they had the potential to be even better because at last they were playing for one another. The Brazil of years gone by, the Brazil of 11 individuals, was a thing of the past.

For Feola and Nascimento, the biggest threat to Brazil was not the French but the feeling prevalent in both the fans and the press that Brazil had only to turn up to book their place in the final. They were worried that the players would believe the hype.

Both the home fans and neutrals had taken to the Brazilians in a big way with people pouring on to the pitch after every game to hug the players as they made their way to the dressing rooms. Even the normally cool Swedes dropped their reserve. Crowds of blondes waited at the side of the tracks to wave Brazilian flags and shout their love for Didi, Garrincha and Gilmar as their train made its way from Gothenburg to Stockholm, where the semi-final and final would take place. The Brazilians knew how to win over the home fans: at the end of the game against Wales, Bellini had grabbed a Swedish flag and led the players in a lap of honour designed to say goodbye to their hosts.

In Stockholm, the manager locked the players away in their Lillswed *concentração*, letting them out only to go to the Solna stadium for training sessions. The French took the opposite approach: days before, the players had demanded to see their wives and girlfriends, and on the eve of the match a group of beautiful French women touched down in Sweden.

France had scored 15 goals in just four games, eight of them coming from prolific striker Just Fontaine. They had the most explosive attack in the tournament, with Raymond Kopa, the French Didi, giving Fontaine able backing. Brazil had scored only six but they had yet to concede a goal, while France had let in seven. Gilmar's apparent invincibility was starting to concern Feola. Both he and Nascimento were afraid the players' heads might go down if they went behind. Feola had to convince them that the important thing was not keeping a clean sheet but scoring more goals than the other side. With Fontaine and Kopa in such fine form, Feola knew the French were a good bet to score and he wanted his players to get the early goal that would give them a boost, just as they had done against the USSR.

They didn't let him down. Didi put a cross over the bar after just 30 seconds and from the resulting goal-kick Garrincha took possession, beat three men and passed to Zito. Zito laid it off to Didi, who passed to Vavá, who scored to make it 1–0. The match was only a minute and a half old.

The goal prompted a period of French possession, and with eight minutes gone Fontaine levelled the scores. The strike lifted France and Brazilian heads dropped, just as Feola had feared. For the next 15 minutes the French were all over them and they could have scored more but for profligate finishing in front of goal.

Didi knew he had to get his side going, and he did so by finally getting the ball to Garrincha, who danced his way around Lerond. The move gave heart to Brazil, who realised that with Garrincha working his magic they had it in them to win the match. Didi took control again, and in the thirty-ninth minute he put Brazil ahead with a trademark *folha seca*. It was plain sailing from there. Pelé scored a superb second-half hat-trick, and although the French pulled a goal back to make it 5–2, Brazil used the second period to show their superiority, much to the delight of the Swedish crowd.

It was years before French defender Lerond saw a recording of the game, partly because he had been told it wasn't something he wanted to see. When he did manage to sit down and view the tape, he realised why. 'It's only now I understand how ridiculous I was,' he commented.

The victory was met with the inevitable celebrations in Brazil. The match had kicked off at three p.m. Rio time and when the final whistle went mountains of paper were thrown from the windows of offices lining the Avenida Rio Branco. Samba schools paraded up and down the streets, giving the city an air of carnival. At last Brazil were in the final – against the hosts Sweden, who had beaten West Germany in the other semi-final. The World Cup was within their grasp.

For Garrincha, though, questions still remained. In the dressing room after the match, he asked Nílton Santos who their next opponent would be.

'Looks like it's Sweden, Mané. It'll be our last game.'

'What? Already?' said a startled Garrincha. 'What a rubbish tournament! The Carioca Championship is much better, you get to play all the teams twice.'

On the eve of the Brazil–Sweden game, Feola arrived in the press room to see a bank of microphones set up on a table at the front of the room.

'What's all this?' he asked one of the radio reporters.

'It's so the players can send messages to their families in Brazil over the radio.'

Feola turned red with anger. He swept his arm across the table, sending the microphones crashing to the floor, and then thundered, 'Oh no they won't. This is not 1954!'

Even though two of the microphones that Feola sent to the ground belonged to stations owned by his boss Carvalho, he did not care. Brazil were one game away from winning the World Cup and Feola didn't need any more trouble. The episode surrounding the shirts had irritated him enough.

Normally, both Brazil and Sweden wore yellow shirts. When it was clear the two teams would meet in the final, officials informed the Brazilian delegation that they would draw lots to decide which of the teams would be allowed to wear its home strip. Carvalho took this as an insult and went to the organisers to request that Sweden, as the home side, follow the established norm and allow the visitors to use their regular strip. The request was denied and a draw was arranged for Friday afternoon. The Brazilians protested by refusing to send a representative to witness it. In the end no one from the Brazilian contingent was there to see Sweden win the right to wear yellow.

Brazil were now faced with the problem of what colour to wear and they had to decide between white, green or blue, each of which had been registered as an official away shirt. The initial idea was to wear white, but this was rejected when officials saw that the players were visibly frightened by the idea. All of them, especially the older members of the squad, associated white shirts with the fateful loss to Uruguay that cost Brazil the 1950 World Cup. Brazil wore white that day and had never worn it since.

It was a lesson for Feola and Nascimento, who saw quite clearly how vulnerable their team of world beaters was to superstitions and myths. In fact, everyone in the delegation was a slave to superstition, including the non-playing officials. Carvalho had continued to wear the same brown jacket and trousers he'd had on when Brazil won their first match: the players joked that they had seen the suit walking by itself along the corridors of the team's Hindas hotel. Several players and officials had their own rituals. Zagalo carried a lucky charm in his sock, and Carvalho held a picture of Our Lady Aparecida, Brazil's patron saint, during each game. The players had a set order in which they would come down for breakfast, get on and off the team bus, and run on to the pitch. The order was so set in stone that even Carvalhaes, who didn't believe in fate, would worry if Gilmar wasn't the last to get on the bus. The spirit of Carlito Rocha was alive and well.

When it came to the shirts, it was Carvalho who took the decision to play in blue, because, he said, it was the colour of Our Lady Aparecida. To add weight to the proposal, José de Almeida recalled that of the five previous World Cup winners, four had worn blue: Uruguay and Italy twice each.

The problem was finding the shirts. Brazil had brought an enormous number of strips with them to Sweden, including literally hundreds of yellow, white, green and blue shirts. But the blue tops were sweaty from use during training and it was deemed unseemly to turn out in the World Cup final wearing dirty strips. So dentist Mário Trigo and Adolpho Marques volunteered to go to Stockholm city centre to buy new ones – Trigo to choose the right shade and Marques to hand over the cash. They eventually found them, and Américo and kit man Assis spent Saturday morning picking the badges and numbers off the yellow shirts and sewing them on to the new blue ones.

Should anyone have been worrying about fate, it was Sweden. The Swedes had faced Brazil twice before in World Cup matches and had lost both times, 4–2 in France in 1938 and 7–1 at the Maracanã in 1950. But Ernesto Santos had watched Sweden play and he handed his dossier over to Feola and Nascimento with words of caution. The Swedes had overcome Mexico, Hungary, Wales, the USSR and West Germany on their way to the final and were rated a fast and skilful team. Wingers Hamrin and Skoglund posed the biggest threat, and although their midfield playmaker Gunnar Gren could control the game, at 38 he was no match for the spritely young Zito. The problem for Brazil, Feola and Nascimento concluded, would be combating nerves. What would happen, for example, if Sweden, roared on by their own fans, scored first? Would heads go down?

Inevitably, Brazil started the game poorly; the players, uncomfortable in their unfamiliar blue tops, gave away possession to the yellow-shirted home side. With just four minutes gone, after a move during which half the Swedish team touched the ball, the 36-year-old Liedholm gave Sweden the lead. It was 1–0.

Two days before the final, when it was announced that Frenchman Maurice Guigue would referee the match, the Brazilian representative at FIFA, Mozart di Giorgio, went to 'congratulate' him on his appointment. Guigue had already refereed Brazil's games against Austria and the USSR, the second of which he had said was one of the best matches he had ever officiated. Guigue liked the Brazilians, he considered the players not only skilful but also disciplined and charming, and when di Giorgio saw he was friendly and happy to chat he casually invited Guigue to come to Rio after the cup on an all-expenses-paid visit. Guigue politely declined the offer.

Guigue had a good game, making just one mistake, one that didn't have any bearing on the result. Even if Brazil had had to contend with 11 biased referees they would have won, so superior were they to the hapless Swedes. When Sweden scored the opening goal – it was the first time Brazil had gone behind in the tournament – heads didn't drop as Feola and Nascimento had feared. Instead, the goal shocked the players into action. Bellini picked the ball from the net and gave it to Didi, who in an attempt to give the players time to compose themselves walked slowly to the centre circle, telling his team-mates, 'It was nothing, guys. Now let's get into these gringos.'

They did just that. Four minutes later Brazil were level, and it was Garrincha who did the damage. He took a pass from Zito, went past Parling and Axbom as if they weren't there and made for the byline, where he crossed the ball to Vavá, who slid it into the net: 1–1. And that was only the start.

The humiliations of 1950 and 1954 were forgotten. This team would not be beaten by ghosts of the past. The Swedish fans, who a few minutes before had been dreaming of winning the cup, were now just hoping to stay in the match. Brazil continued to pressure, and with just over half an hour gone Garrincha and Vavá combined to score a second. Garrincha, by now irresistible, beat three Swedes, hit the byline again and crossed to Vavá: 2–1. He was to reach the byline 15 times during the match, each time causing havoc in the Swedish defence.

Back in Brazil, each second-half goal – from Pelé, Zagalo and Pelé again – sent people into raptures. No one seemed to believe that Brazil were going to be, already were, world champions. There were even celebrations when Sweden scored a second goal to make it 4–2

133

with ten minutes to go. Perhaps because it was, according to the 50,000 fans in Rasunda, well offside. It was Guigue's only mistake, but it didn't stop the CBD from honouring their invitation: later that year Guigue and his family spent a happy holiday in Rio.

A few hours before the game kicked off, Carvalho had called Américo into a corner. 'Mário Américo,' he said, 'soon Brazil will be crowned champions of the world. We need the ball. As a trophy. I am making you responsible for getting it.' With just seconds left on the clock and Brazil 4–2 ahead, Américo positioned himself on the edge of the pitch ready to grab the ball as soon as the final whistle went. Everyone in the stadium was on their feet. As Guigue lifted the whistle to his mouth, Nílton Santos crossed the ball for Pelé to rise and head home the fifth. The Santos star fell to the ground and passed out. Guigue blew for time and Américo ran on to the pitch, still unsure whether to attend to a prostrate Pelé or go for the ball. As he ran, he stuttered to Bellini, 'G-get the ball!' But before Bellini could move, Guigue had grabbed the ball, stuck it under his arm and started walking to the centre of the pitch. Américo left Pelé, ran up behind the referee and knocked the ball out from under his arm. It bounced once, then he picked it up and started running for the dressing room, weaving in and out of players and fans like a rugby player.

It was pandemonium on the field. As soon as the final whistle went people poured on to the pitch. Journalists cried; Feola, Zagalo and Gilmar cried. Joel, another one of those in tears, embraced Garrincha, the only one of the players who wasn't crying. Bellini composed himself for long enough to shout, 'Let's do a lap of honour!'

A huge Swedish flag appeared and the players took hold of the corners and set off for their victory lap, Garrincha and Joel hugging each other at the front of the parade. The response was phenomenal, the gracious home fans cheering as though it was Sweden, not Brazil, who had won the cup.

King Gustav Adolf VI made his way on to the pitch to congratulate the Brazilian team without having any idea of what he was getting himself into. As he shook hands with the last of the sweaty Brazilian players, a grinning Américo grabbed his jacket sleeve and shouted, 'Come here, King, say hello to our chief.' The king laughed and shook hands with Carvalho. He had never been so happy to see protocol so severely breached.

A few moments later the Jules Rimet trophy was presented to Bellini. He would later say that at that precise moment – at half-past one Rio time on 29 June 1958 – he thought of his father, who had suffered a stroke shortly before the team left Brazil. He wanted to cry again but he held back the tears. He took the cup and lifted it with one hand as if he was going to wave it. However, the smaller Brazilian photographers couldn't see over their taller Swedish colleagues and they shouted for him to lift it higher. Bellini raised the cup above his head with both hands – and invented a gesture that is now imitated by sportsmen and women all over the world.

The celebrations were wild, and they lasted long into the night at a special dinner laid on by FIFA for the four semi-finalists at a Stockholm hotel. There was whisky and champagne on tap and no shortage of exotic French and Swedish women. The Brazilians, of course, were the stars of the show, and the players took advantage of the delicacies on offer. Reserve midfielder Moacir asked the journalists to call him Pelé and he had some success in his new role: the 5'4" midfielder was seen disappearing with a 6'2" blonde.

After a couple of days spent recovering and packing their bags, Brazil headed home early on 1 July on a Panair DC-7 piloted by Guilherme Bungner, the same man who had flown them from Rio 37 days earlier. After brief stops in London and Paris, where they got off the plane to drink cocktails and hear congratulatory speeches, they headed for Lisbon, where they paraded through the streets before attending receptions laid on by Benfica and Sporting. The kit man Assis, a 31-year-old ex-boxer, was at one point mistaken for the 17-year-old Pelé and lifted on the shoulders of the cheering crowd.

Eventually someone pointed out that Assis looked a bit too old to be Pelé. They put him down and tried to lift Feola instead. Unsuccessfully.

The next morning the team left Lisbon for Recife in north-eastern Brazil. When they flew over the Brazilian coast a few hours later around noon the city was in the midst of a torrential storm so fierce that the pilot twice aborted landings just as he was about to touch down. When they finally did set foot on home soil the players were stressed and tired after a journey that had lasted 30 hours. Outside on the streets of the city thousands of locals had lined up ready to watch them on the traditional victory parade on the back of a fire engine. The team got on the back of the truck and after hours fighting their way through the cheering throngs they found themselves at the Palacio das Princesas, where someone proposed that local boy Vavá stand as a member of parliament.

The next stop was Rio, where Juscelino Kubitschek was waiting for them at the Palacio de Catete. As they approached the airport, fighter jets flew alongside in tribute, leaving colourful trails of smoke in their wake. On the ground they were waved through customs and straight on to the Rio fire engine that would take them along the Avenida Brasil into town.

By now it was eight o'clock at night. They had been travelling for 36 hours and were exhausted, grubby, sweaty and in need of a bath. Their ties were crooked, the badges were falling off their jackets and their hands were tired from signing autographs on everything from bits of papers to bodies. Bellini's arms hurt from lifting the cup. It was an intoxicating experience for them all, but they really just wanted to get home and see their families. The journey through the massive crowds seemed to be endless, and it got even longer when, just as the players thought they were on their way to the last stop at the palace, the car took an unexpected detour and stopped at the offices of the magazine O Cruzeiro.

It was an ambush. The president would have to wait because the magazine's owners had prepared a big party for the World Cup winners – and without telling them had brought all their loved ones. *O Cruzeiro* had invited wives, fiancées, parents and brothers and sisters from all over Brazil to be at their party, and relatives had been arriving throughout the day on buses sent to pick them up. Some had come the night before from São Paulo, while those based in Rio had joined them during the day. All, of course, except the Pau Grande contingent. Amaro, Mané Caieira, Pincel, Swing and dozens of Garrincha's friends had been at the *O Cruzeiro* offices since nine that morning. When they got there the only people in the building were journalists and office staff, but when the special guests started to arrive Amaro got flustered. He had never seen so many beautiful women in his life. Miss Brazil was there, along with a handful of other beauty queens from across the country. When they were told that Amaro was Garrincha's father they locked on to him, playfully stroking his chin and smiling sweetly.

Although the magazine had bought plentiful supplies of whisky, beer, locally produced champagne and *guaraná*, Amaro wanted *cachaça*, and when he grumbled about the lack of the hard stuff the kindly art director of *A Cigarra*, one of the magazines based in the same building, went outside to try to find a bottle. While he was out looking, Amaro made do with beer, but he became increasingly desperate for *cachaça* and every now and then he would sneak down the back stairs – he was afraid of lifts – and nip into one of Rio's ubiquitous corner bars for a quick dram. In order not to waste his journey he threw back three or four glasses on each trip before stumbling back up the three flights of stairs to rejoin the festivities.

By the time Garrincha and the other players arrived, Amaro and the rest of the family were well oiled. When they walked in, a huge cheer went up and the room filled with the flutter of confetti. An old samba band played 'Cidade maravilhosa' ('Marvellous City'), the hymn to Rio, and photographers were knocked over as they fought to get a prime space on top of chairs and tables.

Bellini lifted the Jules Rimet above his head and the building shook with cheers. At one point the trophy was passed around the room; everyone wanted to touch it, kiss it, drink from it. Little did they know that it was a fake, a copy made by the Uruguayans after they won the trophy in 1950. Uruguayan officials had offered Carvalho the replica when he arrived at Rio's Galeão airport, suggesting that, given the Brazilians well-known love of partying, it might be wise to hide the real thing and take a replica out into the crowds. They warned, however, that the base of the copy was made of wood, not bronze like the original, and must be held with two hands because it was coming loose and could fall off at any moment. It was a miracle that the cup didn't fall apart in someone's hands.

It was almost two a.m. on the morning of 3 July when the players finally left the presidential palace – and 42 hours since they had left Stockholm. The players from Rio went home and the São Paulo contingent spent the night in a hotel before heading back to the city where they would do it all again: yet another open-top parade and another champagne reception at the governor's palace.

For Pelé, Zito and Pepe, the marathon followed them to Santos. Pelé's celebrations finished four days later in his home town of Bauru. The city fathers named a street after him and presented him with the pride of the local industry, a three-wheeler Romi-Isetta car. No one had remembered that, still only 17, Pelé was not allowed to drive.

After leaving Catete, Garrincha and his friends headed for Sandro Moreyra's flat in Copacabana, and from there a convoy of 50 cars and lorries set out for Pau Grande. They arrived in the town just as the sun was rising to the noise of fireworks going off. The local friar, a Flamengo fanatic who would regularly halt services to ask the latest football results, opened the church and rang the bells, vainly hoping that Garrincha might stop by and thank God for the title. Garrincha walked straight past. The town's bars were open, too, because Garrincha had promised to pay for all the *cachaça*, beer and *guaraná* the locals could drink. Someone proposed his name as mayor, a prospect he found hilarious.

It was now eight o'clock in the morning, and Garrincha was starting to show signs of exhaustion. He needed a rest, and he got it at home, where he saw his wife and daughters for the first time before crashing out and grabbing a few hours' sleep. His repose did not last long, however. By midday he had showered and changed and was out of the house again. He took a wad of dollars to settle the mammoth bar bill, then went to the local shop and paid off the tabs run up by his friends. He also went to the church to ask the friar to forgive him for not showing up earlier, and from there he got hold of a bottle of *cachaça*, climbed the hill to the town's football pitch and spent the rest of the day playing football with his mates.

In the days to come, Garrincha would be showered with presents. América Fabril handed him the keys to his house on rua Demócrito Seabra, and although they didn't come with the title deed he felt that the house was now his. At the same ceremony the company gave him a big box of cloth, and a group of wealthy businessmen from the area gave him a small weekend chalet in Piabetá, a small town near Pau Grande. S.C. Pau Grande hung up a brand-new photo of him on the wall. Someone else gave him a cow.

The tributes continued. The president of the Petrópolis Esporte Clube offered him 30,000 cruzeiros, a week's wages, to attend a dinner in his honour at the club the following Saturday. All the food and drink was free and he could bring whoever he wanted with him. 'I'll be there,' he said, so on the Saturday the great and good of Petrópolis turned out for the chance to glimpse the star up close. But Garrincha never arrived. He didn't send word and he was not discovered until the next night, laid out in an alcoholic stupor with Pincel and Swing in their mountain cabin.

Cards poured in from across the world, many of them addressed simply to Garrincha, Rio de Janeiro, Brazil. The post office delivered them to the offices of Botafogo where they were laid out alongside the thousands of other begging letters sent from Brazilians seeking money, jobs and even false teeth.

Garrincha's fame was a boost for Pau Grande. As it spread, the self-conscious little town with the funny name saw itself plastered across the front pages of newspapers around the world. Until then the people of the town had been embarrassed to say where they were from and had, when asked, usually said Raiz da Serra because Pau Grande seemed so weird to people who had no idea of the place. But now it was almost chic to say you were from Pau Grande, the home of the greatest football player in the world. When the state legislature proposed changing the town's name from Pau Grande to Garrincha, the little man was the first to protest. 'Where did they get that idea from?' he asked, genuinely puzzled. 'Pau Grande is such a nice name.'

The players had been promised the world if they won the World Cup: houses, jobs, cars, fridges, washing machines, ovens, free entry into cinemas, football matches and on to public transport, clothes, electric razors, umbrellas, table lamps, water filters and, of course, hard cash. Some companies joined together with banks and opened accounts where grateful fans could deposit money for the victorious team. The players never saw any of the proceeds, but some companies did make good on their promises of gifts. Drago Beds sent a sofa-bed to each player; General Electric made sure each of them got a yellow-and-green television; and Gulliver Bicycles gave them shares in the company and offered them jobs as salesmen. To the companies that made the offers the players' acceptance of their gifts implied an endorsement, and before long they found themselves promoting a number of products ranging from matches to cigarettes.

Garrincha wanted to know about the cars they had been promised, but Nílton Santos asked him, 'What do you want a car for, Mané? You can't drive.'

Garrincha replied enigmatically, 'Oh really? That's what you think!' The cars never arrived.

In fact, the amount of money each player got from the CBD during their cup-winning campaign was only a fraction more than what they would have got at their clubs. Some clever clubs, like Vasco da Gama, made their players sign new contracts before the tournament started to ensure that players whose value increased greatly were still on relatively meagre salaries. Even captain Bellini was taking home a wage negotiated before his inspiring performances had helped bring home the trophy.

In the excitement of the champagne reception at the Palacio de Catete, Juscelino Kubitschek had promised every player a house and a government job. The houses never appeared and the jobs were so inconsequential that few of the players actually took up the offer. The houses were forgotten about until a year later when a reporter asked João Havelange, in the presence of the president, how things stood. Havelange knew nothing about it, and Juscelino was surprised to hear they had still not been handed over.

The president ordered the government bank to give the players preferential mortgages, but the whole process ground to a halt again when the Chamber of Deputies failed to approve the measure. Didi, Bellini, Nílton Santos and Castilho petitioned the head of the chamber, but he baulked. The players would not be given special treatment, he said, because war veterans had complained. The players were already quite well off, the veterans relatively poor. The war had been over for more than 20 years and *they* still hadn't been given the houses *they* were promised. So the players never got their houses. And neither did the veterans.

CHAPTER 10

1958–1959:
The Firecracker Angelita Martinez

'YOU MIGHT BE A WORLD CHAMPION AGAINST THOSE JOKERS IN SWEDEN. But here in Piauí life isn't going to be so easy.'

This was the kind of threat that Garrincha faced when, after returning from the World Cup, he lined up for Botafogo in backwater states such as Piauí. The comments were quickly followed by a steel-capped size ten to the shin, and Garrincha resigned himself to suffering in silence if he was to have any chance of surviving 90 minutes alive. Murderous tackles were not rare in these friendly matches (and Botafogo had no way of avoiding them because they needed the money). Every defender wanted to be known as the man who could stop Garrincha. But Garrincha had the crowd on his side wherever he went and they laughed every time he dribbled the ball around them.

The world champions had hardly had enough time to take a nap on their new Drago folding beds before being called up by their clubs. A fortnight after lifting the trophy in Sweden, Garrincha, Didi and Nílton Santos lined up against Fluminense in the opening match of the 1958 Carioca Championship.

Even then, the clubs with World Cup winners in their ranks could not limit themselves to performing only in the league. The whole country wanted to see them. And they especially wanted to see Botafogo, who, with the purchase of Zagalo from Flamengo for 100,000 cruzeiros, or about $7,000, now had four World Cup winners in their team. The fans knew them by the names Waldir Amaral, the commentator on Radio Continental, had given them: Garrincha was 'the demon with the crooked legs'; Didi, 'the thermometer of the cup'; Nílton Santos, 'the encyclopedia of football'; and Zagalo, 'the little ant'.

Botafogo played on Saturdays or Sundays in the Carioca Championship, and during the week they went to Fortaleza, São Luís, Teresina, Salvador, Vitória, Uberaba, Porto Alegre or Buenos Aires. In the north and north-east, the players were greeted on arrival by huge crowds. They were given a special reception by the mayor, placed on the back of a flat-bed truck and driven through streets lined with adoring fans. At night they attended banquets or political rallies – it was an election year and all their hosts were running for office – and then when it was all over they had to take part in a football match.

In time, the players learned how to get out of at least some of these occasions. When the plane landed one of them would order Garrincha out first and the crowd would follow him, enabling the rest to sneak off to the hotel. Half an hour later, João Saldanha, alleging that Garrincha needed to rest, would apologise to the mayor and take Garrincha back to the hotel. By that time Garrincha had usually discovered where the red-light district was.

Saldanha was not opposed to letting the players have their fun, as long as they didn't stay out too late. His main worry was Garrincha. Every night he would stick his head round the door of Garrincha's room to make sure he hadn't sneaked out. Saldanha thought he had the situation under control: every time he looked he saw him fast asleep dressed in the checked shorts he always wore to bed. Years later, when Saldanha was no longer manager, Garrincha told him that he had paid reserve centre-half Domício to put the shorts on and take his place while he escaped through the window.

The friendly matches were beginning to take their toll on Botafogo's league performances. Vasco and Flamengo, who themselves had more than a few World Cup winners in their ranks, had made winning the league their priority and were tied at the top of the table. Botafogo were near the bottom, and when the league moved past the halfway stage they resolved to cut back on the travelling. That decision helped them to gain ground on their rivals and made the 1958 Caroca Championship one of the most memorable of all time.

With two matches to go, Vasco were four points clear of Botafogo and Flamengo, their last two opponents. They needed only to win or draw with one of them to take the title. But they lost both matches, 2–0 to Botafogo (with a great performance from Garrincha) and 3–1 to Flamengo. With all three teams tied at the top of the league they were forced to play a super championship among themselves to see who would emerge as champion.

At first, the answer was no one. In the super championship, Flamengo beat Botafogo 2–1, Botafogo beat Vasco 1–0 and Vasco beat Flamengo 2–0, so they were all still tied. Another round of matches was required – this time it was called the super super championship. And this time things were different: Botafogo drew 2–2 with Flamengo and lost 2–1 to Vasco, ruling them out of the race. Flamengo needed to beat Vasco in the final match but could only draw 1–1, so the title went to their rivals.

Flamengo were all over them during the last five minutes but couldn't score. It was exciting stuff. So exciting that one man listening to the game on the radio, bohemian factory worker Avelino Gomes, keeled over from a heart attack and died. His daughter was not there to help him. She was in Argentina singing. Elza Soares would come to play a crucial role in the life of the little bird.

* * *

On the eve of the super championship game against Flamengo, with the Botafogo squad grouped together in their *concentração*, Garrincha was nowhere to be seen. The club had allowed the players to spend Christmas with their families on the condition that they be back by the evening of 25 December. They all returned on time except Garrincha.

Saldanha was fairly easy-going when it came to letting the players drink, as long as they didn't overdo it. He knew that if he locked them up in the *concentração* they would manage to find a way of getting booze into the hotel. It was better to let them go out and drink and see what state they were in when they got back. But when Garrincha was still not back the next morning, Saldanha went mad. 'If that son of a bitch isn't back here by four o'clock this afternoon then he's not getting a game tomorrow. He's dropped!'

The club doctor, Nova Monteiro, heard Saldanha's threats and was worried. Whoever heard of a manager dropping Garrincha? He called his son Francisco Eduardo and they got in his Ford 41 and headed for Pau Grande. When they got there they found Garrincha at home – with Pincel, Swing and at least another ten lads from the town, all of them laughing, singing and shouting at the top of their voices.

Without even entering the house, Monteiro looked at Garrincha and said simply, 'Garrincha, we have a game tomorrow. You're coming with me.'

Garrincha tried to focus on the man at the door and what he was saying. When he managed to work out who it was, he responded placidly, 'Yes, sir.'

They drove back to Rio together in Monteiro's car. Garrincha played poorly the next day and Botafogo lost.

Garrincha might have kept a lid on his drinking when he was at the club, but when he was away from it there was no stopping him – and he did his best to rope in his team-mates. On the Mondays after league games, when the players were supposed to be relaxing, he hosted get-togethers in Pau Grande at which Didi, Paulo Valentim and Quarentinha were regular visitors. Garrincha would prepare a *feijoada* and then strip to take part in a kickabout. The other players couldn't believe that Garrincha was risking life and limb on the mounds and craters of the Pau Grande pitch, but he was young, invincible and didn't need to rest. He lived his youth as though it would never end.

When the high jinks in Pau Grande were over Garrincha went back to Rio with his team-mates and headed straight to Iraci's flat. Saldanha knew of Garrincha's double life and even approved of it. The hours he spent with her were hours spent not getting into trouble. His relationship with Iraci was worth celebrating for another reason, too: she kept him far from Pau Grande, where – Saldanha was well aware – all those romantic stories of hunting and fishing were just a pretext to go drinking.

What Saldanha didn't know was that as the end of the Carioca Championship neared, a new threat was circling his most important player: a music-hall firecracker called Angelita Martinez.

Affairs between football players and showgirls were common in the 1950s. The girls were the most beautiful and the most sought after of the era. After Virginia Lane, who had once had an affair with the country's president, the most desirable of all the showgirls was Angelita Martinez. The 26-year-old was no stranger to politicians herself: when she split up with the country's vice president he shot the lock off her door to get into her flat. She was a typically Brazilian beauty with dark hair, small breasts and a pair of hips that defied description. The daughter of a professional football player, the niece of former Corinthians legend Neco, and the former girlfriend of Flamengo defender Pavão, Angelita was said to have the best legs in Brazilian football.

She met Garrincha at the end of 1958, when she recorded a song for the upcoming Rio carnival. The song, 'Mané Garrincha', was a tribute to Garrincha, but the lyrics were weak and without proper

147

promotion it would not have had a chance of becoming a hit. Angelita needed Garrincha to pose with her for photos and accompany her to TV studios and concerts. So one afternoon she went to Botafogo to ask him.

Needless to say, she was a huge success. Wearing a Botafogo shirt over a black swimsuit, and tottering over the grass in her high heels and stockings, when she sang the song she brought the training session to a halt. When the photographers asked Garrincha to pose with her, he picked her up and held her in his arms.

His team-mates tried to take the mickey, but Garrincha knew that they were really just jealous. Many of them were married or engaged and they couldn't even think of getting so close to another woman, especially not one like Angelita. Garrincha, on the other hand, although married with daughters, seemed to have all the freedom in the world. His affair with Angelita began that afternoon, almost as soon as they had taken off their Botafogo shirts.

The first person to sense that love was in the air was Iraci. Garrincha stopped going to her flat at the usual time, and when he did appear he flew in and out shouting excuses about having to accompany Angelita to a dance or to hear her rehearse the song. In fact, Garrincha had almost moved in with her at her flat in Copacabana. She treated him like a king there, wearing satin negligées and expensive perfume and setting the scene with champagne and soft lights. Garrincha was starry-eyed.

Saldanha, however, was less impressed. Botafogo were right in the middle of the super super championship and Garrincha was clearly not getting enough sleep. He would take Angelita from Radio Nacional to the theatre where he waited backstage while she performed. From there they would head off to dinner in Barra da Tijuca, and rarely would they get to sleep before seven a.m. Botafogo did not lose the title because of Angelita, but she didn't exactly help Garrincha prepare for those crucial two games against Flamengo and Vasco.

As if that were not enough, the censor had banned the song 'Mané

Garrincha' from being performed either live or on the radio. The words as they had been written were not the problem; the problem was the crowd were changing the line that said 'Mané who was born in Pau Grande' to 'Mané who was born *with* a *pau grande*'. Angelita had started it by getting mixed up and inadvertently singing the new version, one that to her did Garrincha justice. She had never seen anything like his masculinity. He must have had a good ten inches.

At the start of 1959, in the middle of the whirlwind – the affair with Angelita, the banning of the song, the super super championship – Garrincha had been absent from Pau Grande for some time. Preferring to spend his days off with Angelita at the barbecues organised by her friend Virginia, he had not been home since Christmas. It was only in the middle of January, when he could not avoid it any longer, that he finally returned. With Angelita at his side.

He justified her presence by saying that she was going to the town to perform 'Mané Garrincha' to the people who lived with the song's hero – after all, it was a tribute to Pau Grande as much as it was a tribute to Garrincha. Garrincha had brought stars to his home town before and no one had thought anything amiss. It was different with Angelita, however, as she seemed to make a big deal of simply being there, turning up hours before the show was due to begin and parading through the town in a swimsuit on her way to the river to take a dip with Garrincha.

Pau Grande had never seen a body like it. They may not even have known that the outside world produced such perfect specimens. Half the people in town traipsed after her to the river, jumped in alongside her and tried discreetly to touch her up. The other half closed their windows and tried to ignore the commotion. The women, some of them wiping their moustaches, felt sorry for Nair, and the men, every single one of them, were dying of jealousy.

The couple followed their swim with a tour of Garrincha's childhood haunts, and then they stopped for a drink, first in Dodi's and

149

then in Constâncio's bar. After that, Garrincha took her home for dinner – prepared by Garrincha's sister because Nair wasn't available. When someone asked Nair what she thought of the song about her husband, she replied timidly, 'It's nice. But I'd rather it was sung by Emilinha Borba.'

Nair's humility was not shared by Iraci, who, back in Rio, was suffering from afar. The mistress was not as naive as the wife. The first chance she got, she pinned Garrincha against the wall and demanded, 'What's going on? Are you having an affair with that bitch?'

Garrincha responded with equal fury: 'First of all, she's not a bitch. She is a lady. And second, no one is forcing you to do anything. I don't have to stay with you and you don't have to stay with me. It's up to you.'

Iraci knew very well that she had no choice. She either accepted Garrincha as he was, and waited for the fever that was Angelita to pass, or she left him and returned to Pau Grande with her tail between her legs. She couldn't even complain about the fact that it had been a while since Garrincha had left her money or paid the rent and other bills, for Garrincha wasn't in a position to help: Angelita was addicted to playing cards and he was doling out money to help her pay off her gambling debts.

The romance with Angelita had started before Christmas, exploded over Carnival and dragged on through Lent, but it did not survive past Easter Saturday. Angelita had caught Garrincha eyeing up Virginia Lane but she hadn't said anything. When he realised he was being watched, Garrincha kept his distance from Angelita's best friend. But the other girls at the theatre were not so off limits.

One night, Angelita went into her dressing room and found Garrincha canoodling with another girl. She was carrying a basket of plastic flowers she used on stage, and she threw the basket, a make-up bag, a hairdryer, a pair of clogs and anything else heavy she could get her hands on straight at Garrincha before storming out. Later that same night she asked him to come back – she wasn't used to being cheated on.

It was too late, though. Garrincha had had enough. The initial spell had worn off and the affair had lost its magic. Angelita had given him many nights of pleasure but it was over, and now he had to come to terms with it.

And there was something else he had to come to terms with: a place on the bench.

'Seventy-one!'

Garrincha jumped on and off the scales at the Brazilian *concentração* as if he had stepped on hot coals. Before anyone could get a good look he had shouted his normal weight in kilos and disappeared. But he was not at his normal weight during the training sessions for the friendly against England at the Maracanã on 13 May. He appeared heavy and sluggish and closer to the 74 kilos he did his best to avoid Hilton Gosling seeing.

Garrincha's weight problems had been getting worse over the years. His inability to maintain his ideal weight of 71 kilos was partly down to his compulsion for *mariolas*. Just one of these sweets contained close to 70 calories, and Garrincha ate 20 a day. To compensate, he spent the Friday and Saturday before a game fasting in an effort to lose weight.

But there was another factor that contributed to his battle with the bulge, something more serious than his love of *mariolas* yet one that no one seemed concerned about: Garrincha's love of *cachaça*. On average, a glass of *cachaça* contained 115 calories. Even when he was in the *concentração*, Garrincha drank at least three a day, usually in glasses much bigger than the normal ones. The number of calories Garrincha took in through sugar cane was therefore astronomical. When he wasn't at the club he was free to drink as much as he wanted and the sky was the limit. For a player who relied on his explosive starting bursts to get past defenders, the extra pounds were fatal.

Contrary to what people thought, Garrincha was not very fast. The powerful muscles in his legs meant that his speed off the mark was dizzying, but it didn't take him far. Garrincha could get away from his marker easily, but if the defender went after him he had to stop and do it again to shake him free. The extra pounds robbed him of that quickness and made it possible to do what under normal conditions had been impossible – get the ball off him.

In May 1959, with the Angelita Martinez festival over, Garrincha was fatter and more out of shape than ever. Just as the English were on their way to the Maracanã.

For that game, a simple friendly at home, Brazil called up 22 players 13 days before the match. Playing England was still a big deal; although the fans wouldn't admit it, Brazil still had an inferiority complex when it came to the country that had given them the game so many years before. They were taking the match seriously, and they wanted to beat the only team they hadn't yet beaten in the World Cup. They felt the title was really theirs only if they beat the English.

So no one took seriously the rumours that Garrincha would be dropped for the game. They didn't believe Feola would be that mad. Yet when the sides took to the field the announcer read out the teams and paused when he got to the name of the right-winger – Julinho. As if on cue, the stadium broke out into the loudest chorus of boos in its history.

Julinho had left Italy, Fiorentina, and the Italians' passion for the game to return to Brazil and Palmeiras. All he needed now was his place back in the national squad. An injury had kept him out of the South American Championship, but he was included in the 22 for the England game after a five-year absence. The owner of the number 7 shirt was, obviously, Garrincha, and Julinho was not offended at being his understudy. At the age of 30 he was no longer the best right-winger in the world; that title now belonged to Garrincha, as chosen by European sportswriters, the same men who had elected Julinho in 1954. All Julinho wanted to do now was get out on the training pitch and prove to Feola that he could be counted on in an emergency.

When Feola picked Julinho over Garrincha he warned him he would get a frosty reaction from the fans. Garrincha said the same thing, but Julinho found it hard to believe that the Carioca fans could have forgotten him quite so easily.

The players were preparing to take to the field when the announcer read out the teams, and the huge chorus of boos drifted down the tunnel towards the dressing room. They walked through the tunnel and climbed the steps to the pitch. When Julinho appeared, the jeers got louder. A small brass band on the terraces played the song 'Mané Garrincha' and Julinho almost fell head-first on to the pitch after tripping on a step. The abuse came from 127,000 mouths – the attendance that Wednesday afternoon on a holiday to commemorate the end of slavery. Julinho took the field in tears and refused to speak to the radio commentators who chased after him looking for an interview. When the national anthems were played his legs trembled even more than they had before the Fiorentina–Brazil match a year before. That day he had cried because he was playing against his own country. Now it was worse: he was playing for his country but being treated like an intruder.

The jeers were still ringing around the stadium when the match kicked off, and Julinho responded at once. With his first touch of the ball he left his marker Armfield on the ground. The fans stopped booing. England attacked, but Brazil won the ball back. Henrique crossed the ball from the left and Pelé, Armfield and Julinho, who had timed a late run, all went up for it. Julinho made contact and sent the ball high into the net. The fans at the Maracanã were generous as always: the silence that followed the jeers was quickly replaced with the warmest applause any player could wish to receive.

For the rest of the game, one of the best he ever played, the fans clapped Julinho whenever he touched the ball. In the end, Brazil won 2–0, the second goal from Henrique coming from one of Julinho's crosses.

Only one person watched the game in silence: Garrincha. Both managers agreed they could make only one substitution, and with 44 minutes of the match gone Feola made his, taking off Orlando and putting on Formiga. When he saw the switch, Garrincha walked back to the dressing room, took off his shirt and left the ground. He missed Julinho's second-half show.

When Garrincha had returned from the South American Championship in April 1959, Dr Nova Monteiro had examined his knee and given him a warning: he needed to have the meniscus removed from his right knee. The recuperation would be complicated and Garrincha might not be ready in time for Botafogo's tour to Europe in May. At best, he might recover in time to join his team-mates halfway through the trip. The club gave him the go-ahead to have the surgery and on the appointed day Monteiro, the anaesthetist and a team of nurses prepared to perform the operation to remove the damaged cartilage. But Garrincha was a no-show. He excused himself by saying that his daughter had been ill and rescheduled, and then he stood them all up again.

Dona Maria Rezadeira, Pau Grande's top authority in curing bone and muscle problems with just a needle, thread and a cloth placed over the injured region, had forbidden him from having the surgery. She had told Garrincha that if he went under the scalpel he would never play football again. The way to resolve the problem was through prayer, and by allowing her to do what faith healers across Brazil commonly did: sew a cloth over his knee while she said her prayers in a language known to no one. Garrincha believed her – his own mother had been a faith healer.

Monteiro took off his gloves and washed his hands. If Garrincha didn't want to have the operation now, he was prepared to wait. The state of his cartilage meant that he could keep playing for now, but he could not avoid it for ever. An operation some time in the future was inevitable.

Garrincha spent April under the care of Dona Maria Rezadeira. When he wasn't with her he was playing for Botafogo in the Rio-SP tournament. He then joined the Brazil squad to face England, and the day after the game he set off with Botafogo for Europe. It would be years before the operation was mentioned again.

Brazilian football was all the rage in Europe. After a World Cup that had been shown on European television, there wasn't a Brazilian club side that didn't set out for the Old World with a billing that made them seem as good as the champions themselves. In a bid to make as much money as they could from the trip the men who organised the excursions obliged the clubs to play 20 or 30 games in as many days, forcing them to undertake inhuman schedules; today in Holland, tomorrow in France, the day after that in Denmark – all of it without a break. Europe was filled with Brazilian football teams and players bumped into one another in hotels, airports and sometimes even on the pitch, where they faced off in friendlies. The trips were so tough that by the halfway stage the players were exhausted and embarrassing themselves by losing even to amateur rivals. Eventually, the National Sports Council decided to lay down rules to prevent over-exposure and further embarrassments.

When Botafogo went to Europe on 14 May 1959, the situation had improved somewhat. The club was scheduled to play 16 games in ten countries over the course of 55 days, albeit with stops in 49 cities. Still, anyone looking at the itinerary would have thought the author insane.

Botafogo had been in Umea, in the far north of Sweden, for only one night when the local police arrived at the team hotel looking for Garrincha. His team-mates were used to the uncanny way Garrincha managed quickly to get his bearings in the strangest of places, but this was a record. Umea was halfway to the North Pole.

Soon after arriving in town the night before, Garrincha and two other players had sneaked out of the hotel and not returned until early in the morning. Saldanha was furious, and when they finally reappeared he told them they were dropped for the game against Gimonas a few hours later. In fact, they did play in the end because Sven Lindquist, a friend of Saldanha's and the man who sponsored the Swedish leg of the tour, would not allow him to leave out the biggest crowd-puller.

Nevertheless, Garrincha must have done something serious for the local constabulary to come after him. He just couldn't understand what. With two female officers waiting outside the door, Garrincha sat down and told Lindquist his story. He had met a girl who had invited him back to her house, where he'd drunk an aquavit with her parents. Then, while the parents watched television in the living room, the girl had taken him upstairs to her bedroom, and after a quick romp between the sheets he'd left. He had no idea why the police would want to speak with him.

Lindquist spoke with the officers and managed to get a better understanding of what had happened. The girl's parents were not worried about what Garrincha and their daughter had been up to. Neither were they worried that she might be pregnant – if she was they would raise the child themselves. They just wanted to be sure that Garrincha was the father. At their request, the officers asked Garrincha for a blood sample that could be used in the future for a paternity test, if such a test were necessary. He was not obliged to comply and he would certainly not be arrested. Garrincha agreed, and the police left.

Garrincha's antics both fascinated and irritated his team-mates. Even though he was married, he acted as if he were single. He could publicly paint the town red, go out with as many women as he liked, run the risk of getting a girl pregnant at the North Pole, and no one said a word. It was a different story for the others. Since becoming a big draw Botafogo had added a photographer and a reporter to their delegation, something that enabled the players' wives to keep track of them via the newspapers. When an innocent picture of Zagalo and

Didi kissing Miss Sweden on the cheek was published in the Rio newspaper O *Globo*, Zagalo got an outraged letter from home. Didi's letter was worse: his wife Guiomar detailed how she had run a razor through all his suits.

In the midst of all the off-the-field drama, Botafogo were doing a little better on the pitch, winning 10 of their 16 games and playing some nice football, particularly in the 6–4 defeat of an Atlético Madrid side that featured Puskas. Garrincha lived up to his reputation with a starring role in the 4–1 drubbing of Willem II of Holland and the 4–0 hammering of West German side Sarre. By then, though, Botafogo and Brazilian football had nothing left to prove in Europe. And the players received enough international adulation that they were able to commit the most incredible outrages – like the time when Garrincha, Edson and Chicão relieved themselves on Napoleon's tomb in the Jardin des Invalides in Paris – and get away with it.

Nine months later, Garrincha was given the results of the paternity test from Umea. They were positive.

Just before kick-off, opposing full-backs would now get close to Garrincha and whisper, 'Mané, help me out here. I am about to get married and my contract is almost up. See if you can't take it easy with me, otherwise I'm in trouble.'

The anger Garrincha awoke in defenders seemed to be diminishing. He now inspired only fear. It was written all over the faces of men who were playing against him for the first time. His opponents seemed finally to be realising that Garrincha was a player they needed to worry about.

Garrincha began to hear such appeals before every game. He was sympathetic to the players who were about to marry, or to those who were at the end of their contracts, as long as they didn't provoke him. Cavaquinha, the full-back with Rio side Portuguesa Carioca, was one player who asked for clemency. Garrincha understood, and when they came face to face for the first time he let Cavaquinha take the ball

157

off him. Cavaquinha, however, must have thought he'd won it fairly because he proceeded to nutmeg Garrincha. The ingratitude woke Garrincha up. When he got the ball back he dribbled around him and then spent the rest of the game sticking the ball between his legs. No one knows if Cavaquinha got married. He certainly didn't have his contract extended.

In fact, it was easy to beat Garrincha. If the ball was taken from him cleanly, Garrincha lost interest and waited for his next chance. To him, football existed only when the ball was at *his* feet. Defenders didn't have to ask for clemency, all they needed to do was mark him cleanly, without resorting to violence. If his marker didn't come in with the intention of trying to cripple him, Garrincha wouldn't make a fool of him. He would limit himself to beating him and moving on – just as he did with Flamengo full-back Jordan, the man he repeatedly called the best full-back he ever came up against. When he was asked why he thought Jordan was the best, he answered, 'Because he's not dirty, he goes for the ball. He anticipates what I am going to do and that's why it's hard to get past him.' There were those who thought that Garrincha's admiration for Jordan was his way of telling Vasco's Coronel and Fluminense's Altair to calm their game down. But though the latter pair took no prisoners, he beat them all with the same efficiency, on average seven out of every ten times he got the ball.

It was a passage of play featuring Altair and Garrincha that marked one of football's most beautiful episodes. The Botafogo–Fluminense match during the 1960 Rio-SP tournament was just three minutes old when Fluminense's Pinheiro fell to the ground with a pulled muscle. The ball ran to Garrincha, but instead of taking advantage and playing on, he kicked it out of play so that Pinheiro could receive treatment.

Up in the Maracanã's press box, journalist Mario Filho jumped from his chair to salute Garrincha's sportsmanship. Filho, who had the Maracanã named after him when he died in 1966, was overcome by Garrincha's *beau geste* and pointed towards the field, proclaiming, 'He's the Gandhi of football! The Gandhi!'

But the show was not over. The linesman signalled a throw-in to Fluminense. Altair went to take it, knowing that the ball was by rights not theirs, and deliberately committed a foul throw, giving the ball back to Botafogo. Such sportsmanship was rare for the time, and this rarity was the reason Filho was so lavish in his praise. It was perhaps fitting that the game ended 2–2. No one deserved to lose.

Although he had stopped the game to enable someone else to get treatment, Garrincha would not allow anyone else to return the favour. No one can ever remember him staying down until the stretcher came on. No matter how hard he had been hit, he got up, even if it was only on one leg, and hobbled to the edge of the pitch to wait for the trainer.

Such attitudes served to confirm the image poets and writers had given to Garrincha, that of a naive little bird. But in 1959, a year before he cemented his humanitarian credentials in the Maracanã with Altair and Pinheiro, Garrincha missed the chance to help someone much closer to his heart. His father Amaro.

CHAPTER 11

1959–1961: Sex Machine

THE BLACK CAR WAS ROLLING INTO PAU GRANDE AT LESS THAN 20MPH when the driver suddenly seemed to accelerate unintentionally. The car zig-zagged across the Praça Montese, the town's main square, at precisely the same moment that Garrincha's father Amaro was crossing the road.

As the guard at the factory, it was Amaro's job to walk the streets of Pau Grande guaranteeing peace and tranquillity. It wasn't hard; the streets were quiet and the most he ever had to worry about were bicycles. Pau Grande was a virgin land still so unspoiled by motor vehicles that when a car appeared in the town people ran to their windows to take a look. But fate determined that when an accident happened, Amaro would be the one who was knocked down. And that his son, by some absurd coincidence, would be the driver.

Amaro walked out in front of the vehicle. An experienced driver would have swerved or hit the brakes. But the black car drove straight on, hitting Amaro and throwing him on to the side of the road. The car kept going, past a group of people who were sitting on the *praça* watching the accident as if in slow motion, before pulling to the side of the road further ahead. Garrincha got out and, without even looking at the man lying at the side of the road, ran off in the other direction.

A group of men went after him, and when they caught him they found him drunk, almost catatonic, and with no grasp of what he had done. They were furious. One of them screamed, 'Are you crazy? Aren't you going to help your father?'

But Garrincha was in his own world, and had it not been for Amaro, who had by now recovered enough to stand up and take control of the situation, he might have been lynched.

'Leave him alone,' Amaro said. 'It was my fault. Let's go home.'

In the Pau Grande of 1959, Garrincha could do no wrong. The people of the town ignored his public escapades with Angelita Martinez, they pretended not to know he was having an affair with the wife of one of the factory directors, and they turned a blind eye when he rode to the factory gates on the Gulliver bicycle he got for beating the USSR and tried to chat up the girls leaving at the end of their shifts. When Garrincha tried to sweet-talk the young ladies into taking a ride to the waterfall with him, they rarely knocked him back. More often they'd pretend to be shocked.

'But you're married!'

Garrincha would respond, 'So what? It's not a disease. One day, you'll be married too.'

The girl would laugh and say, 'You're terrible. You're not worth it.' And off they'd pedal towards the waterfall.

Garrincha didn't care how old the girls were; even those that were under age were fair game if he really liked the look of them. In an age when fathers still killed anyone who did wrong by their little girls, Garrincha enjoyed a certain impunity because of who he was. He wasn't necessarily taking advantage of his fame or status; his father had been the same when he was his age, and he wasn't Garrincha.

While Garrincha flirted brazenly with the girls of Pau Grande, Nair continued to do the only thing she knew how to do – have daughters. In August, she gave birth to Denísia, their fifth girl. At the same time, Garrincha was caught by surprise with the announcement of another pregnancy – Iraci's.

When his romance with Angelita Martinez was drawing its last breaths, Garrincha had returned to Iraci, although not with the same élan as before. He was not opposed to her pregnancy, neither did he ask her to have an abortion, but he was not the loving boyfriend of times gone by. He was late paying her rent, he would go weeks without visiting, and he rarely telephoned. When he did sleep at her flat he invented excuses not to have sex with her, behaviour so unusual that Iraci thought he might have caught a sexually transmitted disease. He denied it, but she could see no other explanation; she had never known Garrincha to refuse sex before. He was a machine who would do it any place, any time, with anyone. He even had sex with Nair when he went to Pau Grande.

Iraci got more and more irritated with his neglect, and one night she could take no more. She went to the house of Paulo Amaral, the team's trainer who lived just along from her on rua Gomes Carneiro. She knocked on the door and introduced herself as 'Garrincha's second wife'. Amaral took one look at her, young, beautiful and very pregnant, and gave a resigned sigh. 'Aaaw, that Garrincha! Come in!'

Once inside, Iraci told him the whole story of how Garrincha had brought her from Pau Grande and then got her pregnant. Lately he had stopped visiting her and stopped sending money. The rent hadn't been paid, the electricity had been cut off, and she was hungry. Paulo Amaral called Lídio Toledo, the youth-team doctor, who arranged to have her admitted to a local hospital, where she gave birth the next day. Garrincha had yet another daughter, Márcia.

Paulo Amaral advised her to take the child and return to Pau Grande, but she didn't listen. Not even after receiving a surprise visit a few days later from someone who identified himself as 'a friend of Garrincha'. Although she didn't know him she invited him in, gave him a cup of coffee and showed off baby Márcia. When she told Garrincha later, he didn't know who the visitor was either, but he recognised him from Iraci's description: he was a friend of Nair's brothers sent to see if Garrincha, not content with having a woman on the side, really had had a baby with her, as the rumours in Pau

Grande suggested. Garrincha was not pleased. He went straight to the registrar's office and registered Márcia as his daughter.

In 1959, while Garrincha was scoring with the ladies, Pelé was scoring goals. That year, Pelé played an unbelievable 103 games of football for Santos, Brazil, a São Paulo select and – now that he was 18 and doing military service – the Sixth Coast Guard, the Army and the Armed Forces.

The differences between Pelé and Garrincha were becoming ever more apparent. Pelé hired an agent, Spaniard Pepe Gordo, to run his business affairs, and it was he who forced Santos to renegotiate his contract. Under the new terms, Pelé got 120,000 cruzeiros (about $500) a month and an agreement to review it again a year later.

Around the same time, Garrincha was called to Botafogo to sign a new deal. When he sat down to put pen to paper, he saw that the values had been left blank. Puzzled, Garrincha, for the first time, asked why.

'Wouldn't it be better if I signed after we agree how much I am going to make?' he said.

The club director assured him there was no problem. 'That's just a formality, Mané. This is just to give us time to get you registered with the federation. Don't be afraid of signing. Even Nílton Santos signed a blank contract.'

Paulo Azeredo later filled in the blanks. Garrincha was to get 75,000 cruzeiros (about $300) a month. For three years.

Whenever he went to Pau Grande, Garrincha would provoke Swing, who supported Flamengo, and Pincel, who was a Vasco fan, with promises to destroy their teams in upcoming games.

However, while Garrincha had some great games against the two sides that year, it was Fluminense who won the Carioca title, bringing to an end an eight-year run without the state pennant in their trophy room. Botafogo finished in second place, having lost two of their most important players halfway through the season when Paulo Valentim was sold to Boca Juniors of Argentina and Didi to Real Madrid in Spain.

The soap opera surrounding Didi's transfer to Spain had been going on since the World Cup. Even then Real Madrid was the richest club in the world, and when its president Santiago Bernabeu wanted a player, he would pay whatever it took to get him. One glance at the Real line-up was confirmation of that. They had a foreign legion in their ranks, with players from Argentina, Hungary, France and even Brazil, and they won everything. Real bid $80,000 for Didi, and $250,000 for Garrincha. Only the first bid was accepted. Botafogo decided they could do without Didi but they refused to entertain bids for their star winger. Not that he was interested in leaving. Garrincha knew that the Real side was the greatest team he had ever seen – particularly with their new attack of Canário (ex-América), Didi, Di Stefano, Puskas and Gento – but he could not imagine himself lining up in their famous all-white strip. He was happy in Brazil. And besides, there was another Real Madrid he was more intent on beating – the Real Madrid that played in Pau Grande.

Whenever he went home, Garrincha played for O que vai e mole ('Go Ahead, It's Easy'), a team that featured Arlindo 'Fumaça', Pincel, Malvino and a bunch of other boys who worked, or used to work, at the América Fabril factory. Although they were by far the best team in town, a side comprising the sons of the directors was formed to take them on and challenge their invincibility. The new team, seeking to make it clear that they were a cut above the factory workers, called themselves Real Madrid.

The two sides faced each other several times every year in friendlies, but the official contest – for bottles of *cachaça*, a suckling pig and crates of beer – was played at Christmas. The losers were forced to watch the winners drink their prize and, fearing they might lose and have to spend a few dry hours after the match, Garrincha's teammates got loaded before the kick-off. They needn't have worried; unlike their more illustrious namesakes, the local Real Madrid seldom managed more than a draw.

The game was one of the highlights of the year in Pau Grande, as sacred in its own profane way as the party to celebrate St George, the town's patron saint. The whole town turned out to watch and people came from nearby communities to join in the fun. The *Jornal dos Sports* even sent a reporter to file a match report. To the eyes of the world, Garrincha was in his natural habitat, the one place where he was truly happy.

In Mexico, too, Garrincha felt happy and relaxed, and he was there in January 1960 when Swedish officials travelled to Botafogo to tell him he had a son – a boy called Ulf, born in Halmstad earlier that month. The officials wanted Garrincha to sign a document freeing him from any parental or financial responsibilities, and when he returned he did so with supreme indifference to the news that he at last had the son he had always wanted.

But Garrincha had other things on his mind. He loved going to Mexico in large part because he adored Cantinflas, the little comedian who had risen to fame outside his own country after starring alongside David Niven as Passepartout in the film adaptation of Jules Verne's *Around the World in 80 Days*. Garrincha identified with Cantinflas – they were both small and dishevelled, and they walked around with their shirt-tails out and their trousers at half mast – and Mexico loved him for it. When Garrincha had hit the headlines there in 1957, the local papers had christened him 'the darkie' and written about the headaches he had given Mexican defenders with his bent legs.

The bent legs fascinated the Mexican ladies too, including the wives of some of the local sporting dignitaries who came to pay homage to Botafogo. More than one of them invited him home one day when her husband was nowhere to be seen. One local beauty, an actress, hosted *feijoadas* for the visiting players, and she, along with her equally attractive friend, was as tasty as any black beans or rice. Garrincha's colleagues believe he tried out both of them during one *feijoada* party in 1960. As the *mariachis* strummed their guitars and sang out 'Solamente una vez' ('One Time Only') and 'Quizás, quizás, quizás' ('Perhaps, Perhaps, Perhaps'), Garrincha disappeared with first one and then another.

That trip was just one of those Garrincha made in 1960. After returning from Mexico he went to the Middle East and Europe in April and May with the Brazilian national side. He came home briefly, went to Peru with Botafogo, and then spent the best part of June and July touring the north-east, São Paulo and Minas Gerais. He was back in Rio in August for the start of the Carioca Championship. Which was just as well, because that month Nair gave birth to their sixth child, yet another girl, one they named Maria Cecilia.

As his daughter was being born, his father was dying. Amaro's health had already been deteriorating when Garrincha ran him over the year before. Now he had been diagnosed with liver cancer and his local doctor in Pau Grande had prescribed him medicine and told him to stop drinking. Amaro, though, had little confidence in cures that did not involve alcohol. His alcohol dependence had been apparent for years, and it had now got to the stage that if he did not have a drink when he got out of bed in the morning his hands shook so much he was unable to hold a cup. That August he took a turn for the worse and was ordered to rest in bed. He lost weight, his stomach swelled and he turned bright yellow. On Monday, 10 October, after two months of agony, Amaro died.

The following Saturday, Botafogo were scheduled to play Bangu in Gávea. The club's directors told Garrincha to go to Pau Grande to take care of the funeral arrangements and assured him they would see him at the wake. For a whole day and night people from all over the town came to pay their last respects, including directors of the factory, who turned up in a group. But from Botafogo, there was nobody. Nílton Santos, Renato Estelita, kit man Aluísio 'Birruma', Sandro Moreyra and a few reporters came to express their solidarity, but as personal friends, not as colleagues or club representatives.

Politicians were also conspicuous by their absence. Garrincha had hoped the president might send a representative and he did not want to close the coffin until they had got there. But as the light faded it became clear that no one else would be arriving, and at 5.30 p.m. an official arrived and told him they would have to proceed to the cemetery because it was going to close. It was only then that Garrincha admitted, 'It looks like they couldn't get here after all.' He ordered the coffin to be closed and watched it being loaded on to the back of the hearse, a black Dodge provided by América Fabril.

Garrincha turned out for Botafogo in the Carioca Championship match against Bangu the following Saturday but he hardly touched the ball. Before the kick-off, there was a minute's silence. As always, some fans booed.

When the 1959 Carioca Championship had ended, João Saldanha had resigned as Botafogo manager to be replaced by Paulo Amaral. Saldanha claimed that he had opposed the sale of Didi and Paulo Valentim, and the decision to go ahead and sell two of his prize assets had left him no choice but to resign. The truth, however, was that Saldanha would not have lasted much longer anyway. He had been rubbing the directors and players up the wrong way for some time.

Nevertheless, the team he left to Amaral struggled to cope without him at the helm, and Botafogo had a bad year by their standards. Nineteen sixty was a struggle and the team finished only third in the Carioca Championship. The poor performances came in spite of the fact that the club had re-signed Didi, who had returned to Brazil after an unhappy spell in Spain. Didi had gone to Real Madrid with the intention of masterminding the side, but when he got there he found that Real already had a mastermind in Di Stefano, 'the red arrow'. The two moustachioed geniuses never got on. Didi thought Di Stefano was sabotaging him; Di Stefano thought Didi was lazy and didn't train hard enough. The situation soon became untenable and Didi asked for a transfer back to Brazil, where Botafogo welcomed him with open arms.

The renewal of Garrincha and Didi's once deadly partnership would take a while to gel again, but when it did it was sublime. Nineteen sixty-one was one of the most successful years in Botafogo's history.

In January that year, the club set off on another tour of the Americas, heading north up the Atlantic coast to Central America and then coming back south along the Pacific. For the first time the man who led the delegation was a journalist, Sandro Moreyra. Moreyra brought a whole new approach, dispensing with the *concentração* and giving the players more freedom than they could ever have hoped for. Before they had even left the airport Moreyra announced how the new scheme would work: 'There will be no *concentração* between games. You are all free to do what you want – as long as you remain unbeaten. When we lose, the team will return to the hotel and will only leave to play their next match.'

Moreyra was the boss the players had always dreamt of.

His new system worked a treat. In 45 days, Botafogo played 12 games in Peru, Colombia, Ecuador, Costa Rica and Chile, drawing the first one and winning the other 11, many of them by big score-lines. The only match they struggled in was the final one, against Chilean champions Colo-Colo. The team had arrived in Santiago six days before the game, days that were in theory to be used for resting and training. In practice they had time on their hands, and they were creative when it came to using it, spending nights at the local broth-els, where on at least one occasion Garrincha had a thorough workout with a brunette and a blonde in quick succession.

In spite of the players' excesses, in the end it was manager Paulo Amaral who fell ill and missed the final match. The obvious man to replace him was Moreyra, who fulfilled the fantasy of every sports journalist by taking charge of the team. Colo-Colo were in control from the start and went in 1–0 up at half-time. Moreyra was horrified at the thought that Botafogo's only defeat would come in the one game he was in charge of, and he took swift action. The players were hung-over after several days of enjoying Chilean wine, women and song, and Moreyra, no stranger to hangovers himself, knew just the cure. He sent Aluísio Birruma to buy cognac at the stadium bar, and when the players came into the dressing room after an insipid first-half display he administered his half-time pick-me-up. Botafogo scored three goals in the second half, giving Moreyra the win he so wanted and ensuring that they ended the tour unbeaten. It was taken as proof that sex and alcohol did little harm, and when the players returned to Rio they presented Moreyra with a silver plaque.

Two months later, Botafogo took off again, this time for Europe. On 1 June, as Garrincha was lining up against Standard Liège in Belgium, Iraci gave him – if his previous statements were to be believed – the thing he most wanted: a son – named, of course, Manuel.

For someone who had waited so long for a male heir, Garrincha did his best to hide any joy he might have felt. When he arrived home almost a month later he refused to call his secret son by his name, referring to him instead as 'the baby'. He was so insistent that even Iraci took to calling him that. He paid little attention either to Manuel or Iraci. He didn't talk about his plans for the child's future, or even say if he had any plans. He didn't dream of the day his son would take the field and dazzle defenders with his crooked legs – and he did have crooked legs, just like his father – and he didn't want anyone to know about the child, especially not journalists.

One person who did find out was Nair, and she was inconsolable when she heard the news. Garrincha's girlfriends having daughters was one thing, but the fact that one of them had produced the son she so desperately wanted to give him devastated her. She forbade him from seeing the child or formally registering him as his son. Garrincha complied with her wishes and kept his distance from Iraci's house in Copacabana. But not because Nair told him to. Rather, Garrincha had lost interest in her; she had, in effect, become another Nair. He paid the bills and the rent but Iraci could see what was going on. The final whistle had blown on their relationship.

Botafogo began the 1961 Carioca Championship with one of the greatest forward lines ever seen: Garrincha, Didi, Amoroso, Amarildo and Zagalo. Together, they treated Botafogo fans to a dream season. Opponents were destroyed one after another, and by the halfway stage of the tournament they had opened up a six-point gap on their nearest challengers. Every game was a party. Fans at the Maracanã even hung banners declaring 'Being champions was never so easy'. Botafogo supporters who hadn't been to matches for years came creeping out of the woodwork to see the glorious new side, and the terraces at the Maracanã all of a sudden became the place to be. There was a country-club atmosphere at General Severiano as the sweet smell of success permeated the corridors and wafted on to the playing field.

Botafogo went 22 games without defeat and by a strange twist of fate were declared champions on the day they suffered their one and only loss, a 2–1 reverse against América in the third-last game of the season. Against the odds, second-placed Vasco went down to Olaria by the same scoreline at their home ground São Januario to hand the title to Botafogo. To confirm their dominance, Botafogo beat Vasco and Flamengo in their two final matches.

That championship win marked the start of an epic era for Botafogo and established them as the fashionable team in town. The club identity was an intoxicating mixture of football, literature and café society. Artists, intellectuals, politicians and the upper classes all claimed to be Botafoguenses; all of a sudden everyone was claiming to be a fan.

Botafogo were getting too big even for the Maracanã, and soon they were making their mark in society football, the football of the upper classes. Invented at the farm owned by José Luiz Ferra, the owner of a big construction company and the director of the Botafogo

171

youth programme, society football was an eight-a-side game played by people who were rich, famous or good-looking, and sometimes all three. There was whisky at half-time and a *feijoada* waiting for them when the final whistle went. Doctors, politicians, lawyers, business-men, journalists and photographers played regularly and were joined by players such as Nílton Santos, Didi and Garrincha, as well as by some of the younger prospects such as Jairzinho – and even, on occasion, Pincel and Swing.

Feeling obliged to return the compliment, Garrincha sometimes invited some of the blue bloods up to Pau Grande to take part in his own local kickabouts, and they returned to Rio with tales that confirmed how much at home Garrincha really felt in his bucolic paradise. To use the words in vogue at the time, he was pure, authentic. His house was a hovel but he wouldn't swap it for the Taj Mahal. Sure, he kept his two fridges in the living room, but so what? And yes, the walls were decorated with football pennants and pictures held together with duct tape, but who cared? The friendship of Pincel and Swing meant more to him than the admiration of Presidents Juscelino or Jango. And the simple fact that he continued to travel back and forth on that creaking old train was proof that fame did not have to be corrupting. He could have had all the luxu-ries in the world, but Garrincha preferred to live like a factory worker or a peasant farmer.

Which is not to say that a car would make him any less salt-of-the-earth; in fact it would certainly make his life easier. And just then, the chance to win one came along.

In November, the newspaper *Jornal dos Sports* ran a competition to find the most popular football player in Rio. The player securing the most votes would win a Simca-Chambord car and one of the lucky voters would win an all-expenses-paid trip to the 1962 World Cup finals in Chile. People could vote as many times as they wished, as long as the votes were marked on one of the ballots published in the paper. If they wanted to buy up all the copies of the paper just to get the ballots, no one would stop them. Quite the contrary, in fact: the people who ran the *Jornal dos Sports* would be delighted.

The clubs took the competition very seriously and each one nominated a player to represent them. Botafogo named Garrincha, Vasco named Bellini, Flamengo named Babá and Fluminense named Castilho. Players were allowed to campaign for votes and some went to schools, hospitals, factories, shops and even to TV and radio stations to make their pitch, often with the help of musicians, singers, politicians or other celebrities who gave away autographs or pictures in return for votes. An autographed photo cost 20 votes, a club pennant cost 30. Singers even gave concerts and sold tickets for 50 votes.

It was a hotly contested competition, and when the paper published preliminary results from the first few weeks of voting the numbers were a big surprise. For the man leading the competition was not Babá, who, as representative of the city's most popular team, seemed the obvious favourite. Babá, a brilliant little winger who stood just five feet tall in his studs, was in third place. The man at the head of the pack was Bellini, the Vasco and Brazil captain, who had taken a big lead because the city's Portuguese merchants had bought numerous papers and stuffed the ballot boxes with votes for their man.

Garrincha was in second place, way behind the leader. It was obvious that if he wanted to win he needed to hook up with someone who could bring him more votes. Someone who was popular and in vogue. Preferably a female singer. Songwriter Ronaldo Bôscoli knew just the person and went to Sandro Moreyra with an idea. Garrincha needed the 'bossa negra'. Elza Soares.

CHAPTER 12

1961–1962: Elza

THE MISCHIEVOUS WAY IN WHICH GARRINCHA LOOKED AT WOMEN unnerved them. If he admired their curves he was not shy about giving them a long and obvious once-over that left them in no doubt as to what he was thinking. He didn't have to say a word; his stare said it all.

When he met Elza Soares in November 1961 at her house in Urca, a quiet neighbourhood nestled under Rio's Sugarloaf mountain, he gave her that look. And no wonder. Elza, in spite of being only 5'2" tall, had a body that was crying out to be admired. She might have been small but she had curves that looked as though they had been painted by Di Cavalcanti. Garrincha's gaze discomfited Elza. She was a well-known TV star, the samba sensation whose powerful throaty voice made her sound like a Zulu goddess. She knew she was every man's wildest fantasy, she was just not used to them being as up front about it as Garrincha.

Elza accepted Garrincha's request for help in his campaign without giving it a second thought. After all, Garrincha was famous, respected and much loved. What did she have to lose? She went to record shops and signed autographs and gave out pennants and photos in exchange for votes. She even took her boyfriend Milton Banana's band to Pau

Grande to play a concert for the América Fabril Workers Association.

As the weeks went by, Botafogo were well on their way to taking the Carioca Championship. But despite Elza's efforts, Bellini, largely because of the Portuguese community's backing, was still an almost insurmountable 20,000 votes ahead of second-placed Garrincha in the popularity contest.

Sandro Moreyra, though, had decided that Garrincha must win the car. Botafogo were league champions thanks to Garrincha's brilliance, and it would be an injustice if he were not similarly honoured with the title of best player. Moreyra convinced the directors to bankroll a last-minute campaign, and with the cash they bought tens of thousands of newspapers and lugged them back to Sandro's flat where for three days and nights friends cut out coupons and filled in Garrincha's name.

The strategy worked. Garrincha won the election and the car with 300,247 votes, 54,939 more than Bellini. He was presented with the Simca on 3 January 1962 in the centre circle at the Maracanã just before the annual shield match between the state champions of São Paulo and Rio de Janeiro. Botafogo were about to play Santos, and Garrincha and Pelé did the honours, each man presenting the other with his championship sash.

Garrincha was expected to take the new car for a victory spin around the stadium. But in light of what had happened with his father in Pau Grande – the whole affair had been hushed up and nobody knew – he decided it would be more prudent for someone else to take the wheel. So Santos keeper Gilmar drove the car around the pitch, blasting the horn as he went. When he was finished he parked it behind one of the goals and then had a nightmare as Botafogo hammered the Paulista champions 3–0.

Botafogo followed that success with a ten-match tour of Chile, Mexico and Peru. Before setting off, Garrincha put pen to paper on a new contract and for the first time he was able to see what he was getting before signing on the dotted line. The contract gave him

Glorious Botafogo: famous cartoonist Lan's depiction of the 1955 Botafogo side.

Party time:
Cruzeiro photographed each of the players when they arrived back in Brazil at the end of their 40-hour long journey home, after the 1958 World Cup.

Manchete Esportiva

GARRINCHA DEU "SHOW" NO MARACANÃ: 2 X 1

BOTAFOGO DE PERNAS TORTAS A CAMINHO DO "BI"

Manchete Esportiva

Botafogo 1 X 0 GARRINCHA: "SUPER-SUPER"

Manchete Esportiva

UM PENALTE SALVOU O VASCO

BOTAFOGO 3 FLAMENGO 2 GARRINCHA, O MONSTRO DA RODADA

Putting on a show:
Garrincha makes the cover of
magazines *Manchete Esportiva*
and *Revista do Esporte*.

Love and hate: the tributes to his World Cup winning exploits didn't stop the magazines from focussing on his love for Elza.

150,000 cruzeiros a month – twice what he had been getting since 1959 but still less than $500. One saving grace was that he got a signing-on bonus for the first time: three million cruzeiros, at the time almost $10,000. He left it with the club treasurer and promised to pick it up when he got back from the trip.

In addition to the money, Garrincha left behind yet another daughter, Terezinha Conceição, born at the beginning of December 1961. She was the seventh daughter born to Nair and her arrival caused a commotion in the local press – with each new daughter, the media wrote about Garrincha's lack of a male heir. The superstitious had believed that the seventh would be a boy. For once, Nair wanted a girl, believing the old wives' tale that said a boy born after six girls would turn into a werewolf.

Botafogo returned from their foreign excursion in the middle of February and began their assault on the Rio-SP title with an avalanche of goals. Their attack had been strengthened by the return of Quarentinha, who was back in the side after two years on the sidelines with a knee injury sustained while playing for Brazil. They now boasted a forward line of Garrincha, Didi, Quarentinha, Amarildo and Zagalo, and they were not content with just winning matches, they wanted to win them in style. They toyed with the opposition, delighting the fans but incurring the wrath of referees who thought they were taking the mickey out of their less capable rivals. During Botafogo's 4–1 win over América, for example, the referee threatened to send Garrincha off for beating full-back Ivan too many times. He cited all 11 players in his match report, forcing Botafogo to defend themselves with the novel excuse that they were passing the ball as a way of saving energy.

The men in black, however, were not so rigorous when it came to punishing the defenders who were resorting to ever more desperate means to halt Garrincha's mazy runs. The attacks were becoming increasingly frequent and more violent, and with Brazil due to defend their World Cup title in only a few months Saldanha, who was now a successful radio commentator, was worried that someone would seriously injure Garrincha and put him out of the tournament. The situation had got so bad that he saw it as more of a human-rights issue than a footballing one. He even made an appeal on air for the Society for the Prevention of Cruelty to Animals to protect Brazil's star player. Garrincha survived, and Botafogo walked away with the Rio-SP title.

In March, after some hair-raising driving lessons from friends in Pau Grande, Garrincha drove his new car to Urca to perform the happy task of personally thanking Elza Soares for helping him secure the title of 'Most Popular Footballer in Rio'. He brought with him a 60-kilo bag of beans. Rio was in the grip of a food shortage brought about by a political crisis and Garrincha wanted to give Elza an extra reason to appreciate his visit.

The strategy worked. Until then, Garrincha hadn't made much of an impression on Elza. Like everyone else, she admired him for who he was and what he had done but she thought of him as just a kid, even though at 31 she was only three years his senior. She knew they had both worked in factories before hitting the big time, and she knew they had both married young and had lots of kids. But as far as she was concerned, the similarities ended there.

Compared with her upbringing, Garrincha's childhood had been a picnic. Elza was born in the Rio suburb of Bangu in 1930 and was brought up in the favela of Água Santa, daughter of a washerwoman who was so poor that she had sometimes forced Elza to suckle a goat because she was incapable of producing enough milk to feed her. As a child, Elza picked through the rubbish looking for bones, cans and bottles to sell, and she was not above stealing chickens in order to survive. There were no plates or cutlery at home and she used to eat with her hands out of old tin cans. She taught herself to read, and although she finished primary school she dropped out soon afterwards to work as a maid, the first of a number of dead-end jobs and one in which she was a constant target for the amorous advances of her employers.

When she was 13 she married Alaúrdes Soares, a 23-year-old card player who worked with her father on a building site. Elza's father, a factory worker who preferred drinking and playing the guitar to working, forced Soares to marry her after he raped her. Soares, who was white, hurled racial abuse at her, beat her regularly, raped her every time they went to bed and stole her money for gambling.

But Elza was nothing if not a survivor. In order to feed her children she held down two jobs, one at the local soap factory and the other serving meals at a hospice. When she went out to work she used to tie her children to the leg of the table so that they wouldn't run outside and get lost in the favela. They had little to eat and three died as infants either from hunger or tuberculosis. The first one to survive was João Carlos, or Carlinhos, born in 1948, and three more arrived in quick succession: Dilma in 1953, Gerson in 1954, and Gilson in 1955. By then she was earning enough money as a singer to feed them chocolate milk.

Elza broke into the music world in 1948 when, like many young girls of the time, she signed up to take part in Ary Barroso's star-turn programme on Radio Tupi, one of the era's most popular stations. She requisitioned her mother's best dress and wrapped it around her so as to lose the fabric that had covered her mother's additional three-stone bulk. She tied up her hair and made the long trip to the station's city-centre studio. She looked ridiculous, and when she walked on stage the audience laughed. Barroso asked her, 'What planet are you from, dear?'

Elza didn't bat an eyelid, and replied, 'The planet hunger.'

The programme's villain was Makalé, a young black man in a turban and tunic who would ostentatiously strike a gong to mark the end of the young wannabe's dream of fame. The naive thought it was really Makalé who decided their fate, but Elza, not quite sure about who was making the decisions, kept one eye on him and one on

179

Barroso as she belted her way through a song called 'Lama'. The gong didn't bang. Quite the opposite: Barroso gave her five out of five and a prize of 500 cruzeiros. With the money, she took a taxi home.

In the 1950s, Elza became a crooner with dance bands and learned to combine the cocky swagger of her favela upbringing with the swing copied from the popular American singers of the time. She then became a backing singer, and when her husband died from tuberculosis in 1958 she left the children with her mother to go to Buenos Aires to sing. There, tragedy struck again when her father died while listening to a Flamengo–Vasco match on the radio.

When she returned to Brazil, she went to work at Radio Tupi with the sambista Moreira da Silva, and from there she jumped to Texas, a nightclub near Copacabana, where she was spotted by Sylvinha Telles and her boyfriend Aloysio de Oliveira, the A&R director at the Odeon record label. De Oliveira had her record the song 'Se acaso você chegasse' (If You Were Here), and it was a huge success. Elza had hit the big time at last.

When Garrincha drove into her life with a sack of beans, Elza was taking her revenge on the humiliations and hard times of the past. The one dress she had, an exuberant coral number she washed every day, had been replaced by a wardrobe full of bejewelled, red gowns that Manuelzinho, the manager of an Ipanema boutique, had designed and made especially for her. In another wardrobe was a collection of wigs, while on her dressing table she had enough false nails, eyelashes, perfumes, cosmetics and jewellery, both real and fake, to last a lifetime.

The other thing she had acquired was a man: Milton Banana, the first drummer of bossa nova. Banana was the man who had created the brushed drum sounds to accompany João Gilberto's acoustic-guitar soundtrack, and it was he who had played drums on Gilberto's original recording of 'Chega de saudade' (No More Blues), the song that sparked the success of the bossa nova movement in 1958. Banana helped Elza understand the bossa nova vocal divisions she incorporated into her samba routines and she loved him for it, calling him pet names and refusing to let him pay his share of the bill. As a drummer, Banana was like a metronome, but when he was not holding the sticks he was at the bar. He enjoyed a drink and was never slow to knock them back.

During the first weeks of March 1962, Banana noticed that Garrincha was spending a lot of time at Elza's house. Every time he went there he took sugar or rice or more beans, even though rationing had ceased to be a problem. Like many drummers, Banana didn't say much, but he began to suspect something was going on between the two of them. He already thought his affair with Elza was coming to an end, but if he was going to finish it he preferred not to do it because of another man, and especially not because of Garrincha. He was a fan of his, and a mad Botafogo supporter. Maybe nothing was going on, but whatever it was he didn't like Garrincha visiting his girlfriend.

And then the visits stopped. Garrincha was called into the squad to prepare for the World Cup in Chile. He was going to be a busy man.

The squad chosen to go to the 1962 World Cup was not substantially different from the one that had gone to Sweden four years earlier. Nílton Santos and Zito had shaved off their moustaches. Feola had spent eight months in bed with heart problems and had been replaced by Aymoré 'Biscuit' Moreira. On the technical commission, the psychologist Carvalhaes was gone, replaced by Athayde Ribeiro da Silva, who would neither give the players IQ tests nor go with them to the finals. The principal difference between the two squads was Pelé.

In the four years since winning the World Cup, Pelé had become a phenomenon. His Santos team had won the Paulista championship in 1958, 1960 and 1961, the Rio-SP tournament in 1959 and the Brazilian Cup in 1961. Pelé was the top goalscorer in almost every competition he played in, and in the 1958 Paulista championship he scored an astonishing 58 goals, a record that still stands today.

During these four years, Santos had turned down every offer that had come from the big Spanish and Italian clubs. No one knew how much Pelé made, but it was clear he was by far the highest-paid player in Brazil. In return for his huge salary, Santos made him perform to a punishing schedule, sometimes even playing games on consecutive days. On one European tour in 1959, Santos played on 3 June against Feyenoord in Holland; on 5 June against Internazionale in Italy; on 6 June against Fortuna in West Germany; on 7 June against Nuremberg, also in West Germany; and on 9 June against Servette in Switzerland. Five games in seven days – and they won them all.

Unlike the team that went to Sweden in 1958 as underdogs, the 1962 team would have problems if they didn't return home with the trophy. Brazil was everyone's favourite and no one rated their first-round opponents Mexico, Czechoslovakia and Spain. The 1958 team, although four years older, was basically intact: Gilmar, Djalma Santos, Bellini, Nílton Santos, Zito, Didi, Garrincha, Vavá, Pelé and Zagalo. The only one who wasn't there was Orlando, who was now playing in Argentina. Some of them had turned 30, but the only player it could be said was really getting on was Nílton Santos, who was 37. Pelé was still only 21.

The banter between the players was also much the same as in 1958. When one of them saw Garrincha wearing shorts, he feigned shock.

'My God, Garrincha's been run over!'

Castilho pretended to explain: 'No. His legs are fine, it's his body that's all bent out of shape.'

The reporters assigned to cover the squad's preparations were also the same as in 1958, and they were all looking for new angles on old stories. One of them, Mário de Moraes from *O Cruzeiro*, came up with the idea of inviting singers contracted to TV Tupi to put on a show for the players at the hotel. *O Cruzeiro* would have exclusive access and the show would later be broadcast on TV Tupi. The main problem was getting Nascimento to OK the idea, but he agreed, thanks mainly to the intervention of Adolpho Marques, the squad's treasurer who also worked for the personal department of Diários Associados, the company that owned *O Cruzeiro*. Nascimento signed off the project on the condition that the show finish before midnight and that the artists return to São Paulo the same night. He did not want to hear about women spending the night at the team hotel.

The man charged with putting on the show was Airton Rodrigues, the producer of TV Tupi's *Clube dos Artistas*, and the presenters would be Homero Silva and Márcia Real. The artists chosen to take part were Pery Ribeiro, Agostinho dos Santos, Edith Silva, the trio Sereno, Germano Mathias, the trio Orixá – and Elza Soares.

On the afternoon of Monday, 2 April, a convoy drew into the team's base at Campos do Jordão for the show later that night. There were no dressing rooms where the artists could prepare so some of the players gave up their rooms. Garrincha gave Elza his and tried to reassure her that no one was going to interrupt her while she was preparing for the show. 'I'll be outside keeping a watch on the door,' he said. 'No one is going to get in. Make yourself at home.'

And he solemnly stood guard in the corridor. He didn't know that next door, in Jair da Costa's room, seven or eight players were peeping through the keyhole of the adjoining door and trying desperately not to make a noise.

The show was a hit. In addition to songs and jokes from the groups and comedians, Mário Américo sang and dentist Mário Trigo tried to steal the show with his jokes. They were no match for the professionals, however. Not for Agostinho dos Santos or Pery Ribeiro, not for the young *mulatas* of the trio Orixá, and especially not for Elza.

Wearing a full skirt pulled in tight at the waist, she shimmied her way around the room, stopping in front of Didi, Pelé and Garrincha to shake her hips provocatively and sing 'Não põe a mão' (Hands Off), a 1951 carnival hit she had just re-released. The chorus of the song contained the line 'Don't lay a hand on my guitar', a play on the word guitar, or *violão*, which in Portuguese also meant the small-breasted and wide-hipped quintessentially Brazilian female body. It was suggestive enough at the best of times, but the way Elza sang it drove the players wild.

When the show was over, the artistes said goodbye to the players, wished them well in the tournament and got ready to leave. Elza changed in Jair da Costa's room, once again watched through the keyhole, then joined her colleagues on the TV Tupi bus back to São Paulo.

Or rather most of her colleagues, for two people never made it on to the bus. One of them, Agostinho dos Santos, stayed behind with Nascimento's blessing and even kicked a ball around with the players the next morning. And one of the young *mulatas* from the group Orixá stayed behind for other reasons.

When the bus left, Garrincha said goodbye to Elza, but instead of returning to the hotel he headed off into the hotel's grounds. Hours later he reappeared and, finding the hotel doors locked – Nascimento had imposed a midnight curfew – he knocked on Mário de Moraes's ground-floor window. Mário shared a room with his photographer, and they opened the window and let Garrincha in. He walked through the bar, past the barman Pedro, and quietly climbed the stairs to the room he shared with Joel. When Nascimento came to check on them at six a.m., he was safely asleep.

No one knows how the girl from Orixá got home. Nor how Garrincha, who had spent the day fussing over Elza, managed to arrange a date in the park without anyone finding out.

In that first week of April, the squad moved on to the second stage of their preparations in the Rio town of Friburgo – and Elza turned up to see Garrincha. She wasn't the only one: thousands of other Cariocas got into their cars and turned the almost 100-mile trek into a Sunday outing. So many people arrived to watch the squad train that Nascimento and Marques barred almost everyone from the hotel because they feared the pressure might affect the players.

They made an exception, however, for Elza and President Juscelino, who smiled for the press as if on an election campaign. Elza spent time with the players in the gardens of the Sans Souci Hotel and then watched them train before Garrincha took her to the bus stop so she could catch her bus home. When the bus approached, he grabbed her and gave her a kiss that left her in no doubt about his motives. Elza responded every bit as passionately.

After Friburgo, the players went to the Serra Negra (the Black Mountains), where they spent another week. Pelé liked to play the guitar, and he serenaded his team-mates under their windows. Garrincha, who was more of a Frank Sinatra fan, didn't think much of Pelé's singing and tipped a bucket of water on his head.

The players finally returned to Rio, where the squad was to be named before they set off for Chile. The big unanswered question was which two players would be selected for the right-wing position; Garrincha, Julinho and Jair da Costa were all vying for a place. But Julinho had suffered a groin strain while in Friburgo that had virtually ruled him out of the tournament. Gosling told him he would wait for him, but Julinho did not want to go to Chile unless he was sure he would be available and he set himself his own deadline for being fit. On 14 May, less than a week before the players were scheduled to leave Brazil, he acknowledged that he would not be ready, and once again in tears he asked to be withdrawn from the squad. Just as in 1958, when he had refused the call-up, he was to miss out on the chance of a winner's medal.

A few days before they set off the players were invited to a reception to meet the Rio de Janeiro state governor at the Palacio de Guanabara. Governor Carlos Lacerda kept a colourful garden in the palace's grounds and there the players were captivated by a mynah bird. The bird barked like a dog, wolf whistled, imitated a plane and, according to Garrincha, knew more words than Botafogo goalkeeper Manga. It said, 'It's the palace's!', 'Are you leaving?', 'Goal!', 'Vasco!', 'Hey baby!' and several swear words. Lacerda could see that Garrincha had fallen in love with the bird.

185

'You like him, eh? Then let's do a deal. You bring back the cup and the bird is yours.'

'It's a deal,' said Garrincha.

On the morning of 20 May, the players' families went to Galeão to see them off. Each of them had four or five people to hug and kiss. Garrincha's farewell committee from Pau Grande was 30-strong. In order to follow as closely as possible the departure of four years previously, the squad flew on the same Panair DC-8 as in 1958, and with the same pilot, Commander Bungner. Paulo Machado de Carvalho, chief of the delegation again, had with him the image of Our Lady Aparecida and was wearing his lucky brown jacket (which was by now coming apart at the seams). With such an array of lucky charms, they couldn't fail to bring home the cup.

The first thing Hilton Gosling did when he arrived in Viña del Mar, the Chilean coastal town where the squad was based, was visit Madame Chabela's brothel. Gosling thought it necessary to set up some extra-curricular activities for the players because unlike in Sweden, where girls had sex as if they were eating sweets, Chilean girls were conservative and the players' opportunities to get to know the local talent would be few and far between. Gosling knew they would want more than a few games of table tennis or dominoes in their spare time so he chose 24 women from the government-recommended brothel and examined them, noting down their names and securing a guarantee from the madame that they would service the players and no one else. When he got back to the hotel he told the squad, 'It's only for a change of oil. You are free to go there in the afternoons. It's all taken care of, you don't even need to pay. I want you all back here at seven p.m. on the dot.'

Garrincha went to the brothel that day along with six other players, but it was his only trip there. A few days later the hotel hired a blonde chambermaid who looked a little bit like Anita Ekberg, and from that moment on Garrincha didn't need to go any further than his room. The only one forced to leave was his room-mate Zagalo.

The players were desperate to win the cup again. They did not complain about the hard physical workouts set by Paulo Amaral, and instead of trying to sneak out to hit the town they were happy to sit in the hotel lobby and pretend that manager Aymoré Moreira was Liberace. Each player was so keen to play a role that for the first time in the four years they had been together one of them kicked up a fuss when he found out he was on the bench.

The complaint came from Mauro, a classy centre-half with all the leadership qualities of a captain. Current skipper and first-choice centre-half Bellini had injured himself during a friendly shortly before leaving Brazil, and Mauro had taken his place and acquitted himself well. But when the team to face Mexico in the opener on 30 May was named, a fit Bellini was back in his customary role and Mauro felt he had been hard done by. After all, this would be the third World Cup he had watched from the sidelines. He took Aymoré aside and told him that if he was going to have to miss out again he would rather go home. Aymoré hesitated a moment, then reacted cleverly: 'I was just saying that to boost his self-confidence, Mauro. You're the one who's going to play.' Mauro was satisfied, and Bellini, with characteristic good grace, accepted the decision.

The status of favourites weighed heavily on the players in the opening match against Mexico. Brazil won 2–0 but the performance was far from convincing. In the first half the players seemed to be carrying the Jules Rimet trophy on their backs. In defence, Mauro and Zózimo failed to read each other's game; in midfield, Zito and Didi were like strangers; and in attack, Pelé accidentally caught Vavá in the groin with a wayward shot. The only reason Mexico were not leading at half-time was a fine performance by Gilmar. The Mexican fans spent the interval throwing their sombreros in the air and dreaming of a win over the world champions. But their hopes were crushed in the second half, when Brazil found their rhythm and won with goals from Zagalo and Pelé.

The second game against Czechoslovakia three days later was just as tough. Up against a defence that contained two excellent players in goalkeeper Schroiff and creative midfielder Masopust, Brazil had trouble stamping their influence on the match. Then disaster struck. With 25 minutes of the first half gone, Pelé shot against the crossbar and went down grabbing his leg – he had pulled a muscle in his groin.

At first, his team-mates didn't understand the gravity of the injury. Zito passed him the ball and Pelé, unable to stretch out his leg to trap it, let it run out.

'What's wrong with you, Crioulo?' asked Zito.

'I'm hurt, Zito!' Pelé screamed.

'If you're hurt then get off the pitch!' Zito replied.

Gosling and Américo ran to help him, and although they put ointment on the muscle the pain was such that he couldn't take two steps without almost falling over. During half-time they put ice on it, but with no substitutes allowed Pelé forced himself to reappear for the second half, out on the left wing, where he would do least damage. The Czechs – Lala, Masopust and Popluhar – saw that it was a serious injury and showed him enormous respect: wherever he got the ball, they didn't try to get it back but instead let him pass it to a teammate. The best attacking player on the planet was toothless.

Brazil–Czechoslovakia ended 0–0 and an ill wind appeared to have blown over the squad. The next game against Spain four days later would be decisive: whoever lost would be out of the tournament. The big question was whether Pelé would be able to play.

The fibre of the muscle was damaged and the treatment comprised putting ice on the affected area during the first 24 hours and then covering it with hot towels in the days afterwards. Four days were not enough for Pelé to recuperate but everyone wanted him to be fit for the decider. The parade of people making the pilgrimage to the bungalow where the medical facilities were based was interminable. On the eve of the game Pelé appeared to be improving, but when Paulo Amaral put him through a fitness test the pain returned.

Pelé then offered to commit the cardinal sin of taking a xylocaine injection to allow him to play. Pelé told Gosling he had taken xylocaine while in Europe with Santos, but Gosling knew that if he ran the muscle would tear even further and that the damage could end his career for ever. He refused to give him the injection and Amarildo was named to take his place in the starting line-up.

The 22-year-old Botafogo striker was the difference between the two sides. Although he struggled to settle during a first half in which the Spaniards did everything they could to try to rile him, Didi calmed him down and his goals in the sixty-second and eighty-sixth minutes were enough to give Brazil a 2–1 win and see them through to the next round.

The match was also notable as the one in which Garrincha came to the fore. Until then he had had a fairly quiet tournament. Against Mexico he hardly saw the ball, and against Czechoslovakia, with Pelé injured and Vavá having a poor game, he didn't have anyone to pass to. Against Spain, however, he woke up, and it was from his cross that Brazil got their second goal.

It was in the next match, however, against England in the quarter-finals, that he would play one of the greatest games of his life, just as if he was in Pau Grande.

When Garrincha played for O que vai e mole in Pau Grande no one obliged him to play out on the right wing. It was his ball and his team, even in a sense his town, and he played in centre midfield, as a centre-forward, or wherever he wanted to. Against England he did the same, coming inside and, to the horror of the English, taking on a free role.

He scored Brazil's first goal with his head, a rare occurrence for him. The second goal came when the keeper Springett could only parry his driven free kick and Vavá ran in to hammer home the rebound. And he put away the third with a classic *folha seca* shot from outside the area. Against England that day, Garrincha was at his best and capable of anything. His confidence was especially important

189

in the 3–1 win because before the game some of the players had not
been as cool or collected as they might have been. Zagalo, for example,
had been unable to take a leak while in the dressing room, and it
was only after the national anthems were over that he experienced a
desperate urge to urinate. He couldn't go back down the tunnel, so
he called three players and two photographers over to surround him,
knelt down on the pitch and took a pee right there in the centre
circle.

Garrincha did everything that day except catch the black dog that
invaded the pitch and forced the referee to stop the game. He tried
to grab it but missed, and eventually it was Jimmy Greaves, down on
all fours and barking, who managed to get hold of the animal. The
game started again, and Garrincha took Brazil into the semis where
they would meet the toughest opponent of all. Not because of their
football, but because they were hosts. Brazil were to face Chile.

There was another reason why Garrincha was starting to turn it on.
Elza Soares was in town.

Elza had been invited to Chile by Edmundo Klinger, a Uruguayan
businessman who was helping to organise a musical festival in Avisa,
a holiday resort close to Valparaiso and the Brazilian headquarters.
She arrived with Milton Banana on the eve of the match against
Spain. She watched the game, shouted herself hoarse, and then left
to sing that night on a bill that included Louis Armstrong and his All
Stars. Armstrong, who headlined the show, was in his dressing room
when he heard Elza sing a song called 'Edmundo'. He could not
understand a word of what she was singing but he recognised the
tune as that of 'In the Mood' and was impressed by her. She had a
throaty voice just like his, she was improvising like Ella Fitzgerald,
and she could also sound soft and smooth like Nancy Wilson. But
best of all was the swing she lent the song, a swing that would never
have occurred to his friend Joe Garland, and one that made Glenn
Miller's version seem like a *berceuse*. At the end of the song, Armstrong

waited for her in the corridor, and when she emerged he hugged her and called her 'my daughter'. Elza thought he was calling her his 'doctor'.

The festival organisers had promoted Elza as the Brazil squad's 'godmother' and she went to El Retiro with a sash bearing that moniker in order to be photographed with the players. However, Paulo Amaral would not allow it and he politely asked her to leave. Women, especially this one, interfered with the team's preparations. She managed to speak with Garrincha, who told her he would ask Oduvaldo Cozzi, then working for Radio Guanabara, to take care of her, to pick her up at her hotel and make sure she got to the stadiums for the games.

But that was not all he told her. There was another message. Garrincha said: 'I am going to win the cup for you.'

CHAPTER 13

1962: Pau Grande Revealed

THE IDEA THAT GARRINCHA COULD BE SENT OFF FOR HITTING AN opponent was as unlikely as St Francis of Assisi taking part in a dove-shooting contest or Snow White getting stoned to death for cruelty to dwarves. But that's what happened during the Brazil–Chile World Cup semi-final on 13 June 1962. The man responsible was Chile's brutal centre-half Eladio Rojas.

Rojas had already come up against Garrincha when Colo-Colo played Botafogo and he was not in the mood to be given the runaround again. He realised that to avoid further embarrassment he would have to sharpen his arsenal, and from the word go he kicked Garrincha, elbowed him and even poked him in the eye, all right in front of Peruvian referee Arturo Yamazaki. It made no difference. Garrincha ran rings around him and the rest of the Chilean defence. He scored the first goal with a left-foot shot, the second with another header and laid on the third for Vavá. He was the chief architect of Brazil's 4–2 win and his performance confirmed him as the player of the tournament.

But with 39 minutes of the second half gone and the game over as a contest, Rojas kicked Garrincha once too often and the little man's patience snapped. He got up, walked over to Rojas and, more as a joke than in retaliation, kneed him in the backside. Rojas fell to the ground as if the Andes had come down on top of him. The linesman, who was standing just a few feet away, raised his flag and the referee ran over. After a quick conversation, Yamazaki pulled out his red card.

Garrincha walked off the pitch with his head bowed and the boos of the crowd ringing in his ears. Aymoré Moreira ran to the side of the pitch to meet him and Garrincha turned to the stand from where Elza looked down and gave him a long wave. All of a sudden Garrincha raised a hand to his head and then crashed to the ground, laid out by a stone thrown from the stands. Elza panicked and ran to the front of the crowd, screaming to be let through. A policeman went to stop her; she screamed insults at him and tried to climb over the fence. Two other policemen, hearing the commotion, approached with dogs. Edmundo Klinger arrived just in time to whisk her away.

The afternoon had started so promisingly for Elza. The wife of a Chilean police officer had seen her shivering in the eight-degree cold and offered Elza her mink coat. Elza's eyes had opened wide. She had always dreamt of wearing a fur coat. However, as the game started and temperatures began to rise, Elza had started to sweat and the had taken the coat off. When Garrincha scored the first goal with just nine minutes gone, she'd jumped up to celebrate and thrown it in the air. She never saw it again.

Chile, like Sweden in 1958, were no pushover. To get to the semi-finals they had beaten Switzerland, Italy and the USSR, and they had outstanding players such as goalkeeper Escutti, midfielder Toro and winger Leonel Sanches. But no one would have overcome Brazil that day, even with the help of a referee like Yamazaki. The Peruvian had a terrible game, ignoring some of the worst offences and missing many more. He didn't see the Chileans commit brutal fouls, he didn't give Garrincha a penalty, he chalked off a legitimate goal by Vavá, he gave Chile a non-existent penalty (which resulted in their second goal), and he sent off Garrincha for something silly. But Brazil still won and went on to reach a final showdown with Czechoslovakia. The big question was whether Brazil, who were already without Pelé, would have Garrincha back for the decider.

The Chilean press turned his petty foul into a criminal assault. In a stunning piece of journalistic licence, editorials portrayed him as temperamental, dirty and malevolent, all of which was simply untrue. Garrincha, one of the most fouled players in the world, was not a player who responded violently to attacks or even one who squared up to his assailants. Quite the opposite, in fact. Every time a defender put him on the ground he would get up, laugh and take the ball to dribble past him again.

In those days a sending-off did not mean automatic suspension from the next game, but Brazilian officials were almost certain they would have to do without their genius for the final the following Sunday. On Thursday, the day after the Chile game, the seven members of FIFA's disciplinary committee were due to meet to hear the case. Their decision would be based on the referee's report.

The Brazilians moved heaven and earth to clear Garrincha's name. Journalist Canor Simões Coelho called his old friend in Brasilia, Prime Minister Tancredo Neves, to suggest that 'in the name of the Brazilian people' he send the commitee a telegram asking for a pardon. The President of Peru, Manuel Prado y Ugarteche, got the Peruvian ambassador in Chile to ask the referee to go easy on Garrincha in his report. And the Brazilian man on the FIFA board, Mozart Di Giorgio, wanted the linesman to disappear before the hearing and contacted him with the offer of a ticket home to Montevideo, via Paris. The linesman left Chile the next morning.

Perhaps, though, all their efforts might not have been necessary. Without Garrincha Brazil were in danger of losing the final to Czechoslovakia, and in 1962 few people wanted to see a socialist country (and an amateur one at that) win the World Cup. In addition, FIFA was still grateful to Brazil for hosting the 1950 World Cup finals, a move that had contributed to saving FIFA, which had almost

195

folded in the aftermath of the Second World War. The FIFA disciplinary committee judged cases with one eye on politics, and they were not unsympathetic to Brazil.

Nevertheless, the committee breathed a sigh of relief when, perhaps influenced by the Peruvian ambassador, Yamazaki wrote that 'he did not see the foul committed by Garrincha'. Yamazaki said his linesman 'had to travel' but that he had left him a note describing the alleged foul as 'a typical response'. Garrincha's representative at the hearing was lawyer Mord Maduro, a larger-than-life Central American who had arranged for Botafogo to tour the isthmus several times and knew the team well. Speaking in a high-pitched voice, the 24-stone Maduro brilliantly used the referee's report and the linesman's notes to show how the incident had been misinterpreted. Others followed his lead. Garrincha was absolved by five votes to two and given a symbolic reprimand.

Luis Murgel, the CBD's representative on the committee, had based his defence on the fact that Garrincha had never been sent off before. However, the truth was that Garrincha had been dismissed before – three times.

His first red card had come while playing for Botafogo against Portuguesa de Desportos in a Rio-SP match at the Pacaembu on 20 June 1954. Portuguesa were winning 3–1 when Botafogo's Tomé hit Portuguesa's Ortega. Ortega reacted, and the other players joined in the mêlée. The referee sent off all 22 players and abandoned the match. It is, however, debatable whether or not Garrincha took part in the scrum.

The second sending-off came on 30 November that same year in Belo Horizonte, when Botafogo played local club América Mineiro in a friendly. With half an hour gone in the first half Garrincha exchanged kicks with the América Mineiro full-back Sílvio. Both men were given their marching orders, and even though the crowd protested the referee stuck to his decision and ordered both men off for an early bath.

Garrincha's third dismissal, on 23 June 1956, was also the result of a mass brawl and happened in Spain during a game against Barcelona in which the players, substitutes, managers and trainers were all arrested by police. The Spanish referee, deciding that Botafogo goalkeeper Amaury had started the incident, sent off the whole Botafogo team, including Garrincha.

Had the members of the FIFA commission known about those three incidents their decision might have been different. But they didn't, and with Garrincha free to play Brazil needed only to beat Czechoslovakia to make it two World Cup wins in a row. In the group match the Czechs had played for a draw against Brazil and had succeeded in taking a share of the spoils. This time, however, it would be different. It was the final, and both sides had to play to win.

Garrincha never cared who he was playing against. He wasn't under-estimating his rivals, he simply had a wonderful disregard for tactics, systems or formations. To him, football was very simple, 11 men against 11 men. His team-mates felt very differently, though, and Garrincha couldn't avoid hearing them talk about their opponents. He asked one of them, 'Who's this Czechoslovakia side again?'

'It's the team that drew with us in the first round, the game in which Pelé got injured,' the team-mate replied.

'Ah, that São Cristovão team full of Paulo Amarals?' Garrincha asked.

Czechoslovakia played in white shirts, just like Rio side São Cristovão. And Paulo Amaral would often join in the training sessions to make up the numbers. But even the trainer was puzzled by Garrincha's comment.

'Why did you say they are full of Paulo Amarals?' he said.

'Because they're all big, fat guys who are no good at football,' Garrincha replied.

Though this story of Garrincha's thoughts on his future opponents was true, many other anecdotes were made up right there in Chile by Sandro Moreyra, who was covering the cup for the *Jornal do Brasil*.

Like the one in which Garrincha, at the end of a radio interview with a Spanish reporter, was asked to sign off by saying goodbye to the microphone. Garrincha was supposed to have said, 'Goodbye, microphone.' Moreyra invented the stories, tested them on João Saldanha and had a ball telling them to Mario Filho, whom he didn't like and whom he enjoyed getting the better of. Filho listened to the tales, marvelling at Garrincha's simplicity, and then asked Moreyra's permission to reproduce them in the book he was writing, *The 1962 World Cup*. He had been told that many of the stories were fiction, but Filho preferred to believe them. After all, Moreyra was the journalist who knew Garrincha best. Neither Moreyra nor Filho ever thought the stories would be distorted and twisted so that Garrincha would come to be seen unfairly as an infantile, almost pathetic genius.

While Garrincha was bringing some life to the dressing room, the players were worrying about another problem: the injury to Pelé. In the days he spent on the sidelines, Pelé's condition had improved more than expected. If he really pushed himself there was a chance he could make it to the final. Hilton Gosling, however, would not hear of it. Some club directors approached Gosling on the eve of the game to push him to give Pelé something to play. They threatened him and told him, 'If Brazil loses because Pelé doesn't take the field, then you're out of here.'

Gosling was not afraid. 'I take full responsibility,' he said.

Technically, giving a player an anaesthetic was not doping. But for Gosling, it might as well have been. He was not going to force Pelé to play. Everyone in the squad remembered how Hungary had put an injured Puskas in the team to face West Germany in the 1954 final, with disastrous results.

Gosling might have vetoed Pelé's appearance, but he was not opposed to suggesting otherwise. The Brazilians spread a rumour that Pelé would take his place in the team and the ploy worked; the Czechs were certain Pelé was not in the side only when the teams took to the field. The counter-espionage department worked well and managed to hide another key piece of information from everyone, even the Brazilian journalists. Garrincha woke up on the day of the final with a cold and a fever that registered 39 degrees. He played only thanks to a dose of aspirin. Whenever he got the ball, he danced in front of the three Czechs who moved to cover him before laying it off to Zito or Didi, who passed it forward to release Amarildo or Vavá. By the time the Czechs had worked out that Garrincha was having an off day it was too late.

Just as in Sweden in 1958, Brazil went 1–0 down but refused to let their heads drop. This time it wasn't Didi who calmly carried the ball to the centre spot but Nílton Santos. Brazil equalised two minutes later with a goal from Amarildo, and then Zito put them ahead shortly before half-time. The third, from Vavá, killed off their opponents. The final minutes were a cake walk, with Garrincha putting his foot on the ball and challenging his opponents to come and take it off him. None of them dared.

In Rio, Governor Carlos Lacerda didn't wait for the final whistle to blow. As soon as Vavá made it 3–1 he called his secretary and dictated an urgent telegram for Garrincha: MYNAH BIRD AWAITS YOU IN GUANABARA STOP LACERDA.

Brazil were double World Cup winners. The players did a lap of honour and Mauro lifted the Jules Rimet trophy. Zagalo, Nílton Santos, Gilmar and several others cried again – it was impossible to be blasé with the World Cup. In the stand, Elza Soares fainted when the final whistle blew.

She didn't take long to come to, however, for half an hour later she walked into the Brazilian dressing room singing a song about Garrincha. There was a party going on. Naked players were being hugged by the directors, reporters and fans who were milling about under the showers. Dozens of flag-waving fans were celebrating with champagne, whisky and beer; everyone was laughing and crying. It was the kind of atmosphere into which any new arrival would struggle to make a grand entry. But when Elza Soares walked in wearing

199

a green and yellow satin dress the place fell silent. Just for a moment. Then there was uproar and she was surrounded by naked men – a situation unthinkable in 1962.

The first one to jump out of the shower and grab a towel or a flag was Didi.

'Get that woman out of here!' he shouted.

Some of the players covered themselves up, others tried to hide. All except Zagalo.

'What are you hiding for?' he said. 'It's her problem.'

Elza, indifferent to the commotion she was causing, grabbed Garrincha under the shower and smothered him with kisses. Her satin dress was soaked and clung even more tightly to her body. Garrincha had promised her the cup and he had been true to his word. The cup was hers, everyone else could go to hell.

The squad returned to Brazil on Bungner's DC-8, stopping in Brasilia for an audience with the president. They flew into Rio at the end of the afternoon and repeated the long victory parade on the back of a fire engine. In the centre of the city a fan managed to climb up on to the truck and give Garrincha a bag of sweets weighing almost two stones.

That night, Nílton Santos, Garrincha, Didi, Amarildo and Zagalo went to celebrate at Botafogo. Elza and Milton Banana left Santiago a few hours later on the scheduled flight that also brought home the press. When they touched down in Rio, Banana went home. But Elza joined Garrincha at Botafogo.

For Garrincha, the party continued into the small hours of the morning in Sandro Moreyra's flat. Garrincha had managed to save the strip he had worn for the final. It was still stuffed into a blue CBD bag, and he gave it to Moreyra the next day and made him promise to take it exactly as it was – the shirt smelling with sweat, the socks streaked with dirt, the boots still muddy and bloodstained – and put it on the altar of the São Francisco de Paula church in Petrópolis.

Moreyra locked the bag in a cupboard so that no one would steal it and promised to carry out Garrincha's wishes the next day. Of course, he kept it for the rest of his life.

With the sun about to rise, Garrincha left for Pau Grande. Mário de Moraes took him in *O Cruzeiro*'s car in order to get exclusive pictures of yet another triumphant homecoming. The only problem was that the town had already let off all its fireworks, drunk the bars dry and got tired of waiting for him to come home.

Garrincha was met by Nair. He went straight to his bedroom where Pincel, Swing and two or three others had passed out on his bed. Garrincha took one look at his friends and shouted at de Moraes, 'Look at that! What's the point in having two World Cup winner's medals?'

In the weeks that followed, a blue Simca-Chambord was frequently seen parked in the garage of a house in Urca. It spent its first night in Elza's garage at the end of June, a week after the squad had returned from Chile. She held a *feijoada* for him and his friends from Pau Grande. Halfway through the party Garrincha pulled her into a corner.

'Crioula, I am falling in love with you,' he said.

Elza feigned surprise. 'What do you mean? You're married, you love your wife.'

'No, I've never loved anyone. There are many women after me, including, even today, Angelita Martinez. But I love you.'

Elza continued to play hard to get. 'Ah, that's just the *caipirinha* speaking,' she said.

But Garrincha was not to be denied: '*Caipirinha* or not, I'm telling you.'

Elza then did something that surprised even herself: she sent her children to her mother's house and told her guests that the party was over. When the last person had left she locked the door and there and then the two of them began the most passionate affair of their lives.

They spent the following days locked inside her house together, having sex morning, noon and night. Elza was amazed at Garrincha's powers of recuperation: it took him only minutes before he was ready to go again. They hardly had time to sleep, they rarely bothered to dress, and Elza never answered the phone. Her initial lack of interest in him had turned into a raging passion that burned with sex, tenderness, admiration and a huge desire to protect him.

When she kissed his feet, Garrincha sighed. 'I thought this kind of love only existed in films.'

'You're crazy. Don't you have to go to Botafogo to train?'

'No, I have a sore knee.'

'You've had a lot of women, haven't you?'

Garrincha, who was just as enthusiastic as Elza was, got serious for a moment. 'The past doesn't matter,' he declared. 'What matters is you.'

The affair was no secret to the journalists who had covered the World Cup. The big question was whether Elza had ever been with Pelé. Rumours of a romance between the two circulated in Chile but no one had ever seen them even talking, never mind anything more intimate. With Garrincha, however, it was a different story, and there were plenty of eyewitnesses. She had gone to see him in Friburgo and Viña del Mar and she had given him that show in the dressing room after the final. If their romance continued when they got back to Rio it would not be a surprise. And progress it did – although quietly, thanks to Garrincha, who did his best to keep things under wraps.

During the 1962 Carioca Championship, Garrincha's official address remained in Pau Grande, but his real home was now in Urca, on rua Ramon Franca. He rarely went to the mountains any more and his life was spent in Rio with Elza and three of her sons: 14-year-old Carlinhos, nine-year-old Dilma and seven-year-old Gilson. They all liked him.

Botafogo were chasing their second consecutive Carioca title and Garrincha was only really turning up to play matches, which made Botafogo's new vice president of football, the former presidential bodyguard and police commander José de Oliveira Brandão Filho, more than a little nervous. Brandão Filho had maintained his ties to the police as well as his sense of authority. His temperament did not make him the most popular person at the club. His attitude to hierarchy was taken straight from the barracks and police station; to him, the players were little better than minor employees. It was an attitude that led Paulo Amaral to resign at the start of the season to be replaced by assistant Marinho Rodrigues.

On one occasion, when Garrincha missed training yet again, Brandão Filho got into his car and went to Pau Grande to look for him. If Garrincha refused to come back with him he was quite prepared to make him. But he couldn't find Garrincha in Pau Grande. He was at Elza's house, and Brandão Filho had no idea where she lived.

Garrincha was not the only one standing people up during the second half of 1962. Elza, too, had practically abandoned her agent Marcos Lazaro. She stopped giving concerts outside Rio because she did not want to leave Garrincha's side, even for a short time. By now she was going to the club to look for him, in full view of the other players. Rodrigues advised her to be more discreet and Elza decided he was right; their affair had all the ingredients necessary for a major scandal. But Garrincha seemed determined to go public – he didn't care if he was seen with another woman. Rodrigues took him aside, too.

'Look, Mané, you are not the first married man to have an affair. But why don't you hide it, as everyone else does?'

'You guys might be like that, Marinho, but I am not. I don't need to hide. This is nobody else's business.'

'It's a passing affair. Why take risks?'

Garrincha seemed offended. 'Passing affair my arse.'

But Rodrigues was right to worry. Botafogo were struggling in the league. They were again without Didi: after the World Cup he had asked to be sold to Peruvian side Sporting Cristal, who had promised him the position of player-coach. Edson returned to the side in his place. They lost their opener to lowly Campo Grande without Garrincha, and then drew with Olaria, again without Garrincha, and then Bangu, before going down to Vasco. Before each of the matches Garrincha slipped out of the *concentração* to spend the night with Elza.

Rodrigues authorised a new regime: trainer Tomé would drive Garrincha from the hotel to Elza's house and then bring him back a couple of hours later. When one of the directors asked him if he thought it was a good idea, Rodrigues shrugged his shoulders and said, 'It's better that Mané goes and comes back with Tomé rather than coming back the next day on his own. Because if he doesn't fit in a quickie with Elza, he's in no state to play a game of football.'

In the footballing world, the affair had become notorious. One afternoon, Elza was coming out of the Banco Nacional on the Avenida Rio Branco in the city centre when the traffic lights turned to red and the Vasco team bus stopped. The players recognised her and a few stuck their heads out of the window and shouted, 'Hey, gorgeous!' and other less polite comments: 'Go for it, Elza! Tire Garrincha out for us so we can make sure of that win bonus!'

Elza never told Garrincha.

The car that Garrincha was leaving in her garage was no longer the Simca, which he had finally abandoned, but a silver Renault-Dauphine given to him by the CBD. The prizes promised to the players for winning the World Cup had finally turned up. Until then the only rewards Garrincha had received were a fridge, presented to him by the manufacturers, and the mynah bird Lacerda had promised him. He had picked the bird up on 17 July in front of assembled media.

In addition, *O Cruzeiro* had arranged for the dog that had run on to the pitch during the England game to be brought over from Chile and raffled off among the players. The draw was a secretive affair, and of course Garrincha won. No one complained. Garrincha called the dog Bi, for *bicampeonato*, and took it to Pau Grande.

Finally, at the end of September, the CBD brought the players together at the Palacio das Laranjeiras where, in the presence of the president, they handed out the prizes for winning the World Cup: 150,000 cruzeiros (equivalent to Garrincha's monthly salary) and a new Dauphine for the players, masseuse, kit man and boot man. The directors got a more expensive Simca or an Alfa Romeo.

But the cup only truly started to pay financial dividends for Garrincha when PR agencies began to offer him work as a spokesman promoting goods and services. One of his first jobs was for department store Ducal; one advertisement showed a smiling Garrincha alongside the slogan GARRINCHA WARNS FATHERS: JUST TWO A DAY. An obvious double entendre, the 'two a day' referred to the Monark bicycles Ducal were to raffle off to those who bought their clothes. Another ad came in the form of a comic strip for leather-goods firm Sete Vidas (Seven Lives) and took advantage of the fact that the man who wore the number 7 shirt also had seven daughters, each of whom wore shoes made by Sete Vidas. It was a clever line, but the truth was that until then his daughters had not worn shoes made by Sete Vidas or anyone else – they had walked around barefoot. That changed when Garrincha got paid, because part of his payment was in kind and he took boxes and boxes of shoes to Pau Grande with him.

In August, Garrincha finally remembered to ask Botafogo for the signing-on bonus he had left with them before going on tour in January. Months earlier, back in March, Botafogo had told him that the money was ready to be collected and once again he hadn't bothered to touch it.

One friend was astonished by this. 'It's three million cruzeiros, Mané!'

Garrincha appeared as easy-going as he was uninformed. 'It's at Botafogo, isn't it? Then it's in good hands.'

205

In fact, inflation had eaten away at the cash, and what had been worth $10,000 in January was worth less than $7,000 by the time he decided to pick it up in August. Moreover, Botafogo didn't have the money; they had paid salaries with it so as not to let it just sit there depreciating. Garrincha thought it absurd that the club should pay other people with *his* money. To resolve the problem, Botafogo were forced to ask for a bank loan from José Luiz Magalhães Lins of Banco Nacional.

Magalhães Lins (or Zé Luiz as everyone called him) had come into Garrincha's life shortly after his return from the World Cup, thanks to their mutual friends Armando Nogueira, Sandro Moreyra and Araújo Netto. The three journalists thought that with two World Cup winner's medals under their belts Garrincha and Nílton Santos would be in a position to make money and that both would therefore need someone to look after their financial interests. They were especially concerned about Garrincha, whose innocence when it came to financial matters was almost criminal. The stories he told them about his disregard for money made their hair stand on end. Just after the World Cup in Sweden, for example, Garrincha gave some money to Nair for safe keeping. She stuffed it under the children's mattress and forgot about it. Much later, when they moved the bed, they discovered the money, rotten and stinking after years of bedwetting.

Nogueira, Moreyra and Netto, who were always getting loans from banks themselves, thought it madness. Before history had a chance to repeat itself they convinced Garrincha to gather all the money he had at home and put it into the stocks and shares recommended by Zé Luiz. He went to pick up the cash in Pau Grande with two officials from the Banco Nacional. When they got there they found bank notes in drawers, fruit bowls, stuck in the pages of Bugs Bunny and cowboy comics, under mattresses and even behind the cooker. There were cruzeiros, francs, lira, pounds, pesetas, Dutch florins, Swedish kroner and coins from everywhere Botafogo had played over the years, not counting the Peruvian soles and the Venezuelan bolivares that were now worth nothing. There were also bundles of dollars and innumerable cheques that had never been cashed.

Garrincha put the money in a shoebox, tied it with string and went to hand it over to Zé Luiz. He counted it and discovered that with salaries, per diems, prizes, donations, bonuses and other untouched funds, Garrincha had about $20,000, a sum that would today be equivalent to almost a quarter of a million dollars.

Until then, Elza had never understood why Garrincha was always short of cash. Even now, knowing he had money stuffed under mattresses and rotting in fruit bowls, she found it hard to believe him when he described the squalid living conditions in his Pau Grande home.

'I'll believe it when I see it,' she said. 'It can't be as bad as you say.'

Garrincha swore he was telling the truth. 'You'll see. But if it's as bad as I say, will you still stay with me?'

'Of course I will. But you must be exaggerating.'

Elza soon found out the truth for herself. One Sunday, when Botafogo were not playing, Garrincha took her to Pau Grande for a barbecue. He also invited Nílton Santos and his wife Abigail to come along with them. It was meant to look as if he was simply taking one more celebrity to Pau Grande to see his home town. Elza finally saw Garrincha's home for herself, and the reality was worse than she could ever have imagined.

Nair met them with her hair in curlers and her breath stinking of beer, her favourite tipple. She looked terrible. Her gums were yellow and her dental brace was cheap and disgusting. The children were in a terrible way as well. They were all dressed in hand-me-downs that had turned to rags, some had runny noses, and some had only pants on. The filth startled Elza. The beds looked as if they had never been made. The cushions were stained, torn and smelly. Shoes and flip-flops were thrown under the beds and potties sat in the middle of the room. The tiny bathroom was crammed with bird cages and the floor was a carpet of discarded seeds and droppings. The sink was covered with green stains. The toilet had no seat.

Elza could not understand how Garrincha, normally so careful and well groomed, managed to tolerate life in such a pigsty. At her place in Urca he would take up to four showers a day.

There were two fridges, one in the living room and another in the kitchen, but neither of them contained anything except beer and *batida* cocktails. Garrincha told Elza he was used to finding bits of old sandwich in the chest of drawers. Both cookers were covered in a layer of fat an inch thick.

In the living room, as in many players' homes, there were pennants on the walls and trophies in the cabinet, but they were all covered in dust. A poster of Garrincha taken from a 1953 issue of the magazine *Esporte Illustrado* hung on the wall alongside a portrait of him in an oval frame. There was a horrendous jaguar-print sofa and the cage containing Lacerda's mynah bird sat on top of a sewing machine like a monument.

But worse than the untidiness was the atmosphere of confusion. An uninterrupted stream of people came and went. They all seemed to know what they were doing: the first thing they did when they came in was head for the fridge. The number of brothers- and sisters-in-law, their lodgers and other relatives could have filled a small stadium. Emilinha Borba blasted from the record player: Garrincha replaced it with one of Elza's singles. Pincel, almost unconscious on the sofa, wet himself.

Nílton Santos and Abigail were horrified too. Elza, who had grown up in a favela, found it incredible.

'I can't believe it's like this all the time,' she whispered to Garrincha.

'Usually it's worse,' he said. 'Yesterday, when I knew you were coming, I killed all the insects. I filled a whole shoebox.'

Elza was experiencing what other visitors to Pau Grande had witnessed but had never had the courage to talk about. Like everyone else, she had imagined that Garrincha lived in Pau Grande's lost paradise of rivers, birds and never-ending football matches. Now, though, the myth had been exploded. The best player in the world lived as if he was a substitute for a mediocre third-division outfit.

When she thought about it on the trip home to Rio, Elza felt sorry for Nair. Perhaps it wasn't her fault that she had never had an education. The only thing she knew how to do was make babies. Elza was suddenly struck by the fact that her affair with Garrincha might be a sin. But Garrincha assured her that the marriage had never really existed, that he had married Nair only because he was forced to. And anyway, he said, their relationship was coming to an end; they no longer lived as man and wife. What he never explained was how they managed to produce a daughter almost every year. And that October, Nair discovered she was pregnant again.

Unlike the previous year, when they were six points clear at the halfway stage of the season, in 1962 Botafogo were struggling, and with only a few weeks left of the tournament they were seven points behind leaders Flamengo. The fans were unhappy and rumours started circulating about Garrincha's involvement with Elza. Garrincha denied them, saying that he and Elza were just good friends, but when reporters confronted Elza she refused to confirm or deny the affair. She had managed to convince herself that their romance was not wrong and that she had been brought into the world to save Garrincha. For one thing, she was starting to open his eyes to his salary at Botafogo.

'You don't know how to put a value on yourself, baby,' Elza said. That was what she always called him. 'Don't be a sucker. You shouldn't be earning less than Pelé.'

'But Crioula,' as Garrincha always called her, 'at Botafogo even Nílton Santos signs blank contracts. The directors fill in what they want.'

The question of salaries became an incendiary issue at the club during the second half of 1962. Winning the World Cup for the second time had alerted the players to their market value. They saw very little of the fortunes the clubs were charging to play exhibition matches, and gradually they began to rebel.

The first to speak out was striker Amarildo. He renewed his contract with much better terms to become Botafogo's highest-paid player. Under the new deal he got 150,000 cruzeiros a month (the same as Garrincha) and a ten-million-cruzeiro ($22,000) signing-on fee – more than three times the bonus Garrincha commanded. Garrincha asked Nílton Santos if he thought it was fair that he was getting less than Amarildo. But Nílton Santos – and Zagalo – were more concerned about their own wage packets.

When Zagalo asked for a pay rise, Botafogo responded by telling him, 'Not even Garrincha gets that much!'

Zagalo replied, 'I am not responsible for Garrincha's bad deals. I just want what I think is fair.'

Botafogo were playing their stars off against one another. In the end, Nílton Santos and Zagalo got their increases, but the club could not reach an agreement with Garrincha. Although he had just signed a contract that ran until 1965 he wanted the same ten-million-cruzeiro signing-on bonus that Amarildo had got. Brandão Filho told him to forget it. Instead, they offered him a one-bedroom flat in Copacabana. Garrincha accepted the compromise but he did not feel as though justice had been done. The small apartment couldn't make up for the huge difference between what he got and what Amarildo got.

With five World Cup winners in the side, Botafogo were being paid between $15,000 and $20,000 to play friendly matches outside Brazil – on the condition that Garrincha appeared. Garrincha's status as the big draw became clear in August when they went to play three matches in Bogotá and Cali. The newspaper headlines screamed GARRINCHA IN BOGOTÁ!, not 'Botafogo in Bogotá'.

And he was worth every penny of the fortunes Botafogo were raking in. Botafogo beat the famous Milionários de Bogotá 6–5 in a match some of those present said was one of Garrincha's best ever performances. One particular move in that game became legendary. Garrincha dribbled the ball past Milionários's Argentine full-back Gambetta. Gambetta fell down but got back up again and ran after Garrincha. He fell down again and again but kept getting back up as Garrincha continued to dribble around him. The two tussled so intensely that they kept at it even after the ball had crossed the touch-line. The referee and linesman might have noticed but didn't dare put a stop to the action. It was the essence of football – two great players in an epic battle for the ball. The game was eventually stopped when they were almost on the track surrounding the pitch and the referee woke them from their trance. Gambetta did not return to the field of play. He was substituted.

Back in Brazil, however, it was a different story. Botafogo continued to perfom poorly in the Carioca Championship. In the 1–0 defeat at the hands of Madureira, Garrincha's failure to control a ball that ran out for a throw-in was booed by the home fans. A few days later, against Vasco, he complained that he wasn't seeing enough of the ball and asked to be taken off at half-time. And in a Brazilian Cup tie against Internacional of Porto Alegre, opposing centre-half Cláudio dribbled around him with ease.

All three matches took place inside a week, and disgruntled Botafogo fans, led by the muscled Octacílio 'Tarzan' Batista do Nascimento, started to blame their winger. Everything Garrincha had done for Brazil just a few months earlier seemed to have been forgotten. Tarzan was well connected at the club and he knew about Garrincha and Elza, and about how Rodrigues was helping them get together the night before a match.

What he probably didn't know was that Garrincha's knee was causing him agony. In fact, the pain was so bad that Garrincha had thought about giving up the game altogether. In October he asked Zé Luiz if the money he had invested now matched the 150,000 cruzeiros he got from Botafogo. If it did, he was ready to retire. Zé Luiz told him that wouldn't be a good idea.

Garrincha was an impatient investor, incapable of allowing his investments to accumulate. He cashed in his shares prematurely and more often than not seemed incapable of spending his money wisely. In November, for example, he exchanged his Dauphine and his Simca for a blue Karmann Ghia and still had to make up the shortfall. Botafogo were not pleased to see him with an expensive new car. It seemed absurd that someone who hardly played – and when he did, played badly – was running around in a brand-new motor. Garrincha justified the purchase by saying it had become increasingly difficult to plan his life around the erratic train time-tables to and from Raiz da Serra. Even when he did take public transport he was no longer able to take a nap, thanks to the constant hassle from fans. He also claimed that he used the new car to take his family out in Pau Grande. It was an argument that provoked hilarity at Botafogo. If he wanted to take his seven daughters out, why didn't he keep the Simca or the Dauphine? The Karmann Ghia was a two-seater sports car with enough room only for him and Elza.

The only other woman to sit in the Karmann was Iraci. She did so for the last time in November, when Garrincha took her to the Bar do Pescadores to end the relationship.

'My love,' he said, 'things are starting to get difficult. I am dropping everyone else because of my Crioula.'

Iraci had suspected as much. But she attempted one last roll of the dice.

'But what about me, Garrincha? And what about our children?'

He was cold. 'If I were you, I'd return to Pau Grande.'

On 22 November, the flat on rua Gomes Carneiro was returned to its owner and Iraci set off for Pau Grande, taking her children with little hope for the future. She could not even accuse Elza of manipulating Garrincha to get her out of the picture. Elza didn't even know she existed.

*　　*　　*

The problems surrounding Garrincha's salary negotiations remained unresolved. The Botafogo directors blamed Elza for putting ideas into his head. At first they thought that Elza was just another Angelita Martinez; by the time they worked out how serious the pair were, there was no one at the club savvy enough to deal with the situation.

In the end, Elza was summoned to the club by Brandão Filho. He took her into his office and banged his fist on the table.

'How much do I have to pay you to leave that waster?'

Elza answered with a line right out of a samba song: 'You can't buy love, Dr Brandão.'

Brandão was characteristically rude and aggressive, and he did not let her go without issuing this threat: 'You are going back to the favela.'

Once again, Elza hid the episode from Garrincha.

Flamengo had slipped up during the run-in and come the last day of the season Botafogo were just one point behind their city rivals. They needed to beat them to take their second title in two years. Garrincha, though, was threatening to boycott the match. He sent a message to the directors stating that unless his wage demands were met he would not play.

To Brandão Filho, Garrincha's attitude was intolerable, and the supporters were not happy either. Three days before the big game their fury spilled over into violence and a small group of fans attacked Elza's house. It was hardly Kristallnacht, but stones were thrown and insults were shouted. It was common knowledge that Elza was a Flamengo fan and some thought Garrincha's threats were part of a conspiracy she had hatched to help Flamengo take the title. Elza called the police. By the time they arrived the fans had disappeared.

Garrincha had spent the night in Pau Grande. The next morning, Rodrigues and Tomé went there to persuade him to return with them to Rio and the team hotel; he should play as never before, they said, and then, if Botafogo won the title, sit down and negotiate. Garrincha agreed.

213

He arrived at training in great form and promised he would put on a show during the match. However, later that afternoon he asked Rodrigues if he could spend the night with Elza – something had upset her the night before and she wasn't feeling well. He promised to return early the next day. Rodrigues had no option but to agree, and Garrincha headed off to Urca.

When he arrived there later that Thursday night, he told Elza, 'Crioula, we're going to make love the whole night.'

'But, baby, you have a game on Saturday.'

'Pretend it's a warm-up for the match. Treat me right, I am going to finish off Flamengo.'

The Flamengo manager Flávio Costa thought he had developed a system to neutralise Garrincha by withdrawing Joel (the same Joel who had played in Brazil's 1958 World Cup-winning side and who went on to be one of Flamengo's top goalscorers) and putting Gerson on in his place. Gerson, then just 21, had still not become the star who would be an integral part of the legendary 1970 World Cup-winning side, but he was already a great player – in his usual position, midfield. Flávio Costa pushed him out wide to mark Garrincha. If Garrincha got past him he would come up against Jordan, and if he beat Jordan he would face Vanderlei.

Garrincha ran rings around them all. When the first goal went in, he seemed to have forgotten the controversy that had engulfed him. He hammered the ball past goalkeeper Fernando, skipped past the photographers and ran behind the posts screaming, 'Goal! Goal! Goal! Let's score another one!' They soon did, a Garrincha shot going in off the head of Vanderlei as he tried to block it. In the second half Garrincha scored a third, killing off any chance Flamengo might have had of getting back into the game. After each goal, the referee Armando Marques, instead of running back to the centre circle, walked to the goal and picked up the ball. For a few seconds no one was sure whether he was going to allow it, but it was just his way of calming the fans and preventing the Flamengo majority from slaughtering their rival fans.

Down on the pitch, Garrincha was happy – he was playing for himself and not for Botafogo. He was the star, not the club. When the third goal went in he started doing what he enjoyed most, and what he would never do again – play at playing football. He got the ball and tormented his old friend Jordan: 'Hey, Jordan, come and get me!' For Garrincha, it had ceased to be a league decider. It was a kickabout, a laugh, just like with his mates in Pau Grande.

When the game finished, Botafogo emerging as 3–0 victors, Garrincha was hoisted on to the shoulders of fans and carried off the pitch. He was a hero again, a god, the golden calf. However, something had changed. Garrincha now knew that the fans who were cheering him on and promising him the heavens could be the same ones that had booed him and conspired against him, the same ones even that had attacked Elza's house. He let himself be carried from the field but he no longer wanted anything to do with them.

Worse, his knee was hurting. He was in so much pain that he did not go to the celebration party Botafogo held at the club's headquarters. Local newspapers said he was complying with a vow he had made to go to Pau Grande wearing his strip if Botafogo won the league, but nothing could have been further from the truth. He had indeed walked out of the Maracanã still wearing his shirt and shorts, but he had gone straight to Elza's home, where he spent several days hidden away.

That game would come to be remembered for some peculiar details. Thanks to Botafogo's superstitious kit man Aluísio, the team had taken to the field in the 1962 Carioca Championship tournament wearing long-sleeved shirts. In addition, Garrincha and Nílton Santos had taken to turning over the waistband of their shorts, a fashion the other players had adopted. The long-sleeved tops and turned-over waistbands became one of the presiding memories of that side, and when

Botafogo fans recalled Garrincha, those details would be definitive. Perhaps because that's exactly what they were – final, lasting, definitive. No one could have guessed it, neither Garrincha himself nor any of the 146,287 spectators in the Maracanã that day, but Botafogo vs. Flamengo on 15 December 1962 would, in some ways, be Garrincha's final match.

CHAPTER 14

1963: Fire in the Heart

CHRISTMAS 1962 WAS THE LAST GARRINCHA WOULD SPEND IN PAU
Grande with Nair and his daughters. The traditional O que vai e
mole v. Real Madrid match would also be his last. O que vai e mole
won 2–1, Garrincha scoring a goal that came straight from an indirect
kick and should have been chalked off. His return to Rio was also
notable. It would be the last time he left Pau Grande in relative peace.
For the next 20 years his visits would be contentious and painful, his
presence there resented.

Botafogo were due to leave Rio on 11 January 1963 for their
annual tour of South America. When Garrincha reported back at
the club after a break of almost three weeks, Dr Lídio Toledo examined him and concluded that he was in no fit state to travel. His
knee was even more swollen than usual. The problem was not a
new one. Garrincha had made the side to play Internacional in the
Brazilian Cup only after Dr Nova Monteiro had drained fluid from
the knee. And after several Carioca Championship matches he had
been in such pain that he was forced to spend days on the sidelines
while the swelling went down. The knee had started to bother him
during the World Cup in Chile, and when he got back to Brazil an
orthopaedic specialist had advised him to have an operation, just as

Monteiro had done three years earlier. And, just as before, Garrincha took no notice.

The doctors told Garrincha he had arthrosis; the joint between the femur and the tibia was wearing away. For those of us who use knees for everyday tasks such as climbing stairs or getting on and off buses, such wear and tear will not be apparent for decades, and even among athletes the damage occurs gradually, getting serious only towards the end of a career. But the congenital deformity in his legs meant that Garrincha's arthrosis worsened more rapidly than normal. Every time he wowed the Maracanã with his trademark move of stopping suddenly and twisting his body to fool the defender, the two bones ground together and ripped the cartilage between the menisci.

Any damaged cartilage turned into a foreign body, swelling up to produce sinovial liquid, or water on the knee. Garrincha's knee would balloon up and the pain could be horrific. He knew he had a problem but he wanted to win a second World Cup and a second Carioca Championship before doing something about it. Now, Lídio Toledo told Botafogo that if he didn't have the operation he would require ultrasound treatment, rest and then physiotherapy to build up the quadriceps, the muscles the knee depends on to support the body's weight. With or without the operation, he would have to stay in Rio.

Botafogo, however, had already signed contracts with Uruguayan businessman Severo Maresca to play nine games in Uruguay, Ecuador, Colombia, Peru and Chile. If Garrincha played, they would earn $12,000 for each match; if he didn't, the sum would fall to $8,000. The directors signed the contracts for foreign trips without consulting the manager, never mind the doctor. It was the same story at all Brazilian clubs.

When Garrincha set off on 11 January he did so without having resolved the other problem that was plaguing him either. He wanted to renegotiate the terms of his salary for the last two years of his three-year contract. Renato Estelita, who had returned as the club's director of football, told him everything would be sorted out when he got back from the trip. He didn't actually confirm that Botafogo would meet his demands, but as Garrincha understood it the matter was resolved.

Even with a bad knee Garrincha wanted to travel. He liked being the star of the side and he enjoyed the privileges it brought him when he was on the road. He was, for example, the only one allowed to miss breakfast or lunch without being reprimanded by the manager or other players. And he got an extra bonus from the tour organisers after each game, usually twice the $50 he received from Botafogo.

Though he did manage to play in seven of the nine matches, Garrincha had to be taken off in the second half in several of them. His knee was sore, and on more than one occasion he was forced to drain it and return to the hotel to rest while the other players went out and enjoyed themselves. Not that it bothered him. The first thing he did when he arrived at each hotel was place a framed photo of Elza on the bedside table and put her records on the record player. He was lovesick.

While they were on the road, Toledo took Garrincha for special physiotherapy sessions in four cities: Cali, Medellin, Bogotá and Lima. One of the games, against Deportivo de Medellin, was scheduled for 23 January, but as Garrincha could barely walk the Deportivo directors simply put the kick-off back 24 hours in order to give him more time to recover. The next day, however, his knee was still in a bad way. He shouldn't have even travelled to the stadium, but Toledo succumbed to pressure from the Deportivo president and forced him to play. He lasted 15 minutes before Toledo ordered Rodrigues to take him off.

He recovered in time to play against Milionários de Bogotá on 27 January but he wasn't fit enough to face River Plate, a match that also took place in the Colombian capital. He returned for the game against Sporting Cristal in Lima on 4 February but was again ruled out of the next game, against Colo-Colo in Santiago two days later. Every game he missed made him doubly depressed: first because he couldn't play and second because he missed out on the extra bonus from the tour organisers, which at $100 was 50 times more than the per diem he got from Botafogo.

Garrincha mistakenly thought that if he didn't play Botafogo might think he was shirking his responsibilities and use it against him when the time came to renegotiate his contract. So when Toledo ruled him out of the last match of the tour, against Peñarol in Montevideo on 9 February, Garrincha insisted on playing. 'If you don't pick me,' he remonstrated, 'Botafogo will take the field with 12 players. I am going out there no matter what.' He played poorly in a 1–0 defeat and left the field feeling as if he had a wasp buzzing around inside his knee.

When Garrincha arrived back in Brazil in the middle of February he did not go to his house in Pau Grande, which Nair, then five months pregnant, had redecorated in his absence. Instead he went straight from the airport to Elza, who welcomed him with a loving embrace that was like something out of a movie. Nair took her husband's absence as confirmation he was having an affair with 'that woman', as she had taken to calling Elza.

Garrincha kept his distance from Pau Grande in the weeks after his return, going there just twice, not to see Nair but to appear in a few scenes for a film Luiz Carlos Barreto was making about him entitled *Garrincha: Joy of the People*. Filming Garrincha was proving to be a challenge. Barreto would set a time and a place in Pau Grande, set up his lights and cameras, and then wait; and Garrincha wouldn't turn up. On the two occasions he did manage to film, he got footage of Garrincha dancing the twist with his daughters and drinking *guaraná* with Pincel and Swing in Dódi's bar. But for Barreto, who wanted to make *cinéma vérité*, such scenes were starting to look like fantasy. Real life was getting in the way of the script.

Around the same time as the filming was taking place, Elza went into hospital for plastic surgery. Garrincha went with her, and while there he met Dr Nelson Senise, a specialist in rheumatism and a big Bangu fan. Garrincha complained about his sore knee and asked Senise if he'd examine him. Senise looked at it, took an X-ray, then went to his text books to find out how a man in that state, with his cartilage so damaged, could still play football. When Garrincha returned to see him a second time, Senise drained the excess fluid and injected him with cortisone, then a new drug on the market. He told him that the swelling would go down and that Garrincha needed to rest.

There was little chance of that. Botafogo had hardly touched down at Galeão airport before the Rio-SP tournament was under way. Garrincha was still under treatment and out of the team, but as was the custom he received the full bonus for wins and draws. The problem was that without him Botafogo weren't winning. Rodrigues hoped that Garrincha would recover in time to play both home and away in the final of the Brazilian Cup against Santos. In the 1960s, the Rio-São Paulo tournament was considered less important than the Brazilian Cup because the latter guaranteed the winners a spot in the Copa Libertadores, the most important club competition in South America. Botafogo would never allow Garrincha to miss the final, so if he wanted to rest there was only one way he was going to get it – by disappearing. And, in a manner of speaking, that's exactly what happened.

Garrincha went to Botafogo to ask Estelita about his promised ten-million-cruzeiro bonus. Estelita told him the directors were still discussing the situation. Garrincha suggested they resolve the problem by rescinding his contract or selling him to one of the Italian clubs that were knocking on the door. Estelita warmed to the idea of selling Garrincha, but when he broached the subject with Ney Cidade Palmeiro, who was then sitting in for club chairman Paulo Azeredo, Palmeiro was aghast. 'Are you mad?' he said. 'The fans would burn the place down. Garrincha is part of this club!'

Botafogo's reluctance to resolve the situation one way or another was a bitter disappointment to Garrincha. In his eyes, after all he had done for them Botafogo were refusing either to sell him or pay him what he had been promised. Brandão Filho, though, saw it rather

221

differently. The club's vice president was enraged by Garrincha's insistence that he was owed money and in a telephone conversation he told him that the club owed him nothing, that as long as he was injured his bonus would be reduced by 50 per cent.

Garrincha's heart was by now hurting as much as his knee. He wiped away a tear and said that if that was the way things were going to be then he could no longer report to the club. None of the directors believed him. They all thought he would give in just as he had done in the past. But this time Garrincha did not capitulate. He and Elza packed their bags and left.

Garrincha and Elza drove along the main road that skirts the bay in Flamengo, and listened with some interest to Orlando Batista's sports programme on Radio Mauá. Batista was talking about Garrincha's fight with Botafogo, a fight that was now in its third week. Without him in the side Botafogo had gone five games without a win in the Rio-SP tournament.

Elza was furious – she thought that Batista was taking the club's side. She forced Garrincha to turn the car around; they would go to the radio station and give them his side of the story.

Elza walked into the office, the click of her high heels on the tiled floor making a mockery of the red SILENCE sign. The programme had already finished but Batista and his team of collaborators were still present. They sat down with Garrincha, who told Batista that he was being treated unfairly, that he had given Botafogo his all, that he had played even when he was injured and in pain, and that he had not been adequately compensated. The squad was already in São Paulo for the game against Santos in the Brazilian Cup and Garrincha told Batista he would play only if Botafogo gave him the ten-million-cruzeiro bonus he believed he had been promised, as well as the bonus he was due for winning the Carioca Championship.

When Garrincha had finished, Batista asked him if he would repeat it all on air.

Garrincha replied, 'Of course. I'll tell everybody.'

A few moments later the technicians had taken their places again and Garrincha was repeating his complaints live on air. He even added that during the last tour Toledo had abandoned him, and that he had been left with nothing to eat. They were serious accusations.

A few miles away at General Severiano, sensitive ears were taking it all in. Brandão Filho was livid, and he was not about to back down. He prepared a statement for the press telling them that Garrincha's provocations left them no choice but to fine him 60 per cent of his wage and to suspend his contract. If he did not retract the allegations then the club would neither play him nor sell him. 'He either plays for Botafogo or he'll have to go and play in Pau Grande,' Brandão Filho decreed.

The backlash against Garrincha spread through the club. An internal memo, signed by 'the club's press director', called him a 'scoundrel' who 'was taking advantage of Botafogo'. Even Garrincha's team-mates were irritated. The affair with Elza already bothered them – not because of Nair, who was not a popular figure, but because Garrincha had spent less and less time at the club since Elza's arrival on the scene. He had played fewer games, which in turn meant the other players did not get as many win bonuses.

The next day Pau Grande woke up to find the press at Garrincha's door. They wanted to hear his reaction to the club's sanctions. Garrincha, of course, wasn't there. Nair, in tears and clutching her daughters, told the reporters that she hadn't seen her husband for weeks. 'The last time I saw him he left saying he was going to buy bread and he still hasn't come back.'

One of the reporters, Roberto Garofalo of *O Globo*, decided to pursue the story and went with a photographer to Elza's house in Urca. Naturally, Garrincha was there. He repeated what he had said on the radio and added that if Botafogo stopped him from playing he would become a coach. Garofalo tried to talk him into going to Pau Grande to speak with Nair, and to his surprise Garrincha accepted, although not because of Nair. In addition to seeing his daughters, there was something more important Garrincha wanted to do in his home town: pick up the mynah bird and the dog Bi. Garrincha stayed in Pau Grande for just a few hours before returning to Urca with the animals.

The next night Botafogo lost 4–3 to Santos. It was the sixth game on the trot in which Botafogo had failed to get two points. The bad feeling directed against Garrincha inside the club was becoming hysterical.

The veil of secrecy that had hung over Pau Grande was ripped down by Garofalo's story in O Globo. There was nothing more to hide. The newspapers went knocking on Elza's door. She refused to open it. Photographers climbed trees and pointed their lenses at her windows, and a truck from TV Tupi, with Hilton Gosling's team inside, parked on the street in front of her house. Eventually the couple relented and were interviewed, photographed and filmed in front of the cannons at the nearby Fort São João. The affair was finally public, and the relative peace they had enjoyed was a thing of the past.

Until that point, Elza had sought to remain in the shadows. She had never admitted to having an affair with Garrincha, although neither had she denied helping him to see how important he was to the club. Elza thought it absurd that he wasn't paid what he was worth. She spoke bluntly to Garrincha, oblivious to the fact that they were standing in front of the press: 'Speak up, baby. Ask for the ten million to re-sign. Don't do it for less. They don't make any money without you. You have friends in the press. Teach those people a lesson!'

When the press had dispersed and gone home, Elza's doorbell rang again. It was Angelita Martinez, screaming at the top of her voice.

'You bitch! I want that man back!'

Angelita hammered on the door and created a huge scene. Elza went to the window to confront her. Angelita was not intimidated. Elza threatened to smash a vase over her head: then she threatened to call the police. Angelita screamed and shouted until finally she was exhausted and went home.

The scandal forced the people of Urca to reassess Garrincha and Elza. Until then they had frequently been seen out and about in the area; couples had asked for their autographs, young mothers had handed them their babies to be kissed, and little boys playing football on the streets had passed Garrincha the ball to play keepie-uppie. From that day on, only the children didn't turn their backs on them.

In Elza's house, the phone rang off the hook. 'Home wrecker! Aren't you ashamed to steal a man who's married with seven daughters?' In addition to being accused of breaking up a happy home, Elza was also accused of taking advantage of Garrincha. Many of the callers asked angrily, 'Why don't you just admit that you're after his money?'

If there was one thing that Elza could do without, it was Garrincha's money. Her jobs with the television stations Rio, Tupi and Record earned her five times as much as Garrincha, and that wasn't counting what she made from her shows and record sales. Music always brought in more money than football, but the public, blinded by the packed terraces at the Maracanã, did not know that. In reality, the only way Garrincha would have more money in the bank than Elza was if Botafogo gave him the bonus he was asking for.

But Botafogo's attitude had hardened. The public slanging match had tainted them and the club's image was at stake. If the directors didn't punish him after all he had said they would lose face. Some of Garrincha's friends in the media knew that a player would never win out against a club and they decided to try to make peace. And the only way to do that was through a respected and neutral mediator – Garrincha's financial adviser José Luiz Magalhães Lins. Zé Luiz accepted.

His first move was to get Garrincha and Elza as far away as possible from the front lines of the conflict. The public revolt against both of them was frightening and it served only to strengthen Botafogo's position. Zé Luiz sent them to his cousin's house in the country on the outskirts of the suburb of Santa Cruz. Surrounded by a garden of palm trees, vegetables and a few horses, it was a rustic little place with no electricity or telephone. It had a tiny bed that was so small they couldn't even turn over, but that was fine as they never let go of each other anyway. Garrincha and Elza went there without the slightest idea of when they might leave; their exile could last a couple of days or a week. They would be isolated, with no radio, television or newspapers. Their only company would be the housekeeper, and even then only during the day.

In Rio, meanwhile, Zé Luiz drafted a letter to Botafogo in a bid to find a way out that would allow them both to save face. In the letter, Garrincha 'explained' his behaviour and promised to return to training. It did not mention the contract dispute and there was no formal apology from him for disappearing. Zé Luiz hoped this would appease the club and at the same time protect the image of a player who was a two-time World Cup winner and a national hero. The letter, however, was never sent. Some Botafogo officials had made it known through the press that it would be not be enough – they wanted Garrincha to apologise. The most intransigent was the club's director of sports, Otávio Pinto Guimarães – perhaps because Garrincha had given him the nickname 'The Coathanger'. Rail-thin and straight-backed, Pinto held his cigarette holder in his gloved hand and was in no mood for mincing his words: 'We are waiting for Garrincha to come and apologise personally. He can come whenever he likes. The Botafogo offices are in the same place they always were.'

It was an impasse. The club wanted to put Garrincha in his place, to show him who was boss.

As Zé Luiz continued to negotiate in Rio, Garrincha and Elza waited at their rural hideaway. It could even have been considered an unexpected honeymoon, but within days of their arrival the stress began to take effect, with tragic consequences.

Elza was three months pregnant, and when she suddenly started bleeding Garrincha was terrified. He had no car and he needed to get her to a doctor. So he jumped on a horse and was all set to head for Santa Cruz when Elza stopped him. Feeling against them was running so high that she feared he might get lynched. Instead, she lay down and told Garrincha to go and collect some leaves from a jacaranda plant and some lemongrass. He squeezed the fluid from the jacaranda leaves and made her some juice to halt the haemorrhaging. The lemongrass helped to calm them both down and Elza soon felt better, but she would not see a doctor to confirm a miscarriage until she got back to Rio.

Back in the city, Zé Luiz was still trying to bring Garrincha and Botafogo together. This time he enrolled the help of Ademar Bebiano, who as well as being a well-known Botafogo fan was also the owner of Nova América, a factory started by some former employees of the América Fabril plant. Bebiano drafted a second letter that, without humiliating Garrincha, did just enough to satisfy Botafogo. The suspension and the fine would be forgotten, Garrincha would return to training and, most importantly, the club agreed to pay him ten million cruzeiros.

Botafogo were due to play Santos again at the end of March in the second leg of the Brazilian Cup final and they needed to win to force a third, deciding match. Zé Luiz went to his cousin's house to tell Garrincha that they had worked out a solution to suit all sides. However, because of a few lingering doubts, not to mention the continuing hostile public opinion, they decided Garrincha should wait a few days before returning to Rio.

Dr Toledo, still angry with Garrincha, went to the house to examine him and found that his knee was in good enough condition to enable him to play. He just needed to get in shape, lose a few pounds and build up the muscles in his legs. Goalkeeper Adalberto, one of the few players sympathetic to Garrincha's predicament, went to the hideaway each day to help put his team-mate through his paces. Some reporters were allowed in to see him, and newspapers printed photos

227

of Garrincha, dressed in a grey Botafogo tracksuit, running past rows of towering coconut palms.

The next day Garrincha played well in the 3–1 win that forced the third game. The fans seemed to have forgiven him. But the goodwill didn't last. In the decider two days later at the Maracanã, Santos hammered the home side 5–0 to take the trophy. Garrincha had a nightmare and was booed off the park along with the rest of the team. The two days' rest had simply not been enough.

Worse, the truce reached courtesy of Bebiano's letter had merely papered over the cracks. The episode had prompted a review of all Garrincha's past indiscretions and transgressions: the break-outs from the team hotel, the missed training sessions, and the days when team officials had had to go to Pau Grande to look for him. What had once been looked upon with good humour as simply part of the Garrincha legend was now being called indiscipline. To Brandão Filho and Pinto Guimarães, that indiscipline had been rewarded when they agreed to pay Garrincha his signing-on fee. Their relaxed attitude had changed completely. The affair with 'the singer', for example, was to them conduct unbecoming of someone who wore the black and white stripes. Many directors refused to shake Garrincha's hand or even to acknowledge him.

However, if Garrincha thought the climate at his club was chilly he was not prepared for the cold front that was about to move in and cast black shadows over his personal life.

When they returned from the country, Garrincha and Elza found a pile of anonymous letters awaiting them. Some threatened physical violence; many wished ill luck on 'the home wrecker'; all of them were bitter and aggressive. The abuse directed towards Elza's children at school, even from their teachers, got so bad that she had to transfer them to another one far away from Urca.

Radio stations were also capitalising on the scandal, Radio Tupi running a retrospective on Elza's life and career and others giving air time to people who called in vowing 'to kill that black woman'. One

TV station asked famous playwright and fanatical Fluminense fan Nelson Rodrigues to write a soap opera about the case. (Rodrigues refused.) Stations were inundated with new records about men who leave their families for other women. One song released by samba singer Noite Ilustrada was typical: 'Go home / Show you are a champion / Hug your children / Get down on your knees and ask for forgiveness.' Another explicit condemnation came from the singer Núbia Lafayette in her song 'Three Tears', which told the story of a housewife who made her living as a seamstress after her husband ran off with another woman. Halfway through the song a child's voice begs, 'Come home, Daddy.'

In a bid to make some easy money, Odeon, Elza's record company, suggested that she record 'I Am the Other Woman', a song originally recorded in 1953 by Carmen Costa, who was having an affair at the time with married samba singer Mirabeau. In a disastrous lapse of judgement, Elza agreed, and the record came out in April 1963, at the worst possible moment. The lyrics read: 'He is married / I am the other woman in his life / Living it red hot / Because he doesn't get everything at home / He is married / I am the other woman in his life / The one that everyone defames / That this unforgiving life mistreats / And without pity covers in mud. / Whoever condemns me / As though I were / A woman who lost her way / I see myself in his life / But I don't have him in mine. / I have no name / I come with a wounded heart / But I have more class / Than someone who never knew how to hold on to their man.'

When she heard the song after its release, Elza wanted to curl up and die. In February, when she went into the studio to record it, the words had seemed innocent; now, after all that had happened, its message was highly offensive, and although she tried to recall the record it was too late. It was in the shops and on the radio, and it was a disaster. To many of those who condemned the romance with Garrincha, the record seemed to mock them. Worse than that, it seemed to make fun of the victim, Nair. Even those who had given

Elza the benefit of the doubt now turned against her. Her friend, popular television presenter Chacrinha, broke the single in front of the cameras and DJs removed it from their turntables. Whenever they had played it the switchboards had lit up with complaints.

Back in Pau Grande, meanwhile, the last angel had been expelled from paradise. For the first time ever, the people of the town lined up en masse against their most famous son, dragging up all the old affairs, his history as a poor father and his reputation as a terrible worker. Everyone had a story to tell.

On rua Demócrito Seabra, Nair and her seven daughters posed for photographers every day, usually with Garrincha's picture in the oval frame behind them. The stories' headline was always the same: COME BACK, MANÉ! – even though Nair had never called him that. She did her best to spare him, instead blaming 'that woman' for having 'turned his head', a head she had not long before said was completely empty. One of the photos fell into the hands of ex-Botafogo president Luís Aranha, who held it up during a TV sports programme and appealed to Garrincha to go back to his family.

The *Cássio Muniz Show* on TV Tupi went one better by inviting Nair to come to the studio with her daughters for an interview. At first Nair refused because she felt ashamed, but the producers convinced her and sent a vehicle to Pau Grande to pick her up. Nair, the driver, the reporter and the seven girls all piled into the car and drove to Rio.

Even with the cameras turned off, the simple matter of their entrance into the studio was emotional, and problematic. Nair and her daughters' appearance was horrendous, too much even for a sensationalist programme that went out of its way to cause scandal. The family wasn't fit to appear on television and the director had to pay for someone to go and buy dresses for the children. Eventually, with the girls in new outfits and Nair's hair and make-up given special attention by the production crew, they finally went live.

The impact was perfect: the pregnant woman, ugly, poor, and with seven daughters, dumped by the famous husband who had left her for a woman she had once invited into her own family's home. Nair was almost unintelligible, but when she cried the tears were real.

Garrincha and Elza did not tune in to the programme but they did have to deal with the repercussions. A whispering campaign went into overdrive; radio and television stations received calls saying that Elza had killed Garrincha and then herself, or vice versa. Reporters rushed to the house to check it out. The information of a double murder was passed on to the emergency services in the early hours of the morning and police and ambulances rushed to the address. Elza and Garrincha were woken up so many times one night that they had to go to Copacabana and sleep at the home of Manuelzinho, Elza's wardrobe assistant.

A few days later, Elza's daughter Dilma, then only ten years old, was sleeping in the yard at the side of the house when someone drove past and shot at the building. The bullet flew over her head and into the water tank above. Elza heard the bang and ran outside but the car had already disappeared. She asked the police for protection, but the evident lack of co-operation by the officer at the other end of the line convinced her there was only one thing to do: they had to get out of Urca.

That same April, Elza took her children, Garrincha, the mynah bird and the dog Bi and moved to Ilha do Governador, a neighbourhood far from the city centre.

Manuelzinho helped them find their new house, a pink-coloured place with a veranda and a small image of the Sacred Heart high up on the front wall. It was situated on rua Domingo Segreto, a street so new it had not even been paved. It had two storeys, three bedrooms, and several bathrooms. Elza cleaned out her bank account, Garrincha pitched in, and they scraped together enough to meet the three-million-cruzeiro price tag. They had no phone and were uncontactable – as far as they were concerned the fewer people who knew where they were the better.

Elza's romantic fantasies were realised during those first few weeks on the Ilha. They broke two beds in fewer than 30 days and eventually bought a reinforced iron one because that was the only kind capable of standing up to the almost constant activity under the immaculate and fragrant silk sheets. The baths they took together lasted hours. When they needed something, Elza rang the bell and called the butler or the servant she had hired. In addition she employed a team of cleaners; she did not want to see one speck of dirt on the sofas or Wedgewood crockery.

Elza was the opposite of Nair. She might have been a samba star and a regular on television, but if she ran her finger across the furniture and didn't smell furniture polish she would put an apron on, tie a scarf around her head and get down to work. On more than one occasion, surprised visitors arrived to find her on her knees with a scrubbing brush in hand. Her house had to be spotless.

In order for the man to match the house, Elza got all the old clothes Garrincha had brought from Pau Grande and made a bonfire with them in the garden of the house. Ripped shirts with different coloured buttons, underpants darned by Nair, moth-eaten suits, trousers that had shrunk – they all went up in flames. Then she made an appointment with the manager of a clothing shop in Copacabana and took Garrincha there. She bought him suits, dress shirts, casual shirts, Italian ties, an English sweater, a silk robe and beautiful slippers. Garrincha happily played along, and even helped her carry the bags home, but he rarely wore the new outfits. At home or in the local bars, he spent the day in shorts, flip-flops and a hat made out of a newspaper, just as he always had. The pyjamas Elza gave him never left the drawer; he only ever slept in the nude.

Elza marvelled at his health. Garrincha seemed immune to temperature, both hot and cold. He would regularly go out in the pouring rain with no coat on and return home without even sneezing. She also thought it was strange that he never appeared to sweat. Garrincha laughed: 'I am an Indian, I was brought up in the wild.' She fussed over his appearance, taking him to a dentist who treated the gaps and arches. Under the circumstances, Garrincha had great teeth.

Elza hired a cook to prepare meals for the rest of the family. Garrincha's food, however, was down exclusively to her. Elza insisted on making his favourite dishes: fish cooked in coconut milk, chicken in a dark sauce, pea soup. Years of travelling with Botafogo and Brazil had helped him get over his old preference for pasta with beans and the fridge was always filled with things to keep Garrincha happy. Elza liked to see him eat. He was well mannered, he knew which cutlery to use, and he always wiped his mouth with his napkin after taking a drink.

'You eat like a prince,' she told him.

Elza reserved special treatment for him. When he came back from training – on the rare occasions he worked out with the team during April and May 1963 – she washed, massaged and kissed his feet. She spent all her time whispering sweet nothings in his ear. And that wasn't all. Privately, she had big plans for him.

Elza had made friends with Luiz Filipe Figueira, a teacher and old Botafogo fan who lived close by on the Ilha. Elza asked him to give Garrincha some basic lessons in English, reading and general knowledge. Garrincha wasn't stupid but he had gleaned his education from conversation, not from reading. He only ever cast his eyes over newspapers or Donald Duck cartoons. He could add and subtract but not multiply or divide. He found it difficult to write a cheque. When it was a large sum or if it involved decimal places he would ask someone else to fill it in for him to sign. Nevertheless, Elza maintained a fantasy that by the age of 30 Garrincha would be able to sit a university entrance exam and get a degree in law or medicine. Figueira twice managed to get him to sit down in front of a book for half an hour. That was his record.

In her own way Elza was introducing Garrincha to a world that, for all the stamps in his passport, he didn't know existed. Elza, for example, never left her house to get her nails done, she had a manicurist come and do them for her. It was the same with the hairdresser. And she had Manuelzinho design clothes for her or she sent off for them to be made.

233

The two of them avoided going out, which was fine by Garrincha. He didn't like the beach and he wasn't interested in going to restaurants or nightclubs, even though he was a good dancer who could pick up steps with little effort. He didn't even go to the movies much, because the actors he liked – Cantinflas, Mickey Rooney, Gina Lollobrigida – didn't make many films. He didn't watch football on the television and didn't even watch the highlights programmes on a Sunday night. He preferred to watch boxing and never missed the show *Ring Rio*. Every time someone landed a big punch he would shake his head and say, 'You have to be really stupid to get involved in that sport.'

Elza's mother Rosária moved in with them. In an exception to the norm, mother-in-law and son-in-law adored each other. The two of them chased each other around the house with slippers in hand, play-fighting, giggling and trying to slap each other.

For Elza, a happy home was built on abundance. Everything was exaggerated, even the coffee, which she filled with sugar. One day she went out to buy a pair of trousers and came back with 12 pairs. Garrincha thought her love of clothes was out of hand. He certainly did not share her passion. 'I was born naked,' he would say, 'now I am dressed. And that's fine.' Simply hearing the word 'naked' set them off again, and they would get rid of their family or visitors and run for the bedroom.

It was too good to be true. And, just when the magazines started to write about the 'peace they had found together', they began, like magnets, to attract each other's ire.

Nair now had the support of dark forces. A *macumba* priest from Bahia called Derê told reporters that Garrincha was the victim of a 'gang of wrongdoers led by a woman' who had 'tied his legs'. On 16 May *O Dia*, the only newspaper to give the story any credit (the others preferred to pretend that the popular Afro-Caribbean religion did not exist), published a front-page piece under the headline ELZA BURIES GARRINCHA'S UNDERPANTS IN CEMETERY.

Derê went to Pau Grande and installed himself alongside Nair. He guaranteed that Garrincha would return. He waved his hands about mysteriously in front of her face and advised her to be on the lookout for dishonest *macumba* priests who would come after her and try to take her money. He made her promise to trust only him. He was close to Pedra Preta, a powerful *macumba* priest more adept at undoing spells, and he had her visit Nair as a way of impressing her. Derê gave her money for a first session to undo the spells, which included a big stock of *pemba* powder and the sacrifice of goats and roosters. From then on, he would always be in Nair's life.

What Derê did not know was that Elza had her own *macumba* priest, her good friend Alberto, a Bahian who lived and worked on Rio's North Side. Well known in the artistic community, Alberto's presence evened out the *macumba* war. Whenever they felt bad vibes coming from Derê's black goats Elza and Garrincha went with Araty, the man who had discovered Garrincha in Pau Grande 11 years earlier, to visit Alberto. Garrincha also had his own spirit woman, the fat and happy Oscarina, and it was to her he entrusted his knee.

Botafogo would have preferred it had Garrincha placed his faith in trainers Tomé and Adalberto. The pair had drawn up a special exercise programme that involved carrying 33lb weights up the stairs at Botafogo and cycling while wearing weighted shoes. But for every five sessions they scheduled, Garrincha turned up for only one. There was no continuity to the programme.

When he heard Garrincha was at General Severiano, Carlito Rocha came out of retirement and went to give him some encouragement. The towering Carlito looked to the sky and told Garrincha, 'God willing, you are going to play again. Repeat after me, God willing!'

Garrincha intoned obediently, 'God willing!'

Later, though, Carlito admitted he was fighting a losing battle: 'It's no use. His heart is on fire.'

If Carlito could have seen Garrincha returning home after a workout he would have seen the exact source of the flames. Elza would find him in front of their house, slumped over the wheel of his car in pain. He could hardly climb the front steps. The fire was burning inside his knee.

In addition to her fears over his knee, Elza was beginning to worry about the role alcohol played in Garrincha's life. She was well aware that he was always drunk, whether there was reason to be drunk or not. One look back at their best moments showed that there had always been a bottle between them. It had started with the *feijoada* just after the World Cup in Chile, when she had sent all her guests home so they could be alone. Garrincha had drunk gallons of the special *caipirinhas* she had prepared for her visitors. It was the same at their home in Urca, where Garrincha was rarely seen without a glass in his hand. Sometimes, when they ran out of booze, he asked her to go out and buy some more. To avoid getting caught short, she started taking alcohol with her wherever she went, along with the Frank Sinatra records he had given her.

When she left the Bon Gourmet club one night and saw he was three sheets to the wind, she asked him, 'Why do you drink so much? Don't I make you happy?'

Garrincha replied, 'One thing has nothing to do with the other.'

And it didn't, but it had everything to do with the hole that had opened up in his life since the end of Botafogo's South American tour in February. With no fixed schedule at the club, no training sessions to go to and no realistic chance of playing football in the foreseeable future, Garrincha had plenty of time on his hands. What had until then been a pleasurable pastime had become a compulsion.

His friends from Pau Grande had kept their distance from Urca; they felt it was Elza's house and were apprehensive about entering it, showing up only when she told them Garrincha had invited them. The house on the Ilha do Governador, however, belonged to them both, and Pincel, Swing and their friends would arrive without warning. They'd spend the whole day drinking, miss the last train home and stay the night. When they woke up the next morning the party would start all over again.

When Elza went into the studio or left town to play shows outside Rio, Garrincha was the king of the castle, the governor of the island. Tomorrow did not exist, and money was the last of his worries. Nothing could cloud his happiness.

CHAPTER 15

1963–1964: The Curse on
Garrincha and Elza

FROM THEIR TABLE AT A PAVEMENT BAR IN PAU GRANDE, TWO OF
Nair's relatives saw Garrincha and Elza's Volkswagen Beetle roar into
town at 50mph. One of Garrincha's daughters had contracted measles
and he had come to visit her. When he walked alone into Nair's
house a few minutes later it wasn't difficult to work out that he had
left Elza at Irene's, one of the few friends who had not turned their
backs on him when the scandal of their affair broke. Nair's relatives
went straight over, intent on venting their rage. Irene, realising what
was going on, refused to open the door but they pushed their way in
and, with their breath stinking of alcohol, began to hurl abuse at Elza.
They did not expect to get it back in spades.

They accused her of breaking up a happy home. Elza wanted to
know what happy home – the one where everyone lived off Garrincha's
money, where he couldn't even find a clean pair of underpants? One
of them called Elza a liar; Elza responded by accusing them of being
parasites. A fight then broke out, with Elza throwing a glass ashtray
and running to the kitchen to arm herself with a knife. Only
Garrincha's timely intervention stopped anyone from getting hurt. He

put his ill daughter down on the sofa, convinced the intruders to leave, and he and Elza got into their Beetle to go home. However, before he could even start the engine the pair were after them again, trying to roll the vehicle into a ditch. Fortunately, Garrincha was able to get the car started and they sped off before any real damage was done. But things were now getting serious. When they reached the Ilha, they bought a gun.

The news of the attack made headlines, and Garrincha admitted that if it was up to him he would never go home again, a comment that did not win him much sympathy in Pau Grande. And while he was bidding farewell to the town, lawyer Dirceu Rodrigues Mendes was making his introductions. Mendes was after business, and he offered his services to Nair free of charge. Garrincha was worth a lot of money and Mendes knew that Nair and her daughters had a right to 50 per cent of everything he owned. All she had to do was show him the green light.

Mendes had an office on Rio's busy Avenida Rio Branco and was famous in the legal community for his extravagant lifestyle. He rode around the city in an orange-and-blue-coloured Cadillac. He smoked cigars, told the time with an expensive Patek-Phillipe pocketwatch and wore a Derby hat to cover his baldness. He had served with Brazilian forces during the Second World War, and to hear him tell it the Nazis must have shuddered at the sound of his name. When he ran for student president while at law school in the 1940s he tried to organise a parade of camels and elephants along the main street in Catete, a neighbourhood not far from Botafogo. The rector put a halt to the planned stunt but Mendes had not lost his sense of showmanship. In Nair, he had found a client who perfectly suited his penchant for making headlines.

Nair's simplicity and lack of worldliness was even more obvious in the presence of lawyers. She was uninformed even about her own situation; the only things she ever read were horoscopes and trashy magazines. In an era when televisions were found only in the fanciest homes, Nair heard about Garrincha's antics thanks to her neighbours' gossip. Mendes told Nair to accuse Elza of exploiting Garrincha and of forcing him to buy a mansion while his wife and children were going hungry. The money that Garrincha gave her now was nothing compared to the millions he made from football. Moreover, he was living with another woman, even though he was already married. That was adultery, and enough to win a separation order in court.

Nair didn't know what to think. She wasn't sure if she wanted to divorce Garrincha. In fact, her only hope was for him to give up Elza and return to live with her in Pau Grande. She was about to have another baby and this time she was sure she would produce not just one son but two – a fortune teller had assured her of twin boys.

Garrincha and Elza, meanwhile, had their own lawyer, Dr Rubens Marçal. When Marçal heard that Mendes had been to see Nair, he went to Pau Grande armed with a written statement formalising the division of their joint goods and property. He wanted Nair to sign it and therefore avoid the possible allegation by Mendes that Garrincha was committing adultery. Nair was confused. The last thing she wanted was to separate from Garrincha. Marçal explained that the document was provisional and would ensure that Garrincha paid her a generous pension until the formal divorce came through. Nair was ready to sign until siblings prevented her.

Marçal returned to Rio and persuaded Garrincha to return to convince Nair to sign. Once again, Nair's family was hostile. Garrincha preferred to let Marçal deal with the case on his own. He would sign whatever he needed to but he didn't want to get involved personally or, if he could avoid it, see Nair again. When he wanted to see his daughters they waited for him at Irene's house.

If his reputation had hit rock bottom in Pau Grande, it wasn't much better at Botafogo. The club had given him two months to recuperate from his knee injury and he had not taken advantage of it. He almost never went to training and he refused even to think about having an operation. Botafogo were scheduled to go to Africa and Europe at the end of May 1963 and he would have to go with them because, once again, the club had signed contracts that were dependent on his appearing. Garrincha asked to be excused from the trip, claiming his knee was still giving him trouble. New president Sérgio Darcy refused.

The squad was to leave from General Severiano and go straight to the airport at Galeão. But at the appointed time Garrincha was missing, and this time the directors did not go to the Ilha, let alone Pau Grande, to look for him. If Garrincha didn't travel, he would have to face the consequences. They set off without him for the airport. The door of the Air France flight was about to close when a VW Beetle appeared on the tarmac and drove slowly towards the stairs of the plane. A smiling Garrincha got out, made his excuses to Renato Estelita and sat himself down alongside his team-mates. He didn't get a ticking off, for Estelita was relieved that he had turned up at all. But Garrincha had done what he had set out to do – scare Botafogo.

Shortly before they left Brazil a representative sent by Gianni Agnelli, the millionaire owner of Fiat and Juventus, tabled a one-million-dollar offer for Garrincha. This time the bid came from three clubs, Juventus, Internazionale and Milan, all of whom would take him for a year. They all wanted the honour of saying Garrincha played for them. It was a big transaction for all three and a tribute to the best winger in the world.

When he heard of the offer, Lídio Toledo told Paulo Azeredo, 'You know what I think? I think you should take the money and run.' But the decision was out of Azeredo's hands. He was no longer president of the club and the men who had replaced him were not about to sell Garrincha, even if it did appear to be good business. Furthermore, the Italians were at the same time offering two million for Pelé and Botafogo thought the difference too great, pretending to ignore the fact that Pelé was just 22 and Garrincha was almost 30.

The Juventus coach at the time was the ex-Botafogo manager Paulo Amaral. No one wanted to see Garrincha in a Juventus shirt more, but he was obliged to warn his employers that if Botafogo did agree to sell the transaction should be conditional on Garrincha's passing a fitness test in Italy. The Italians had no idea his knee injury was quite so serious.

It didn't take them long to get suspicious. Botafogo played two matches in Florence on that trip, losing to Palmeiras on 8 June and drawing with Yugoslav side Vojvódina on 16 June. Juventus had scouts at both games and Garrincha played poorly. They lowered their offer to $700,000.

What the men from Turin didn't know was that between the matches in Florence Garrincha had gone to Paris to play two other games, against Anderlecht on the 11th and Racing on the 13th. After playing Palmeiras, Botafogo took the train to Milan and from there flew to Paris. Garrincha sat for nine hours on the train and for several more at the airport, and then on board the plane. By the time he arrived in Paris he was in great pain. The man responsible for organising the tour had taken Garrincha aside in Paris and offered him money not to play. If Garrincha didn't turn out, Botofogo would be paid only half the agreed fee, and he was proposing to give Garrincha a cut of the money he saved. Garrincha was affronted by the dishonesty, and even though his knee was in a bad way he forced himself to strip and play. It was a brave act that would cost him.

He played against Anderlecht after having the fluid drained from his knee and then two days later he turned out against Racing. That match was followed by a lengthy train trip back to Florence and his fourth game in seven days. It was no wonder the Juventus scouts were disappointed; the Turin shroud could have performed better than he did. Only Garrincha knew the sacrifices he had made. 'I wanted to cry every time I kicked the ball,' he later told Elza.

Lídio Toledo took advantage of the team's presence in Florence to call on Dr Oscar Scagliette, the director of the Florence Orthopaedic

Centre and the man considered the best orthopaedic surgeon in Europe. After examining Garrincha, Scagliette declared that the best procedure would be to perform an osteotomy on the tibia in order to align the knee. But since his patient was Garrincha – whom Scagliette, like all Italians, knew and admired – surgery was out of the question. He would take months to recover and Garrincha was no longer a *bambino*. So Scagliette suggested a course of treatment based on corticosteroid injections.

In 1963, corticosteroid was as new and revolutionary as the Beatles. It was a violently powerful anti-inflammatory that was harmful to the cartilage and therefore used only in cases of acute inflammation. The injections could be given four times a year at most, and only then at regular intervals, and should be followed by placing ice on the wound, 48 hours' rest and physiotherapy to work the quadriceps in the thigh. It was neither a cure nor a palliative but rather a reinforcement of the real treatment, the physiotherapy.

Toledo gave Garrincha the first injection on 16 June in Florence on the morning of the match against Vojvódina. He drained the fluid from the knee in the team hotel and then gave him the first shot of xylocain; shortly afterwards he gave him another of hydrocortisone. Just as with Dr Senise six months earlier, the injection straight into the knee did not hurt. Garrincha was given an ice pack and told to rest. Two days later, he could start exercising.

Botafogo's next game was the last one of the trip and came against Karlsruhe in West Germany on 19 June, four days after Garrincha's treatment. Garrincha was ruled fit to play but he had a bad game. He was not the player he once was, and he never would be again.

On 4 June, as Garrincha was on his way from Rome to Florence, a reporter approached him with some news. Nair had given birth in Petrópolis. To no one's surprise, it was another girl: Cíntia.

'What a pity,' Garrincha said. 'I would have preferred a boy. I was going to call him Carlos.'

When he got back from Europe, Garrincha did not go to Pau Grande to see his new daughter. He had no idea what kind of welcome he would get. Or perhaps he didn't have time. For Botafogo arrived back from Europe on 23 June after a month on the road and were travelling again just four days later, this time for a 15-day, six-game trip to South America. Players of all ages – Garrincha, Nílton Santos, Quarentinha, Amarildo, Zagalo, Rildo, Manga, Aírton, Jairzinho and Arlindo – were being pushed to the limit by the club's gruelling schedule. The married players never saw their wives, fathers never saw their children, and those with injuries never got the break they needed to recover.

Toledo warned Botafogo that Garrincha's knee injury was serious enough to merit his missing the trip. Once again, his advice was ignored and Garrincha was on board the plane to Peru. He played in the first game, a Copa Libertadores tie against Alianza on 30 June, and then in the friendly against Didi's Sporting Cristal on 4 July. The next day, after arriving in Colombia, Garrincha's knee was swollen like the limb of a circus freak and he had to be sent home. Back in Rio he went straight to hospital, where the doctors who examined him were categorical: he must not kick a ball for at least 30 days.

That did not mean that he was to stay away from Botafogo; in fact, the doctors wanted him there for physiotherapy and other exercises. But on the first day he was supposed to meet with the club doctors Garrincha didn't show up. For a whole month he made appointments with Toledo and failed to keep any of them. Finally, he just disappeared. Elza was shocked. She had made a point of taking him to the club each morning and dropping him off. Garrincha had been waving goodbye, and when she was gone he had been hopping into a taxi and going to meet his drinking buddies on the North Side.

The release that same month of *Garrincha: Joy of the People* could not have come at a worse moment. The images of Garrincha winning the World Cup single-handedly in 1962, just one year earlier, and of the goals he had scored for Botafogo seemed like echoes of a time

245

long gone. The Garrincha portrayed in the film was a character from a fairy tale: the genius with a soul as free as a bird who went from rags to riches yet never forgot his humble roots. In the eyes of the public, that character no longer existed.

In his place stood a man who had abandoned the mother of his children for a famous singer, who had fought with his club over money, and who no longer flew free but sped around in a sports car. It was Dorian Gray in reverse. In less than a year, the man had replaced the myth, and no one liked the man. Even the title was a misnomer because Garrincha was no longer a joy to anyone, not even to himself.

The film bombed.

On 19 August, one month after the release of *Joy of the People*, Elza and Garrincha were driving Irene's son Nelson to the bus station when Garrincha tried to overtake and narrowly missed driving into the path of an oncoming bus. He slammed on the brakes, throwing Elza head-first into the windscreen. As the blood started to flow from the wounds where her teeth used to be, she heard voices outside the car.

'Shit, she's still alive. Why doesn't she just die?'

Eleven days later, on 30 August, Garrincha was in the car with Elza and their friend Ari when he was involved in another crash. He was on his way home from visiting his daughters in Pau Grande when a boy ran out from behind a bus parked on the hard shoulder. Garrincha wasn't able to stop in time and he smashed right into him, sending the child flying through the air.

Hours later, after they had rushed the injured boy to hospital, Renato Estelita and Rubens Marçal accompanied Garrincha to the local police station to give a formal statement about the incident. They had their fingers crossed – Garrincha did not have a driver's licence.

Garrincha was lucky. He was charged with causing injury by care-less driving and driving without a licence, but he was not detained – because he had helped the boy and, of course, because he was

Garrincha. The only way he could have avoided hitting the kid was if he had been driving a lot more slowly, or if he had been sober.

The accident got a lot of press coverage and did nothing to improve Garrincha's image. In his column in the paper *Ultima Hora*, Antonio Maria used the accident as a way of telling Garrincha that his bad luck had begun only after he accepted the mynah bird. Maria had nothing against the bird, but he warned Garrincha to get rid of it or his streak of ill fortune would continue.

It seemed as if everyone except Garrincha was hitting the big time. Dino da Costa, Vinícius and China had been transferred to Italy, Paulo Valentim had gone to Argentina and Vavá was in Spain. The recent sale of Amarildo to Milan for $400,000 had put paid to any chance of Garrincha going to Europe in the near future. The Italians had stopped making offers.

With the money they got for Amarildo, Botafogo went to Flamengo and offered Gerson a salary of 150,000 cruzeiros and a signing-on fee of ten million, exactly the same as Garrincha. On the day he was unveiled to the press at General Severiano, someone at the club suggested he pose for photographs with Garrincha's boots. It appeared symbolic, as if the old star had died or retired and the new signing was coming in to take over. The only problem was that Garrincha was alive and at that very moment sitting with his knee wrapped in towels in the physio's room. Gerson held the boots for the photographers – they both wore size 41 – but he declined to put them on; they were completely misshapen.

The boots were badly distorted because of the millions of jinks, feints and crosses Garrincha had performed up and down the right touchline. Those moves had brought Botafogo a plethora of titles and trophies, but if Garrincha was unable or unwilling to keep it up, the club would find someone who could. And they were looking not only to Gerson. Coming through the ranks from the juniors was Jairzinho, a 19-year-old prospect who had starred in the youth side that had won three Carioca Championships.

The Garrincha soap opera seemed never-ending. The fans were sick and tired of picking up the papers and reading that he was having this treatment or that and he might be back in time to face this team or that. Just as they were getting their hopes up again, another story would appear about how Garrincha had failed to keep an appointment with the doctor.

His recklessness came in spite of efforts from Toledo and Elza to get him fit again. During the second half of 1963 Toledo drained the knee on two more occasions, allowing him to play four games. When he did turn up for treatment Garrincha underwent therapy involving jets of water, infrared and heat. He worked out to build up the muscles in his thighs, but half an hour in the gym was by now sufficient to cause both his knees to swell. At home, Elza made him spend the day with his knee either covered in ice or wrapped in hot towels. She also tried to put him on a diet as his weight had risen to 11 stone 11 pounds, at least half a stone more than normal. In terms of the effect on the arthrosis, it was as if he had been eating lead. He needed to slim down.

'What a load of nonsense,' Garrincha complained, referring to the best-selling book of the time, *Calories Don't Make You Fat*. 'Everyone knows that calories don't make you put on weight.'

In August, Garrincha wore his strip only once, for a match against Santos in the Copa Libertadores, and even that appearance was more about psyching out his opponents than actually kicking a ball. Santos had won the competition and the World Club Championship the year before and Botafogo knew that if they were to stop Pelé and co. from retaining the trophies, they needed Garrincha in the side. But Botafogo needed the Garrincha of old, not the man with the dodgy knee who couldn't reach the byline. Santos won 4–0.

Elza continued to come up with alternative therapies, and at the end of September she convinced Garrincha to go to Guarapari in Espirito Santo, the state just north of Rio, to try out the sand treatment there. Rheumatics and paraplegics had buried themselves in

Guarapari's mineral-rich sands and emerged with a new lease of life. Botafogo gave him permission to spend two weeks there and Garrincha planned to sit with his knee in the sand twice a day for two and half hours each time. Unfortunately, it would only have worked had Garrincha turned up in dark glasses and a wig. Because when the newspapers announced that he and Elza were coming to town, fans turned out in huge numbers and made it impossible for him to walk even the short distance between the hotel and the beach. He had to stop every few seconds to sign autographs and the whole city insisted he visit their shops, clubs and homes. During his first three days in the town, he made it as far as the beach only once, and when Botafogo found out what was going on they ordered him to come home.

The hostility towards Elza in Rio had not diminished during her short absence from the city. She continued to receive anonymous letters and people even shouted abuse at her as she walked down the street. Groups still stood outside her house to accuse her of breaking up homes or exploiting Garrincha. One night in June, while Garrincha was in Europe, she had seen a crowd gathering outside her house and for the first time she had feared they might try to force their way in. She got her gun, went out on the veranda and fired three shots in the air. The mob dispersed, but the neighbours in what was normally a quiet suburb did not get the message. A few minutes later one of them knocked on her door with a warning: 'Elza, please be careful. There's some madman running about with a gun.'

With Mendes acting for Nair and Garrincha desperate to resolve the issue, it wasn't long before the two sides reached an agreement. It was a wonder Garrincha left the court with his shirt. Under the settlement reached in August 1963, Garrincha gave Nair their house in Pau Grande and everything in it; half the value of the flat on rua Barato Ribeiro; their country cottage in Piabetá along with the three houses built on the adjoining land; land they owned in Fragoso; and a pension of 50,000 cruzeiros a month for her and each of his daughters, a sum

249

that totalled 450,000 cruzeiros a month. The last item on the agenda would be difficult to provide, for Garrincha earned only a third of that with Botafogo. Garrincha's lawyer argued that it was too much and got it reduced to 200,000 in exchange for an immediate payment of two million cruzeiros in stocks, plus five million which the judge awarded at a November 1964 hearing to ratify the initial accord. In exchange, it was ruled that Garrincha could keep the house on the Ilha do Governador (which, although it belonged to Elza, was registered in his name); a Volkswagen; the rest of the shares; and the dog Bi, which Garrincha had insisted be included in the settlement so that Nair couldn't claim him afterwards.

Still Mendes was not satisfied. He demanded half the value of the car, half of the remaining shares and 25 per cent of all future earnings, including salaries, bonuses and signing-on fees. His intention *was* to get Garrincha's shirt. To the despair of his lawyer, Garrincha agreed to it all except the percentage of future earnings. In addition, the judge ruled that Garrincha could not take the children to Rio on the days he was given visitation rights. Nair did not want them 'frequenting Elza Soares's house', and the judge agreed. Garrincha would have to see them in Pau Grande, the one place where he was least welcome.

Mendes still had decks of aces up his sleeve. Three weeks later, he requested an audience with the judge in order to set a provisional pension for Nair. The judge agreed and Mendes asked Nair to attend the hearing with all of her children, even the baby. He arranged to meet them in the city centre, and from there they would walk to court. Two of Nair's brothers helped her travel into town to the prearranged meeting point from where they walked along one of the city centre's busiest streets, the girls following behind Nair, who carried baby Cíntia on her shoulder. Everyone knew they were Garrincha's family and a huge crowd followed behind them. It was exactly as Mendes had planned. The girls wore new dresses and clean shoes and carried crocheted bags. People offered them money; some even threw coins on the ground in front of them. For Mendes, it was a triumphant procession; a large number of those accompanying them took Nair's side against Garrincha. It more than made up for the thwarted attempt to parade with camels and elephants 20 years earlier. The judge awarded her a provisional pension of 100,000 cruzeiros a month.

Garrincha was told of the decision but he didn't care. He did not look like a man who was giving away everything he had earned in ten years as a professional footballer. In fact, he was euphoric. If that was the price to pay for liberty then he would pay it, never mind the accompanying humiliations. With his future earnings secure, he had nothing to worry about. It was all down to him and his legs.

His legs, though, were the last thing he could rely on. In that season's Carioca Championship Garrincha played in just three of the club's 22 matches. He produced few moments of inspiration and even then they were not from his trademark dribbles but from dead-ball situations, like the goal he scored direct from a corner against São Cristovão. Botafogo finished the championship in third place behind Flamengo, who beat Fluminense in the title decider.

Furthermore, the house on the Ilha do Governador, bought to serve as a refuge from the ill winds that were buffeting them from all directions, was not proving to be the safe port they had envisaged. On New Year's Eve 1963, Garrincha and Elza had a few friends round and prayed that 1964 would bring them more luck than the 12 months that had just gone by. A band played and Elza's hits blasted from the record player. Shortly before midnight, Elza went into the yard to get some of the ice they had left outside in buckets. When she climbed the steps to enter the house the fireworks were going off to signal the arrival of the New Year. All of a sudden, it seemed that a rocket had gone off right beside her – she felt something whizz past her head. She ran into the house but later discovered what it was that had almost hit her. It was a bullet. It was one more secret she kept from Garrincha.

*   *   *

In previous elections, all the politicians in Magé, no matter what party they were from, had gone to Pau Grande to pay homage to Garrincha. Garrincha had received them all, and when they had asked if they could have their picture taken he had agreed then turned and run as fast as he could – it was his way of getting away from people he considered a monumental pain in the neck. Every four years they would slap him on the back, send him baskets of food and sometimes even goats and pigs. When the election was over they would disappear. Like everyone else who lived out in the country, Garrincha regarded most politicians with contempt.

In 1955 he had voted for Juscelino Kubitschek, who won; in 1960 he had voted for Marshall Henrique Lott, who didn't. Garrincha voted for whoever Sandro Moreyra told him to vote for. During the unrest that followed President Jânio Quadros's resignation in 1961 Garrincha was the most apolitical celebrity in Brazil, although no one had the bad taste to ask him what he thought of the situation. Even when vice president Jango took over from his boss Jânio and the military started getting restless, Garrincha carried on as normal. He was busy trying to win another World Cup for Brazil as well as leagues and cups for Botafogo. The only thing he and Jango had in common was Angelita Martinez, and Garrincha wanted nothing to do with her.

Elza was different. As a singer, she was acquainted with people heavily involved with politics, and she was a friend of Jorge Goulart and Nora Ney, two well-known communist sympathisers. Moreover, she was a big hit on Radio Mauá, whose strongman Raimundo Nobre de Almeida was a close friend of Goulart's. At Nobre's suggestion, Elza had participated in several of Jango's campaigns. In 1960 she recorded a jingle for his vice president Miguel Gustavo, and in 1963, during the referendum over the parliamentary system versus a presidential one, she did the same for the presidential camp. When voters ditched the parliamentary system, Jango phoned her house in Urca to thank her personally.

The activism was not enough for Brazil's secret police to open a file on her, but she was certainly viewed with suspicion. In 1961, Elza was declared 'the Queen of the Metal Workers' after a memorable show at the union's headquarters. Around the same time she went to a barbecue at the country ranch of a left-leaning local businessman. To her it was just a barbecue with friends, but to the promoters every piece of beef that came off the grill was helping to raise funds for the Communist Party's clandestine newspaper *Novos Rumos*.

On 30 March 1964, Elza was among those with Jango during the crucial last moments of his presidency. Goulart was to speak before an audience of radical soldiers at the Automobile Club in the centre of Rio. Watching the speech on television, the hard-line anti-communist generals waited to see if he would order the soldiers to maintain discipline or if he would be vague as usual. When he spoke he appeared stoned – it was later said that he had drunk a whisky spiked with Dexamil before taking the stage – and his speech was interpreted as a tacit incitement to revolt. The address was so suggestive that it was feared the sergeants and the other non-commissioned officers would march to the Palacio de Guanabara and attack Governor Carlos Lacerda, one of Jango's fiercest political opponents. But the soldiers did not attack. When Jango finished speaking they walked next door to another room to watch a show performed by, among others, Elza Soares.

The next night, 31 March, the tanks moved on to the streets and 24 hours later Jango had been overthrown. Many people who were linked to him and his regime, and even many who were not, were persecuted. In the early hours of 20 June, ten men broke into Garrincha and Elza's house on the Ilha. They tied up Elza's bodyguard and forced Elza, Garrincha, Elza's mother Rosária and Elza's three kids to strip naked and stand facing the wall while the house was turned upside down. They didn't say what they were looking for, but amid the confusion and the shouted threats Elza heard them mention Jango's name. The deposed president had fled to Uruguay the day after the coup. The men found nothing and they eventually left, but

253

not before one of them had pulled the mynah bird from its cage and wrung its neck.

They could have been the same people who had got together once in a while to harass the couple. But these men were armed and identified themselves as members of the DOPS, Brazil's MI5. The DOPS did not waste their time with small fry such as Garrincha and Elza but there were some freelance volunteers aligned with the organisation, and some others with the army and navy, who had taken it upon themselves to go after 'subversives'. But there was no way of identifying their attackers; they did not leave calling cards.

A conveniently sanitised version of events appeared in the local newspapers two days later. The reports said that unidentified men had broken into the couple's house while they were sleeping and killed the mynah bird. According to the story, they were so quiet that Garrincha and Elza only realised what had happened when they woke up.

Elza did not want the news to become politicised and Garrincha played down the episode, saying their attackers must have been 'Botafoguenses or people from Pau Grande'. Nair, when she heard about it, accused Elza of having the mynah bird killed because her *macumba* priest had said it was bringing her bad luck.

It was hardly relevant. With or without the mynah bird, Garrincha and Elza's bad luck would continue to hang over them like a dark cloud.

CHAPTER 16

1964–1965: The End of the Knee

THE CUPBOARDS WERE BARE IN THE HOUSE ON RUA DOMINGO SEGRETO, and the fridge that had been overflowing with food and drink now had just a few bottles of water on the shelves and not even a lettuce leaf in the vegetable drawer. The local grocer had cut Garrincha and Elza's credit and the friends who were once regular fixtures in the front room had made themselves scarce. The miniature Jules Rimet trophies Garrincha was presented with for winning two World Cups had been pawned in Copacabana along with his trophies and Elza's gold discs. They were out of work, and the money was all gone. They only survived thanks to Elza's friend Manuelzinho, who brought them fruit, salami and coffee.

The television stations had stopped calling Elza. Anyone suspected of having any links to the deposed government, even professional links, was being frozen out. It wasn't that they feared Elza would get up on stage and start singing political jingles. But her ties to the old regime were clear, and those ties, especially when coupled with the damage done by her affair with Garrincha, were enough to make the TV executives reconsider hiring her.

Elza also had problems with the clubs on Rio's North Side. At one point, a mob armed with sticks and stones had threatened to stop the show if Elza took the stage. She escaped on the floor of a taxi after being helped out of the back of the club and over a wall. On two separate occasions the crowd had shouted her down, and she arrived to perform at one club only to hear the manager tell her he had removed her name from the list of the night's attractions.

In addition to being banned from clubs, her record sales were plummeting. Fortunately, she ran into a lucky streak on the *jogo do bicho*, an illegal but popular numbers game. The money wasn't much but it was enough to put some food on the table and give her a bit of breathing space. She won so often that the *bicheros*, the men who ran the games, banned her from placing bets. She had a taxi-driver friend make bets for her at different points across the Ilha, but the *bicheros* soon cottoned on and he was banned too.

In order to find work, Elza travelled to São Paulo, taking Garrincha with her. Their bad luck followed them. At the first hotel they went to, the Hotel Lord on rua das Palmeiras, they were denied a room because 'they were people of colour'. Elza kicked up a huge stink in reception, registering a complaint with the police and contacting the newspapers. Even in São Paulo, it seemed, they could not get a hearing.

Elza's only option was to give up singing or to play in places where people were so starved of top-class performers that she would be welcomed with open arms. In the second half of 1964, she set off to do a series of shows in the north-east. It was as if she had been black-balled in London and was now heading to North Wales. There, she gave shows where she could, even on the backs of flat-bed trucks. But at least she made money, the first part of which she used to pay the bills back home in Rio; the rest went on paying three months' worth of pension that Garrincha owed Nair. He was behind on his payments and in danger of going to jail.

In March, while Elza had been singing at pro-Jango political rallies, Garrincha was in Bolivia with Botafogo on a short tour that took in four games in La Paz and one in Cochabamba. He returned to a country shaken by the military coup and spent three weeks resting

his knee. In April and May he played seven times in the Rio-SP tournament. Or rather, he took to the field. Occasionally he'd get the ball
and sometimes he would try to play; mostly, however, he laid it off
to team-mate and stood where he was. The fans were furious at his
listless performances and chanted, 'Go home!' They were unaware
that they were watching a farce produced on the training ground by
Botafogo's new manager Zoulo Rabelo.

Rabelo was an intelligent and sensitive man. He instructed the
players to give the ball to Garrincha only when necessary and to let
him dictate his own pace. When Garrincha was feeling up to it he
could attempt a dribble; when he wasn't he could pass the ball back
to a team-mate who should understand the situation. Essentially, that
meant Botafogo were taking to the field with ten men, but Rabelo
also knew that Garrincha was capable of springing a surprise. And he
was right: in the seven matches he took part in Garrincha scored
three goals, against Flamengo, Santos and Bangu.

Nevertheless, when the ball arrived at Garrincha's feet his first
instinct was to panic. He knew that no matter how little he moved
he would go home in agony. Worse still, he had no idea when the
pain would subside and if it would allow him to play again. In the
past he hadn't cared, because Botafogo were obliged to pay him no
matter what. But now he had no choice. He had to play, under the
terms of the new contract he had signed at the start of the year, which
gave him a 150,000-cruzeiro base salary and 100,000 cruzeiros for
every game he played.

It was hardly a fortune, but he needed the money. So much so
that often during the Rio-SP tournament he forced himself to play
when he shouldn't have. In one game, against Vasco on 15 April, he
was so bad that the Vasco fans sang a song about their full-back having
Garrincha in his pocket. His ego was beginning to hurt almost as
much as his knees.

At the end of May, Brazil were due to take part in the Nations
Cup, an international tournament played at the Maracanã and

Pacaembu against England, Argentina and Portugal. The manager was Vicente Feola, the same man who had taken a chance on Garrincha years before. A recall for the winger would mark his first international appearance since the World Cup final in Chile nearly two years earlier. In years gone by, Garrincha's return to the team would have been cause for celebrations, but the situation was different now; many people at the CBD thought Garrincha was past it, and the stories of his drinking habits were starting to do the rounds. It was not an easy decision for the selection committee but, with João Havelange and Carlos Nascimento in favour of his recall, he made it into the squad.

When the day arrived for the players to meet, some inside the CBD were betting on Garrincha being a no-show – and, of course, he was. One director was furious: 'Get rid of that loser! We're not going looking for him like we used to do before.'

Garrincha was granted a stay, though, and he appeared the next day. He told people that his house on the Ilha had no phone (which was true), that he had seen no newspapers or television (not so true), and that he had made a mistake with the date. No one believed him, but it didn't matter. Before he could even unpack his bags, Hilton Gosling sent him to have his knee looked at by the CBD's doctors. Nine of them bent over him like the doctors in Rembrandt's *Anatomy Lesson*, and they didn't like what they saw. The doctors identified arthrosis in both knees and an acute inflammation of the tendons in the thigh – a result of the consecutive games he had forced himself to play in April. He was going to need cortisone, ultrasound and short-wave treatments as well as 20 days of rest and physio. He was ruled out of the match and sent home. Argentina humiliated Brazil 3–0 at the Pacaembu and walked away with the Nations Cup.

With Garrincha behind on his payments, a judge ordered Botafogo to subtract 40 per cent of his salary and pay it directly to his ex-wife. Nair never got it.

Nair didn't have a bank account, but Mendes did, and he convinced her she would see the money more quickly if it was paid into his account. In the end, less than half of what he received was passed on to her. The cash, according to Mendes, went on office services, expenses and, incredibly, taxes, even though under Brazilian law pensions were exempt from taxes. Nair, though, accepted his explanations without question as well as his contention that the best way to make up the difference was to squeeze more out of Garrincha.

The constant drain on his finances meant that Garrincha needed to play football and earn money. But the 20 days of rest ordered by the CBD doctors turned into almost two months, and it was mid-July before he played again, in Buenos Aires during Botafogo's four-game tour there. The pain was still bad and he managed only two matches before returning to Rio in agony. He also ignored the pain in order to play in the first two games of the Carioca Championship, but he was a pale shadow of his former self. Botafogo drew the first match 0–0 with América and lost the second 3–1 to Campo Grande, both small teams they were accustomed to beating. More than ever before, the seriousness of his injury was becoming public; every couple of weeks he was out there on the pitch at the Maracanã where the fans and the press could see the reality of his injury up close. After every frustrated attempt to dribble the ball his hand went to his knee, causing outrage among the press and even some fans. To them, it looked as if Botafogo were forcing Garrincha to play.

The truth was exactly the opposite. In fact, Garrincha was desperate to stay in the side and there was no shortage of young wingers bidding to take his place. But Botafogo had forced him to play before and the club was an easy target. At this point, the directors were extremely sensitive to criticism that they were using Garrincha. When journalist Armando Nogueira began a campaign in the *Jornal do Brasil* in support of his friend, he got anonymous phone threats: 'You either stop or we will eliminate you.' The phone rang at his house at all hours of the night with voices threatening him and his wife.

259

Nogueira believed they were coming from friends of Brandão Filho, the director Nogueira had criticised for his truculence and insensitivity, and even his dress sense. Nogueira was forced to change his telephone number.

The crisis was reaching boiling point. On 27 July, Toledo gave Garrincha an ultimatum: he had to have an operation or he would never play for Botafogo again. The problem was only going to be resolved by opening the knee and extracting the damaged cartilage. Doctors, nurses and physios were all tired of seeing him being taken to the cleaners by centre-halves and then being carried off to have his knee wrapped in hot towels.

Elza, too, had had enough. She was the only one who saw the tears before and after each game and she begged him to ignore the people praying for his recovery and have the operation. Eventually, thanks to Elza's constant nagging, Garrincha gave in and agreed to go under the knife. But even though the doctors were delighted, Toledo warned him that surgery alone was not enough; the operation's success would depend on how he behaved in the weeks after the operation. He would have to rest, turn up at the club when required, and actually do the exercises the doctors told him to do. Toledo tried to get him to sign a form 'promising to follow the post-operation treatment to the letter'.

His request irritated Garrincha. He hadn't wanted to have the operation in the first place, and he used the demand as an excuse to change his mind. 'I am not signing anything,' he said, 'and there will be no operation. What do they think? That I am irresponsible?'

That was exactly what people thought. Garrincha wasn't disciplined enough to live up to his promises, follow schedules or stick to diets. He was used to doing exactly what he wanted and getting away with it. When his legs were younger he had made up for his irresponsibility with mesmerising dribbles and goals. Now, with his legs giving way, his lack of discipline was counting against him.

The operation was postponed. His knee had improved slightly and

Garrincha wanted to play again. Toledo was against the idea and appealed to Botafogo not to let him play until he had had the operation, but they ignored him and Garrincha turned out against Madureira on 9 August. It took almost a month to recover from that. His next game was against Fluminense on 6 September, and when he came off the pitch at the end of the match the knee was so bad that it looked as if he might never set foot on a football pitch again.

Since he was playing one match then sitting out the following five or six, Garrincha asked Botafogo to pay him as if he were participating in every match. 'I hurt myself playing for Botafogo. It's more than fair,' he said. Ney Cidade Palmeiro, who had taken over as president after Paulo Azeredo's ten-year reign, agreed, on condition that he have surgery and follow the post-operation treatment. Garrincha accepted Palmeiro's conditions, but asked once again to delay the date of the surgery. Palmeiro said that was fine.

Three weeks later, Garrincha set the day for the operation. And when he announced the details to the doctors at Botafogo their jaws dropped. He was going to have the surgery with a doctor from another club.

Garrincha's friend Jaílton, a midfielder with América, had told him about his club's orthopaedist, Dr Mário Marques Tourinho. Tourinho had spent most of his career performing cartilage operations on injured football players, Jaílton told him, and had already carried out the operation on more than 2,000 people, including half the América side, all of whom had made it back to full fitness. Jaílton took Garrincha to see Tourinho at his office at the Red Cross hospital in Lapa, near Rio's city centre. There, the doctor asked him, 'Are you sure you want to have the operation?'

'I'm sure,' Garrincha answered, not really knowing where he got the courage from to sound so certain.

'Then let me have a look at you.'

According to Tourinho, Garrincha's arthrosis was in the initial stages – something that was common in players over the age of 30 (Garrincha was almost 31). The problem, he said, was the menisci. Once they were gone, the arthrosis should slowly start to get better, he said – an opinion that contradicted what the previous orthopaedists had said about Garrincha's knee. Tourinho, however, did stress that the only way Garrincha would get better was to look after himself and complete the post-surgery exercises and physiotherapy prescribed by the doctors. Garrincha agreed completely.

Tourinho was optimistic. He hoped not only to get Garrincha playing again but also to get him back in the national side in time for the 1966 World Cup. He was so keen he even waived his fee. All Garrincha had to do was pay the hospital expenses.

He also told Garrincha that it was only right he inform Botafogo of his decision to have Tourinho carry out the operation. And Tourinho, for his part, personally called Toledo to give him the diagnosis, which Toledo graciously accepted. He felt betrayed, but he could not disagree after trying for two years to get Garrincha to have the operation.

Ney Palmeiro, however, was in shock. Garrincha's decision had thrown up a lot of unanswered questions. Who would pay for the operation? Not Botafogo. And if there was a problem and Garrincha couldn't play again? Botafogo would pay the price. What about insurance? And why, after turning down Botafogo's constant appeals to go under the knife, had Garrincha agreed to have the operation done by an outsider? When Ney Palmeiro heard Garrincha answer that final question, he finally gave in: 'Jaíton tells me that it won't hurt if Dr Tourinho does it.'

The surgery took place two days later, on 29 September, at the Red Cross hospital in Lapa, and took an hour and ten minutes. Tourinho sliced open Garrincha's right knee like a fruit and extracted the internal and external menisci. The internal meniscus was wrecked and the external was going the same way. The doctor confirmed that the arthrosis was almost insignificant. The surgery was photographed with cameras that went so close to the action that they were almost inside Garrincha's leg. The scenes were like something out of a Vincent Price movie.

Garrincha spent three days in hospital with no official contact from anyone at Botafogo. The club made no comment other than to insist that the responsibility for Garrincha's recuperation rested with the doctor who had carried out the operation. The only Botafogo representative to visit him in hospital was the director of football, João Citro, and even then he went as a personal friend, and after visits by officials from Flamengo, Vasco and Fluminense.

Elza, however, was a constant companion. She spent three days sitting alongside him, stroking his head and face, feeding him his meals, shaving him, watching over him as he slept and having kittens if he so much as breathed more heavily than normal. She went home only twice, to take a bath and to see her children, and when she did so the more daring nurses lined up to watch him as he slept. Under his green pyjamas, they could catch a glimpse of his unusually big erection.

Garrincha's friends from Copacabana put together a list of people who would help pay the hospital bills, and as he was leaving the clinic someone from Zé Luiz's office turned up with a cheque for 400,000 cruzeiros. In fact, Elza had already paid with the money she had got from Radio Mayrink Veiga. Zé Luiz's emissary insisted she take it anyway. The offer came at the right time. As Garrincha was climbing the steps of his house, with Elza supporting him on one side and Sandro Moreyra on the other, he was told that Botafogo were fining him 70 per cent of his monthly salary for disobeying them and having the operation with another club's surgeon.

Thirty-eight days later, on 4 November, Tourinho gave Garrincha a clean bill of health and handed him over to the doctors at Botafogo. He went to the club, did a few exercises, and all seemed well. And then, just when it looked like he would finally have some peace in which to work on a comeback, the black clouds moved in overhead once more. Nair's lawyers tried to seize his house. The five-million-cruzeiro cheque he had given her as part of the divorce settlement had bounced.

Garrincha needed cash, and he needed it fast. He sold the rest of his shares, getting the best price possible, and transferred the money to his bank account. But between the money arriving in his account and writing a new cheque to Nair, Garrincha spent with characteristic generosity and irresponsibility. And, as usual, he didn't bother to balance his chequebook. So when Nair went to cash the new cheque, that bounced too. Her lawyer asked the judge to seize Garrincha's house and he agreed. If he didn't get the five million cruzeiros in five days, his house would be put up for auction.

Garrincha went to the Botafogo directors and asked for a loan, one he offered to repay with the signing-on fee from a future contract or with his part of a transfer fee. Ney Palmeiro and Brandão Filho turned him away. They still felt betrayed by Garrincha's decision to have Tourinho carry out his operation and they were not interested in hearing about his personal problems.

Moreyra tried to convince them with a political argument: 'How do you think it looks for Botafogo if one of its players has his house seized? Especially Garrincha. Think about it, this news will go all round the world.'

'They can go to hell,' said Brandão Filho. 'He can work it out with that woman of his.'

As Moreyra had warned, the news did go all round the world, and it was embarrassing for all concerned. But it also caught the eye of Alfredo Monteverde, the owner of Pon to Frio, a chain of shops that sold household appliances such as fridges, washing machines and televisions. Monteverde contacted Garrincha and discreetly offered him money on the condition that his identity not be revealed. Garrincha happily accepted and offered to repay him in some way. For the next two months he appeared in Pon to Frio adverts. His house was safe.

Back at Botafogo, the directors felt that if they had to put up with Garrincha's behaviour off the pitch then at least they should make him play on it. They charged the club's new trainer, Admildo Chirol, with bringing him back to full fitness. Head of the medical department, Dr Nei Mendes de Morais, Ney Palmeiro's son-in-law, told Chirol, 'The physical aspect is down to you. But the medical side of things is something else. If he wants so much as an aspirin, he has to ask Tourinho.'

Botafogo's doctors had still not forgiven Garrincha for going behind their backs to have the operation, but they couldn't be sure that if they had carried out the operation themselves the result would have been different. With or without menisci, Garrincha's arthrosis was continuing to grind away inside his knee. It wasn't long before the swelling returned – and it wasn't as insignificant as Tourinho had believed.

The arthrosis hampered the work of Chirol, whose job was to strengthen Garrincha's thigh in order to reduce the burden on the knee joint. His right leg was thinner than his left as a result of muscle atrophy, and to make matters worse he had put on weight – he was carrying nine pounds more than before. Garrincha spent the rest of 1964 in physiotherapy, and in 1965 he played his last 23 games for Botafogo. Or he pretended to.

It was a tumultuous time for the club and they hired and fired several managers, none of whom was able to count on Garrincha for important matches. In 1965, he was good only for the foreign tours, such as the one in January to Peru and Mexico. But if the club believed that foreign crowds would be more tolerant of a crippled Garrincha they were mistaken: the Peruvians and Mexicans had seen him when he was in his prime and the fat, clumsy man on the wing was not the Garrincha they knew and loved. Botafogo sent him home halfway through the tour.

When the rest of the team got back to Rio, the press got hold of an internal memo written by Citro, the director of football who had led the trip. The memo said that Garrincha was unable to play football, but that his situation 'should not be revealed as he could still be sold'.

265

The rumour doing the rounds at the time was that Santos had tried to buy him for $500,000. But even though Santos were said to have given up the attempt, it was a hard story to believe. That same week, in the São Paulo State Championship, Pelé scored eight goals in an 11–0 drubbing of a team from Ribeirão Preto and four more in a 7–4 defeat of Corinthians. Why would a team like Santos want a player so obviously in decline?

When he heard about the memo, an exasperated Garrincha asked, 'If I am finished and not worth anything then why not give me a free transfer? Why ask for so much?'

By the middle of 1965, Botafogo had stripped Garrincha of all his old privileges. With Jairzinho, Rogério, Biachini and Sicupira all vying for a chance to wear the number 7 shirt, he could no longer command a regular place in the side even when fit. He was stung by the humiliation and eventually, when his contract was up, he approached Citro with a new proposal – to go to Mexican club Veracruz on a free transfer, spend a year there and return to end his career with Botafogo.

Citro refused even to consider the idea. He was not going to let Garrincha go on a free transfer so that another club could get a last good year out of him. So Garrincha came up with another pay-per-play proposal: 400,000 cruzeiros for every game in Brazil and two million for each one abroad. The club's older directors knew that a pay-per-play deal would be a financial disaster for Garrincha and managed to convince their colleagues on the board that their ageing star deserved a more charitable deal. The contract offered to Garrincha in April 1965 – 800,000 cruzeiros per month and 150,000 per game – was a good one, and he accepted it. As far as Botafogo were concerned, Garrincha should have been rubbing his hands at the deal.

He certainly had little else to celebrate. His life with Elza on the Ilha was becoming a nightmare. It seemed as if everyone knew where they lived, and on Sundays anyone who went near there to visit friends, to fish or even just to hang out paid a visit to 'Garrincha's house'. Most people looked on from afar, but some were more daring and would shout insults and abuse. Even the house itself continued to be a cause for upset: every time Garrincha fell behind on Nair's pension Mendes threatened to come and seize it.

It was not the idyllic home they had dreamt of. In the two years since they had moved in Elza had been attacked, the house had been invaded by armed men, it had been seized by lawyers, an encyclopedia of abuse had been thrown at them and the letter box had been filled with anonymous threats. The final straw came when Elza found a *macumba* spell under her bed. She was terrified. Anyone who could break into her house was capable of doing a lot worse than casting a spell.

So in April, Garrincha gave Bi to a friend and he, Elza and her children left the house and moved into a rented flat in Ipanema. They wanted to start afresh.

'Let's swing it / Let's sing it / Let's dance samba / Let's swing / And leave life's sadness behind. / How does love begin? / It begins with swing / How do you cure pain? / Singing. / So let's swing / And leave life's sadness behind.'

It might not have been 'The Girl from Ipanema', but it wasn't bad for a beginner. Released on Elza's record label it was called 'Prescription to Swing' and was written and sung by 'Manuel dos Santos (Garrincha)'. The idea came from a 1964 song called 'Balançamba' in which duo Menescal and Bôscoli sang, 'If you can't swing, ask Garrincha to teach you how.' Garrincha decided to do just that.

In truth, Garrincha had whistled a tune and Elza, with hundreds of lyrics in her head, had helped him write the words. Months later Elza recorded another song written by Garrincha called 'Round Foot'. But although 'Prescription to Swing' was a minor hit, neither record brought the singer – and certainly not the composer – much glory.

The two songs were part of Elza's plan to depict Garrincha as a cheery and optimistic man who was overcoming his recent setbacks. She had managed to hide his increasing tendency to hit the bottle, one best shown by his inability to wait until lunchtime to have his first drink. By now, Garrincha was pouring himself a *caipirinha* after breakfast, and his drinking had not been helped by the fact that when they moved to Ipanema, Pincel and Swing had practically moved with them. When Elza complained about his drinking in the mornings, Garrincha shot back, 'I like my lime, Crioula. Does there have to be a specific time when I do the things I like to do?'

By counting his intake, Elza calculated that Garrincha was drinking more than a litre of hard alcohol every day. She had no idea how he managed to drink so much and not get drunk. At Botafogo, where he trained in the afternoons, no one imagined that the man Chirol was putting through his paces every day could have that much alcohol in his bloodstream. They knew he drank, but they didn't know how much. If they had, they might have understood why it took so long for him to recover from injury.

Their new home at 371 rua Visconde de Piraja, in the heart of Ipanema, was their first apartment and the walls were not as thick as those in the house they had owned together on the Ilha do Governador. There, they had not had to censor themselves when they made love. Here, though, it was different. When their neighbours on the fourth floor banged on the walls with slippers in order to get them to keep the noise down they realised everyone could hear what they were doing.

During his first few years with Elza, Garrincha was a model of fidelity; he got rid of all his mistresses and never thought of replacing them with others. His passion for Elza neutralised his desire to sleep with anyone else. If there was any playing around at all then it was with the servants or cleaners when Elza was on tour – something she must have worked out because when she returned from one trip she fired them all. When she was around, Garrincha didn't want to know about anyone else. They were not shy; they would go at it even when friends were around, at one point sneaking off for a quickie while Miéle and Bôscoli sat in the front room. They came back 15 minutes later, straightening their clothes and with a smile on their faces.

But while Garrincha and Elza's sex life kept them deliriously happy, the tax man also had reason to be delighted. The authorities had discovered that Garrincha owed them 12 million cruzeiros in back taxes. After taking interest and the recent currency devaluation into account, he owed 44 million cruzeiros, or about $22,000 at the exchange rate of the time. The only place he could imagine finding that amount of money was at the end of a rainbow.

A representative of the court turned up at Botafogo every day hoping to speak to Garrincha about his debts. But Garrincha was wise to him and left instructions with the security and doormen to detain visitors at the entrance and then come inside and tip him off. The men who worked the door at Botafogo were experienced in such ruses; there was always someone there trying to force Garrincha to pay Nair. By the time they let the official into the dressing room or on to the training pitch Garrincha was long gone, having disappeared out of a side door. Nevertheless, despite his diversionary tactics, he was perplexed to find that he owed money. 'I didn't know I owed anything,' he said. 'When I travelled with Botafogo or Brazil, they always put a "paid" stamp in my passport.' Garrincha didn't realise that the stamps were provisional ones given to anyone travelling with the club or national side. Without them, one could not leave the country.

Had Garrincha really thought about it, he would have recalled that he had never filled out a tax-return form. This hadn't been an issue before 1964 because until then no one in Brazil was required to pay taxes, not even professionals such as judges or journalists. But when the military came to power they shook things up and the man in charge of Brazil's Inland Revenue went after those who owed money.

Many people were hit in the crackdown. At Botafogo, Nílton Santos, Didi and Zagalo also had enormous debts. They had public support, though, with many people asking why the IRS should go after these relatively small fish when there were so many sharks swimming around with impunity. Writers Nelson Rodrigues and Paulo Mendes Campos appealed to their friend Roberto Campos to pardon the players as national heroes, invoking the US government's decision to waive the huge debt incurred by ex-heavyweight boxing champion Joe Louis. Campos, though, was the Minister of Planning, not the Minister of Finance, and even had he been he wouldn't have lifted a finger to help. If the government gave amnesty to the stars at Botafogo they would have to do the same for players at other clubs. Then judges and journalists would want the same treatment. Moreover, any amnesty would have to be approved by Congress, and following the recent political turmoil that wasn't a likely scenario.

To clear their names, Nílton Santos, Didi and Zagalo paid up, even though it meant taking a big chunk out of their savings. Nílton Santos sold an apartment he was building in Botafogo and Didi and Zagalo cleaned out their bank accounts. Garrincha, though, didn't have that kind of money, or anywhere to get it from. He was rescued thanks to the timely appearance of another guardian angel. This time his saviour was João Havelange.

In 1965, the CBD president was sure of two things: one, that Brazil would win the World Cup for a third consecutive time in 1966; and two, that with that prize under his belt nothing could stop him being elected president of FIFA in 1970. With Pelé, and possibly Garrincha, a third title was in the bag. There was nothing to stop Pelé going to England to defend the trophy, but Garrincha was not the player he had once been and he needed help. The CBD would do anything possible to help him get back to the sort of form that had won them the cup in Chile. The first step was to pay off his debt. The second was to get him back in the national side and motivated to turn it on again.

So Garrincha paid the tax man and made Feola's squad for the short tour to Algeria and Europe in June. He played in the three warm-up games at the Maracanã against Belgium, West Germany and Argentina and travelled with the squad on 11 June. However, his best performance of the tour came in the airport's departure lounge, where he put on a scene for photographers with his passionate send-off for Elza.

Garrincha featured in the first two matches of the tour, against Algeria in Oran and against Portugal in Porto: he played poorly in the first and was unrecognisable in the second. The final two matches were against Sweden in Solna and the USSR in Moscow. Feola, if he could have, would have dropped him for both games. He didn't want Garrincha to lose heart by producing sub-standard performances in matches with nations against which he had done so well in the past. He managed to rest him for the Sweden game, but he put him on in place of Jairzinho – the young winger who had taken his place in the Botafogo side – for the second half of the match against the USSR. The Soviets needed only a few minutes to see that the player who had destroyed their 'scientific football' just seven years earlier was finished.

Garrincha's return to Brazil was not as triumphant as his departure. The fans had listened to the games on the radio and seen the pictures on television. All their illusions had been shattered. Havelange, though, thought they needed to persist. He wanted Garrincha to be 'saved' for the 1966 tournament, and to do that he came up with the extraordinary idea of buying him from Botafogo. The CBD would turn Garrincha over to a team of coaches, preferably in São Paulo, who would hone him into prime physical condition for the tournament. All of which implied that Garrincha was a certainty to go to England, even with the World Cup still 12 months away and even though he would spend a year without playing any competitive matches. Somebody, though, must have talked Havelange out of it, because the idea was dropped before Botafogo were even approached.

Garrincha returned to Botafogo, and after a month of inactivity he played out his last glorious moments at the club. Manager Daniel Pinto put him in the side for three successive Guanabara Cup matches against América, Flamengo and Vasco. To the surprise of doctors and with no apparent explanation, Garrincha was back to his brilliant best, playing with no pain and no swelling. His single goal sunk Flamengo, yet again, on 22 August. Between games he underwent a punishing training regime and suffered no adverse reaction. In the training games of attack against defence he went past Rildo with ease, and Rildo was Nílton Santos's successor at full-back. It was a miracle. It looked as if Garrincha was back. Only no one could say for how long.

Botafogo, worried that his new-found form wouldn't last, left him out of the next few Guabanara Cup games in order to make sure he was available for their lucrative friendlies in the provinces. Garrincha rebelled and refused to travel, saying, 'I'm not good enough for the Maracanã but I'm good enough for the provinces? They're better off sending someone else. There are loads of right-wingers around here.' Garrincha failed to turn up for the trips to Barra Mansa, a small town west of Rio, Vitória, the capital of Espirito Santo state, and Salvador, the capital of Bahia. He wanted to prove he was still competitive and capable of playing at the highest level, and he believed that his only stage was the Maracanã. Botafogo didn't see it quite the same way and fined him.

Once again, war broke out between Garrincha and his club. Garrincha started turning up late and missing training sessions. He was ordered to train with the reserves, and then in October he was banned from Botafogo entirely. The directors turned their backs on him when he sought them out and the situation worsened to the point where Carlito Rocha advised the club to let him go. Even his team-mates turned against him. Their trips were cancelled when he refused to travel and they missed out on easy bonuses.

Their attitude was hardly fair. On the one hand, they didn't like it when Garrincha was picked to play in competitive matches because it was like playing with ten men. But then they were happy for him to be in the team for friendlies against the weaker provincial sides because his presence, like a bear at the circus, guaranteed a big crowd, higher gate receipts and a bonus.

The players also snubbed him in other ways. As she did every year on 18 October, Garrincha's official birthday, Elza laid out a new linen tablecloth, bought a cake shaped like a football pitch, and invited round friends, journalists and team-mates for a celebratory drink. This year, though, only Nílton Santos and trainer Admildo Chirol turned up. There were more players there from other teams than from Garrincha's own. When the Botafogo players saw Chirol's photo with Garrincha in the paper the next day they gave him the cold shoulder too.

Nineteen sixty-five marked the end of the great Botafogo side. The team had lost Didi, who was forced to end his career in Peru. Nílton Santos retired in March, aged 39, angry at directors who refused to give him a testimonial. Zagalo was increasingly hit by injury and also hung up his boots, becoming the youth-team coach. Gerson and Jairzinho had established themselves in the first team but were not yet international stars. The team created by Renato Estelita and João Saldanha in 1957 was no more.

Like his good friend Nílton Santos, Garrincha would also miss out on a farewell match. His last appearance for Botafogo was on the opening day of the Carioca Championship against Portuguesa on 15 September. It was a Wednesday night, and 5,309 people turned up at the General Severiano stadium. The crowd was almost within touching distance of the players but Garrincha had never been further from the fans. There was no love, not even any hate, between them, just a mixture of pity and indifference.

When he took the field that night, neither they nor Garrincha knew the game was to be his last in a Botafogo shirt.

'Garrincha, I trust you. Iraciara.'

When Garrincha got to his car he found that the door was already

273

open. On the back seat was a little dark-skinned girl of no more than six months with a note sticking out of her nappy. Someone had left her for Garrincha to find. He took the child home, and when no one claimed her, he and Elza decided to keep her as their own. That version of the story, published in *O Cruzeiro* at the end of 1965, was dramatic, but it wasn't true.

Iraciara – or Sara, as she was called – was in fact born not far from the home of Alberto, one of Elza's closest friends in Colegio, a neighbourhood on the North Side. Her father was 16 and her mother just 14; there was no way they could look after her. They gave the baby to Alberto, who in turn asked Garrincha and Elza if they would raise it. They agreed, and went to a registrar in Copacabana officially to declare the baby their 'natural daughter'. The real story was no less moving than the one published in *O Cruzeiro*, but perhaps the fantasy was easier to accept. It was a pity that Alberto had been left out of it.

It was Alberto, in his role as *macumba* priest, who advised Garrincha and Elza to get out of Rio. By now the whole city, and not just Botafogo, had turned against them. Alberto believed they could make a fresh start in São Paulo. Corinthians had shown an interest in buying Garrincha many times, and when the club's manager Oswaldo Brandão – who went to *macumba* priests and knew of Alberto – heard Garrincha might be available, he fought to sign him.

But there were other, less mysterious forces pulling Garrincha towards Corinthians. In January 1966, the club was entering its twelfth year without a title and president Wadih Helu needed to make a big-name signing to pacify those who were ready to force him out of St George's Park on the end of a lance. The fans believed Garrincha was back in form, and they were desperate to have him.

Garrincha would later say that Botafogo sold him to Corinthians without consulting him, but in fact Jango's government had passed legislation in March 1964 making it illegal to sell a player against his wishes and ensuring that the player on the move received 15 per cent of any transfer fee. On 6 January 1966, a week before signing terms,

Garrincha went to São Paulo for a medical exam and posed for photographs with a Corinthians shirt. His price tag was 220 million cruzeiros (about $100,000), or one tenth of what the big Italian clubs had offered just two years earlier. The 15 per cent came to 3.3 million cruzeiros and was paid by Botafogo. No one from the club came to see him off. The directors were happy to see the back of him.

On 14 January, Garrincha put pen to paper on a two-year deal with Corinthians which gave him a monthly salary of 200,000 cruzeiros and a signing-on bonus of 12 million to be paid in 24 monthly instalments of 500,000 cruzeiros. It was a package equivalent to 700,000 cruzeiros, or a little more than $300 – less than he had been earning at Botafogo, but at least he would play, get paid bonuses and receive a percentage of what the club got for foreign friendlies. And then there were the fans, who turned out in great numbers to welcome him at the city's airport.

When Garrincha got off the plane two local journalists again had him pose for photos with a Corinthians shirt, this time as a fully signed-up player. Few people noticed that it wasn't a number 7 but a number 10 shirt they had hurriedly picked up from Rivellino, who lived just around the corner from the airport.

Corinthians gave Elza and Garrincha everything they had agreed to. They picked up the tab for Garrincha and Elza's move to São Paulo, enrolled her kids in a good school, and found them a flat that met with all Elza's specifications: a big living room, four bedrooms, all already decorated and in one of the city's most chic neighbourhoods, in front of the bar Roma in Higienópolis.

When Elza saw the new flat, she threw open the curtains and windows and announced to the directors and journalists trailing behind her, 'I am going to start life afresh here.' However, she was not taking any chances. As soon as her visitors left she had Alberto wash down the flat with the sea salt used in Afro-Brazilian religions to ward off evil spirits.

The next night, Alberto had more work to do. Brandão took him

275

to St George's Park after all the players and officials had gone home. The only people there were security guards and no one saw them walk out on to the pitch. Brandão asked Alberto to look for buried frogs under the playing surface as only a *macumba* spell could explain why Corinthians had gone so long without a title. With his ability to see the unseeable, Alberto immediately went to one of the goals and started digging, and there, a little below the surface, he unearthed some small bones wrapped in a bag tied with butcher's twine. He replaced the soil and guaranteed that Corinthians could from now on depend only on themselves if they wanted to win a trophy.

To avoid any financial complications, Garrincha wrote a letter to Corinthians formally requesting that the club deduct the rent from his salary every month. It was 430,000 cruzeiros, more than half his pay, but with the revenue Elza was making from performing they did not envisage having money problems. He also instructed them to discount Nair's pension – 200,000 cruzeiros – and deposit it straight into the bank.

When all Garrincha's commitments were met, he was left with 70,000 cruzeiros a month, or about a tenth of what he was paid. More than ever before, he would depend on his ball skills to keep him alive.

CHAPTER 17

1966–1967: Finished

ELZA AND GARRINCHA HAD BEEN IN THEIR NEW FLAT FOR LESS THAN a week and already the neighbours were threatening to call the police. They had never seen, or rather had never heard, anyone make such a racket in the bedroom. They went at it all night, stopping only occasionally for 15-minute breaks to get their breath back. For Garrincha, sex was a sport that gave him as much pleasure as football. The neighbours were not impressed.

Garrincha and Elza never felt at home in São Paulo, and during their first few months there they returned to visit Rio several times. Elza was also travelling to other states every weekend to perform. She didn't want to; if possible she would have spent every minute at home in order to keep Garrincha under control. His new club didn't know it but his alcoholism had intensified over the previous 12 months. When he was in Ipanema, he had no longer restricted himself to drinking at home, where Elza could see him. Several times she had woken up to find he had sneaked out and gone to the bar on the corner for a drink. It was not uncommon to see him sitting there at eight a.m. nursing a huge *batida* cocktail. He eventually stopped going there because it was also a popular spot for other famous actors and personalities. He didn't like to be seen drinking in public.

Elza had hoped that being in a new city and playing with a new club would help Garrincha recover his enthusiasm for football and in turn help him stop drinking, or at least persuade him to cut back a bit. At the start of his stint in São Paulo, Garrincha really was enjoying himself, but by then he couldn't have stopped drinking even if he had wanted to. Even his friends from Rio, who knew how much he loved a tipple, were shocked when they arrived to visit and saw him open the door with a drink in his hand. They knew it meant only one thing: that Elza was on the road. Garrincha never dared to drink so heavily in front of her.

Elza tried to put temptation out of harm's way by getting rid of all the alcohol they had in the house but she never trusted Garrincha not to sneak in some supplies and she would undertake periodic sweeps of the flat looking for a secret stash. Even though she never found any, she was still suspicious, and she was right to be. Garrincha had taken apart the easy chair in little Sara's room and for months he had a secret bottle of *cachaça* hidden in there. Whenever Elza left the apartment he would undo the tacks, pull the *cachaça* out and take a slug straight from the bottle – he knew she would sniff the glasses when she returned. Then he would suck mints to mask the smell on his breath.

Elza eventually found that particular hiding place, but Garrincha soon came up with others. When she wasn't there he would empty bottles of tonic water and fill them with *cachaça*. Or, like Ray Milland in *The Lost Weekend,* he would tie a bottle to a length of string and hang it out of the bathroom window.

By now, Garrincha wasn't drinking for pleasure. His body needed alcohol: only another drink would get rid of the shakes that hit him when he woke up in the morning. Those who saw him after he'd had his first drink of the day would never have noticed any difference. And, for a while, few people in São Paulo realised he had a problem.

Garrincha arrived at Corinthians tipping the scales at 12½ stone, more than a stone overweight. Before the club signed him he was examined by orthopaedist João de Vicenzo, who X-rayed his knees and found nothing wrong; he needed only to lose some weight and recover the muscle strength in his right leg. In order to do that, the club put him under the guidance of specialist fitness trainer Haroldo Campos. Campos had him lift weights with his leg and prescribed a diet that would enable Garrincha to start training with the rest of the squad in 30 to 45 days' time.

The whole city had faith in Garrincha's ability to regain top fitness and only a few of them had any reservations about his age. Garrincha was by now 32 years old, but in São Paulo there were players such as Djalma Santos, who was almost 37, Mauro, who was 36, and Dino Sani, who was 33. All of them were older than Garrincha and still going strong. And of course, everyone knew about Stanley Matthews, who had retired the year before aged 50.

Even though he was drinking heavily, the exercise regime helped Garrincha slim down. He wore a plastic shirt during training, lifted 220lb weights with his leg, and took part in workouts with all the enthusiasm of a youngster trying to break into the first team. He wasn't ready to play a competitive match – he was still playing only one half of matches in training – but the pressure from the directors and the fans forced Oswaldo Brandão to put aside his scepticism and name him in the team for the game against Vasco at the Pacaembu on 2 March, just 40 days after his arrival at the club.

That week, Elza went to all the bars around St George's Park to beg the owners not to serve Garrincha if he came looking for a drink. The waiters laughed – Garrincha was already a regular. Elza persisted. When Garrincha went with the rest of the players to the team hotel on the eve of the match she booked a room in order to keep an eye on him. She didn't want to take any risks.

On the night of his debut, several Carioca residents in São Paulo went to the Pacaembu to lend Garrincha their support. Neivaldo, Pampollini and Cacá, all formerly of Botafogo, and Dida and Henrique, both ex-Flamengo, were there to cheer him on. They were all friends of Garrincha's, even Neivaldo, whom Garrincha had kept out of the Botafogo side for eight years. When he was asked if a player as good as he was minded always being on the bench, Neivaldo was offended. 'I wasn't kept out of the team by just anyone,' he countered. 'I was kept out of the team by Garrincha.'

A crowd of 45,000 turned out to see Garrincha make his debut and they were eager to see him put on a good show. They didn't have to wait long to see him involved in the action. With his first touch Garrincha gave the ball away, and with his second he was easily dispossed by Vasco centre-half Oldair. He got past Oldair shortly afterwards but fell over the ball, and the defender cleared the danger. Garrincha then took another pass, but he couldn't control it and it ran out for a throw. The game was less than five minutes old and he had done nothing right. The crowd murmured uneasily and his teammates, perceiving the unrest, thought it best to keep the ball from him for the next 15 minutes. When they gave it back to him, Oldair robbed him and then dribbled round him so nicely that Garrincha fell on the ground. The terraces fell silent. When half-time came, Pampollini, Cacá, Dida and Henrique didn't stick around. They were so embarrassed that they went home, and Neivaldo hadn't even stayed that long: he had left the ground with tears in his eyes after only ten minutes. It was perhaps just as well. In the second half Garrincha hardly touched the ball, and when he did he got rid of it as quickly as he could. Vasco won 3–0.

The next game came eight days later at the Maracanã against Botafogo. Lining up against him were Manga, Rildo, Gerson and Jairzinho. Botafogo hammered Corinthians 5–1 and Garrincha's threat was nullified by Rildo – the same man Garrincha had run rings around in training just a few months previously – with laughable ease.

In his next game on 21 March there was more disappointment: a 2–1 defeat to Palmeiras, with Garrincha missing a penalty two minutes from the end.

There were some bright moments. With Garrincha in the side,

Corinthians beat São Paulo and Flamengo, drew with Santos and ended up winners of the Rio-SP tournament. Or rather joint winners, because Corinthians, Botafogo, Santos and Vasco were all tied at the top of the table and with the World Cup looming there was no time to play the deciders. All four clubs were declared champions, although none of them put it on their pennants. Not even Corinthians, who needed to record a triumph more than most.

Around the same time, Garrincha had something worth putting on his own personal pennant – his new marital status. His formal separation from Nair – divorce was still not legal in Brazil at the time – had come through on 27 November 1965, and in March the following year he and Elza filled out the forms that would enable them to marry at the Bolivian embassy in Rio. The process was not cheap, but it was straightforward. Brazilians paid Bolivians living in Santa Cruz de la Sierra for permission to use their names in a civil marriage ceremony. Cristían Chavez Pedraza and Mercedes Abrego Justiniano were the Bolivians chosen to represent Garrincha and Elza, and permission came through on 11 March. One week later the embassy informed them that the documents confirming them as married were ready. On 31 March, they went to the embassy to pick up their wedding papers.

Elza and Garrincha knew that the marriage counted for nothing in Brazil but it was a gesture both wanted to make. For them, it was a piece of paper that recorded their eternal love.

'Without Garrincha there will be no third World Cup.'

Nílton Santos repeated the statement over and over to reporters. But in private he wasn't so sure. And the reality would prove that with or without Garrincha, Brazil did not prepare for a World Cup in England, but for a farce.

At the end of March, the CBD announced a squad of no fewer than 45 players, 46 counting Amarildo from Italy, the first footballer playing outside Brazil to make the national side. Of those, 24 would be cut before the plane took off. Of the remaining 22, nine players would have previous World Cup experience: Gilmar, Djalma Santos, Bellini, Orlando, Altair, Zito, Dino Sani, Garrincha and Pelé – and all of them bar Pelé were there not because they were playing well but because they had been good servants. The CBD wanted them to become three-time World Cup winners. The top men at the confederation thought the 1966 World Cup would be a walk in Hyde Park.

Feola, whose heart condition left him in a more precarious state than ever, was manager again. Paulo Amaral refused to return as trainer and was instead given the assistant manager's job. His post as trainer was filled by João Havelange's son-in-law Rudolf Hermanny – a judo professor, not a football trainer. Higher up the ranks, Paulo Machado de Carvalho lost the battle of egos with Havelange and refused to lead the delegation. One of the names floated to replace him was Zé Luiz, but he turned down the opportunity. With no other options, Havelange himself offered to take on the task of leading the delegation and bringing home the cup. From the moment the team first met up at the Hotel das Paineiras on 12 April until the day of their opening match against Bulgaria on 12 July, they would have three months in which to train, find a settled side and get ready to defend the trophy.

They had never been given so much time and they were confident of victory. The CBD paraded the squad all over the country, as if on a premature lap of honour. Dozens of cities had fought for the privilege of hosting the squad but the CBD limited themselves to choosing just four: Lambari, Caxambu, Teresópolis and Serra Negra. They were all sleepy provincial towns, ideal for retirees and newlyweds. But the only place they got any peace, not counting the flyovers of the Brazilian Red Arrows, was Lambari.

On arriving in Caxambu on 19 April, the players found themselves in the middle of a war. The town was not happy that the squad had gone to Lambari first and had prepared a festival of events designed to humiliate their rivals. For ten days the players ate at banquets, watched school parades, hoisted flags and watched foundation stones being laid in buildings that would become fountains, crèches, and even a dentist's clinic. The town's female choir sang serenades outside the players' hotel at one in the morning, preventing them from getting any sleep. When Feola tried to impose some order the locals started calling him 'Fatso', and Feola got so angry he threatened to punch somebody. At the training sessions open to the public, the fans booed the players and Paulo Amaral threatened to jump over the fence and lay into them.

In Teresópolis, the squad was welcomed by the town's mayor with a band, a committee from the Lions club and a performance by Horácio, an amateur trapeze artist who rigged up two trapezes from local buildings and threw himself off holding on with his legs. That same week, a well-known TV presenter offered a fortune to anyone who could bring Pelé to a TV Globo studio, and with tens of thousands of people just down the road in Petrópolis there was concern that someone desperate enough for the money would kidnap him and take him there. To make matters worse, Gerson had drunk so much mineral water in Lambari and Caxambu that he developed kidney trouble and was out of action for a week.

Garrincha, of course, had his own troubles to deal with. While he was in Lambari and Caxambu, his letterbox back in São Paulo was filling up with court summons regarding Nair's petition to adjust her allowance. With Elza travelling and away from the flat, the letters went unread, and the first Garrincha knew of them was when Mendes burst on to the airport concourse as the players met up before heading to Teresópolis. After elbowing his way through the reporters, photographers, players and fans, he poked Garrincha in the chest and tried to force him to sign a judicial order obliging him to appear before the judge.

When he heard the commotion, Carlos Nascimento tried to remove the lawyer. Mendes, however, was not intimidated. He whipped out the ID that proved he was a judge and declared that just one call to

283

the police would result in Nascimento being arrested. A devastated Nascimento backed down; he had never seen anything like it in all his time with the national team. Garrincha, deeply ashamed, signed the document right there in front of his team-mates. Mendes wanted Nair's pension increased from 200,000 to 700,000 cruzeiros a month, an amount equal to Garrincha's entire salary with Corinthians.

The 46 players at the CBD's disposal were enough to make up four teams and still have a couple of subs left over. In three months of preparations, they played countless matches against one another, as well as against Brazilian club sides and rival international teams. In not one of the games did the same side play twice. Every possible line-up was tried and tested.

Cuts, however, were necessary, and week after week heads rolled as the squad was trimmed to get closer and closer to the final 22. But even when the squad left Brazil on 17 June it comprised 27 players: the final five would be cut in Europe. In the midst of this sinister lottery, the players didn't concentrate on playing as a team: they were more interested in excelling individually and avoiding the chop.

Only two players didn't go all out to impress the manager: Pelé, because he didn't have to, and Garrincha, because he no longer had the skills to. In training, he avoided the byline as if it were infested with rattlesnakes. When he got the ball, he laid it off again as quickly as he could. If he found himself in the box with no defenders near he might shoot or fire in a perfect cross, but if he had to dribble past a marker, and that marker was Rildo or Paulo Henrique, he knew he'd be dispossessed. The two other candidates for the position on the right wing were Jairzinho and Paulo Borges of Bangu, one of the era's hottest prospects. Borges was so fast they called him 'the gazelle'. But Feola sacrificed him in order to hold on to Garrincha.

During one of their rest periods before the cup, Garrincha went home to São Paulo and confessed to Elza that if it were up to him he'd rather not go to England. He knew he no longer had what it took to play in the World Cup finals. But there was nothing he could do. He had to go, as he explained to Elza: 'If I don't go and Brazil lose, they'll say it's my fault.'

Elza could have come up with professional reasons to go to England and be by her husband's side. But she thought it best to stay in Brazil – if Garrincha played poorly she'd get the blame. Instead of spending her money on an airline ticket to London, she bought candles, stayed at home and prayed for a miracle.

But no amount of candles or prayers would have been sufficient for that Brazil side. In Europe, they played six times prior to the finals: once in Spain, once in Scotland and four times in Sweden. They scored a barrowload of goals and were fêted by the press. One English newspaper wrote, 'Left-backs of the world unite. Garrincha has returned.' But *Sun* journalist Peter Lorenzo had seen Brazil play in Spain, Scotland and Sweden and saw things more realistically. The Swedish teams Brazil had hammered were hardly tough opposition. His conclusion: 'Bellini and Garrincha are dead.'

Even Brazilian spy Ernesto Santos was pessimistic. After giving Feola a dossier that lauded the superior fitness, teamwork and football of England, West Germany, Hungary and Portugal, he told his boss to forget about seeing the Jules Rimet trophy back in Brazilian hands: 'We'll need a miracle if we're to win the cup again.'

It was all happening in London in 1966. Mary Quant had invented the mini skirt. The Beatles were about to record *Sgt Pepper's Lonely Hearts Club Band*. Italian director Antonioni had just filmed *Blow-up*, after painting the London grass because he didn't like its natural colour. Men and women were parading down Carnaby Street with the same haircuts and violet suits: from behind it was impossible to tell them apart. Thousands of youths took LSD and thousands more pretended they did. High culture was out and high fashion was in. Everything was mad, modern and psychedelic in swinging London.

The Brazilian team didn't get as much as a sniff of that swing.

Their base was in Lymm, 188 miles outside London. It had all the hallmarks of Charlotte Brontë country – dark, distant and sad. Someone had told the players it was unsafe to go out at night and many of them were afraid to set foot outside the hotel. Instead, they stayed in their rooms, which were singles, not doubles, so they were on their own, and they hated it. They had no television or radio and none of them spoke enough English to be able to read the papers. The hotel was depressing, and they wouldn't have been surprised to hear the ghostly sound of chains rattling along the corridors. The food was just as bad. The players had heard a rumour that they were being served horse meat and the majority opted to eat only potatoes and cabbage. They were unhappy and isolated. It was hardly the ideal atmosphere in which to be preparing for the World Cup.

The training ground was an hour from the hotel by train. They had been playing together for three months, but neither Feola nor Nascimento had decided on their ideal first team. And they never would: in the three games Brazil played during the tournament they used 20 of their 22 players. The team changed from game to game and no one understood why, not the reporters, not the players, not even the manager or his assistants.

Brazil scraped a victory in their opening game on 12 July, beating Bulgaria 2–0 with Garrincha and Pelé scoring from set-pieces. As they had feared, they lost the next match, on 15 July, 3–1 to Hungary. After that defeat the players went to Feola and asked him to come to a decision about the squad once and for all. They didn't care who was in and who was out, they just needed to know; the uncertainty was driving them mad. At that, Nascimento deposed Feola and assumed control of the side for the last game against Portugal on 19 July, axing nine players, including Garrincha.

Some 5,000 Brazil supporters made the three-hour train journey from London to Liverpool to watch their side play. Two huge containers with tambourines and drums had passed through British customs on the eve of the Hungary game, only being given the all-clear after officials had been convinced that what was inside was not going to be used for voodoo. If the customs men had waited any longer they would not have needed to open the containers at all. After losing to Hungary, the majority of the fans went ahead and booked their flights back to Brazil on 20 July, the day after the Portugal game.

To qualify for the next round, Brazil needed to beat Portugal by three clear goals. No one in London, not even those high on LSD, believed such a scoreline was possible. And they were right. The Portuguese, managed by Brazilian Oto Glória, had Mozambiquan centre-forward Eusébio in their line-up and they dispatched Brazil 3–1.

The 1966 World Cup might have been a disaster, but it was momentous for at least one reason. The Brazil–Bulgaria game marked the end of the most magnificent chapter in Brazilian football history. Brazil's opener was the last match in which Garrincha and Pelé played together for the national side.

Since the first time they had played side by side in a yellow shirt, at the Pacaembu in 1958, coincidentally also against Bulgaria, they had never been on the losing side. Brazil had lost with Pelé in the side, but never when the two of them were on the field at the same time, and never when Garrincha was on the pitch. Brazil–Bulgaria in 1966 was his fifty-ninth cap, and his record until then was 52 wins and seven draws. His first loss came in the next match, against Hungary. It would also be the only one, because it was to be Garrincha's last appearance for Brazil. The unbeaten pair continued unbeaten because Pelé missed the Hungary match through injury: and in the third game, against Portugal, Pelé played but Garrincha didn't. If the statistics were anything to go by, Havelange was right in fighting to have Garrincha play alongside Pelé. Together they were invincible.

This World Cup was the last Brazilians would follow by radio, for in 1966, television was still rare, and although taped highlights were shown two days after the matches took place only 21 million people watched, half of them crowded into their neighbours' houses to see the action. In contrast, 60 million people listened to the games live on the radio, including Elza and her son Carlinhos in São Paulo. When Garrincha put away a free kick in the sixty-seventh minute of the match against Bulgaria, Elza dispatched Carlinhos to the post office to fire off a telegram: BRAZILIANS DELIRIOUS OVER YOU STOP KISSES IN THE HEART STOP CRIOULA. But in reality Elza was a woman in love using poetic licence to encourage her husband. The fans were hardly delirious. The team was a huge disappointment.

In the three and a half months he spent with the national squad, Garrincha worked hard in the knowledge that it was all or nothing. He knew this might be his last chance for a cap. He took part in all the training sessions, did special workouts and lifted tons in order to reinforce the muscles in his legs. Off the field, and to the surprise of many, his behaviour was also impeccable. Even when the players were given time off and allowed to stray from their base, Garrincha never left his room. But he was using the time to drink. Garrincha had managed to smuggle a bottle of booze into his hotel room. He could no longer get through the day without it, especially first thing in the morning. And it wasn't only because he was far from his wife and his home. It was the same desperate situation back in Brazil. When he returned to São Paulo at the end of July, no one could stop him.

On 9 October, as the teams were lining up for the Santos–Corinthians game, Zito told Garrincha, 'Don't try any fancy stuff with me or you'll get it.'

When they played together for Brazil they were good friends, but it was a different story now they were on opposing sides. The photo of Zito's tackle on Garrincha became a classic: Zito, his villainous eyes shining, his teeth gritted and his arms outstretched like a ptero-dactyl; Garrincha in mid-air, falling, with a desperate look of pain in his eyes. Zito had caught him on the knee. Years later, Garrincha would rub the place where Zito had caught him and say, with no trace of either rancour or fondness, 'Thanks, Zito.'

The 3–0 defeat by Santos was Garrincha's last game for Corinthians, but not because of Zito's crunching tackle. That appearance was only his third for the side that year, and even then the previous two games had been friendlies in Spain where his presence in the side guaranteed the club a bigger pay day. Oswaldo Brandão had left the club to be replaced by Argentine Filpo Nunes. Nunes felt no obligation towards Garrincha and soon relegated him to the reserves. Before long he was not even in the running for a spot on the bench.

Nevertheless, Garrincha outlived Nunes. In the second half of 1966 the Argentine was fired and replaced by Zezé Moreira. Garrincha was delighted: the new manager was an old friend of his and he had high hopes of regaining his place in the team. But not even Zezé's arrival was enough to get him his place back. His knee might not now be swelling after every game but he didn't have the speed over the first few yards, or the balance, the mobility or the stamina Zezé had seen in years gone by and the new man refused to put Garrincha back in the starting line-up. He discreetly told his friends in Rio, 'It's sad to say it, but Garrincha is finished.'

The fans who were fighting to oust Corinthians chairman Wadih Helu used Garrincha as a weapon, accusing Helu of wasting the club's money. Helu, however, survived the attacks and never let Garrincha down. He gave him the wage increases he had promised – his basic salary at the end of 1966 had risen to 500,000 cruzeiros – and he paid him the agreed bonuses. Altogether, counting wages, bonuses and signing-on fees, Garrincha earned 12 million cruzeiros at Corinthians that year – all for playing just three matches.

In December, Garrincha asked to be put on the transfer list. He wanted to go back to Rio, and Helu gave him his blessing. Garrincha still had a year of his contract to run but even Helu could see no reason for his staying. He could not let him go for free, of course, as the fans would only accuse him of wasting the club's money again. So he agreed to sell him for 300 million cruzeiros and waited for offers to arrive.

Unfortunately, none was forthcoming. No one wanted a player as useless as Garrincha.

Garrincha and Elza returned to Rio in January 1967 and rented a beautiful house overlooking the Lagoa, the city's picturesque lagoon, on Avenida Borges de Medeiros, 3207. They didn't know it yet but they would spend the following years living off Elza's money.

Garrincha knocked on the doors of many clubs looking for an opportunity for a comeback. The doors opened for him, but only the legend was allowed in; the professional who stubbornly refused to retire was left out in the cold. The first to disappoint was Botafogo. The side was now trained by Zagalo and Chirol and his former team-mates offered a warm welcome, giving him permission to work out with the team in order to keep himself fit until another club made an offer. Garrincha took part in two or three training sessions, coming on as a sub in games between the reserves and the youth team. But if he was dreaming of coming home he was deluding himself. This was the new Botafogo of Gerson, Rogério, Jairzinho, Roberto, Paulo César and Carlos Roberto. With those names in the side, Botafogo would win the Carioca Championship in 1967 and 1968 and once again provide the players that formed the backbone of the Brazilian side. There was no room for someone who had played back when Biriba was a star.

With no chance of a comeback at Botafogo, Garrincha went to Fluminense, a team now managed by Evaristo, the man who had played alongside him in the Botafogo–Flamengo select that had beaten Honved ten years earlier. Evaristo had no space for him, so Garrincha went to Vasco and spoke to their boss Gentil Cardoso. Cardoso, who had been Garrincha's first ever coach, remembered him with fondness but couldn't offer him anything other than a place in a Vasco side that was due to play a friendly in São Paulo.

If there was a lesson in these repeated refusals, Garrincha didn't want to learn it. Moreira and Cardoso, who knew him so well, could see that his career was over. Zagalo and Evaristo, his old team-mates, had known when it was time to hang up their boots and turn their attention to coaching, but Garrincha continued to drag his unwanted legacy from club to club, embarrassing friends who had never expected to see him begging for a game.

For the first time, Garrincha spoke of the possibility of a testimonial. The game would be between a Brazil XI and a Rest of the World Select, with the proceeds split evenly: half to him and half to his daughters. It would be an elegant way of sparing him any further financial embarrassments. He would simultaneously help his daughters and assure his own future – if he didn't fritter away the cash.

The project, however, never got off the ground. Garrincha was furious when he heard that the CBD, who would sponsor the game, were planning to withhold his share of the proceeds for five years. 'I am not a child,' he said. 'They either give me the money or they tell me straight up that they don't want to give me it.' There was also the suggestion that he walk across the pitch with his daughters, an idea that didn't please Elza: 'Why don't they just have him pass a collection plate around the terraces?' Garrincha said he wanted a testimonial, not charity, and vetoed the idea. 'I don't need to say goodbye,' he insisted. 'I still have years of football in me.'

But even Brazilian kids could see that Garrincha didn't have any football left in him – he didn't even make their table-football teams. Worse than that, people were starting to lose respect.

At TV Tupi, where Elza was appearing every Friday night on Bibi Ferreira's show, Garrincha would sit patiently and wait for her to finish her rehearsals. He sat at the back of the stage with his head bowed, bothering no one. But his presence was not always appreciated, and one Friday a young man from production came up to him and demanded he move.

'You can't stay here. Get out!'

Garrincha got up and left without saying a word.

Marília Barbosa, one of the other singers performing that day, witnessed the incident and was horrified. Even though she was only 19 she knew very well who Garrincha was and what he stood for. She was saddened by the humble way in which Garrincha accepted the order to move.

Elza continued to try to rein in his alcohol intake. She managed to stop him from drinking at home and was encouraged to see him take pleasure in fishing again. Garrincha crossed the road to the lagoon every afternoon and brought back a net full of fish to prove he really was spending his time fishing, not sitting in a corner somewhere throwing them back. But he would return with a new air about him, the euphoria of someone who had had a few. When Elza confronted him, he denied it. She knew he wouldn't interrupt his fishing every 15 minutes to head for the bar, so she surmised that he must be taking a bottle with him. When she decided to follow him one day, she discovered that he had buried a bottle of *cachaça* in the sand at the edge of the lagoon. Elza actually caught him in the act of digging it up, but it didn't seem to upset him. He had an answer for everything: 'Have you ever seen anyone fish without having a drink, Crioula? The fish would be offended if I didn't have a nip!'

In the middle of the year, Garrincha at last found a club that would have him: Portuguesa, a small club from the Ilha do Governador. Businessman Aderbal Savóia had arranged for the club to play 17 friendlies in western Brazil and Bolivia – on the condition that Garrincha go with them. Portuguesa got 800 new cruzeiros for each game, which, with the government having cut three zeros off the old cruzeiros (an accounting measure after inflation sent the currency soaring), was equivalent to 800,000 old cruzeiros. Garrincha was paid separately, and more than the other Portuguesa players: 1,000 new cruzeiros per match. By the time he got back to Rio three months later he would be owed 17,000 new cruzeiros, or close to $6,000.

Garrincha and his new team-mates went by plane from Rio to Goiânia in central Brazil and then south by train through Mato

Grosso state to Santa Cruz de la Sierra, Cochabamba and La Paz. In each city, the fans turned out to see Garrincha and ended up seeing only the man marking him. He started every game with a few tricks and at first the opposition's full-back was worried, but it took only a few minutes for the defender to discover he had nothing to fear and he was soon dispossessing his more illustrious opponent with ease. At that point, Garrincha lost interest and waited for the half-time whistle to blow so he could go off and let Almir Lima come on in his place. He was booed off the pitch in the first game in Goiânia and in the majority of the others.

Not that he cared. The games were just friendlies and the players were allowed to do pretty much anything. His colleagues didn't seem to mind either, not when he didn't train with them and certainly not for having a couple of bottles of cognac in his hotel room.

Almir Lima was his room-mate for the trip. Every morning Lima watched Garrincha wake up with the shakes; he could hardly light his cigarette his hand trembled so much. He was unable even to have breakfast without first gulping down a brandy and lime.

In the town of Três Lagoas, Garrincha met a dark-skinned beauty who was a dead ringer for Elza and he took her with him to their next stop in Campo Grande. The team travelled by train in the first-class carriage, except for Garrincha, who had secured a private cabin for himself and his new lady. When they got to Campo Grande he bought her a ticket back to Três Lagoas.

He rarely went out with his team-mates at night, preferring to stay in his room drinking. One of the few occasions he did venture out was in Corumbá on the Bolivian border where he paid the madam of a brothel to give him and the other players the run of the place. It cost him a whole game's salary. When he left La Paz at the end of the tour in December he was in for a shock. The businessman who had signed him up with the promise of big bucks had disappeared without paying him a penny.

During his month on the road, Garrincha did not pay Nair her

monthly allowance. His payments had been getting gradually less reliable, particularly since Corinthians had stopped automatically debiting his account. Mendes waited for the situation to become untenable
and then kicked up a fuss. In January 1968 the newspapers reported
that Nair and her daughters were starving. They owed money to the
local grocer, butcher and cobbler. They were getting by thanks only
to Nair's siblings. In order to buy food, the girls were selling off the
presents – radios, clothes and cushions – that Garrincha had brought
them from Europe the year before. There was no money for medicine when they got ill and any health problems were treated with
home-made potions. Their oldest daughter Terezinha had lost a finger
in a work accident at the factory and couldn't work. More than ever,
Pau Grande wanted to drown Garrincha in Dove Doze, the town's
well.

At Mendes's request, judge Áureo Bernardes Carneiro summoned
Garrincha to appear at a hearing on 27 January. He didn't turn up
and didn't send a lawyer to represent him. On 2 February, Mendes
formally asked the court to arrest him and the court accepted, setting
Garrincha's debt at 2,600 new cruzeiros and giving him a month to
pay up or face jail. But Garrincha continued to ignore the court, and
when the judge heard arguments on 6 March he sentenced him to
three months in prison. When reporters turned up at his house to
inform him of the judge's decision, Garrincha appeared genuinely
surprised. 'Why are they doing this to me?' he said. 'No one came
looking for me or questioned me, and yet they find me guilty.'

That was not quite true. In fact, Garrincha had received the first
summons asking him to appear in court, and he had even signed it.
But that did not mean his comments were purely cynical: he was drunk
when he signed the paper and had not even bothered to read it. It was
no excuse, but his no-show could indeed have been a result of his
knowing little about what was actually going on. The truth was that
with no work and no money he did not have the 2,600 new cruzeiros
– almost $1,000 – he needed to pay Nair. His understanding of the

divorce settlement was also confused. 'If they come to arrest me,' he said, 'I will go with a clear conscience because under the settlement I don't have to pay an allowance if I don't have a contract to play football. And if I am in jail, I can't pay because the prison side doesn't pay bonuses.'

Elza, meanwhile, had been on tour in Mexico for two months and was about to go to New York to sing at the carnival balls at the Waldorf-Astoria. She had no idea of the storm brewing in her absence. Without her, Garrincha passed his days in an alcoholic stupor and was unable to think straight. It didn't even occur to him to call his new lawyer, Dr Roberto Pontes. Pontes found out about the latest scandal only when the stories appeared in the newspapers the next day.

Mendes alleged that Garrincha had stopped paying Nair's allowance in April 1967. But Pontes, who had jumped on the case after his rude awakening by the papers, showed the judge receipts, countersigned by Mendes, that proved Garrincha had paid Nair in both May and June. He might even have paid other months, but those were the only receipts Garrincha could provide – he was not one for paperwork. Time was running out if they were going to stop him going to jail.

Court officials were typing up the arrest warrant when someone from Zé Luiz's office found the judge and handed over a cheque for 2,600 new cruzeiros. Just like in the films he had watched when he was a kid in Pau Grande, where the hero escaped just seconds before his car fell over the edge of the cliff, Garrincha had been pulled back from the precipice.

From that particular precipice, at least. There would be others. The wheels were still perilously close to the abyss.

CHAPTER 18

1968–1969: Blood on the Motorway

WHEN GARRINCHA LOOKED IN THE MIRROR IN JUNE 1968 HE SAW WHAT the fish must have seen when they looked up at him through the murky waters of the Lagoa: a grotesque and deformed caricature of a man. He was two stones overweight, flabby, swollen, and had big bags under his yellowing eyes. Two thick creases had developed on either side of his increasingly bulbous nose. He had lost control of his drinking. Elza was out of town performing, and with no one to keep an eye on him he was hitting the bottle morning, afternoon and night. The only time he emerged from his alcoholic stupor was when he tried to live out the fantasy that he could still play professional football.

In the first six months of 1968 several foreign clubs expressed an interest in signing him. A New York club called Toro contacted him through Elza's agent. Garrincha did not reply. Boca Juniors from Argentina and Nacional from Uruguay wanted to see him, and he went to both countries to train. Both clubs took one look at him and decided it wasn't worth the gamble. Atlético Junior from Barranquila in Colombia opted to give him a chance and sent him a plane ticket and a cash advance. It was a disaster. After his one and only appearance for the team, fans gathered outside the stadium and tried to attack him. He was sent home after only a week.

The news that Garrincha was going to Colombia in August piqued the interest of Nair's lawyer. In June, Mendes had talked the state governor into giving Nair's dependants 250 new cruzeiros every month until Garrincha could get his financial affairs in order. At the same time, Nílton Santos convinced Botafogo to chip in with a monthly stipend of 200 new cruzeiros. But when Mendes heard that Garrincha was leaving Brazil he became worried that he might sell everything and disappear. So on 19 August he petitioned a judge once again to seize Garrincha's assets. This time, though, Mendes was too late – there were no more assets to seize. The house Garrincha owned with Elza on the Ilha do Governador had been lost to a loan shark. The couple's chronic financial disorganisation had cost them in the past, but until now the losses had been small. This was their first big loss, and it would not be their last.

When João Saldanha and commentator Jorge Curi heard that Garrincha was signing with Flamengo they thought it was a joke. It was too ridiculous to be true.

However, the news they had got from Radio Nacional was confirmed. Three Flamengo players, Silva, Carlinhos and Paulo Henrique, all of whom had played alongside Garrincha during the 1966 World Cup, had asked manager Walter Miraglia to give him a chance at the club. Miraglia consulted with trainer José Roberto Francalacci, who told him that if they gave him a few months he could get Garrincha back into shape even if only to play friendlies outside the city. So Flamengo announced that if Corinthians would release him from his contract they would sign him. Corinthians tried to negotiate, initially hinting that they would sell him only for 300 million old cruzeiros, but after a few weeks they gave in and sent Garrincha to Flamengo on loan.

Flamengo did not sign Garrincha out of kindness. The club had not won the state championship for three years, they were in financial trouble, and no one wanted to pay them to travel for friendlies.

Garrincha's presence would be a big draw for the side when they went to play in the north and north-east. His recovery, though, was so complicated that Francalacci had to ask the club's two doctors to help out. They were too busy to devote the time needed to get Garrincha back into shape, so Francalacci asked orthopaedist Paulo Calarge to assist him. Calarge, who was a Fluminense fan, wouldn't get paid, but that didn't discourage him. The chance to rehabilitate a superstar everyone thought was finished was a fascinating challenge.

Garrincha arrived at Flamengo on 21 September 1968, less than two months after being unceremoniously chased out of Colombia. His weight had ballooned to more than 13 stones. Calarge measured his legs and found that his right leg was just over one inch longer than his left, not two inches as had been previously believed. Calarge manufactured special inserts for his shoes to compensate for the difference, and to reduce the stress on the pelvis and therefore the pressure on the shorter leg. The arthrosis had worsened and new fragments of bone were now loose in the joint. Another operation was pointless as it would just be a quick fix, like the one performed by Tourinho. What Garrincha needed was to lose weight and build up his leg muscles in order to reduce the rate at which the arthrosis was developing. It was not mission impossible.

Calarge imposed only one condition. 'First things first: you have to stop drinking.'

Garrincha nodded his head.

Just as he had done during his first few days at Corinthians, Garrincha worked hard at getting back into shape. Every day, Francalacci would be alongside him in the gym or as he ran along the beach at Leblon. Sometimes they would go for a sauna at the nearby Monte Líbano club, where Garrincha would sweat out enough alcohol to leave his fellow users half cut. No matter what their programme for the day entailed, Francalacci picked him up in the morning and handed him over to Elza when they were finished. She played her part by joining him on a macrobiotic diet, working out alongside him in their gym and even skipping with him. She had vowed to shave her head if Garrincha played football again, and she did just that.

Francalacci's main concern was how to control Garrincha's drinking. He began by warning the other players not to go to bars with him or even to sit down and share a *guaraná*. Then he turned his attentions to Pincel and Swing, both of whom would wait for Garrincha to finish training and take him for a drink afterwards, just as they had done in the days when he played for Botafogo. Francalacci took them aside and told them it had to stop.

'Lads, you like Garrincha, don't you? If you do, do me a favour and don't come round here looking for him any more.'

They listened, and stayed away from the ground. But no one could stop them going to Garrincha's flat. The fact was that Garrincha could not live without them.

Until then, all attempts to rehabilitate Garrincha had floundered because no one, not even the doctors, knew how to diagnose alcoholism. When they told him he needed to stop drinking, they genuinely believed he would be able to stop, that it was simply a question of deciding when to drink and when not to. Even after he arrived at Flamengo no one thought to put him on a treatment programme, without which playing football or doing anything else was destined to fail.

Doctors prescribed Antabuse, a drug that reacted with alcohol to produce vomiting, nausea, rapid heartbeat and other unpleasant effects. Elza was instructed secretly to mix it in with Garrincha's food, and when he had a drink after taking it for the first time he was on the street and didn't know what had caused him to vomit. When he drank secretly at home and then threw up in front of Elza she was scared and eventually told him what she had done. Garrincha was furious, and Elza never gave it to him again.

In return for Elza and Francalacci's efforts, Garrincha promised to try to drink less, and he seemed to be managing to curb his intake, although some people still reported seeing him drinking in bars close to Flamengo's training ground in Gávea. Francalacci even discovered that Garrincha was drinking right in front of him using his old trick of pouring *cachaça* into a bottle of tonic water.

Flamengo remained confident that he would turn himself around and gave Garrincha a generous contract that included a 50,000-new-cruzeiro signing-on fee, 3,000 new cruzeiros per game (in lieu of a fixed salary), and an additional 500 new cruzeiros monthly allowance. Garrincha asked for and got a new grey Galaxie car to replace his 1960 Ford Comet, which he had crashed once again on the Rio-Magé road a few months previously. The contract ran until 31 June 1969.

The partnership between Garrincha and Flamengo had the potential to be a good one for both sides, but there was also a symbolic aspect to the unlikely relationship. Although he had been a Flamengo fan as a child, as a player Garrincha had been the club's *bête noire*. During his 12 years with Botafogo, Garrincha played against Flamengo 38 times, winning 15, drawing 11 and losing 12. There wasn't a lot in it until you looked back and remembered the games. The image that most stuck in the minds of Flamengo fans was of Garrincha skipping effortlessly past Jordan, and they would not forget that almost all of the 12 goals he scored against them were crucial ones – especially the brace he got in the 1962 final of the Carioca Championship when Botafogo won 3–0. Garrincha seemed to have an Indian sign over Flamengo. Even when he went to Corinthians, a club for which he played few matches and won even fewer, he was in the side that beat Flamengo 3–1 in 1966. Now, at the age of 35, he would finally be turning out for the team he was used to beating.

Some 70 days after starting his treatment, on 30 November 1968, at a trim 11 stone 2 pounds and having played only one warm-up match, Garrincha made his debut for Flamengo against Vasco in the Taça de Prata, or Silver Cup, as the Brazilian League Championship was then called. Both teams were doing poorly in the tournament, so poorly that they had scheduled the meaningless mid-table encounter to take place on a Saturday night. The presence of Garrincha, however, had energised the city.

The spectacle was impressive; hours before the game people made their way to the stadium in cars, trains, buses and on foot. Everyone wanted to see Garrincha play. The official attendance was put at 79,694, but perhaps as many as 20,000 more fought their way into the lower terraces. Pelé was a guest of honour in the stand.

When Garrincha walked on to the pitch he received the biggest ovation of his life. Eberval, the Vasco full-back charged with marking him, was trembling with fear. The reporters who followed Vasco couldn't see why he should be afraid. Eberval could snuff out Garrincha simply by standing his ground, but the full-back lacked confidence and was scared that he'd be humiliated. When Garrincha dribbled past him for the first time, the photographers behind the goal heard Vasco centre-half Fontana scream, 'Stop being a wimp, get into him!'

Until that point, Eberval had marked Garrincha fairly, and although he was nervous he had done well. But after taking the heat from Fontana, Eberval's tactics changed and he laid into Garrincha. The next seven or eight times he got the ball, Eberval pushed, kicked or stamped on him. Once, the Vasco player even punched Garrincha in the stomach, right in front of the referee, who didn't pay the slightest bit of attention. The crowd didn't like it, and Eberval and Fontana were booed even by their own fans, many of whom wanted to see Garrincha do well. At the end of the first 45 minutes Garrincha twisted his ankle in a hole left by a divot and didn't come out for the second half. When he left the pitch he got an even bigger ovation than the one that had greeted him 45 minutes earlier. The fans wanted to believe they had seen a resurrection, and that if it hadn't been for Eberval's violence Garrincha would have hit the byline whenever he had wanted to.

Those 45 minutes were enough for the city's Museum of Sound

and Image to award him their annual Athlete of the Year award. It was ironic because Garrincha was in reality no longer an athlete; he had become more of an artist, an actor who simulated playing football. Garrincha took advantage of the prize to complain that he had been forgotten, and to allege – falsely – that the CBD hadn't invited him to the recent dinner to commemorate the tenth anniversary of the 1958 World Cup win. The dinner had taken place in July in a restaurant in Leblon, and Garrincha, like all the other members of the side, had been invited. The envelope marked with the CBD's badge had arrived at his house on the Lagoa but was thrown in a drawer without even being opened. Once again, Garrincha was refusing to take responsibility and blaming other people for his own mistakes.

In January 1969, thanks solely to Garrincha's presence, Flamengo set off on a marathon tour of nine games in 18 days that took them from Dutch Guyana (now Surinam) to the Brazilian cities of Manaus, Belém, Natal and Salvador. Garrincha played games on alternate days, a schedule that would have been too much even for a player in his prime. When he did play, though, he didn't do much, and when the crowd applauded after he'd dribbled past a defender he was quickly subbed so that they would be left desperate for more. In Manaus, against Fast Clube, he scored a goal, and the match ended there and then when the crowd invaded the field and hoisted him on to their shoulders.

It was on that trip that Flamengo discovered that Garrincha didn't really have a desire to play football any more. All his work under the direction of Calarge and Francalacci had served only to show in that one game against Vasco that he was not finished as a footballer. But what happened after he had proved his point didn't seem important to him. On the trip up north he returned to his old ways, slipping the reins he himself had imposed. The doctor shared a room with him on the trip, but to Francalacci's despair Garrincha abandoned his diet and returned to satiating himself with food and sex. Halfway through the trip he even caught gonorrhoea. Needless to say, he hit the bottle hard too. In Manaus, he let the crowd carry him right out of the stadium and no one saw him again until he turned up at the hotel hours later, dead drunk.

On his return to Rio in the middle of February, it took Garrincha almost a month to get back into shape. During that time he and Elza were forced to vacate the house on the Lagoa when the landlord ended their tenancy, and they moved into a flat in Copacabana a few blocks from the sea.

The 1969 Carioca Championship soon got under way, and although no one believed he was able to play in competitive matches, Garrincha held his place in the starting line-up, perhaps because he was still such a huge draw. Whatever the reason, Flamengo were unbeaten in their first four matches, up to and including a 1–0 win over Campo Grande at the Maracanã on Saturday, 12 April.

The day after that game, Garrincha drove to Pau Grande to visit his daughters. His adopted daughter Sara and his mother-in-law Rosária went with him. Death caught up with them on the way home.

Whenever Garrincha went to Pau Grande to see his daughters he would drive to the corner of his old street, peep the horn, and a few seconds later the girls would appear and funnel into his car. He would take them for a drive, and then on the way home stop off to buy them chocolate. While they picked out sweets, he would go to Dódi's bar, where he played cards with his old buddies and threw back three or four Garrincha-sized cachaças. When he was finished he'd shout for the girls to get back in the car and then drive them home again. The visits lasted a little more than two hours.

Sometimes Nair would be out on the veranda when he dropped the girls off, but he tried to avoid any contact with her. He almost always had someone with him, either his Portuguese friend Manuelzinho, one of Elza's sons – Carlinhos or Gilson – or, once Pau Grande had accepted it as inevitable, Elza herself.

That Sunday, though, no one wanted to go with him. Not Manuelzinho, not Edgard Cosme, who lived with them in Copacabana, not Elza's sons, and especially not Elza. The night before she had dreamt of a car accident and two bodies on the side of the road. She did not want to be in a car, especially when she knew that Garrincha would be well oiled by the time he drove home. Garrincha dismissed her fears with a laugh, and his mother-in-law Rosária offered to bring Sara to keep him company.

They arrived in Pau Grande, where Garrincha carried out his regular Sunday ritual. When he was finished, he dropped the girls off and set off for home. Rosária and Sara were alongside him in the front, while a cage containing a bird someone had given him sat on the back seat. It was almost seven p.m., and it had just got dark.

On the main motorway that connects Rio and São Paulo, a lorry carrying 132 sacks of potatoes turned out of the tax office set up at the side of the road to monitor cargo trucks. Garrincha was approaching at more than 50mph with his headlights switched off. When he saw the lorry loom out of the darkness in front of him it was too late to do anything. He tried to swerve but he was going too fast and he rammed straight into the back of the truck. The Galaxie somersaulted three times, throwing Rosária through the windscreen.

The men working in the tax office heard the crash and managed to flip the upturned Galaxie over and pull the blood-soaked bodies of Garrincha and Sara from the wreckage. They knew immediately who they were dealing with because Garrincha was screaming at the top of his lungs, 'Help me! I'm Garrincha! I'm Garrincha!'

By an amazing coincidence, the first car to stop was a Galaxie driven by Vasco director José Bento de Carvalho. The scene he found was like a disaster area, with people milling around and sacks of potatoes all over the place. Garrincha was wandering about in a daze, and it was a few moments before he saw the lifeless body of his mother-in-law sprawled out on the road, her head almost severed from her body. Crying, he ran over and hugged her. 'My mother-in-law! My mother-in-law!'

He was in a severe state of shock, and someone had to talk him into getting into the back seat of Bento de Carvalho's car. All the way to the hospital, Garrincha cried and tortured himself for not believing in Elza's premonition. And he continued to shout: 'I don't want my mother-in-law to die! I want to see my daughter!'

Another car had stopped and taken Sara to hospital. She appeared to have only minor cuts but they were worried she might have more serious internal injuries. Rosária's body, meanwhile, waited for an ambulance to arrive from the town of Nova Iguaçu on the outskirts of Rio. The truck driver had fled the scene, but his registration number had been noted down.

When they reached the hospital, Garrincha was taken to the third floor by two nurses. Bento de Carvalho phoned Vasco chairman Reinaldo Reis to break the news and Reis called his counterpart at Flamengo, Veiga Brito, who rushed to the hospital. When he got there, he hugged Garrincha, who wouldn't stop blaming himself for what had happened.

'I killed my mother-in-law. My God, why did I do that?'

Doctors examined Garrincha and found that he had small cuts on his body and a wound on his forehead right between his eyes that would scar him for the rest of his life. Sara, meanwhile, had broken two bones in her left leg and was transferred to another hospital in Copacabana where she was kept overnight. Bento de Carvalho waited for the doctors to release Garrincha and then drove him home.

The press had got wind of the incident and cars filled with reporters followed them to Garrincha's flat in Copacabana. Elza was not at home and their nanny was on holiday. Flashes went off and reporters shouted out questions, but Garrincha did not want to be photographed; at one point he threw himself to the floor and covered himself with a beach mat. One by one the reporters got the message and left as Garrincha slowly calmed down. Bento de Carvalho didn't want to leave him alone but Garrincha insisted he was fine and that Elza's children would soon be home. The Vasco director reluctantly departed.

A few hours earlier, Elza had been at home when the telephone rang.

'Hello? Is that Garrincha's house? Look, there's been an accident in São João de Meriti, everyone was killed!'

Elza had been speechless. Stunned and with no clear idea of what she was doing, she had fled. When she came out of her trance she was halfway to the Santa Rosa Theatre where she was appearing in the show *Elza of All Sambas*. She had walked for miles without realising it. She went into the theatre, where she approached her colleagues. All she could say was, 'Everyone was killed. Everyone was killed.'

Her friend Clara Nunes, a well-known singer, managed to calm her down and take her home. But the house was empty, Garrincha had disappeared. The accident was by now being reported on the radio, and before long the flat was filled with friends from the world of soccer and samba. A tearful Garrincha called to tell Elza that he was OK but that he didn't want to come home. He didn't say where he was. He kept calling back, each time in tears, and it was only during one of the later calls that he told her he was in The Garden, a restaurant frequented by Flamengo players.

Edgard Cosme and a few others went to get him but found only a drunk man too scared to go home. It was early morning before they convinced him to leave. When he got back to the flat, he threw himself at Elza's feet.

'I killed my mother-in-law, Crioula. The person I most loved in the world after you.'

He lay down on the bed and cried. Elza stroked his head but her son Carlinhos was not in the mood for pardons. He didn't mince his words.

'Drunk! Murderer!'

The next day, while Elza was burying her mother in Rio's Caju cemetery, lawyer Ernesto da Luz Pinto Dória called on Garrincha. Dória said he had come on behalf of Dr Oscar Stevenson, a professor of law at the Universidade do Brasil, to offer him free legal representation. 'From now on you can count on us,' Dória told him.

They got involved for the first time two days later, when Garrincha went to São João de Meriti to help the police. At the station, Garrincha met the truck driver, a white-haired, 61-year-old father of four named Benedito Faria Sales. Sales had been driving lorries for 42 years and had left his home town of Taubaté in São Paulo state six hours before the accident occurred. He swore he was lucid and awake in spite of having spent the afternoon on the road, and he was clearly upset at what had happened. He hugged Garrincha and told him he would do anything not to have hurt him.

Garrincha, still worn out and upset, calmed him down. 'It's all right,' he said.

Sales's other worry was how to pay for the 132 sacks of potatoes he had lost when they fell off the truck. Garrincha promised he would organise a whip-round at Flamengo to help him pay.

When police questioned him about the details of the accident, Garrincha denied he had been drinking and the investigator did not labour the point; he was more interested in determining whether or not Sales had checked his mirror before pulling out on to the road. Other eyewitness testimony was contradictory and confused, but everything suggested that the two of them were at fault. Both Garrincha and Sales were fingerprinted and charged with manslaughter. When officials asked Garrincha to strip for a body search, he said that he didn't have the time as he had to get back to train with Flamengo. What he really wanted was to get out of there, and the police let him go after giving him a cursory once-over.

Before he left, the police handed over the items they had found in the destroyed car: the image of a saint Garrincha had hung from the rearview mirror; the battered cage with the dead bird inside it; and a piece of false tooth that almost certainly belonged to Rosária.

Garrincha took the saint and went with Elza to visit Sara. He tried
to joke with the girl, telling her that his nose would now be even
flatter than Elza's, but no one was laughing.

He returned home in a state of depression and spent the day in
bed, without saying a word and not eating or even drinking. Elza
checked them into a hotel in order to get them away from the friends
and reporters besieging the house. Garrincha wasn't drinking, at least
not in front of Elza, and the images of the accident continued to
haunt him.

Once, Garrincha woke her up in the middle of the night and asked,
'Crioula, do you think this was my fault? Do you think I killed my
mother-in-law?'

Elza put aside her own pain and tried to console him. 'You didn't
kill anyone,' she replied. 'It was destiny. It could have been me at the
wheel.'

'I never did anyone any harm, I never wished anyone any harm.
Why is this happening to me?'

In an attempt to convince him she didn't hold him responsible, or
simply to stimulate him, Elza tried to seduce him. However,
Garrincha's depression was so profound that he wasn't interested in
sex. After a week in the Hotel Riviera they went home to Copacabana.

The depression continued, and not even the thought of playing
football could inspire Garrincha. Flamengo's doctors Cotecchia and
Calarge, together with Francalacci, visited him and tried to convince
him to start training again. He had two months of his contract left
with Flamengo and there was no way it would be renewed if he wasn't
playing football. The doctors told him the road to recovery was
through kicking a ball, but his apathy was total.

In the time he had been absent from the game Flamengo had
appointed a new coach, Elba 'Tim' de Pádua Lima, a star with
Fluminense in the 1930s and 1940s and one of the best coaches in
the country. Tim was considered a master strategist capable of changing the course of a game with subtle tactical alterations. But when

he arrived at Flamengo he made it clear that Garrincha would not figure in his plans. Not because he was a drinker – Lima drank almost as much as he did – but because he believed that while Garrincha might still be a draw for provincial friendlies he wasn't up to playing in the Carioca Championship. Moreover, Flamengo had just signed a talented new winger from Argentina, the 21-year-old prospect Doval. Garrincha's Flamengo adventure was over.

Garrincha started drinking again, this time more than ever, but his depression did not lift. Elza's three eldest kids moved out because they couldn't stand to be around him any longer. One afternoon, when he was alone in the flat, Garrincha locked himself in the bathroom, turned on the gas at the water heater and sat down to die.

By chance, Elza and the nanny arrived home a short while later and smelled the gas the moment they opened the door. They ran to the bathroom, forced open the door and found Garrincha still alive. They opened the doors and windows and made him drink some milk. Elza didn't call the doctor – the last thing they needed was more bad publicity – but the story that Garrincha had committed suicide somehow spread across the city. Elza was forced to invite the press into her house to prove he was still alive. In doing so she quashed the rumours, but it was not the end of the affair. Garrincha would try again.

The flat in Copacabana had brought them nothing but bad luck, so in June they decided to move again, this time to a beautiful house in Jardim Botanico, a lush residential area situated right under the outstretched arms of Christ the Redeemer. They paid the 150,000-cruzeiro down payment with Garrincha's signing-on fee from Flamengo and the money Elza had made from a recent national tour. The remaining 150,000 was to be paid within six months.

The house was beautiful. Built on several levels, there was a spacious living room, a pool, and a tropical garden with monkeys and possums from the nearby Tijuca Forest. Carlinhos, Dilma and Gilson, having forgiven Garrincha for their grandmother's death, moved back in with them. Elza wanted life to start afresh, and to prove to the world that she and Garrincha were happy she decided to throw a huge house-warming party.

It was a spectacular blow-out worthy of the names on the invitation. Some 200 people joined them in an orgy of whisky and champagne, turkey, shrimp and caviar. Once everyone had arrived, Elza made her grand entrance, appearing on the landing in handmade *palazzo* pyjamas and blowing kisses to her friends as she made her way down the stairs. In the living room below, Garrincha fingered his shirt collar and complained that he didn't see the point in spending 10,000 cruzeiros they didn't have on such extravagances. He had nothing in common with most of the people there; all they wanted to talk to him about was football. One of the city's top gossip columnists wrote about the party and made it clear that in spite of the tragedies that had dogged them Elza and Garrincha were still happy together. Until, that is, the morning after, when the old bones of contention quickly resurfaced.

The problem was the same one as always: Garrincha's insatiable appetite for drink. Pincel and Swing continued to exert as bad an influence as ever and they had been joined by others: Fluminense players Oliveira and Flávio and Vasco's Mário Tilico. None had met a drink he didn't like. Tilico drank so much he sometimes passed out, forcing Elza to revive him with chicken soup. When she realised Garrincha's new companions were playing an increasingly influential role in his destruction she banned them from the house and once again scoured the place for any remaining alcohol.

It wasn't enough to stop Garrincha. Elza suspected that her butler Homero was hiding booze for Garrincha and she kept finding bottles stashed away in secret hideouts. She found bottles in the water tank, in the garden, and even tied to stones at the bottom of the swimming pool. He was even still using the oldest trick of them all and pouring *cachaça* into empty bottles of tonic water. In that, even her son Gilson was an unwitting accomplice: 'Gilson, go and get your father's tonic water . . .'

On the morning of 1 August, Elza answered the phone and heard an anonymous voice at other end of the line: 'Go to the theatre tonight and anything could happen, nigger.'

Elza didn't pay much attention – she had been a target for anonymous threats ever since she had started going out with Garrincha. So, as always, Garrincha dropped her off at the theatre and then picked her up again when she was finished. But when they got on to the dual carriageway that runs around the Lagoa, two cars tried to cut them off by the side of the central reservation. Garrincha panicked and accelerated away, forcing them on to the side of the road. Elza swore she saw hooded men carrying guns.

The next day an unsigned letter arrived at their house: 'You both have 24 hours to leave the country. If you don't, we are going to come after you.'

They couldn't understand who would be threatening them. Nobody, perhaps not even Nair, saw Elza as a home wrecker any more. If anything, Brazil had progressed so significantly that she was now lauded for having risked her career for love. And nobody hated Garrincha, a semi-retired footballer who had become so linked with failure that when clubs offered players farcical new contracts they would say, 'Don't try that with me, I am not Garrincha.'

Lawyer Ernesto Dória asked police to guarantee their safety, and although they were given assurances that they would be protected, no real measures were taken. They hired a private security guard, fearing that the threats were not political but from a gang of kidnappers who wanted to seize them and scoop a rich ransom. The security guard was immediately called into action when, just three days later, he spotted a man trying to climb through their second-floor window. The guard shot his gun in the air to scare off the intruder and immediately came under machine-gun fire from two accomplices who were backing him up on the other side of the garden wall.

Police arrived the next morning and saw that the shots had ripped through the windows and taken chunks out of the piano. The newspapers called it a robbery, just as in June 1964 when they were attacked on the Ilha do Governador.

Garrincha and Elza did not know who wanted to harm them. And they didn't want to. All they knew was that if they wanted to stay safe there was only one way out, the same route that had been taken by many Brazilians during those lead-filled years of dictatorship: the road to Galeão airport.

To reassure those who had taken a disliking to them, Garrincha and Elza announced they were leaving Brazil. Elza signed a contract to perform shows in Italy, and Garrincha, who had been given a free transfer by Corinthians, planned to play friendlies in Europe until he could find a new club. It worked; the threats stopped.

They wanted to leave Brazil with their house in Jardim Botanico secure, but without the 150,000 cruzeiros necessary to make the final payment they needed to find a quick way to make some money. Elza's solution was to take up the idea of a testimonial match again. This time the game would not just be a farewell from football but a farewell to Brazil. Her country, she was convinced, owed it to her man.

Together, they went to speak with Otávio Pinto Guimarães, the new president of the Carioca Football Federation. When they met, Elza got straight to the point: she wanted the federation to help them get the money they needed to buy their house. They suggested the match take place between Brazil and Peru, whose manager Didi had already agreed to the idea; all the CBD would have to do was arrange and pay for the Peruvians to come to Brazil and pay their flights and accommodation. Pinto Guimarães, however, was not overly enthused. 'It's risky,' he said. 'What happens if it rains?'

Garrincha wasn't in the slightest bit surprised at Pinto Guimarães' lack of enthusiasm and he suggested they go over his head and talk with João Havelange, then the president of the CBD. By now they had given up on the idea of a testimonial and were instead hoping the CBD would simply lend them 150,000 cruzeiros. To Elza, it wasn't a risky deal; she was simply seeking their help in securing a house for a two-time World Cup winner. She fully intended to pay them back.

But the CBD was not a bank. At the time, 150,000 cruzeiros was worth $35,000, a hefty sum of money. Not only that, Havelange had helped Garrincha out not long before by generously paying off his tax bill. Now, all Elza and Garrincha had to offer by way of collateral was their word. Havelange thought about it for a few days and then invited Garrincha for a meeting. After making him wait outside his office for several hours, Havelange called Garrincha in and gave him the bad news. It was not going to happen.

On hearing they had been rejected, Garrincha reacted the only way he knew how – by hitting the bottle. When he didn't return home that night Elza put two and two together and spent hours in a taxi going from bar to bar looking for him. Eventually she found him drunk and in tears on the steps of a church in the city centre.

A month later, in the middle of January 1970, Garrincha and Sales went on trial accused of causing the accident that had killed Elza's mother.

Although Garrincha's lawyers Oscar Stevenson and Ernesto Dória put up a brilliant defence, reminding the judge of the debt the nation owed their client, it wasn't enough to sway him. He found both Garrincha and Sales guilty and sentenced them to two years in jail. As it was his first offence, the judge gave Garrincha a suspended sentence and gave him special dispensation to travel on the condition that he present himself either to the Italian authorities or the Brazilian embassy in Rome once every six months. Stevenson and Dória appealed against the sentence while Garrincha and Elza boarded a plane to Italy.

For Elza, getting Garrincha out of Brazil was the only way to save him. His depression had become almost constant, and though she managed to coax him into something approaching a lighter mood whenever they left the house, the moment they walked through the front door again he threw himself on to the sofa. He could spend whole days morosely chugging back bottles of booze. Elza thought his depression was due to the accident a year earlier; she did not consider that it might be a consequence of his chronic alcoholism – not necessarily the cause of it – and that if he continued to drink he would take his depression to Italy.

They left for Rome on 24 January 1970, leaving Elza's children – Carlinhos, 21; Dilma, 17; Gilson, 15; and Sara, just five – to look after the house in Jardim Botanico. Elza did not want her family to go with her because she was unsure how long they would be gone. If things worked out she planned to have them come and join them.

But they had barely touched down when they got bad news from home. A judge ruled that because they had failed to pay the outstanding portion of the loan for the Jardim Botanico house, the property would be returned to the original owner. A court official arrived one day and forced Carlinhos to sign a writ obliging them to vacate the premises. Elza's children were out on the streets and their furniture, belongings, and the trophies Garrincha had won for performances the world over, were seized by authorities.

In one of the drawers was the paper from Corinthians guaranteeing his free transfer.

CHAPTER 19

1970–1971: Roman Fag-Ends

In the lobby of Rome's Hotel Imperial, Garrincha struck matches and set fire to the flowers that sat in the middle of the table. The petals crackled as they burned and Garrincha giggled. Elza playfully slapped his hands to get him to stop. The last thing she wanted was to upset him. At least he seemed happy.

Italian entrepreneur Franco Fontana had put them up in the Imperial while they looked for a more permanent place to live. The hotel was popular with Brazilians and Elza had to fight to stop Garrincha from accepting their invitations to drink. Not that he needed any encouragement; he was creative enough himself. The hotel employees knew who he was, and although he didn't speak a word of Italian he had soon set up a clandestine network of friends to provide him with alcohol. His principal suppliers were the barman and the waiters. They knew that when he asked for tea, he wanted cognac, so in front of Elza he drank 'tea' and when he was alone he drank grappa.

In the midst of her hugely successful first run of shows at the Sistine Theatre – she won rave reviews from local reporters who dubbed her a sexy and swinging Vesuvius – Elza asked Maria Eunice, the wife of the *Jornal do Brasil*'s Rome correspondent Araújo Netto, to help her look for an apartment. Finding the right place was not easy. Elza was hard to please. 'It has to be the flat of a prima donna,' she said. 'Otherwise, no one will respect me.'

They scoured the seven hills for a place but it was a struggle finding somewhere suitable. When Elza found a flat she liked, it wasn't in the right neighbourhood; when she found a neighbourhood she liked she couldn't find the right flat. Eventually, she came across the perfect home: a sumptuous place on the via Bevagna, close to the homes of actress Monica Vitti, film director Michelangelo Antonioni and several of the TV journalists who enjoyed superstar status in Italy. Elza used Fontana's first cheque to pay three months' rent and buy furniture from B&B and Cassina, the chicest new design shops. She threw a house-warming party for local musicians and media personalities and kitted herself out with a new wardrobe designed by Rina, an award-winning stylist. She even got herself two white fur coats. All on credit. She was, after all, a star. Losing her house and belongings in Brazil had not dulled her passion for splashing out on the finer things in life.

Garrincha, meanwhile, whiled away his time doing very little. He had gone to Italy in the hope of signing with an Italian club, as either a player or a coach. But the transfer orgy of the 1950s and 1960s, when Italian sides signed the best players in the world, was over, and he knew it would be difficult to get a decent contract. Still, he believed that someone might make an exception for him. And if they didn't then he still hoped he might at least be signed on a game-by-game basis, even if only for friendlies.

The months passed, however, and the only interest came from the Italians who would stop him on the streets, hug him and invite him into bars and restaurants for a meal or a drink. To the older generation, the goals he had scored for Botafogo and Brazil were firmly ingrained in their memories; to the younger generation he was a legend. Wherever he went the locals were constantly screaming 'GARRINCCIA!' with the Rs spat out like bullets from a machine gun and the Cs sounding like sneezes.

Unable to persuade any managers to give him a trial, Garrincha took advantage of Elza's trips, both in Italy and further afield, to look for a new team. In April 1970, when she went to Portugal, Garrincha paid a visit to Benfica to inform them of his availability. Feigning insouciance, he turned up at the Stadium of Light in a jacket and dress shoes and ended up kicking a ball about with Eusébio. Benfica offered him a traditional Portuguese dinner of cod and red wine but explained that they did not sign non-Portuguese nationals, which at the time was true. They neglected to say that even if they did, a team that still boasted most of the Portuguese side that had finished in third place in the 1966 World Cup would not have space for a man so obviously in the twilight of his career.

Elza decided to take charge of the situation and arranged lunches and dinners with the directors of clubs she thought might like to have Garrincha in their side. But when they sat down to eat, they saw that the man across the table was a pale shadow of the player he had once been. Sometimes the shadow wasn't even sober. When he met with the chairman of second-division side Avelino, he drank too much wine and Elza resorted to kicking him under the table to try to get him to stop. Garrincha responded by screaming at her to stop kicking him and throwing back another glass of wine, the fateful one too many that sent the room spinning and turned his voice into a slur as thick as *quattro formaggios*. He did not make a good impression.

He managed to get a few games, but only with amateur sides and school, factory or union teams who paid him a few lira for the honour of having him don their shirt. Garrincha pretended to enjoy the games but in reality it was depressing: the matches took place on weekday afternoons on terrible pitches in front of empty stands. Garrincha usually went to the games with Netto but sometimes he was driven there by Chico Buarque, a celebrated and hugely popular Brazilian singer-songwriter who was also living in exile in Rome. Netto had introduced them to each other and Garrincha often visited Buarque at home, where they would drink grappa together and discuss football

319

and music. Buarque's flat was one of the few places Garrincha risked venturing out to alone. He still hadn't got his bearings, didn't understand a word of Italian, and refused to learn.

The only other people he visited on his own were Netto and former Botafogo player Vinícius. Except for visiting friends, he had little else to do, and he spent most of his free time either wandering the city and popping in and out of bars, or staying at home and watching the television. His relationship with Elza was deteriorating and their fights were more frequent and more violent. She protected him in public, but behind closed doors she no longer accepted his excuses for drinking.

In June Garrincha had the perfect excuse to sit in front of the television and drink without fear of getting it in the neck from Elza. The World Cup was on in Mexico. Garrincha was nervous. In the previous three tournaments Brazil had relied on his dribbling, but his place on the wing had now been filled by Jairzinho, the player he had watched rise through the ranks at Botafogo and take over from him. Only two of his old team-mates were there seeking a third winner's medal: Pelé, who was now 30, and Zagalo, who had become manager.

For Brazil's opening match against Czechoslovakia, Garrincha sat in front of the television and shouted encouragement to Jairzinho as though he could hear him: 'Come on, my man! Play for the jersey!' Jairzinho might not have heard, but he did respond, scoring two goals in the 4–2 win. Garrincha was happy, but when Jairzinho went on to score in every match – including the 1–0 win over England – he no longer felt the need to cheer Brazil on. He ended up watching the rest of the games in silence, slowly swilling the ice around his glass of cognac. Seeing Jairzinho being sent down the wing by Gerson didn't excite him. Perhaps he was seeing the end of an era – his era – that until recently he had refused to believe was really over.

The era was brought to a definite close a month later with one of the most painful tributes he had ever received. TV Tupi were going live with Brazil's first ever satellite broadcast and the executives asked

Protector – Jose Luiz Magalhaes Lins takes a stroll with Garrincha at the country cottage where he was hidden away during the controversy at Botafogo.

Home sweet home – Elza attempts to give Garrincha the love and affection a two-time World Champion deserves.

The glory and pain of 1962: against England, above, and in the dressing room after being sent off against Chile.

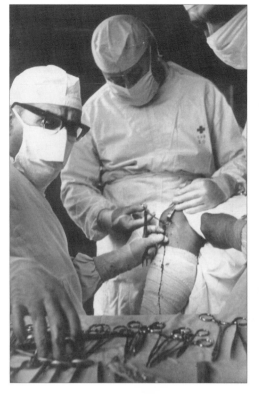

The long-awaited operation.

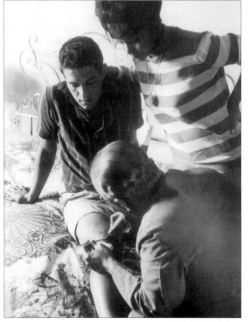

Post-op: Surgeon Marques Tourinho removes the stitches from Garrincha's knee. He would never be the player he once was.

Motorway tragedy: Garrincha's Galaxie is a write-off after the crash that killed his mother-in-law.

On trial: Garrincha and the lorry driver attempt to explain how the accident happened.

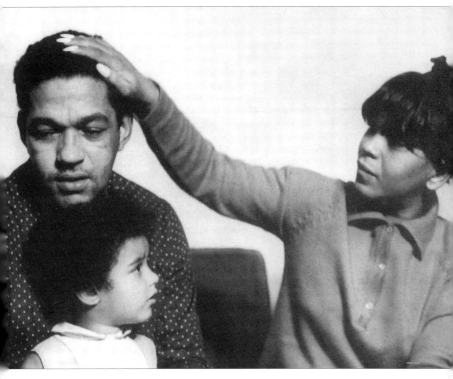

Depression: Elza and Sara try to console Garrincha after the accident. But it shook him badly and he would go on to attempt suicide.

Flamengo pick up Garrincha in September 1968, at the age of thirty-four.

Above left, married again: Vanderlea takes centre stage as Garrincha's 15-year union with Elza comes to an end.

Above, with Livia, his daughter with Vanderlea. The two never had a chance to get to know each other. Garrincha died the day before her second birthday.

The zombie-like figure of Garrincha waves to the fans at Rio's carnival.

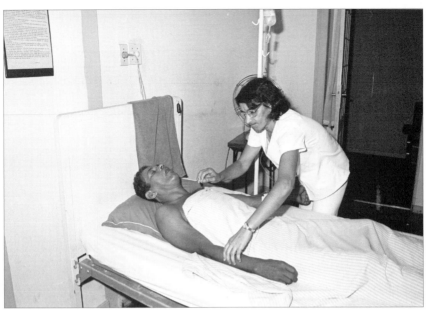

Hospitalised 15 times in 4 years, Garrincha frequently spent nights in the care of doctors hovering between life and death.

Fans gather to watch the funeral cortège go by.

Pincel grieves over the death of his friend. He would soon join him.

Garrincha and Elza to be their special guests from Portugal, where she was doing some shows. Director Mauricio Sherman was planning to surprise Garrincha by asking him to wear the shirt Jairzinho had used in the World Cup finals. Sherman was surprised at how apathetic and distant Garrincha was when they met a few days before the show, but that was nothing to how he felt when Elza called him shortly before they were supposed to go live and told him Garrincha wouldn't be able to appear.

'I don't think it's going to work, Mauricio. My baby isn't well.'

Sherman froze. 'What do you mean? He's the reason we're here!'

He rushed over to their room and found Garrincha legless. Elza tried to explain: 'He got a little carried away when I went out to rehearsals earlier.'

Garrincha was so drunk he could hardly open his eyes. Sherman rushed off to find something to sober Garrincha up – they needed him to appear on television that night. He and his assistant went from chemist to chemist, eventually finding a glucose and complex B pill that worked well enough to allow Garrincha to guest on the show. He was *compos mentis* but he didn't appreciate the surprise invitation to wear Jairzinho's top. He put it on, but later said to Elza, 'What a cheek. If they think he's good, then what about me?'

Elza was by now run off her feet, struggling to cope with the aftermath of Garrincha's drinking sessions and at the same time working to maintain the momentum she had gained after arriving in Europe. The Italians loved her. With her throaty and suggestive voice, she could make the most ordinary words sound funny or sexy, and even though she never understood Italian she made up for it with a sensuality that crossed continents. She moved every inch of her body and the crowds left theatres with their hands sore from clapping.

Nevertheless, Brazilian artists found it difficult to succeed in Italy at the start of the 1970s and Elza's initial impact soon began to wear off. The Italian taste for popular music was still stuck somewhere around 1914, and while exotic singers such as Elza often made a big

321

splash when they first hit the scene the novelty quickly wore off and they were soon discarded in favour of the old romantic ballads that remained as popular as pizza.

Fontana cancelled a $60,000 summer tour after newspapers complained that Elza was taking work away from local singers (Elza had blabbed about the contract to journalists). He tried to compensate by arranging dates in Rome, Milan and Turin, but the offers were drying up. As if that wasn't bad enough, her backing band was on the point of revolt; they had arrived in Rome in the middle of winter with no money to buy warm clothes and their salaries had not been paid on time. She had just flown her family over from Brazil, too, and to cap it all she was constantly having to fight off Fontana's amorous advances.

In the autumn of 1970, the gondola was taking on water at an alarming rate and Elza knew that if she didn't take action she would go under. She owed money to her band, the rent was late, and she had to make outstanding payments on the clothes and furniture she had bought on arrival.

Her relationship with Garrincha was also floundering. He, too, was stuck in a vicious circle. Had he been able to remain sober he might have made some money to help alleviate their financial difficulties, but that seemed impossible. He spent more and more time drinking, which in turn caused his self-esteem to plummet, which gave him more reasons to drink. Elza stopped bailing him out, but it didn't make any difference. Garrincha didn't need money to drink: there was no shortage of Italians who considered it an honour to stand him a grappa. He only needed money to smoke, and without that, or the heart to bum cigarettes, he began to pick up fag-ends on the street.

The struggles contributed to making the atmosphere between them untenable. Every time they spoke they seemed to be on the verge of a fight. Their friends could see it was just waiting to happen, and when it finally did, right there in their flat in front of Elza's children, it was about drink. Elza, at the end of her tether, scratched Garrincha's face with her nails, drawing blood. Garrincha hit back, punching her in the face and breaking her teeth.

For a few seconds they were both in a state of shock. Neither Garrincha, with his face a mess, nor Elza, spitting bits of broken brace from her mouth, could believe they had attacked each other with such ferocity. Garrincha phoned Elza's Italian teacher, Anna Maria Piergilli, and she rushed over to find Garrincha with his face covered in dried blood and Elza crying in the corner. She took Elza to a dentist who fitted her with a brace that enabled her to keep a date on Italian television later that night.

While Elza was flashing her million-watt smile as if nothing had happened, Garrincha slunk off to drown his sorrows with Netto and his wife. The couple had been called to keep the peace between Garrincha and Elza before, but when Garrincha appeared with scratch marks down his cheek they knew the situation was serious.

'I am going to leave Crioula,' Garrincha told them.

It wasn't the first time they had heard him threaten to leave her, but they knew that he was just mouthing off. It would never actually happen.

Elza's son, however, was all in favour of a break-up. When Elza returned from the television studio that night, Carlinhos gave her an ultimatum: 'That's enough. Either he leaves or I go back to Brazil.'

Elza tried to appease him. 'You have to understand, Carlinhos. He's a good man. It's the drink that makes him do these things.'

Carlinhos was not convinced, and a few weeks later he was back in Rio. Elza remained by Garrincha's side.

Not that Garrincha was there for her. He had given up on himself. Alone in the flat he filled the bath up to the rim and lay back with a bottle of cognac. He finished it off and waited for unconsciousness. Once again, Elza arrived just in time. She saw that the bathroom door was closed and when he didn't answer she barged it open with her backside and pulled him from the water. The next day Garrincha got up eager to eat breakfast. He couldn't remember a thing.

* * *

In Brazil, the first rumours about Garrincha's situation were starting to circulate and most of them were true: that no one wanted to sign him, that he had been reduced to picking cigarette ends from the gutter, and that he, Elza and her children couldn't afford even to feed themselves properly. Reference was never made to the fact that it was his drinking that had caused his downfall, and that it was now starting to interfere with Elza's career. In reality, Elza was not so hard up that she couldn't afford to feed her children, but she was refusing to go on tour for fear that if she left Garrincha alone he might try to kill himself again.

Elza put a brave face on the situation. All the interviews she gave to Brazilian newspapers were marked by an optimism that hid the bitter reality. She repeatedly told reporters that Garrincha 'had got a rough deal', that he 'was playing brilliantly' and that 'he had lots of years of football left in him'. She knew it was all lies. Garrincha didn't have years left in him, he barely had 15 minutes in him, and that was all the time he spent on the field in those few friendlies for which he was still being paid.

The rumours continued to spread, and they saddened many who remembered Garrincha as the man responsible for some of the happiest times of their lives. One of them, Salim Simão, a journalist and Botafogo fan, went to the government to see if they would help. Simão's appeal to help Garrincha in some way resonated in the corridors of power, and it eventually reached the ears of Emílio Garrastazu Médici, the country's president. The idea that someone as famous as Garrincha was going hungry in Europe was not good for Brazil's image, so Médici got in touch with the embassy in Rome to ask if they could find some kind of job for him. The ambassador suggested that the Brazilian Coffee Institute (IBC) hire Garrincha as a 'coffee ambassador' to help boost sales at the international trade fairs.

The head of the IBC office in Milan was a São Paulo shoe magnate called João di Pietro. Di Pietro had been in Milan only a short time and he was not enjoying himself. He had personal and professional reasons for wanting to get back to Brazil, and when the ambassador suggested he hire Garrincha he saw the meddling as an ideal opportunity to kick up a fuss that might result in his getting a transfer home. The ambassador's idea was to have Garrincha appear at the Brazilian stand at trade fairs, where he would attract visitors and present them with a bag of coffee. It seemed like the perfect union of two of the best things Brazil had ever produced. The suggested salary was $1,000 a month.

Until then, the position of 'coffee ambassador' had not even existed and di Pietro did not like the idea of creating it just for Garrincha, let alone giving him a salary that was only $200 less than his own. To award him such a good position and high wage just for serving coffee would cause bad feeling among the other employees who were earning less than half that, di Pietro argued. He could not have had a better pretext for telling his superiors that if Garrincha was hired, then he would resign.

When he spoke to Elza, however, he was more direct: 'I don't want a drunk working here.'

In Rio, Simão asked José Luiz Sattamini Neto, the former head of the Milan office and now the IBC's executive director, to help resolve the problem. When he didn't show any enthusiasm about hiring Garrincha, Education Minister Jarbas Passarinho intervened.

Like many people, Passarinho thought Garrincha was a better player than Pelé, and he got on the phone to Brasilia, Rome and Milan. At the same time, his wife, who was visiting Rome, went to see Elza and assured her they'd work something out, even if it meant that the Education Ministry would pay his wages. Passarinho's intervention did the trick. Garrincha became the IBC's latest employee in Milan, and di Pietro got to go home, just as he had wanted.

In October, Garrincha returned to Brazil to sign his employment contract, then went back to Italy with enough *cachaça* and beans to see him through several Italian winters. When he got back, in spite of all the efforts that had been made to get him a job, he turned out to be as good an employee at the IBC as he had been at América Fabril.

The Milan office had jurisdiction over Italy, France, Switzerland, Yugoslavia and Spain, and every year the IBC would visit those countries and take part in around 20 fairs. They didn't expect much of Garrincha. Everyone knew his appointment was a symbolic one designed to help him get back on his feet. Garrincha was not even obliged to go to all the fairs, he just had to go to enough of them to show that he was taking the job seriously. In his first year, he went to three: in Bologna, Zagreb and Marseille.

In Bologna, a Brazilian overheard a conversation between Garrincha and an Italian who had gone up to greet him.

The Italian asked, 'Is this Brazilian coffee really any good?'

Garrincha didn't know how to lie. He responded, 'I don't know, I never drink it. I know that Brazilian *cachaça* is good.'

When Elza realised that he was ducking out of travelling she started taking him to the airport. Had it been up to her Garrincha would have taken his new role more seriously and represented Brazil at all the fairs. But even with Elza's mothering he managed to get out of doing any work. On at least two occasions Elza packed his bag and delivered him to the airport only to discover later that he hadn't boarded the plane.

The first time, Elza started to get concerned when he didn't phone to say he had arrived safely. After two days she was out of her mind with worry. Anything could have happened to him, and in fact it had, only a lot closer to home than she imagined. Someone called her from a dodgy hotel near Rome's airport asking her to come and pick him up. He had gone to the bar in the departure lounge, started to throw back the drinks, and ignored the calls to board the plane. Rather than face Elza's ire, he had checked himself into a hotel and planned to pretend that he had travelled. Two days and countless bottles of wine later, a hotel employee found him in his room in an alcoholic stupor. Elza went to pick him up, and the fighting started again.

The second crisis came when Garrincha missed another plane and checked himself into another hotel. Elza was in the process of roasting a side of beef at home with Dilma when the meat fell from her knife into the boiling fat. She was badly burned all over her face and arms and had to be rushed to the accident and emergency unit. When she got a call to come and rescue Garrincha, she turned up with her face covered in bandages. When they removed them a few days later the nurses could hardly hide their shock. It was not a pretty sight and the only answer was to have plastic surgery, for the second time. She couldn't sing for a month.

With so many setbacks and so little money it was only a matter of time before they were evicted from the flat on the via Bevagna. Cassina seized their furniture; the furrier took the white coats; and Rina, knowing that used clothes were no good to her, grumbled 'Porca puttana' ('Fat whore') and swallowed the loss.

One of those most interested to hear that Garrincha had a job was Nair's lawyer. Between January and October of 1970 Garrincha hadn't paid Nair a penny, so Mendes asked a judge to force the IBC to withhold a percentage of his salary. The judge agreed to the request and started debiting $220 a month from his net pay.

Nair, however, often saw very little of the money Garrincha gave her: Mendes's free services in fact cost her two-thirds of her monthly income. Sometimes he would go months without contacting her, and when he did pay her the money arrived incomplete or with 'discounts'. Nair signed the receipts without reading them – she didn't understand a word – and Mendes took care of the accounts for her. Nair didn't know anything about the financial technicalities; she even thought she was getting the money from President Médici.

In Europe, Garrincha had no idea that his daughters, who still worked for América Fabril, were trying to survive by selling fabric made by a factory whose fortunes had fallen so far that they could only afford to pay their employees in kind. With everyone trying to

327

get by in the same way there was a glut of cloth and life was a struggle. The savings and property Garrincha had left his daughters in the divorce settlement had disappeared and the family survived thanks only to the support of Nair's relatives.

In Milan, where they had now moved in order to be closer to the IBC office, Garrincha's concerns were more immediate.

'Luiz Felipe, can you give me a sub until the end of the month?'

Advances were normal in football so Garrincha didn't think anything of asking Luiz Felipe Matoso Maia, the new head of the IBC office, for a few lira to see him through until pay day. Luiz Felipe had trouble making Garrincha understand that government agencies couldn't hand out money quite as easily as football clubs, and he ended up lending Garrincha $30 or $40 out of his own pocket. Although Garrincha was always sure to pay him back on time, the money he borrowed was quickly spent on essentials for the house, and whatever was left over would be spent on drink.

The IBC office was close to the piazza Babila, right in the heart of Milan. Although Garrincha didn't have to go there very often, Elza decided to set herself up in a serviced flat nearby. She couldn't afford to rent a fancy apartment any more and there was no need anyway, as she was touring again – and towing Garrincha along with her – to Switzerland, France and Spain.

In Madrid, Garrincha was asked to appear on Spanish television on 18 July to commentate on Pelé's farewell appearance for Brazil in an international against Yugoslavia. Farewell matches were a sensitive issue for Garrincha. All the big stars of his era – Di Stefano, Puskas, Gilmar and Pelé, to name just a few – had been given one. When Pelé did a lap of honour around the Maracanã with the crowd chanting 'Stay! Stay! Stay!' Garrincha had a huge lump in his throat. But he did not let it show. He refused to complain about the CBD's refusal to recognise him, and the only hint of discontent came when he lamented what he regarded as Pelé's premature retirement from international football: 'Silly, isn't it? With so much football left in him.'

In September, after a possible tryout with French side Red Star had fallen through – by this time the 37-year-old had resorted to telling people he was 33 – Garrincha managed to get a game for a Rest of the World Select in a testimonial for Soviet goalkeeper Lev Yashin, who was hanging up his gloves at the age of 41. The only youngster on the field in Milan was Tostão, scorer of two goals in the Rest of the World's 4–2 victory.

Shortly after that match, Garrincha and Elza decided to return to Rio. They were increasingly aware that they had missed finding El Dorado, if indeed it existed, and there didn't seem any point in carrying on in Europe. Elza owed money to shopkeepers, designers, her landlord and even her friends. There were occasions when if she hadn't taken a train or a plane and travelled to do a show on Friday night she would have been up to her neck in debt by Monday morning. Garrincha's salary at the IBC had become even more vital for keeping them solvent.

To make matters worse, Elza's children were struggling. Her daughter Dilma had received a grant to study in England, but Gilson had not adapted: he was forgetting his Portuguese and spoke hardly a word of Italian. Elza was stressed and unhappy, and the sex machine that was once Garrincha had spluttered and broken down. Europe had long ceased to be a shop window filled with women and Garrincha had long ceased wanting to buy anything.

It was touching and at the same time sad for him to listen to friends such as Vinícius, now retired and rich in Rome: 'I owe Garrincha everything, he made me who I am. If it hadn't been for him, Napoli would never have bought me back in 1955. Whatever he needs, he will get from me.' Garrincha, loosened up with ten cognacs, got melancholy and sentimental when he heard such statements. He hugged Vinícius, or whoever else was paying the tribute, and almost broke down in tears. 'You are a good man,' he said. 'You're on my side.'

The man who had made life hell for thousands of defenders had now made life hell for himself.

Towards the end of 1971, entrepreneur Abelardo Figueiredo went to Rome personally to invite Elza to take part in a mega-production he was calling the Brazil export show. The extravaganza was to feature musicians, singers and dozens of plumed and scantily clad dancers, first in Rio, then in São Paulo and then overseas. For Elza, it looked like a way to get back to Brazil. Figueiredo paid for her ticket back to Rio, and a whip-round organised by Netto raised enough money from people such as Chico Buarque, Jorge Ben, Vinícius, Amarildo and Netto himself to pay for Garrincha, Gilson, Sara and Elza's aunt Altina to join her on the flight home.

On 10 December, after one year and 11 months of exile, Garrincha and Elza arrived back at Galeão. In the interviews they gave shortly after touching down they told reporters that they were tired of being harassed and taken advantage of. They had no idea how prescient they were being, for two days later their lawyer Ernesto Dória had to hide Garrincha away. Mendes had asked that he be jailed for failing to pay Nair's pension.

CHAPTER 20

1972–1974: The Love of the Crowd

MENDES WAS SO CERTAIN OF VICTORY IN HIS CASE AGAINST GARRINCHA that he had arranged for police to wait outside the TV Tupi studios and arrest him when he left the Flávio Cavalcanti programme.

Garrincha had been invited to appear in a televised debate between Mendes and Ernesto Dória, which had come about after one of Garrincha's friends, journalist Sérgio Bittencourt, heard Elza complain about how Garrincha was being harassed by lawyers. The public perception was that by not paying Nair, Garrincha was allowing his family to starve. Bittencourt, however, had heard Elza angrily refute those suggestions. 'That woman need not want for necessities,' she'd insisted. 'When they separated, Garrincha gave her a house, a flat, land, stocks and shares, and money. Everyone knows my money kept him going. It is not fair that with all our sacrifices, his family is still living in misery.'

If what she said was true then there was something wrong somewhere. So Bittencourt decided it would be a good idea to have the two lawyers thrash the issue out on TV in the presence of Garrincha. It was a risky strategy, but if Garrincha really was innocent it would do wonders for his image. And whatever happened, it would make for sensational television.

Neither lawyer took any prisoners. Mendes described the poverty in which Nair and her eight daughters lived, the youngest of whom, now eight years old, hardly knew her father. The audience was moved, with good reason. But then Dória listed all that Garrincha had given to Nair. Where had it gone? He produced the receipts to show that the IBC was automatically withholding 20 per cent of his salary for Nair. The suspicion that the money had not gone where it was supposed to go hung in the air, and the audience took Garrincha's side. A defeated Mendes almost collapsed. Dória, who was well liked inside the police force, asked for their men to be removed from outside the building, and Garrincha left, tearful and triumphant.

Months before, when Garrincha was still in Italy, Dória had won another significant victory for his client when his appeal against Rosária's manslaughter conviction was granted. Garrincha was absolved and the sentence was quashed. Dória also managed to get Garrincha another year's work with the IBC, even though he was in Brazil. All of a sudden, things seemed to be looking up. The judicial threats hanging over Garrincha's head were removed, he had a job, and Elza was about to perform in Abelardo Figueiredo's successful Brazil export show. There was nothing to stop them being happy.

Figueiredo, however, didn't think Garrincha was happy. Every time he went to visit them at their new flat in Copacabana, Garrincha was complaining. Within days of their arrival the flat had become the republic of Pau Grande with the unfailing presence of Pincel, Swing and a host of others who came, drank and left again, barely pausing to say hello. But not even that reminder of home could lift Garrincha's spirits.

He seemed even worse at Elza's show in Rio. While Elza set the place ablaze with her presence and her voice, Garrincha curled up in the dressing room, indifferent to the hubbub. When she finished her stint, Elza ran off stage to be with him. Figueiredo saw that Elza was like a mother to her husband, protecting him as if he were an orphan she had found walking the streets. But she also kept a sharp eye on him because the waitresses who worked backstage made it clear they would drag him into the corner first chance they got.

The Brazil export show finished its two-month run in Rio and moved to São Paulo, where they played dates throughout March 1972. But the show's success came to an abrupt halt when its foreign investors objected to the participation of the dark-skinned girls. Figueiredo insisted they were an integral part of the troupe and the show never left Brazil. However, even if the show had gone on with Elza to Canada, it would have been without Garrincha. He had been signed by Olaria.

It was impossible to fathom what whim, pride or blindness made Garrincha believe he could still play professional football. A comeback had seemed improbable when he left Flamengo in 1968, yet now, four years older and even more alcohol-ravaged and depressed, Garrincha was insisting he could still do the job. And he had found a club that agreed.

Or rather a company: Ponto Frio, the electric- and household-goods firm that had helped him hold on to his house on the Ilha do Governador in 1964 when the bailiffs had threatened to seize it. The man who had come to his rescue then had passed away in 1969, but the company's commercial director was a friend of Olaria's principal benefactor Álvaro da Costa Melo. Using Pon to Frio money, Olaria paid Garrincha 5,000 cruzeiros a month and a share of the gate when they played big teams. The club was one of Rio's smaller sides but it had its sights set on challenging second-tier clubs América and Bangu for a place higher up Rio's footballing heirarchy. Signing Garrincha would help them command respect and bring them important publicity.

His debut came against Flamengo at the Maracanã on 23 February 1972. It was a Carioca Championship game on a rainy Wednesday night but the numbers on the scoreboard showed an impressive crowd of 49,276 people. Unfortunately, they had not all paid to see Garrincha;

instead, most of the fans had won tickets in a free draw held at the nine Pon to Frio shops spread throughout the city. But in the end it was unimportant: Pon to Frio sold a lot of fridges and Garrincha still got a nice cut of the gate money. And the embarrassment everyone had feared did not materialise.

Quite the opposite, in fact. Garrincha even beat his old friend Paulo Henrique a few times. Perhaps the Flamengo defenders gave him too much respect – sometimes they looked like as if they were about to doff their caps and wave him past – or perhaps they thought he was incapable of causing any damage. Whatever the reason, Garrincha told manager Roberto Pinto he wanted to stay on for the second half, and he was on the pitch when Olario took the lead in the fifty-fourth minute through a goal from Gessé. When the ball hit the net, the scenes were unprecedented. Instead of congratulating Gessé, the Olaria players ran to Garrincha to celebrate and he was buried under a pyramid of players. Pinto saw his chance and held up Garrincha's number. He ran off the field to warm applause from the crowd. The Flamengo players lined up to shake his hand as he departed, and some fans even cried. Doval equalised for Flamengo with 70 minutes to go but the match had lost its spark when Garrincha left the pitch and the sides played out a 1–1 draw.

No one spoke about 'the return of Garrincha'. Even though he had not exactly exerted himself, his knee was swollen and painful. He could clearly play only in carefully selected matches, which suited Olaria just fine.

Garrincha did not need to force himself to train but he made an effort and went to the training ground every day. No one asked him to, but he did two or three laps of the pitch, almost always walking. He enjoyed taking part in the pranks organised by the younger players, who never made him the target of their horseplay. He was sad, though, and the sadness was never more evident than when he told Pinto, 'I am really sorry I can't do what I used to, Roberto.'

Between February and August, Garrincha played ten league and friendly matches for Olaria, winning two, drawing four and losing four. He scored once, in a friendly against Comercial de Ribeirão Preto, and his last two games were against Botafogo, the final one coming on 23 August 1972, ten years after he had almost single-handedly won them the Carioca Championship against Flamengo.

Even though Olaria wanted him to keep playing, Garrincha knew it was time to retire from professional football. Privately he told Elza that he was starting to feel embarrassed about playing competitively. It wasn't so bad in friendlies, where he was up against people who knew him, but he felt ashamed at being out there when vital points were at stake. And there was another reason for wanting to retire: he had become a grandfather for the first time – his daughter Edenir had just given birth to Alexandra – and being a professional football player and a grandfather felt weird.

Garrincha was developing a conscience about football that he would never have when it came to alcohol. That same year, when someone asked him if he was still drinking, his denial, the typical alcoholic's response, served as confirmation: 'I am not drinking any more. I have had my fill. I just take a *caipirinha* now and then.'

At the beginning of March 1973, Garrincha was in Toron to playing *futbol de salão* with a local side called The Italians. He played two matches at $1,000 a time, but if he had any illusions about swapping the harder surface for the full-size pitch they didn't last long. *Futbol de salão*, a type of indoor football popular in Brazil, proved even more difficult than the real thing; the ball was smaller, heavier, and always in play. Just when he thought he would get a minute to catch his breath the ball was coming straight for him again.

When he got back to Rio, Garrincha accepted an offer from former Internacional player Ivo Hoffman to take part in a long tour of Brazil's provinces. In each city he would turn out for the local side against an obscure opponent. It would be nice to think that Garrincha was giving something back to the rural community by showcasing his

335

talents in some of Brazil's less affluent areas, playing against little-known sides so that one day the locals could boast of having been on the same pitch as Garrincha. But the truth was less romantic. It was bitter, and at times depressing. Garrincha played for the money, 4,000 cruzeiros per match, or about $600. He was the star turn in a travelling circus. The tour took him to almost 60 Brazilian cities to play matches on dirt fields where the crowd stood not in stands but on nearby hills. Even nets were few and far between. He travelled by train, plane, car and boat. When a player came off he had to give his shirt to the sub.

Garrincha usually played only during the first half, and even making it to half-time was a miracle for him. Wherever he went he was met by local authorities bearing industrial quantities of *cachaça* and local produce. Women of all social classes offered themselves to him, much to the chagrin of their husbands and boyfriends. Sometimes he went to the red-light district and ended up sleeping there, intoxicated by the cheap odours.

Often the organisers didn't have enough money to pay him his full fee and sometimes he would get into fights with fans; on one occasion he reacted angrily after someone insulted Elza and the fight ended with Garrincha almost being thrown through a hotel window. Such problems were a rarity, though; almost everywhere he went he was treated well. Not that he could tell where he was. Every city seemed the same to him. When he travelled through Quebrangulo on his way to play a game in Palmeira dos Índios he didn't even realise he was passing through the town where his father and grandparents had been born.

When Garrincha's wages got too heavy to carry from town to town, Hoffman took the money to the bank and wired it to Rio, where Elza added it to the savings they were putting aside to buy their flat. But in reality, it was a humiliating job. Elza could not stand to see him ambling about the pitch when so many other players who were not worthy of lacing his boots were retiring with glory and gratitude.

Gratitude. The word made her think again about a testimonial that would allow Brazil to show Garrincha how much they loved him and enable him to hang up his boots once and for all. She had tried twice before, in 1967 and 1969, and failed both times. This time she was going to get it right.

Elza and her journalist friend Edgard Cosme met with Gilbert Pereira de Oliveira, the vice president of the Foundation to Assist Professional Athletes (FUGAP), an association set up to help older players cope with life after football. Oliveira spoke with two reporters from the influential Radio Nacional, both of whom told him that a campaign could succeed only if they got the press on their side, as this would convince the CBD and Carioca Federation to back the idea and in addition give them the publicity necessary to fill the Maracanã. Cosme and Oliveira also took Elza to meet the country's most important radio reporters and newspaper columnists and all of them pledged to support her, on the condition that a portion of the takings go to Garrincha's daughters.

The idea was to stage a match between the World Cup-winning side of 1970, with Garrincha on the right wing, and a Rest of the World Select. There were practical problems to overcome, however. The CBD would have to pay for the foreigners to come from Europe and the Rio authorities would have to waive their customary 30 per cent cut of the gate money for the use of the Maracanã. A date was set for 19 December and the match was given the title 'The Gratitude Game'.

And then the problems started. The CBD delayed for two weeks before telling the organisers that they could not get the European players they wanted because their clubs would not release them in the middle of the European season. Instead, they came up with the idea of forming a select side comprising foreigners playing in Brazil. But even that was going to be costly because the foreigners – and the Brazilians – were spread throughout the country. The CBD was not co-operating. Players read in the papers that they would be asked to take part but that the confederation did not formally solicit their participation. And the confederation had not asked the players from the 1958 and 1962 teams if they would take part in a game against a select from that era.

With just ten days to go before the match was scheduled to take place, Oliveira took control of the operation and asked the clubs to help out. Flamengo offered their hotel for the players who travelled. Botafogo gave them their bus for transportation. Volunteers went to the airports to meet and greet those coming from further afield. The Ministry of Education paid for travel expenses and dozens of Brazil's top musicians, including people such as Chico Buarque, Jorge Ben and Paulinho da Viola, offered to perform for free in a pre-match show. The press talked and wrote about the game every day, and radio reporters, the real stars of the time, went out of their way to publicise it. Private companies pitched in, many firms giving away tickets to employees as Christmas presents. Pon to Frio bought no fewer than 30,000 tickets. There were no complimentary tickets available: even reporters and photographers had to pay their way in.

It was again proposed that Garrincha carry out a lap of honour with his daughters, but he and Elza vetoed the idea, saying it was exploitation. Then the CBD refused to let the Brazil side play in their official strip, saying that it was not an official match, and the team was instead forced to wear a yellow shirt without the traditional CBD badge or the stars that Garrincha had helped put above it. The confederation's entire contribution was $1,000: the Carioca Federation, still run by Otávio 'Coathanger' Pinto Guimarães, didn't even give that much.

Nevertheless, the day before the game the proceeds had reached $100,000, a sum that was enough for Garrincha at last to put his life in order. It was suggested that Nílton Santos help him run his financial affairs, but his old team-mate was having none of it. 'No way,' he said. 'No one can help Garrincha with his money. One day the money is going to run out and I'll be the one that gets the blame.'

There was at least one person who didn't want to run the risk of seeing Garrincha fritter away his new fortune: Nair's lawyer. Even though he had read in the papers that a share of the gate money would go to Garrincha's daughters, Mendes asked a judge to guarantee that the money would go through him first. To Mendes's surprise, Garrincha was in court for the hearing and an agreement was reached under which the money would be channelled to the girls' bank accounts via FUGAP. The remaining cash would go to his account, part of which would be used to buy houses for his daughters. Mendes was not happy with the arrangement and he tried to get Garrincha's son-in-law to convince his wife to lodge an appeal on behalf of Nair and her daughters. He was worried, and he was right to be. The game promised to be a huge money earner.

On the night of the game, Rio was buzzing. It was not just a football match, it was a spectacle. People were delighted to be able to help the man to whom they were so grateful. A sea of 131,555 people filled the circular stadium. The terraces were bedecked with flags from every club, draped and waved by fans who had come to pay tribute. On the track in front of the stand, one of Garrincha's friends had arranged a floral display reading 'Mané, Joy of the People'. When Elza saw the stadium filled with people and love, she exclaimed, 'Now I can die happy!'

On the pitch, Barbosa, Bellini, Orlando, Nílton Santos, Zito, Zózimo, Julinho, Vavá, Quarentinha, Zagalo, Adalberto, Pampollini, Altair, Maurinho, Sabará and other former colleagues played in the warm-up match. Some were greying, others were going bald, but all of them were capable of making the ball do whatever they wanted – when they had the strength.

Just like the man they had gathered to honour.

Félix; Carlos Alberto, Brito, Piazza and Everaldo; Clodoaldo, Rivelino and Paulo César; Garrincha, Jairzinho and Pelé. It was the legendary team from 1970, with Gerson and Tostão making way for Garrincha on the right wing and his successor Jairzinho at centre-forward. Both the Brazilians and the foreigners spent the day together at the Flamengo *concentração*. Without Garrincha's knowledge, Edgard Cosme had convinced the opposition full-back Bruñel to let the star of the show beat him once or twice, and he played his role perfectly: in the eighteenth minute he let Garrincha push the ball through his legs and the crowd went wild. On two other occasions, Garrincha controlled the ball, and with no one near him swung in perfect crosses for Pelé and Jairzinho. The Vasco goalkeeper Andrada was not about to co-operate, though. He had never recovered from being the man in goal when Pelé scored his thousandth goal.

With half an hour gone, as had been agreed, referee Armando Marques stopped the game to let Garrincha do a lap of honour. Garrincha ran towards the terraces filled with thousands of hands waving farewell. Tears fell from many eyes, although not from Garrincha's – no one ever saw him cry. The fans didn't shout 'Stay! Stay! Stay!' like they had for Pelé; instead they chanted his name – 'Garrincha! Garrincha! Garrincha!' – as though they were pronouncing it for the first time. When he had completed his lap of honour he stopped in front of the *geral* terrace, the standing-only area at pitch level where the entrance fee was cheaper and where the hardcore fans gathered. He tore off his boots, his socks and his shin pads and one by one threw them into the crowd. When he had removed everything bar his shorts, he ran to the dressing room surrounded by a huge crowd. He saved his shirt for one of his closest friends, the *macumba* priest Alberto.

Garrincha was in the dressing room when Pelé beat four men and slipped the ball past an advancing Andrada. It was one of his greatest goals and a worthy tribute to Garrincha. But nothing that happened after that, not even Luis Pereira's goal that gave Brazil a 2–1 win, was of any importance, except perhaps the announcement that the night's takings totalled 1,383,121 cruzeiros, or almost $230,000.

Throughout the second half the Maracanã tunnel appeared to be swallowing people. Friends and acquaintances made their way into the dressing room where they gave Garrincha medals, trophies and even birds. People he had never seen before kissed him, hugged him and pushed cheques into his shirt pocket. Shortly before midnight, Garrincha, Elza and a group of friends left the stadium and went to a club in Leblon, where Elza was singing. The night ended at four a.m. when Garrincha – surprisingly sober, just as he had been on the eve of the match – took Elza home to their flat in Copacabana.

The next morning, Garrincha went to the bank and opened an account with the cheques he had received the night before. He had no ID or social-security number but the bank manager was co-operative, although not so co-operative that he allowed Garrincha to take the money out immediately, as he wanted to. He had to wait until the cheques cleared before he could get his hands on the cash, the manager explained. Garrincha nodded and headed off towards the North Side. An hour later he had used his new chequebook to pay 25,000 cruzeiros for a blue Chevette. He went to Oliveira's house and asked him to return to the dealer with him. When he got there, he pointed at the car and laughed. 'It's yours, my good man.'

Those who had heard the Maracanã loudspeakers announce the night's taking could have been forgiven for thinking that Garrincha had left the stadium with the cash in his pocket. But in fact the money was handed over to him a week later on 27 December after the relevant parties had taken their cut. Of the 1,383,121 cruzeiros taken at the gate, the Inland Revenue walked away with 8 per cent, or 110,649; another 13,120 went to FUGAP; 6,865 went on the cost of printing the tickets; and 254,494 was set aside to open nine accounts for Nair and his eight daughters. The cheque finally presented to Garrincha was worth 997,993 cruzeiros, or $166,000.

Before the game, Pelé, considered an astute businessman by his fellow players, had offered to have his assistants help Garrincha invest the money. Garrincha had politely turned down the offer, saying he

341

already knew what he was going to do with it. Which was exactly what many people feared.

At the start of 1974, Garrincha made good on his promise to his daughters: he bought one-bedroom flats for Edenir, Denísia, Marinete and Juraciara; small houses for Maria Cecilia, Terezinha Conceição and Cíntia; and a place in Pau Grande for his eldest Terezinha, who was by now married with twins. The purchases cost him 270,000 cruzeiros, leaving him, in theory, with about 700,000 to do with as he wished.

The first thing he did was take 200,000 cruzeiros in cash along with 400,000 he got from the sale of his and Elza's flat in Copacabana to buy a house in Barra da Tijuca, an up-and-coming neighbourhood to the far west of Rio. He still had 500,000 cruzeiros remaining, enough to bring him 10,000 cruzeiros a month in interest alone if he left it in the bank. It wouldn't be enough to get him invited to Onassis family parties, but it would ensure he wouldn't have to worry about where his next lunch was coming from.

Or his next drink.

Garrincha drove his 1963 Oldsmobile into the garage of his house and found his usual parking space occupied – by a car wrapped up as a present. Underneath the huge bow was a blue Mercedes. A second-hand one, but a Mercedes nonetheless, as grand and palatial as a cathedral. It was Elza's present to him, and he did not understand.

'Why such luxury, Crioula?'

'It's going to be good for you, baby. People will respect you more.'

Garrincha took it for a spin but he didn't seem happy.

'Do you think that a person is superior because he drives a Mercedes?' he asked. 'You can be superior in a VW Beetle. All this is good for is attracting thieves.'

Garrincha ended up putting his birds in the back of the car and taking them out to Recreio dos Bandeirantes, a largely rural area out past Barra da Tijuca. He liked to set the cages down in the middle of the forest to make the birds feel at home. When he arrived back at his house the back seat was covered with water, birdseed and droppings.

Elza got the message, but she did not give up on her hope of seeing Garrincha live an active, sober and respectable life. She still wanted to believe that if Garrincha had something with which to fill his time, he would stop drinking. But the Garrincha Elza dreamt of – a responsible middle-aged man who worked nine to five, came home to the wife, put his slippers on, drank a brandy and then went to sleep – was as improbable as his becoming the doctor or lawyer she had imagined when they'd first met all those years ago.

In March 1979, Elza and Garrincha took the first steps towards buying O Bigode do Meu Tio (My Uncle's Moustache), a steakhouse and nightclub that was to become the worst business deal of their lives. The club had been a huge hit but the owner had no time to run the place and was looking to sell up. Elza convinced Garrincha to buy it, and together they paid 400,000 cruzeiros, 160,000 in cash with the rest to paid in 30 instalments of 8,000 cruzeiros. Another 100,000 went on refurbishing the place. Elza's dream was to turn the club – they were going to call it 'O Garrincha' but changed their minds at the last minute and opted to name it 'La Boca' – into a temple of samba and football, a place where Elza would sing and Garrincha would meet and greet dignitaries, artists and sportsmen. Its financial success, Elza believed, would give Garrincha the freedom to start playing friendlies again the way he had once done, for free, for the sheer joy of it.

Garrincha had lost interest in football. He hardly bothered to watch that summer's World Cup in West Germany. Brazil were lucky to qualify from their group and they beat Argentina 2–1 in the quarter-finals, but when they came up against the majestic Dutch in the semis they had met their match. Garrincha could hardly have cared less. When a reporter asked him what he thought of Brazil's right-winger Valdomiro, Garrincha responded with vague platitudes. He had no idea who Valdomiro was.

La Boca brought nothing but misery to their financial situation. Elza and Garrincha knew as much about running a nightclub as they did about running NASA. Customers who went there in the hope of seeing the couple often returned home disappointed. Elza had to do other shows to make money, and when people found out she wasn't going to be singing at La Boca they cancelled their reservations. Garrincha refused to let his old friends pay and he didn't help the cash-flow situation by demolishing the stocks of Cointreau. Waiters and chefs were not paid on time and some of them took Elza and Garrincha to court to demand their wages. Even when the place was full it didn't actually make them any money: all the profits went directly towards paying off their debts.

The list of creditors grew, and although Elza took out covering loans the bills kept arriving. Salaries, taxes, electricity, gas, water, telephone. They couldn't meet the monthly instalments of 8,000 cruzeiros and in September the original owner sued them. By Christmas, it was clear that the club was bankrupt. When they did finally make the decision to sell, the business was in such a mess that they couldn't find a buyer. The place was abandoned, and in February 1975 trucks arrived to seize the assets.

The thousands of dollars that kind fans had given to Garrincha in the Gratitude Game were disappearing faster than they had come through the turnstiles.

CHAPTER 21

1975–1977: Elza Loses the Fight

IN MARCH 1975, NAIR DIED IN PAU GRANDE. SHE HAD CANCER OF THE
uterus and it was diagnosed too late. She had never been to a gynae-
cologist in her life.

Nair was only 38, but no one would have taken her for a year
under 50. Her two oldest daughters, Terezinha and Edenir, were both
married with kids; the other six – Marinete, 18; Juraciara, 17; Denísia,
15; María Cecília, 14; Terezinha Conceição, 13; and Cíntia, 11 –
were adolescents. They all still lived together, the eldest working in
América Fabril, which was on the verge of closing down, and the
youngest wearing hand-me-downs. Although they had spent their lives
being photographed, they were a million miles away from the celebrity
lifestyle enjoyed by their father. They were naive and vulnerable;
some of them still giggled with embarrassment when questioned by
reporters. Almost all of them had dropped out of school. Life had not
exactly been a bed of roses.

Garrincha hadn't known Nair was ill. A month earlier, when she
was taken into hospital, relatives had had to club together to raise the
100 cruzeiros for an ambulance. No one asked Garrincha for help.
He didn't visit her in hospital and he didn't go to the funeral.

When Nair died, Garrincha, with Elza's support, asked a judge to grant him custody of his youngest daughters. The judge consented, and all except Marinete, who stayed in Pau Grande with Edenir, went to São Paulo to live with them in a new four-bedroom flat they rented especially. The youngest girls had never been to school and couldn't read or write, or even tell the time. They were menstruating but had never been given sanitary towels. Elza shaved their heads to rid them of lice, bought them new clothes and tried to teach them the basic everyday skills that most people take for granted, such as answering the telephone. She forced the girls to take a bath every day and didn't mind when they used almost a whole bar of soap – each. Against all expectations the girls got on well with Elza. She wasn't the stepmother from hell but a woman who took them to the hairdresser and let them raid the fridge whenever they wanted.

After the club venture had failed to perform, Elza had gone to São Paulo to perform in a series of shows organised by impresario Reginaldo Corumba. She made good money from the tour, but because she was paying out a fortune to sustain families in both Rio and São Paulo by the time the end of the month came around she had very little left.

She had insisted that Garrincha go with her to São Paulo. Anything would be better than leaving him at home to take advantage of her absence and hit the bottle again. But while she was out working, Garrincha spent the day lying on the sofa staring at the ceiling. When he did go out, it was to the local bar to drink *traçados*, cocktails of *cachaça* and vermouth. Elza thought his new depression was brought about by loneliness. She was happy that he was far from Pincel and Swing, but she did not know how long the funk would last, so when her contract with Corumba expired she returned to Rio.

There, everything changed again. They sold the Mercedes and the house in Barra in order to pay off some of the debts run up at La Boca, and with the remaining money they bought a second-hand Galaxie and a house in Jacarepaguá, to the far west of the city. Edgard Cosme and Manuelzinho never ceased to be amazed at their ability to wheel and deal and somehow emerge from the worst financial situations with money in their pockets. They lost houses and cars and then went out and bought new ones. Even more incredible was the number of people they supported.

The house in Jacarepaguá had 12 rooms yet still barely managed to house the huge crowd that had gathered around them: Garrincha, Elza, his five daughters, her three children, her sister, her aunt and her three nieces and nephews – and that wasn't counting the maids, the driver Edson and two or three lodgers. Only Elza was earning any money and everything she made went towards feeding them. Every month they devoured 120 kilos of rice, 90 kilos of beans and 80 kilos of sugar. Even bird feed was a major expenditure: by now Garrincha had more than 200 feathered friends.

But even the pleasure he took from watching his birds was not enough to lift him out of his depression. Alcohol is a violent depresser of the nervous system; all alcoholics, sooner or later, get depressed. And the more depressed Garrincha became, the more he drank to escape from the darkness. In Jacarepaguá, far from civilisation and with no responsibilities and nothing much to do, Garrincha started to down oceans of alcohol. The only time his body was rested was while he was sleeping, but when he woke up he needed to drink even more to make up for the time his body had gone without. He got up in the morning in a cold sweat, his hands shaking and his heart pounding. He would go out to bars or friends' houses and drink, and when Elza found him she would drag him home by the scruff of the neck. She refused to allow him to leave the house so he sat in the garden and drank from bottles his friends had thrown over the wall during the night.

One of the side effects of Garrincha's drinking was incontinence. He would wake in the middle of the night, head for the bathroom and relieve himself against any tiled wall in the belief that he was urinating into the bowl. Sometimes he didn't even get that far and he would wet the bed or himself as he staggered to the toilet.

His sexual problems were also gradually getting worse. When he was sober he wasn't interested in Elza; when he was drunk he wanted her at all costs. He could maintain an erection while under the influence but it was difficult for him to ejaculate. Sometimes he fell asleep during intercourse.

He began to sweat profusely, and he left a smell of alcohol everywhere he went. It seemed as if alcohol was seeping from every pore. He paid less and less attention to his personal hygiene and could go a week without shaving or taking a shower. Elza had to force him to wash, and even to eat. Consuming solid food caused him to throw up, especially in the morning. He looked like a man whose internal organs were literally being pickled.

Elza continued to hide the extent of the problem from the rest of the world. She booked the two of them into a hotel, believing she could force him into cold turkey. But Garrincha rattled like a cocktail shaker and Elza was so frightened that she abandoned the plan after two days and took him home. When friends recommended she check him into a treatment clinic, she baulked, fearing that if the press found out it would demoralise him.

Her solution to getting him sober again was to have a baby. When she decided to get pregnant she thought first of the risks. Garrincha was a physical and emotional wreck and that could cause complications in the unborn child. Moreover, the chance of her getting pregnant was slim because her Fallopian tubes were obstructed. Nevertheless, she decided to take the chance. She made Garrincha promise that if she got pregnant he would stop drinking, or at least try to cut down. He did, and in what was a much-needed break for his body Garrincha controlled his intake for nine whole months.

The child was to be her eighth, and the first since the birth of Gilson 20 years earlier. Elza was determined to do everything possible to ensure a complication-free pregnancy and she spent almost the whole nine months in bed resting. The doctors who first examined her advised her to terminate the pregnancy, but she refused. She needed something in her life since her recording career had come to a halt the previous year when Odeon, the record company that had discovered her and given her her first hit with 'Se acaso você chegasse' in 1960, rescinded her contract. She planned to restart her career with a small label but for the moment she needed a project, and the baby was it.

Cutting back on the drink enabled Garrincha to get into decent enough shape to make some money playing for a team called the Milionários – the Millionaires. The Milionários were formed in Rio in 1954 by ex-goalkeeper João Mendes Toledo and named after the Colombian side of the 1940s and 1950s that was banned by FIFA for contravening transfer laws and offering big sums of money to sign whichever stars took their fancy, Argentinian greats Di Stefano, Pedernera and Nestor Rossi among them. Toledo's Milionários featured a host of former World Cup winners: Nílton Santos, Bellini, Djalma Santos, Pepe, Vavá, Orlando and Oreco, all of them now retired and with grey hair or respectable paunches. As the brains behind the organisation, Toledo knew what he was doing. He had an address book with the names of dozens of mayors and the date on which their city or town celebrated its founding. When the date approached he called them and offered to bring the Milionários to town as part of the celebrations. The mayors, many of whom were from a generation that still considered Nílton Santos, Bellini and Vavá national heroes, went to great lengths to raise money for their illustrious guests. With Garrincha in the side, the fee for bringing the Milionários to town tripled.

Toledo took the side to hundreds of small towns and cities in Brazil's far-flung provinces and to many more in the prosperous cities that surrounded São Paulo itself. It was not unusual for the team to play 30 games a year, a number that increased in 1975 when Garrincha became a regular attraction. Or as regular as Garrincha ever was.

In order to ensure he would actually turn up to play, Toledo drove from São Paulo to Rio to pick Garrincha up. When the game was

349

over he brought him home. His fee was $400 per match, twice what his team-mates got. Not that he was in it for the money. He gave the distinct impression that all he was interested in was drinking and playing football. Although he wasn't always able to do both.

No matter how much his team-mates kept an eye on him, Garrincha always managed to find a drink before the game. Sometimes he would pretend to go to the toilet then sneak into the kitchen to put away two or three quick shots. Toledo took to asking someone to accompany him to the bathroom, but Garrincha made his excuses and slipped out to the local bar. Before long he didn't even bother to pack his football boots and played in whatever was available. If they were the right size, great; if they weren't, that was fine too. The Milionários were there not to win games but to entertain – although they usually did win, or at least draw, more often than not after Garrincha had been subbed in the first half and they were back to playing with 11 men.

For Garrincha really struggled. With no strength left in his legs, his corner kicks didn't even reach the penalty box, and he rarely risked trying to dribble the ball. Even though Bellini asked opposing defenders to let him beat them once or twice, he frequently beat himself. During one game in Rio Preto he tried to take the ball past the full-back and simply collapsed on his knees. Someone in the crowd shouted, 'That man is drunk!' People started booing and Toledo pulled him off. Garrincha didn't even know what had happened.

Even more painful – and it wasn't an infrequent occurrence – was when fans screamed abuse. 'You son of a bitch! You never came here when you were good. You only appear now, when you've got one foot in the grave!' The insults embarrassed the mayors and presidents of the local clubs they were playing and they approached Garrincha afterwards to apologise. Local businessmen gave the players gifts, and in addition to his wage Garrincha came away with bags full of beans, cheese, dried meat and fruit. His huge family were certainly not going to die of hunger.

And he was not going to die of thirst. He never came away without a bottle or two of the local *cachaça* as well.

Manuel Garrincha do Santos Júnior was born on 9 July 1976 at the Balbino Clinic in Olaria on Rio's North Side. It was a Caesarean birth and the child emerged in perfect health, weighing in at just over nine pounds. Most importantly, it was a boy, as Elza always said it would be. Garrincha went with Elza to the hospital and as soon as the child was born he kissed her and took off for Paraná, where he was due to play for the Milionários. When he got to Videira, where the match was to take place, the city had already hung a banner across the main street congratulating him on the birth of his son.

Garrincha only made it back to the maternity ward four days later, and when he arrived he was very drunk. When Elza saw him falling over flowers and nurses, she gave him an ultimatum: 'You are going to have to choose. It's either the drink or your son.'

Garrincha did not respond.

There was more trouble on the horizon. A registrar refused to register the child's name as Garrincha, alleging that Garrincha was a nickname and not a proper name. A lawyer from Elza's new record company Tapecar had to go to the registrar's office and convince the man to allow Garrincha to call his son by whatever name he wanted. Worse still two months later Elza was arrested at the Tapecar offices after she failed to pay one of the creditors from the La Boca deal on time. Police handcuffed her and tried to put her in the back of a squad car but she refused, and they ended up taking her to the station in a taxi. Manolo, the head of Tapecar, sped off to get the money, but it was six in the evening and all the banks were closed. Elza spent hours surrounded by men who seemed to be growling at her. Milk spilled from her breasts while her son sat at home screaming to be fed. She was eventually freed at two a.m. when they managed to raise the cash. Anyone else would have been traumatised. For Elza, already a victim of attacks, death threats and kidnaps, the episode was no big deal.

To all intents and purposes, Garrinchinha was Garrincha's first son. Brazilians remembered the eight daughters he had had with Nair in a sequence that was as cruel as it was monotonous. He was said to have a son in Sweden, but in spite of the positive paternity test no one really knew if it was true – and even if it was, he was as far away as the northern lights. His other son, Neném, the child he had had with Iraci in 1961, was known only to those in Pau Grande. Unlike Márcia, the daughter he had had with Iraci in 1959, Neném had never been registered as Garrincha's child.

Iraci, in spite of feeling hard done by, was always loyal. In 1962, when she was ditched after Elza arrived on the scene, she returned quietly to Pau Grande with her children. Neném was 18 months old at the time and Garrincha never saw him again. Life was not easy for Iraci. With no way of sustaining herself and her children, at one point she proposed they all commit suicide by drinking poison. But Márcia and Neném wept before they drank their glasses of deadly *guaraná*. Iraci was overcome with regret and managed to pick herself up and carry on. She married a humble América Fabril worker named Clésio, who adopted her children as his own. She followed Garrincha's career from a distance – his demise as a player, his stint in Italy, the Gratitude Game – and it never occurred to her to ask for the same things Nair had for her own children.

However, Neném would not stay hidden much longer. That year, aged 15, skinny, with crooked legs and bags of talent, he was spotted playing football in Pau Grande by Fluminense director José Lemos. He stood out thanks to his legs, and the fact that he was a right-winger.

Lemos asked who the kid was and someone answered, 'That's Neném, Garrincha's son.'

'You're joking!' said Lemos.

'Everybody knows that.'

Lemos spoke to the kid after the game and Neném took him to meet his mother, who told him the whole story. Lemos was thrilled and promised Neném he would take him to the club and have him work with the youth-team coach Pinheiro. The story even reached the pages of O Globo, which ran a full-page feature on him. Everyone who saw the photo could see that Neném was the spitting image of his father.

Everyone, that is, except Elza. Three months after giving Garrincha a son she did not want to know about other children just because they had crooked legs. She tried to be logical, but she was angry. 'Do you think', she argued, 'that mother would take 15 years to look for the boy's father? Especially when the father is Garrincha? The boy is going to play with Fluminense and she is trying to get him some publicity. It's evil.'

Garrincha, however, could not deny that he knew 'dona Iraci', that he had given her a house, food and clothes in Rio and that he was also the father of Márcia, Neném's sister. His refusal to recognise the boy stemmed from the fact that he had lied about his relationship with her: 'We had broken up already. One day she turned up saying she was expecting my baby. I said that she couldn't be right. We had already separated and I wasn't sure if the baby was mine. Just look at the birth certificate.' The fact that he hadn't admitted to paternity didn't mean the baby wasn't his. And Garrincha couldn't confess (because Elza would have killed him) that in the years after splitting up from Iraci he had gone to Pau Grande a few times and given her money, which Iraci accepted because Clésio earned next to nothing. It was true he had never seen Neném again but he heard about him from Márcia, to whom he had given biscuits when he visited his daughters.

Now, years later, when Garrincha pretended not to know the truth about Neném, no one believed him. 'He looks like me, doesn't he? Botafogo had a guy with bent legs who called himself Garrinchinha. He was almost as old as me, but they said he was my son too.'

But the similarities between Garrincha and Neném were so obvious that within two years he had to admit to being the boy's father. At the request of television he even let himself be filmed kicking a ball about with the kid at Fluminense.

By that time, though, Elza was out of his life.

Ulf Lindberg, Garrincha's Swedish son, was the subject of a magazine article published in Scandinavia in June 1977. A Swedish woman who lived in Rio was sent the pictures by her sister-in-law, who was Ulf's teacher, and she passed them on to Garrincha and the Rio magazine *Fatos & Fotos* (Facts and Photos). The pictures showed a 17-year old with light skin and powerful legs playing keepie-uppie. The wide nose and fleshy lips were unmistakably Garrincha's. It was not the first time he had seen his Swedish offspring. Garrincha had received photos from the boy's family, but they had cut all links at the end of the 1960s and since then he had heard nothing. Now, though, Ulf had resurfaced. With the pictures was a tender letter from Ulf telling his 'dad Garrincha' that 'he'd like to meet him and hear his news'.

Had Ulf known, he'd have asked for anything but the latest news from Brazil. Because Garrincha's news was all bad.

Garrinchinha, now a year old, had not brought the harmony his mother and father had hoped he would. In fact he had brought discord, and violence. Elza's ultimatum, 'the drink or the baby', had had no effect. Now, more than at any time in his life, Garrincha had no control over himself and he did not take kindly to Elza's attempts to get him to stop drinking. At the slightest complaint he would storm out of the flat and head to the nearest bar. When he returned hours later he would restart the argument in order to feel victimised and justified in his drinking. His attitudes were the typical responses of an alcoholic.

Garrincha was a danger to Garrinchinha. Even when he was relatively sober he would squeeze him tightly without releasing him, almost burn him with the tip of his cigarette, and playfully throw him three feet into the air. A frightened Elza would stop what she was doing and tear the baby away from Garrincha, angering him and provoking a tug of war over the child. With the baby on her shoulder, Elza would take Garrincha's abuse and the baby would cry.

Garrincha slapped Elza in July 1977. It was the first time he had taken his anger out on her since their scraps in Italy. As the month went on there were more slaps, and for other reasons: he suspected she was cheating on him with her record producer. Paranoia is a side effect of alcoholism, and betrayal is another almost inevitable consequence. For the first time in their 15 years together, Elza sought refuge in the arms of another man. The man she had once loved more than she loved herself no longer existed.

From August onwards, the violence occurred almost daily, and the rumours about their battles spread to the newspapers. Elza denied them, but her close friends knew they were true. So true in fact that Elza, fearing for the safety of Garrinchinha, rented a flat in Copacabana to which she could escape when Garrincha got threatening. On the 15th, the situation became untenable, and with Garrincha out of town on a trip with the Milionários, she packed a bag and moved out. She hoped her husband would see he was losing his family and come to his senses.

When Garrincha arrived home he was surprised to see them gone. He did not know Elza had rented another place and it took him two weeks to find them. When he finally tracked them down on 30 August, he tried to break the door down. Elza eventually opened it and he ordered her to take the baby home. She refused, so he knocked her to the ground and laid into her with punches and kicks. What he had never done to the opponents who attacked him he was now doing to the only woman he had ever loved. Elza managed to grab Garrinchinha and flee the building via the back door with her dress ripped and her face and body hurting from the blows. It was the end of Garrincha and Elza.

It was also the end of Garrincha.

When Elza returned to the flat with two police officers early the next morning, he was gone. Fearing for her life, she had gone straight to the police and an officer had told her that Garrincha would be charged with assault. If found guilty he would face between two and four years in prison. When she heard the possible sentence, Elza refused to let the doctors examine her.

The police went to look for Garrincha in Jacarepaguá, but he had already been and gone. He was hiding in the house of his neighbour, Charles Borer, Botafogo's new president. He spent one night at Borer's and then checked into the O.K. Hotel in Copacabana while Borer tried to sort out the mess with the authorities. Garrincha spent three nights there, leaving only to go to Borer's office nearby. When he was convinced that Elza was not going to press charges, he returned home. Elza never would.

Garrincha spent the next few weeks in mourning. Elza refused to see him, and when he did manage to contact her, she wouldn't listen. Borer suggested that Garrincha take her to court for fleeing with their son but Garrincha wanted only reconciliation, and that was the last thing on Elza's mind.

Instead, she offered to help Garrincha and his family financially, on the condition that he keep his distance. The question was where. The house in Jacarepaguá where he lived with the rest of his and Elza's extended family was no longer his as Elza had put it up as collateral in exchange for loans given to her by her new manager Calil. When she could not pay him back, she lost it – the third such house to disappear.

Calil let Garrincha stay in the house until September. Without Elza, however, there was a stampede to leave. It wasn't long before his solitude was complete.

CHAPTER 22

1977–1982: The Mangueira Zombie

GARRINCHA WAS ALONE IN JACAREPAGUÁ. HIS DAUGHTERS RETURNED to Pau Grande and Elza's family and friends went their own way. Elza sent removal men to pick up her belongings and they took everything except the few trophies and medals Garrincha had managed to hold on to. With the house cleared of furniture – there was not even a bed – Garrincha slept on the floor on a towel or a beach mat. There was no fridge and nothing to eat, and even if there had been there were no plates off which to eat or pots or pans with which to cook. Garrincha let his birds go and checked into the Ambassador Hotel in the city centre. He spent a month there, still bitter at Elza for leaving him and taking their son. He believed she had left him for another man and he spent his days drowning his sorrows, leaving the hotel only to pick up prostitutes on the street downstairs.

On his forty-fourth birthday Garrincha finally managed to speak to Elza on the phone. He invited her to come and spend the day with him but she refused, so Garrincha called and asked Edgard Cosme to come and visit him at the Ambassador with Vanderléa, the widow of their mutual friend, former Vasco winger Jorginho 'Carvoeiro' ('Coalman').

Garrincha had met the 28-year-old Vanderléa when she and

Carvoeiro had visited Garrincha and Elza at their home in Jacarepaguá earlier that year. Shortly afterwards, however, Carvoeiro died after an agonising bout with cancer, and a month after that Elza left Garrincha. Garrincha liked Vanderléa and wanted to meet her again. Two weeks later, in November 1977, he moved into her house in Bangu.

In Bangu, Garrincha felt as if he was at home. It was a staunchly working-class area populated by people who had grown up in the shadow of a big textile factory founded by the English at the start of the century. There were chimneys on the horizon and a football pitch next to the factory, and people cycled to work every day. But this was not the verdant rural Rio of the 1930s and 1940s, rather an industrialised suburb on the city's gritty West Side. In place of the hillside breezes, the temperature in Bangu was a permanently stifling 100 degrees; the leaves never moved and the only birds were suffocating in their cages. Instead of charming cottages there were high-rise estates from whose windows the residents hung their underpants and bras.

Vanderléa was employed in the factory and, like Nair, worked in the cloth section. Destiny had come full circle and was tightening its grip on Garrincha in the most ironic way possible. But though their backgrounds were similar, Vanderléa was nothing like Nair. For Vanderléa de Oliveira Vieira was a well-built, bossy and clever girl who lived with her retired docker father, her brothers, and her son Wendell. Garrincha was just one more member of the family. He did not wish it to be any other way.

In their first few months together, Vanderléa had to get used to some of Garrincha's unusual habits. One of them was his custom of not wearing underpants. Perhaps it was so that he had one less article of clothing to take off, because there were times when his libido was such that he went after Vanderléa several times a day. But principally she had to get used to his alcoholism. Vanderléa, like Elza, wasn't much of a drinker. She knew Garrincha drank before she set up home with him, she just didn't know how much. It took her a while to discover that she needed to be strict.

Garrincha got up at six a.m. every morning and went out, ostensibly to buy breakfast but in reality to have his first drink of the day. He came back with bread and milk but by mid-morning he had gone out again. Although there were no bars on his street he had a few favourite hangouts just around the corner. Sometimes he gave flowers to Vanderléa on his return before taking a nap to recharge his batteries for the serious drinking ahead.

When Garrincha was late coming home, Vanderléa knew he would return accompanied either by his friends or by the police. Many times he came back having wet himself, and he often arrived at the house after banging his head on a tree or having fallen and scraped his knees or arms. Even when he was at home he was not safe: he would fall asleep with a cigarette in his hand and burn his chest, stomach or leg.

Vanderléa noticed how Garrincha described everyone he met as a 'good guy'. It was his way of not speaking badly of anyone and of avoiding having to remember names. To recall all the people he had come across would have required an encyclopaedic memory, and what Garrincha remembered was not enough to fill a notebook. He could recall the names of the sides he had played against but he had trouble recalling what he'd done the day before. Sarcastically, or out of habit, even those who had hurt him he classed as 'good guys'. And he had the same response for everything, even when he wasn't happy: 'Right.'

His lack of interest in what was going on around him was evident: it was as if he had an invisible veil over his eyes. But he eventually found something to shake him from his torpor when the Rio director of the Brazilian Assistance Legion (LBA), one of the country's best-known charitable organisations, came to him with a proposal to help run a football clinic for underprivileged children.

At the beginning of 1978, the LBA wanted to create a network of soccer schools for disadvantaged youngsters. The schools would be run by famous ex-players, and Garrincha's was the first name to be mentioned as a potential coach. Everyone knew Garrincha needed a job and the LBA thought that involving him in the new project was just what he needed. They were unaware of his alcoholism, which was just as well, as by now he could not go more than a few hours without drinking and that made it difficult for him to fulfil commitments and keep appointments. But the LBA believed that getting Garrincha on board would attract other former players. And it did. After he signed on, Nílton Santos, Jair Rosa Pinto, Vavá, Alcir, Barbosinha and Denílson all followed.

Garrincha was enthusiastic about the offer. He was going to do what he had always considered his true vocation: help kids and pass on to them his fantastic array of tricks. At the press conference to announce his participation he never let go of the ball. When photographers asked him to kick it about for the cameras, he made his excuses: 'Keepie-uppie was never my thing. It's Nílton Santos that's good at that. I'm best with the ball on the ground.' It was true. Unlike Nílton Santos, who could keep a matchbox or a bottle top in the air for hours, Garrincha never knew what to do.

Garrincha's role as the LBA's 'community development and social recreation assistant' was to promote vaccination campaigns, distribute milk to poor families and, most importantly, to visit the schools the LBA was setting up in five Rio suburbs.

His first day of work in the field in Duque de Caxias on the outskirts of the city was like a tribute to him. The nightly news broadcast pictures of mothers and fathers embracing him, proud that he had been put in charge of their children. The kids knew who he was and they couldn't take their eyes off his legs. Garrincha spent the day preparing for his appearance in order to make a good impression, and he even gave a short speech: 'I am not going to give you anything or take anything from you. I am only going to give guidance in the best way possible.' And he spoke of the dangers of alcohol, tobacco, drugs, insensitive bosses, signing blank contracts and injections in the knee. When they stopped for a break, he stood in the middle of the pitch and lit a cigarette.

In his own peculiar way, Garrincha tried the best he could to do a decent job. When his car spent weeks in the garage after he had crashed it while leaving the airport after a Milionários game, he took a taxi all the way out to Duque de Caxias or Nilópolis, another working-class neighbourhood on the edge of the city, rather than disappoint his young charges. Instead of having the driver leave, he asked him to keep the meter running while he gave the kids a lesson. He paid the bill himself, and when the LBA found out about it they arranged for a driver to take him to and from subsequent appointments. On more than one occasion Garrincha used the car to take a woman to a sex motel near his old home in Jacarepaguá.

The LBA took Garrincha to the launch of soccer schools in several cities, and the warm welcome he got at each of them was impressive. A huge crowd turned out to see him in Gama, near Brasilia, and when he appeared on a busy city-centre street in São Paulo he caused enough of a commotion to stop the traffic.

The simple fact that he had undertaken to participate might have inspired many of his admirers to offer their services as volunteers as well, but, just as in his other jobs, Garrincha was anything but an exemplary employee. Sometimes he didn't even turn up, and often when he did he spent more time in the bar opposite the ground than on the pitch. Vanderléa tried to take control of the situation by preventing him from drinking at home, but Garrincha pretended not to hear, so Vanderléa broke all the bottles in the house. He went to the bar on the corner and had the barman mix bottles full of *traçado* which he took home and hid behind the fridge, under the cooker and inside the fuse box. Whenever Vanderléa turned her back, Garrincha sneaked a swig.

He had managed to hoodwink Elza and he thought he could do the same with Vanderléa. But the years of uninterrupted drinking were catching up with him. One morning in 1978, right there in front of Vanderléa, he was overcome by sweats and convulsions. It was the first outbreak of chronic abstinence syndrome. Or, in plain English, the result of having gone five or six hours without a drink.

Doctors from the local clinic were called and they managed to sedate him and take him away for treatment. He remained in hospital for a week under heavy sedation. The LBA was paying for his treatment and they were worried about his future. Garrincha, after all, was an LBA employee, and they wanted to make sure he was seen by reliable doctors. The top men in the Rio organisation got in contact with a US-educated neurologist at the Enio Serra Clinic in Laranjeiras, just 200 yards from Fluminense's home ground. The doctor, a 29-year-old named Carlos Henrique de Melo Reis, agreed to go with a psychologist and visit Garrincha once a week at his home in Bangu.

The first few months were almost a complete waste of time. Every Wednesday, Carlos Henrique and Olga, the psychologist, drove out to Bangu to discover that Garrincha wasn't there. After several weeks of fruitless trips they tried another tack and sent a VW van to bring him to Laranjeiras. That plan failed because when Garrincha saw the van coming he made himself scarce. He would often go a whole month without seeing the doctor.

Eventually, very slowly, the relationship between the two men started to improve. In the first few conversations they had together Carlos Henrique tried to find out what was bothering Garrincha and to discover what had led him to seek refuge in alcohol – only to come to the conclusion that nothing seemed to bother Garrincha. Garrincha didn't complain about his childhood, or Botafogo, or money, or even the fact that he was no longer capable of doing the things he once could. 'I don't drink because I miss football,' he said. 'To be honest, I don't know why I drink. I just know that if I drink two drinks, I want to drink four.'

When he felt confident enough to open up to Carlos Henrique, Garrincha admitted that no one was to blame for his career coming to a premature end. To the doctor's surprise, he confessed that he was so desperate to play football that he had asked to be given injections, and he acknowledged that although he was aware that Sandro Moreyra's stories had turned him into something of a retard in the eyes of the public, he didn't really care. To be honest, the public's portrayal of him as a naive fool was quite convenient. Everyone loves a fool, which is often what gets them off the hook.

But alcohol didn't let Garrincha off the hook, and he had developed chronic alcoholism. It didn't matter why he had started drinking or when: he had by now reached the point where his body had become chemically accustomed to receiving huge amounts of booze every day. He needed alcohol to survive like a fish needs water. Garrincha couldn't *not* drink. Before, he had drunk in order to feel good: now, he drank in order not to feel bad. When he went a few hours without a drink, his body reacted accordingly, as if there were some wild beast inside him fighting to get out. It was chronic abstinence syndrome, a hundred times worse than his old morning shakes.

In January 1979, Garrincha suffered more convulsions and was admitted to the Enio Serra Clinic again. He spent just 24 hours under observation before being sent home with a battery of pills that were supposed to help stabilise his condition. The main medicines reduced anxiety and repressed the central nervous system in the same way alcohol does; an anti-allergy drug made him drowsy; and an antipsychotic controlled the aggressive impulses drunks sometimes experience. All were to be used for short spells, because not only did they have side effects – facial tics, trembling hands and hardening of the muscles – they could also be addictive. Moreover, they would only work if he stopped drinking. If he didn't, the combination of the drink and the pills would be equivalent to drinking twice as much as usual.

But Garrincha wasn't taking the tablets. He was throwing them away or hiding them under his tongue and then spitting them out, and all the while continuing to drink. Vanderléa tried to force him to take them and the two of them got into fights. She kicked him out of their bed and made him sleep in the back bedroom; depriving him of sex was the harshest punishment she could impose. But instead of realising that it was the drink that drove a wedge between him and the women he loved, Garrincha preferred to see it as intolerance on their part, and in an unwilling show of self-pity he threatened to leave her.

When Vanderléa called his bluff and told him to go ahead, he decided to carry out his threat. In April 1979, the only place he could run to was Pau Grande. The first option was to go home, to the house now occupied by his married daughters. They didn't want him, though. All the hurt of the past was still fresh in their minds and they didn't want to know about his current suffering. So Garrincha turned to the woman who had never stopped waiting for him: Iraci.

It was two o'clock in the morning when he knocked on her door, but she let him in. Drunk, with his face swollen and his arms grazed from a recent fall, she hardly recognised the man she had lived with for so many years. Seeing him like that was painful. He was bent double and could hardly walk without tripping over, his skin was dull and yellowing, his voice was tired and his breathing difficult. He was incapable of speaking coherently; every time he tried to put together a long sentence he gave up after the first few words. He was unshaven, his hair was filthy and his breath reeked of alcohol.

When he woke up the next morning he looked even worse. He shook so much that he needed two hands to lift the glass of *cachaça* to his mouth. Iraci tried to get him to eat something but the thought of solid food in the morning almost made him throw up. He was probably vomiting blood. The alcohol had started to eat away at his insides.

Garrincha spent a week with Iraci. As with Elza and Vanderléa, he became dependent on her and was afraid to be left alone. When it seemed as if he had gone to sleep, Iraci would try to tiptoe out to the shops. But Garrincha always heard her and in a slurred voice would ask, 'Where are you going, sweetheart?' Iraci had to return and sit with him.

In the hours just before the sun came up, the time when he felt best, he would invite her to take a walk with him. Out there on Pau Grande's dark and empty streets, with the silence broken only by the animals and the scraping of their flip-flops, he would get all sentimental. 'I was very ungrateful with our son. I want him to take my surname.' Neném was 18 now and training with Fluminense. But when Garrincha spoke to him about taking his name, the boy responded, 'You don't need to, Dad. My face is my birth certificate.'

A few days later, Vanderléa's Chevette appeared in Pau Grande. She had come to get him. Garrincha never said whether he wanted to go or not but he got in the car and headed back down the road to Rio. In the years to come he would return to Iraci many times, and he would always leave with Vanderléa when she came to collect him.

On 30 July that same year, the LBA's VW van raced from Bangu to Laranjeiras in record time. Garrincha's life was in danger. He was suffering from arterial hypertension, sweating, diarrhoea, dehydration, malnutrition (his weight had fallen to seven and a half stones), pneumonia, palpitations, vomiting, convulsions, aural hallucinations and delirium tremens. Almost all of the symptoms were consistent with chronic abstinence syndrome.

Delirium tremens is its most serious manifestation. Those suffering from it believe they are being attacked by spiders, snakes, rats, cockroaches or other repulsive animals. The sense of fear is indescribable. Garrincha thought there were spiders on the roof that were about to fall on him and bite him to death. The attacks can last for hours and even days, and are capable of causing heart or respiratory failure. Garrincha's breathing failed him and he had to be intubated for 48 hours.

In the past, doctors had treated delirium tremens with a straitjacket, but the modern cure was sedation. Nevertheless, Garrincha lived through hours of terror before the medics were able to get to him. When he finally came round after being sedated and realised he did not have the strength to get up and get a drink, he gulped down the nurses' alcohol.

When doctors allowed him to receive visits, he did not recognise Nílton Santos and Sandro Moreyra. The medics cancelled further visits for a time, and when they were reinstated Iraci turned up with Márcia, Neném and three of Nair's daughters. Fourteen-year-old Sara also made the pilgrimage. It was a scene that brought together a whole cast of characters from his past; six children by three different women had turned up to see him.

Garrincha took advantage of such occasions, more often than not in the presence of reporters, to make firm promises, of a sort: 'I swear I will not drink again. I mean, I swear I won't drink any more *pinga*. Now I am sticking to beer. I've had enough of *pinga*.' He was lying, and he knew it. He didn't like beer, his body needed spirits.

Carlos Henrique knew his recuperation would be possible only if he admitted he had an incurable disease, and he tried to get Garrincha to go to a meeting of Alcoholics Anonymous. Members of two AA chapters had already visited him and representatives of two others had been in touch to try to get him on the programme. Their efforts, however, were in vain. Garrincha didn't consider himself an alcoholic.

Garrincha spent ten days in the Enio Serra Clinic. When he was discharged on 10 August he went to a government-sponsored retreat run by Lindalva, the wife of radio commentator Orlando Batista, in the hills near Rio. The couple invited him to stay as long as he wanted and Carlos Henrique signed off on the idea, believing that if Garrincha could spend three weeks off the drink he would see how much better he felt and finally attribute the improvement to the dry spell.

The clinic, however, was for recovering drug addicts, not for recovering alcoholics, and it had all the accompanying facilities, including a swimming pool, a gymnasium – and a bar. Carlos Henrique knew he could not close all the bars in the world for Garrincha but he could ask the barman not to serve him and hope that Garrincha couldn't convince him otherwise. Which, of course, was exactly what happened. Garrincha went up to the bar, pointed at a bottle of Campari and told the man, 'The doctor says you've to give me some of that red stuff. He says it's good for my liver.' And just like that almost two months' work went down the drain.

Garrincha, like all alcoholics, had convinced himself that if he could go a few days without a drink it would prove he was not an alcoholic, and he wouldn't need to stay in the clinic. To that rationale he added other justifications for checking out: the kids from Duque de Caxias 'needed him'; the Milionários fee dropped without him.

Three days after leaving the clinic he went to Pirapozinho in São Paulo state to play for them. And, unsurprisingly, he started drinking again. On 28 December he was taken into hospital again with abstinence syndrome. He was released the next day. Such stops in hospital gave him a quick break. They didn't even make the papers. And they were all paid for by the LBA.

The next month, January 1980, doctors started to worry about the number of domestic accidents Garrincha was having. On one occasion, while completely out of it, he tried to open a window by punching it with his fist. In another, when Vanderléa locked herself in the bedroom after a fight, he tried to break down the door with a knife. When he couldn't get in he went out and got drunk and had to be rushed to the Enio Serra. Carlos Henrique and the other doctors were always on call.

On 11 January he was back under their care again suffering from delirium tremens and haemorrhages in his digestive system. He spent 12 days in the clinic, but on 8 February, two weeks after being released, he was back again, this time in a serious condition. He had to be intubated to help him breathe and eventually he spent a week under sedation. He was released with strict orders to take his medicine, but by this stage the drugs only turned him into a zombie.

367

Garrincha was released on a Thursday. Three days later, on 17 February – Carnival Sunday – the whole of Brazil watched aghast as he made his way along the sambadrome, the famous avenue along which Rio's samba schools parade each year, on the front of a float, dressed in Brazil's number 7 shirt. The thousands of people who watched him from the stands, and the millions more watching live on television, were stunned. It wasn't the little bird they were looking at. It was the living dead.

In August the previous year, when Moreyra had asked Carlos Henrique if Garrincha would be able to parade with the Mangueira samba school, the doctor had said he had no objections. He could not, however, have had any idea how things would turn out.

All of Rio's top samba schools parade along the sambadrome's open-air avenue every year with costumes and floats related to a specific theme, and Mangueira's theme this year was a tribute to Brazil entitled 'What is ours'. Garrincha was scheduled to appear as the star attraction on a float entitled 'From the park to the Jules Rimet'. He was to be paid 32,000 cruzeiros, or around $700, for taking part, but according to Moreyra, the one who came up with the idea, Garrincha was going not for the money but to see 'that he was still loved'.

When he left the hospital just days before the carnival was due to start it was clear he was still suffering from the effects of Carlos Henrique's medication. On Sunday, when Sandro went to pick him up and take him to Mangueira, it should have been clear that he was not able to parade. He was out of it. Garrincha, however, insisted the show must go on. 'Once we get going I'll be all right,' he said.

Garrincha spent the whole of Sunday afternoon sitting on a bench watching the school prepare for its extravaganza. Mangueira was the eighth school to parade, which meant that their floats would not enter the sambadrome before six a.m. the next morning. Garrincha took his medicine and spent at least 16 hours sitting waiting; two of the school's directors took turns to sit with him. He did not drink.

The plan was to have Garrincha stand on the World Cup float and wave triumphantly to the crowd. But shortly before they set off it became apparent that expecting him to stay upright was a risky proposition, and that nothing about his appearance was triumphant. The medicine had left him conscious but almost catatonic, with no reflexes and no mobility in his muscles. The most sensible thing to do would have been to send him home. But in the frantic atmosphere of a samba school preparing to hit the avenue common sense is in short supply, so with Moreyra's help the directors decided to sit him down on the edge of the float and hope he would not fall off.

When the float turned into the sambadrome, the crowd roared. But as it began slowly to make its way up the avenue people saw Garrincha up close and the applause turned to amazement. He was a zombie, asleep, indifferent, sweating profusely and with a vacant expression etched on his face. Sometimes he meekly waved a red handkerchief – which served only to highlight the difference between him and the 'Joy of the People' the crowd had expected to see.

Pelé, who was watching from one of the VIP boxes overlooking the avenue, saw Garrincha and shouted, 'Mané! Mané! Mané!' The float was pushed closer to the box in order to give the two old friends a chance to interact, and Pelé threw Garrincha a Hawaiian necklace. It fell on the float alongside him but he never even noticed. It was only then that Pelé realised the state Garrincha was in. TV pictures showed Pelé shaking his head as if to say, 'Oh my God . . .'

Elza Soares was also watching from a VIP box. When she saw Garrincha out there exposed to the pity and derision of millions, she ran from her box and tried to get to him. A security guard stopped her by pointing a gun at her chest.

The parade lasted 90 minutes, and they were the longest 90 minutes of Garrincha's life. When it finally ended, Mangueira's directors lifted him from the float and tried to get him out of the area and away from the reporters who were trying to interview him. His legs could hardly take his weight and he was barely able to put one foot in front of the other. As they waited to find him a cab, one of the reporters heard him ask, 'How did it go? Did people like it? The school was fantastic.' He had no idea how sad his appearance had been.

One of the directors asked him if he was all right. Garrincha responded as though someone were answering for him: 'Everything is fine . . . everything is great.'

Eventually they managed to flag down a taxi, but the driver didn't want to pick them up. One of the directors said, 'But it's Garrincha!' The taxi driver didn't believe him and stuck his head out of the window to make sure. It *was* Garrincha. Or the man who used to be him.

Garrincha's pitiful parade through the sambadrome had brought tears to the eyes of millions of people watching the spectacle both in Brazil and overseas, but the sad scenes were particularly troublesome for the LBA. With his condition now clear to everyone, it was becoming more and more difficult for them to justify spending so much money on his medical bills.

In the days following the carnival, the men in charge of the LBA sheepishly asked their counterparts at AGAP, a federal organisation set up in 1977 to provide assistance to former football players and other professional athletes, if they would assume responsibility for his care. Although they said they could continue to pay Garrincha a salary, the LBA acknowledged, with some embarrassment, that they could not continue to pay his hospital bills.

AGAP had very little cash themselves, and certainly not enough to cover Garrincha's stays in hospital. So the programme's director went to the Brazilian Football Confederation (the CBF, which had replaced the CBD in 1979) to ask the president, Giulite Coutinho, if the confederation would contribute. Coutinho agreed to pay for his treatment as long as AGAP shared the financial responsibility.

In February and March footballers and medical professionals met on three separate occasions to see what they could do to help. Carlos

Henrique and other doctors from the Enio Serra Clinic, representatives from AGAP and the LBA, and a host of football players that included active stars such as Zico and Júnior and past greats such as Pampollini, Tomé and Félix, all wanted to be involved.

One of the priorities that emerged from the meetings was getting Garrincha back among friends who could keep an eye on him and try to keep him sober. Carlos Henrique believed he was lonely out in Bangu and that the atmosphere there didn't help him stay teetotal. The committee of friends decided to try to get Garrincha to move back to Rio's South Side, where he would be closer both to his old friends and to the Enio Serra Clinic. They appointed Félix, the goalkeeper in the legendary 1970 World Cup-winning side and the man who ran AGAP's veterans team, to act as a kind of guardian, someone who would spend time with him and perhaps even get him fit enough to play for the AGAP veterans team.

A friend of Francisco Horta, a judge and one-time president of Fluminense, allowed Garrincha the use of a flat in Laranjeiras rent-free, and he, Vanderléa, her son Wendell and Marinete moved in. A local member of parliament, the former football player Ítalo Bruno, arranged the move from Bangu for free.

The protective circle almost worked. For seven months in 1980 Garrincha stopped drinking.

It had nothing to do with the hypnosis treatment one of the doctors at the Enio Serra Clinic had tried on him, because Garrincha refused to allow himself be hypnotised. Rather, seeing friends make such an effort to help him enabled him for the first time to see what life without alcohol could be like.

He was in hospital between 5 and 14 March, and when he emerged dry he swore not to take what Carlos Henrique called 'the first sip'. When he felt like reaching for the bottle, which was almost every day, he went to the clinic, conveniently located just 200 yards from his new home. There, he sat around charming the doctors and nurses and flirting with the female staff. He started to train children again under the LBA soccer-schools programme and looked healthier than he had done in years. He was even going to be a father again; Vanderléa was pregnant.

Félix arranged a string of games for the AGAP veterans, and with Garrincha as the star attraction they went north to Bahia, west to small towns and cities in the interior of São Paulo state, and out to Goiás in the centre of the country. Félix roomed with him and was a first-hand witness to his newfound sobriety. Garrincha woke up without the shakes and had a hearty breakfast instead of a morning tipple for the first time in ages. A full recovery seemed more than possible.

One highlight came on 31 May when the AGAP team opened the new society football pitch at Rio's Jockey Club in front of 2,000 socialites. But the biggest moment of the new phase came at the Maracanã on 6 June before the 1980 Brazilian league championship decider between Flamengo and Atlético Mineiro. A crowd of 140,000 people saw Garrincha help the AGAP veterans defeat a team of famous singers in the warm-up match. Needless to say, Francisco Horta had briefed the opposition on their role in the proceedings before the match began.

In June, Garrincha decided he wanted to leave Laranjeiras and move back to Jacarepaguá, where he had found a house where he could raise birds again. The CBF paid the rent and the bill for necessary repairs and Ítalo Bruno once again arranged the move free of charge.

Soon after that, Garrincha travelled to rural São Paulo with the Milionários. Félix and his friends at the AGAP did not want Garrincha to travel with them because they wouldn't be there to keep an eye on him. The temptations on these trips were numerous. Before the games, merchants and businessmen lined up to have him open shops or promote new products, services for which they were prepared to pay good money, sometimes twice what he got just for taking the field with the Milionários. Inevitably, they laid on parties and offered him a drink. Back in Rio, surrounded by family, friends and doctors who cared for him, Garrincha was immune to the temptations. But in November, far outside that protective circle, they finally got the better of him.

Somebody – a player, an official or a businessman – convinced him that having gone so long without a drink, having just the one would not do him any harm, and Garrincha drank the fatal shot of *pinga*. For the rest of the trip he threw back everything that was put in front of him.

When Milionários owner Toledo saw the state he was in he got on the phone to AGAP and told Gilbert, the association's supervisor, that he was putting Garrincha on the next flight back to Rio. He asked him if someone from AGAP could go and meet him at the city's Santos Dumont airport, so Gilberto called Ademir Menezes, the former Vasco and Brazil striker, and asked him to pick him up. Menezes jumped in his car and went to the airport with the intention of taking Garrincha straight to the Enio Serra Clinic. Garrincha was nervous and agitated as he got off the plane, and when Ademir tried to embrace him he lashed out, kicking him and refusing to get in the car.

Three weeks later, on 20 December, Vanderléa, who was by now eight months pregnant, called AGAP again. Garrincha was attacking her and urgently needed to be admitted to hospital. Acute alcoholic psychosis, characterised by extreme agitation and aggression, was one of the effects of Garrincha's abstinence syndrome. Patients suffering from the condition are confused, and although they talk a lot their words make no sense. They become headstrong, won't listen to others, and stubbornly refuse to take their medicine or to seek treatment. Nurses from the LBA arrived at Garrincha's home and managed to get him to return to Laranjeiras with them, but he wouldn't be fooled and refused to let them give him a sedative. They were forced to lie, telling him that the sedative was really something for his liver.

Garrincha remained in hospital for 25 days under almost permanent sedation and was forbidden from receiving visitors. He was eventually released just in time to see Vanderléa give birth to Lívia, on 21 January 1981. She was the fourteenth child (and eleventh girl) he knew of, but he was thought to have others in Curitiba, Porto Alegre and, of course, Pau Grande. The birth of a new child, just like the arrival of the previous ones, did nothing to change him. It might, however, have prompted him to seek out the woman he had never forgotten: Elza.

Vanderléa knew that during the three years they had been together Garrincha had tried to contact Elza. Garrincha told Francisco Horta that Elza was the love of his life, and Horta thought that if Elza would take him back, Vanderléa would stand aside and Garrincha might save himself.

Not everyone liked Vanderléa, and Horta was one of them. He thought that by kicking Garrincha out of bed, hiding his money or locking him in the house until he took his medicine, she was hurting someone who needed to know he was loved. Horta appealed to her to take a look at the way she was treating him.

'You can't do that,' he said. 'He's an idol!'

'That he is,' replied Vanderléa. 'But you go and sleep with him when he's drunk.'

In April, Horta bumped into Elza at a barbecue in Urca and told her that Garrincha needed to see her. 'Mané opened up to me. He needs you. Would you meet with him?' Elza said she would. She was single again after splitting up with Gérson, the record producer she had lived with for the last few years. She wanted Garrincha back too, and she suggested that a meeting take place in São Paulo, where she was performing in a series of concerts. Horta spoke with Garrincha, and he went to meet her at the city's Normandie Hotel.

They spent hours together in her suite, where Garrincha told her he loved her and was delighted when he saw the surprise she had brought for him: Garrinchinha, who was by then almost five years old. It was the first time he had seen his son since they had split up, and it would also be the last. Elza's nanny took the boy away, and when they were alone again, Garrincha drank the mini-bar dry. They tried to make love. Garrincha was able to get an erection but he could not ejaculate, and at the end of the afternoon he was exhausted.

Elza needed to get Garrincha back to Rio, but he was tired and drunk and she was afraid to take him on a plane, so she booked them a carriage on the train. When they pulled into the station in Rio they were met by a huge scrum of reporters, photographers and cameramen. Someone had tipped them off. Garrincha wasn't ready to be seen with Elza so he did a runner, fleeing across the tracks and heading home to Jacarepaguá.

When she saw their arrival on the nightly news, Vanderléa asked him, 'What's going on here?'

Garrincha tried to brush it off. 'Ah, that's an old story. I don't know where they got that footage from.'

Vanderléa, however, knew better, and she made Garrincha call Elza while she listened in on the extension.

Garrincha tried his best to put on an act. 'Crioula, stop chasing me, all right?'

When Elza, who had no idea Vanderléa was listening in, replied, Garrincha was sunk. 'What are you on about, baby? Wasn't it you who came to see me in São Paulo?'

On 6 May, Vanderléa called the AGAP and asked them to come and collect Garrincha again. He was drunk, and he needed to be taken to hospital. Félix went to Bangu – they had moved back there a few days earlier at Garrincha's insistence – and found Garrincha face down on the bar.

'Let's go, Mané,' Félix ordered.

Garrincha didn't object. He downed his Campari and got into the car.

Félix drove him to the door of the Enio Serra and said simply, 'We're here. You know where it is. All you have to do is go in.'

And Garrincha calmly walked in for yet another three- or four-day stay in hospital.

Garrincha kept having to go back into hospital because Carlos Henrique was not able to treat his chronic alcoholism as he wanted, by checking him into the clinic for a long and dry period monitored by the AA. He was able to treat him only as an emergency patient whenever he turned up at the clinic suffering from the worst symptoms. He had saved his life on at least three occasions, but he knew that no matter how many times he helped him Garrincha would start drinking again when he got out. Enio Serra was not a specialist clinic. There was no way to stop him leaving and going for a drink whenever he wanted.

During one stay, in March 1982, a group of friends were getting ready to leave after visiting him when Garrincha said, 'Go to that bar on the corner and I'll meet you there in a few minutes.' The four friends went to the bar, not really believing what they had heard. Yet sure enough, a few minutes later Garrincha appeared, dressed in the same hospital-issue short-sleeved T-shirt and shorts. He had simply walked out. They chatted for half an hour and then the friends left. Garrincha said he was going to hang around a bit longer.

Hours later he was seen sitting in the stands at Fluminense's training ground watching the youngsters practise. At the edge of the pitch a group of boys were dreaming of a future in football and waiting for their trial to start.

CHAPTER 23

The Last Bottle

LESS THAN A YEAR LATER, GARRINCHA WAS DEAD.

In the ten months between March 1982 and the last day of his life he was admitted to hospital eight times, and each time it was as dramatic as it was desperate. In addition to the already horrible diseases battering his body, he was hit by alcoholic haemorrhagic gastritis, early cirrhosis, cardiomegaly, dementia and several other ailments brought on by alcoholism.

And yet there were still some happy times during those last few months.

No one would have believed, for example, that he would parade in carnival again, this time in Bicas, Minas Gerais, where he stood on a float dressed in a Brazil strip and waved tenderly to a crowd who had last seen him play a friendly there on the eve of the 1962 World Cup.

Even more remarkably, he almost went to Saudi Arabia as an assistant to his old Botafogo team-mate Adalberto, who was then managing El Ahlei. Two Arabs from the Gulf came to Bangu to talk terms, but the deal fell apart when Adalberto felt it prudent to warn his old friend, 'There's one thing, Mané. They don't drink there. It's banned. They cut your hands off.'

Garrincha just about fell off his chair. 'Are you nuts? I don't want to go there!'

In reality, there was no way back. After a series of relapses at the start of the year, Garrincha was admitted to hospital for his longest stay yet: 54 days, from 15 March to 7 May. It cost the CBF 2.6 million cruzeiros, around $16,000, and was instrumental in the confederation's decision to halt subsequent payments. His stays in hospital were simply too frequent and too long, and Giulite Coutinho could no longer convince his colleagues that the expense was merited. Garrincha did not help by buying packets of cigarettes for the other patients and putting them on the CBF's bill. The confederation did not abandon him completely, however, and continued to pay the rent on his home in Bangu until Vanderléa and Wendell moved out two years after his death.

The withdrawal of CBF aid meant that Garrincha now had to leave the private clinic in Laranjeiras and go to a state hospital. After he was found lying drunk in the street, Brazil's Social Security Minister guaranteed that there would always be a bed available for him as long as he needed one. Garrincha, though, didn't care: 'I drink and you put me in hospital. I get out and I drink again and you put me in hospital again. Why do you want me to keep returning to this shitty life?'

On 31 August, an ambulance was called once again. Garrincha had passed out on the street and medics had to pick him up and rush him to hospital. Doctors diagnosed him with acute alcoholic psychosis and unquestionable mental decay and transferred him to another clinic after a week. He spent a month there, and was allowed to go home at weekends. One night, however, he couldn't wait for the weekend to arrive and went back to Bangu. There, he collapsed in a square and was taken to hospital after Gilbert and the reporter Oldemário Touguinhó found him and called an ambulance.

While they were together, Gilbert told Oldemário that Garrincha was the result of an incestuous relationship between his father and one of his sisters. It was a ridiculous story, but Oldemário published it in the *Jornal do Brasil*, then Rio's best-selling broadsheet. According to the article, such a thing 'was possible because he had never been someone who behaved like a normal person'. The article shattered Garrincha, who was in hospital when it came out. 'I thought he was my friend,' he said of Oldemário.

In fact, Oldemário had been friends with Garrincha for more than 20 years and he thought the world of him. His source for the shocking declaration was Gilbert – not that Gilbert was in any position to comment. He had simply misunderstood a conversation about physical anomalies and congenital mental defects and thought the case applied to Garrincha. Needless to say, it had no basis in fact. How could Garrincha have been born to one of his sisters if Rosa, the eldest, was only eight and a half years older than he was?

After Garrincha was released from hospital once more at the start of November, the football magazine *Placar* arranged what was to be his final encounter with Pelé. The meeting took place at the luxurious Copacabana home of Pelé's friend Alfredo Saad and brought together the two living legends of Brazilian football, one of them healthy, prosperous and glowing, the other bloated, poor and lacklustre. A whole sea had passed under the bridge since that unforgettable Brazil–USSR match in Gothenburg 24 years earlier.

The two chatted about football and had their photo taken together (Pelé playing the guitar, Garrincha pretending to play the *cavaquinho*), but one of the most memorable aspects of the reunion was the way in which Garrincha cheekily insisted on teasing Pelé by calling him 'King'. 'Hey, King,' he said at one point, 'don't you have a few coins to spare? You've got loads of greenbacks.' He wasn't being serious, and Pelé knew it.

To the surprise of many the two of them got on famously. Though they had never been friends off the park – they were too different – those who had thought Garrincha might be bitter about Pelé's success were wrong. He was not, and Pelé did not attempt to patronise him, even though it would have been natural to.

When the meeting ended, they hugged affectionately and went their own ways – Pelé, off down the yellow brick road, and Garrincha straight towards the last bottle.

'Hey, lads, take it easy on me, I haven't kicked a ball in four months. A Merry Christmas to you all.'

With these words, Garrincha walked on to the pitch in Planaltina, 30 miles outside Brasilia, to play one more game of football. It was Christmas Day, 1982. The mere thought of his putting on a pair of football boots and attempting to kick a ball was ludicrous. Just a week before he had spent six days in hospital. But there he was, lining up for local side Londrina against the Brasilia branch of AGAP. He was supposed to appear for just 20 minutes but he played the whole first half of a 1–0 defeat. It was his final game.

He spent three days in Brasilia – enough time for him to try to chat up the 63-year-old maid in his hotel – before returning to Bangu to do his last drinking. He was in a bad way, but he still managed to appear at a party the LBA held for 30,000 underprivileged kids at a stadium in Bangu on 10 January 1983. They were the last people to chant his name.

Two days later, a desperate Vanderléa called Edgard Cosme and begged him to come and help her. Garrincha was trying to kill her with a wooden stick. Cosme called an ambulance and rushed over to find Garrincha naked, angry and in no mood to listen to anyone. When Cosme tried to calm him down Garrincha threatened to thrash him.

The ambulance arrived and the medics eventually managed to restrain him on a stretcher and cart him off to hospital. Six days later, on 18 January, he was helped to the door of the clinic and released. He didn't know it but he had a little more than 24 hours to live.

*   *   *

On the final day of Garrincha's life, 19 January 1983, he did not drink any more than usual. He spent the morning and the early part of the afternoon out of the house, but he felt strange and had to return home to lie down. He got up an hour later at around three p.m. but fell over and hit his face on the ground. When a bruise appeared over his left eye, Vanderléa called the doctor, afraid that when the worst of the hangover wore off he would attack her, just as he had done several times over the previous few weeks.

The ambulance arrived at a quarter to five to find Garrincha delirious and obviously in agony. The medics strapped him to the stretcher and took him to the local hospital, but two hours later the medicine they had given him was not having the desired effect so they transferred him to another clinic in Botafogo. On the way there he mumbled incomprehensibly and complained of a headache. At 7.40 p.m. he was taken to the ward for alcoholics with psychiatric problems, and after putting him on a drip, the nurse left him. The lone star had never been more alone.

By now, his organs were in revolt, his body as far as it could be from being capable of darting down the right wing, as evasive as the Scarlet Pimpernel; of the sudden stops that caused studs to screech; of the circus twists that made his muscles and bones look as though they were made of rubber; or even of the deadly power of his shots at goal. He was incapable of giving or receiving pleasure from the women he still found attractive, and of enjoying the *cachaças* he still intended to drink. His body had given up.

In the early hours of the following morning a pulmonary oedema took him. When the nurse came at six a.m. to take his pulse his heart had stopped beating. The little bird was dead.

Acknowledgements

MANY PEOPLE WHO PLAYED AN IMPORTANT ROLE IN GARRINCHA'S LIFE are no longer with us. Garrinchinha, his son with Elza Soares, drowned in the river Imbarie near Mage on 11 January 1986, aged eight. He was on his way to play a game of football in Pau Grande when the car he was in left the road and plunged into the river, trapping him underwater. Neném, Garrincha's son with Iraci, also died in a car accident, in Fafe, Portugal on 20 January 1992. He was 28. After playing with Fluminense he was transferred to Portuguese side Belenenses and from there to Switzerland. He was in Portugal on holiday when he perished. Pincel, Garrincha's great friend, died in Pau Grande in 1984. That same year, his former team-mate Paulo Valentim died penniless in Buenos Aires. Another close friend, Gilbert, died in 1993. All three died as a consequence of their alcoholism. Sandro Moreyra passed away in 1987 and João Saldanha died three years later, during the 1990 World Cup in Italy. Dirceu Rodrigues died in the mid-1970s – as one of the most controversial figures in Garrincha's life his help would have been fundamental in preparing this book. Angelita Martinez died in 1984.

Happily, many close friends still remain and were prepared to open their files and tell their stories. Among them are doctors, ex-girlfriends, fans, friends, journalists, lawyers, photographers, singers, and former players, managers and directors.

All the names below collaborated by giving their time and information. The majority patiently and cheerfully submitted themselves to my often long and time-consuming investigations. To them, my heartfelt thanks.

Here is a detailed list:

In Rio, in São Paulo and in Rome:

Adalberto (Adalberto Leite Martins); Ademir (Ademir Marques de Menezes); Abílio de Almeida; Afonsinho (Afonso Celso Garcia Reis); Altair (Altair Gomes de Figueiredo); Paulo Amaral; Waldir Amaral; José Maria de Aquino; Araty (Araty Vianna); Araújo Netto; Adib Elias Avvad; Maria Consuelo Ayres; Badeco (de Os Cariocas); Milton 'Banana'; Marília Barbosa; Luiz Carlos Barreto; Bellini (Hideraldo Luiz Bellini); Ney Bianchi; Cecil Borer; Charles Borer; Chico Buarque; Luiz Carlos Cabral; Otelo Caçador; Paulo Calarge; Doalcei Camargo; Roberto Campos; Norah Cardoso; Áureo Bernardes Carneiro; Carvalho Leite (Carlos Dobbert de Carvalho Leite); Gilberto de Carvalho; Joaquim Vaz de Carvalho; José Bento de Carvalho; Admildo Chirol; Canor Simões Coelho; Carlos Heitor Cony; Cléa de Araújo Corrêa; Rivadavia (Rivinha) Corrêa Meyer Filho; Reginaldo Corumba Filho; Edgard Cosme; Célio Cotecchia; Giulite Coutinho; Francisco Pedro do Coutto; Sergio Schiller Dias;

Didi (Waldir Pereira); Djalma Santos; Ernesto da Luz Pinto Dória; Romero Estelita; Félix (Félix Miéle Venerando); Alberto Ferreira; Sebastião de Andrade Figueira; Abelardo Figueiredo; José Roberto Francalacci; Ernani de Freitas; Marco Fulniô; Roberto Garofalo; Gerson (Gerson de Oliveira Nunes); Gilmar (Gilmar dos Santos Neves); Gílson (Gílson Mussi); Oswaldo de Azevedo Góes; Luís ('Chupeta') Gomes; Ricardo Augusto Gosling; Jorge Goulart; Alberto Helena Jr.; Jamil Helu; Wadih Helu; Hans Henningsen;

Francisco Horta; Lêdo Ivo; Jairzinho (Jair Ventura Filho);

Joel (Joel Antônio Martins); Jordan (Jordan da Costa); Judber Jorge; Julinho (Julio Botelho); Nubia Lafayette; Juan Giu Lamana; Virginia Lane; Michel Laurence; Almir Leite; José Louzeiro; Jards Macalé; Fátima Macedo; Alexandre Madureira; Marina Mafra; José Luiz Magalhães Lins; Luiz Felipe Matoso Maia; Carlos Marcondes; Marinho (Marinho Rodrigues); Adolpho Marques; Humberto Mascarenhas; João Máximo; Augusto Mello Pinto; Claudio Mello e Souza; Francisco Dionísio (Chico) Mendes; Luiz Mendes; José Messias; Miéle; Mário de Moraes; Edevaldo de Souza Moreno; Álvaro Barros Moreira; Zezé Moreira; Léa Moreyra; Sandra Moreyra; Claudio Moscoso Morize; Maneco Müller; Neivaldo (Neivaldo Pinto de Carvalho); Sebastião Nery; Jader Neves; Carlos Niemeyer;

Nílton Santos; Arnaldo Niskier; Raimundo Nobre de Almeida; Armando Nogueira; Djalma Nogueira; José Albano da Nova Monteiro; Orlando (Orlando Peçanha); Otávio (Octavio Sergio de Moraes); Pampollini (Américo Pampollini Filho); Jarbas Passarinho; Anna Maria Piergilli; Marcelo Loesch Pinto; Percival Pires; Arthur José Poerner; Luiz Roberto Porto; Carlos Henrique de Melo Reis; Pery Ribeiro; Richard (Richard Ferreira); Roberto Pinto; Joffre Rodrigues; Lolita Rodrigues; Sabará (Onofre Anacleto de Souza); Abigail ('Biga') Batalha dos Santos; Danilo dos Santos; João Luiz Sattamini Neto; Nelson Senise; Mauricio Sherman; Geraldo Romualdo da Silva;

Elza Soares; Almir Souza Lima Jr; Hideki Takizawa; Lídio Toledo; Tomé (Antonio Corrêa Thomé); Tostão (Eduardo Gonçalves de Andrade); Oldemário Touguinhó; Manuel ('Manuelzinho') Aguiar Vaz; Vanderléa de Oliveira Vieira; Zagalo (Mario Jorge Lôbo Zagallo); Maurice Zimetbaum; Ziraldo;

In Pau Grande, Fragoso and Raiz da Serra:

Dulcinéa de Abreu; Rubens de Abreu; Arlindo 'Fumaça'; Iraci Castilho; Camilo Coutinho; Glória Coutinho; 'Dódi' (Jorge) Bento;

Cirllo Cunha; Gaudêncio Ferreira Filho; Léa Ferreira; Madalena
Marques Fonseca; Luiz de Freitas (special thanks); Laerte Leocornyl;
Celeste de Mattos; Luiz Carlos Morgado; Tereza Morgado; Fernando
Mozer; José Mário Neto; Nelson 'Coreto'; Octaciano Ramos; Roberto
'Galo'; Roberto Leite Rodrigues; Rosa dos Santos.

Other invaluable contributions came from friends who provided texts
or photos and from people who helped track down sources. Without
their help and suggestions this book would not have been possible.
Again, in alphabetical order:

Marcos Antonio Americano; Ítalo de Assis; Álvaro Barcelos; Tarlis
Batista; Israel Beloch; Afonso Borges; Gilberto Bueno; Rosa Canha;
Régis Cardoso; Pilar Guido de Castro; Eduardo Chouahy; Edilberto
Coutinho; Domingos Antonio D'Angelo Júnior; Mauricio Dias; João
Carlos de Camargo Éboli; Claudinei Ferreira; Fernando Pessoa
Ferreira; Walter Fontoura; Janio de Freitas; Ivson; Juca Kfouri; Laís
Pimenta de Lacerda; Lu Lacerda; Laco (Luiz Alberto Chaves de
Oliveira); Ricardo Locatelli; Elisa Luzzato; Rodrigo Flávio de
Magalhães; Paulo Marcello; Gilson Martins; Luiz Filipe Carneiro de
Miranda; Geneton Moraes Neto; Fernando de Morais; Leda Nagle;
Miguel Paiva; Sebastião Pereira Jr; Luiz Alberto Piccina; Paula Planck;
Luiz Puech; Sueli Queiroz; Augusto Falcão Rodrigues; Oswaldo
Sargentelli; Maria Angélica Seixas; Jairo Severiano; Carlos Stabile;
Mario Telles; Silvio Tendler; Jorge Vasconcellos; Daisy Mara Bastos
Vianna; Humberto Werneck.

Ivonete Rodrigues da Silva, Karla Profeta da Luz and Irene Campos
(*Diários Associados*); Tatiana Constant (*Jornal do Brasil*); Christina
Konder, Maria Célia Fraga and Djair Mattos (*O Globo*); Francisco
Moreira Machado and Osmar Esch (*Jornal dos Sports*); Francisco de
Sousa (*Carreio Braziliense*); Flaminio Lobo (livraria Dantes, RJ);
Alexandre Maluf and Neuza de Oliveira Piquis (Instituto Médico-
Legal, RJ); Eliane Furtado de Mendonça (Arquivo Público do Estado

do Rio de Janeiro); Moacir Medeiros de Santana; Silvia Regina de Souza (Biblioteca Nacional); Plínio Melo e Ibsen Spartacus (TV Cultura de SP).

A special word of thanks goes to journalist Antonio Roberto Arruda, from *O Globo*. With his researcher's soul, he combed through files and archives checking names and dates and on the way came across some precious gems. It was he who discovered that Garrincha had been sent off three times before the 1962 World Cup in Chile.

Estrela Solitaria (this book's Portuguese title) had curious origins. The idea of writing a biography came to me in December 1992 shortly after I published *O Anjo Pornografico*, a biography of the playwright Nelson Rodrigues. With no backing or advance I worked on the book throughout 1993. Then, in January 1994, football fanatic Carlos Alberto Reis, then the head of the Rio Stock Exchange, said he would love to read a biography of Garrincha and mentioned my name as a possible author to journalist Jose Roberto Alencar (a man to whom I owe countless thank yous). Alencar made contact and it was with his help that I secured the funding without which the book would never have been possible. Carlos Alberto Reis's enthusiasm and help to see *Estrela Solitaria* see the light of day means that it also partly belongs to him. His successor at the stock exchange, Fernando Opitz, was also a great help.

The two and a half years I spent living with Garrincha's memory awoke in me an admiration that I first felt on a distant Sunday in 1958 when I saw Botafogo beat Flamengo 3–2 at the Maracanã. That was the day I discovered that even the most ardent Flamengo fans also have a place in their heart for Garrincha.

Career Statistics

This is the most complete list yet published of the games played by Garrincha. It was compiled by reporter and researcher Antonio Roberto Arruda, with the help of archives from the *O Globo* and *Jornal dos Sports* newspapers and records from the Rio State Football Federation, the Brazilian Football Confederation and the National Library. The list does not include games played by Garrincha as an amateur for S.C. Pau Grande or semi-professional matches for teams in Petrópolis, all of which came before he joined Botafogo. Similarly, it does not take into account the dozens of friendlies he played in from 1972 on. In many of those exhibition games, Garrincha took the field for no more than 15 minutes.

Key to Brazilian states featured:

AL – Alagoas
AM – Amazonas
BA – Bahia
CE – Ceara
DF – Brasilia
ES – Espirito Santo

GO – Goias
MG – Minas Gerais
PA – Para
PB – Paraiba
PE – Pernambuco
PI – Piaui
PR – Parana
RJ – Rio de Janeiro
RN – Rio Grande do Norte
RS – Rio Grande do Sul
SC – Santa Catarina
SP – São Paulo
SUR – Surinam

1953		GOALS
21/06	Botafogo 1–0 Avelar	1
28/06	Botafogo 5–1 Cantagalo	0
12/07	Botafogo 5–0 São Cristóvão	1
19/07	Botafogo 6–3 Bonsucesso	3
26/07	Botafogo 5–1 Canto do Rio	0
02/08	Botafogo 1–2 Fluminense	0
09/08	Botafogo 3–0 Portuguesa	2
15/08	Botafogo 1–4 Vasco	0
22/08	Botafogo 3–1 Bangu	0
30/08	Botafogo 2–1 Olaria	0
07/09	Botafogo 3–0 Flamengo	1
13/09	Botafogo 3–1 América-RJ	0
20/09	Botafogo 1–1 Madureira	1
27/09	Botafogo 2–0 Bonsucesso	2
04/10	Botafogo 4–0 Canto do Rio	1
11/10	Botafogo 3–0 Portuguesa-RJ	3
18/10	Botafogo 3–1 Madureira	1
24/10	Botafogo 6–0 Bangu	3
01/11	Botafogo 1–1 Flamengo	1
08/11	Botafogo 1–1 América-RJ	0
17/11	Botafogo 1–0 São Cristóvão	0
22/11	Botafogo 3–1 Fluminense	1
29/11	Botafogo 1–2 Vasco	1
05/12	Botafogo 4–3 Olaria	0
08/12	Botafogo 1–4 Bahia select	0
18/12	Botafogo 6–1 Asas-MG	2

		GOALS
21/12	Botafogo 1–1 Bangu	0
27/12	Botafogo 1–1 Vasco	0
	1954	GOALS
02/01	Botafogo 0–1 Fluminense	0
09/01	Botafogo 0–1 América-RJ	0
14/01	Botafogo 3–2 Uberaba-MG	0
20/01	Botafogo 0–1 Flamengo	0
24/01	Botafogo 2–2 Vitória-BA	1
01/02	Botafogo 2–0 Minus Gerais select	0
03/02	Botafogo 3–0 Democrata-MG	0
14/02	Botafogo 1–1 Remo-PA	0
17/02	Botafogo 3–0 Remo-PA	1
21/02	Botafogo 4–2 São Paulo	1
13/03	Botafogo 2–4 Palmeiras	1
16/03	Botafogo 2–2 Atlético-MG	0
19/03	Botafogo 3–2 Atlético-MG	1
23/03	Botafogo 1–4 Flamengo	0
31/03	Botafogo 4–1 Sport-MG	0
04/04	Botafogo 5–1 Fluminense	0
17/04	Botafogo 4–3 Palmeiras	0
21/04	Botafogo 2–2 Internacional-RS	0
25/04	Botafogo 3–1 Fluminense	1
27/04	Botafogo 7–0 Rib. Junqueira-MG	1
15/05	Botafogo 0–4 Fluminense	0

19/05	Botafogo 3–5 Vasco	0
23/05	Botafogo 1–2 Corinthians	0
30/05	Botafogo 2–2 Palmeiras	0
01/06	Botafogo 4–0 Guarani-MG	1
05/06	Botafogo 2–3 Santos	1
12/06	Botafogo 0–1 Calouros do Ar-CE	0
13/06	Botafogo 2–0 Ceará	0
17/06	Botafogo 2–1 Flamengo	0
20/06	Botafogo 1–3 Portuguesa-SP	0
26/06	Botafogo 5–1 São Paulo	0
30/06	Botafogo 1–3 América-RJ	0
18/07	Botafogo 4–1 Deportivo (Colombia)	1
25/07	Botafogo 2–0 Milionários (Col)	0
01/08	Botafogo 2–1 Nacional (Col)	1
07/08	Botafogo 3–1 Nacional (Col)	0
08/08	Botafogo 2–1 Santa Fé (Col)	0
10/08	Botafogo 2–0 Quindio (Ecuador)	1
12/08	Botafogo 2–1 Valdez (Ecu)	0
22/08	Botafogo 3–1 Olaria	1
29/08	Botafogo 2–0 Madureira	0
05/09	Botafogo 3–1 Canto do Rio	0
07/09	Botafogo 2–1 Passense-MG	0
12/09	Botafogo 4–2 Portuguesa-RJ	1
19/09	Botafogo 1–3 Vasco	0
25/09	Botafogo 2–3 Fluminense	0
02/10	Botafogo 0–0 Bonsucesso	0
16/10	Botafogo 2–4 Bangu	0
23/10	Botafogo 1–1 América-RJ	0
07/11	Botafogo 1–1 Flamengo	0
14/11	Botafogo 5–0 Madureira	1
20/11	Botafogo 2–0 São Cristóvão	1
27/11	Botafogo 5–2 Bonsucesso	1
30/11	Botafogo 2–0 América-MG	1
05/12	Botafogo 2–1 Portuguesa-RJ	0
12/12	Botafogo 2–3 Flamengo	0
15/12	Botafogo 2–3 Internacional-RS	1
19/12	Botafogo 5–1 Canto do Rio	1
22/12	Botafogo 2–4 Vasco	0
30/12	Botafogo 3–3 Bangu	1

1955		GOALS
09/01	Botafogo 3–0 Olaria	0
12/01	Botafogo 5–2 Santos	3
15/01	Botafogo 1–3 Fluminense	0
22/01	Botafogo 1–3 América-RJ	0
27/01	Botafogo 3–3 Fluminense	0
02/02	Botafogo 1–1 Vasco	0
05/02	Botafogo 2–1 Bangu	0
09/02	Botafogo 0–2 Flamengo	0
13/02	Botafogo 2–4 América-RJ	1

09/03	Carioca select 3–2 Pernambuco select	1
13/03	Carioca select 4–0 Minas Gerais select	0
23/03	Carioca select 6–1 Minas Gerais select	1
27/03	Carioca select 1–3 São Paulo select	0
31/03	Carioca select 3–4 São Paulo select	1
09/04	Botafogo 3–1 Portuguesa-RS	1
13/04	Botafogo 1–3 América-RJ	0
16/04	Botafogo 3–2 Palmeiras	1
20/04	Botafogo 2–1 Vasco	0
24/04	Botafogo 3–0 Rio Preto-SP	2
28/04	Botafogo 1–1 Fluminense	0
01/05	Botafogo 0–3 Santos	0
05/05	Botafogo 0–0 Flamengo	0
08/05	Botafogo 1–1 São Paulo	0
11/05	Botafogo 1–0 Corinthians	0
15/05	Botafogo 2–2 Real Madrid (Spain)	0
	Debut in Europe	
19/05	Botafogo 3–3 Atlético Madrid (Spain)	0
22/05	Botafogo 4–1 Santa Cruz (Sp)	1
24/05	Botafogo 1–2 Tenerife (Sp)	0
29/05	Botafogo 3–3 Valencia (Sp)	1
01/06	Botafogo 2–4 Racing de Paris (France)	0
05/06	Botafogo 2–2 Murcia (Sp)	1
08/06	Botafogo 5–1 Reims (Fr)	1
11/06	Botafogo 3–2 Racing de Leinz (Fr)	1
14/06	Botafogo 5–2 Alliancen (Denmark)	2
19/06	Botafogo 6–1 Holland	1
22/06	Botafogo 6–2 Grasshopper (Switzerland)	0
29/06	Botafogo 4–0 Juventus-Torino select (Italy)	2
06/07	Botafogo 3–2 Roma (It)	1
09/07	Botafogo 1–0 Dinamo de Praga (Czechoslovakia)	0
12/07	Botafogo 2–0 Slovan (Cze)	0
14/07	Botafogo 1–0 Spartak (Cze)	0
16/07	Botafogo 1–1 Banik Ostrawa (Cze)	0
14/08	Botafogo 1–3 Bonsucesso	0
21/08	Botafogo 1–0 Olaria	0
28/08	Botafogo 2–0 Madureira	0
04/09	Botafogo 0–1 Flamengo	0
07/09	Botafogo 0–0 Atlético-MG	0
11/09	Botafogo 3–2 Canto do Rio	0
18/09	Brazil 1–1 Chile	0
	Debut for the national side	
24/09	Botafogo 1–3 América-RJ	0
01/10	Botafogo 4–3 Bangu	0
09/10	Botafogo 0–1 Portuguesa-RJ	0
14/10	Botafogo 0–1 Náutico-PE	0
16/10	Botafogo 1–1 Santa Cruz-PE	0
18/10	Botafogo 2–2 Sport-PE	1
22/10	Botafogo 0–1 Fluminense	0

391

30/10	Botafogo 2–3 Vasco	0
06/11	Botafogo 2–2 Bangu	1
20/11	Botafogo 2–2 Fluminense	1
27/11	Botafogo 1–1 Bonsucesso	0
04/12	Botafogo 3–0 Olaria	1
21/12	Botafogo 2–0 Americano	1

	1956	GOALS
08/01	Botafogo 1–0 Madureira	0
14/01	Botafogo 1–4 América-RJ	0
18/01	Botafogo 3–1 Americano	0
21/01	Botafogo 3–0 São Cristóvão	0
29/01	Botafogo 1–2 Vasco	0
04/02	Botafogo 1–2 Flamengo	0
26/02	Botafogo 3–0 Santo Antônio-ES	1
03/03	Botafogo 5–0 Colo-Colo Itabuna-BA	2
04/03	Botafogo 2–1 Itabuna select	0
11/03	Botafogo 2–1 Americano-RJ	0
14/03	Botafogo 2–1 América-MG	1
15/03	Botafogo 5–1 Uberaba-MG	1
17/03	Botafogo 3–2 Uberlândia-MG	1
18/03	Botafogo 2–1 Araguari select-MG	0
20/03	Botafogo 2–0 Atlético-MG	2
01/04	Botafogo 0–1 U.D.A. (Cze)	0
02/04	Botafogo 2–0 Norkopping (Sweden)	0
09/04	Botafogo 2–2 Fulham (England)	1
17/04	Botafogo 2–1 Burnley (Eng)	0
19/04	Botafogo 3–2 Brentford (Eng)	0
22/04	Botafogo 2–6 Honved-Kimitz (Hungary)	0
29/04	Botafogo 2–2 Espanhol (Sp)	0
01/05	Botafogo 0–1 Valencia (Sp)	0
08/05	Botafogo 1–0 Oviedo (Sp)	0
10/05	Botafogo 3–0 Celta (Sp)	0
13/05	Botafogo 4–3 Córdoba (Sp)	0
23/05	Botafogo 4–3 Rott Weiss (Germany)	1
30/05	Botafogo 3–0 Racing de Paris (Fr)	0
02/06	Botafogo 2–0 Le Havre (Fr)	0
05/06	Botafogo 3–0 Nuremberg (Ger)	0
08/06	Botafogo 5–1 Troyes (Fr)	0
09/06	Botafogo 1–1 Stade de Reims (Fr)	0
13/06	Botafogo 2–3 Saint Etienne (Fr)	0
18/06	Botafogo 2–0 Racing de Leinz (Fr)	1
20/06	Botafogo 4–0 Sedan (Fr)	1
23/06	Botafogo 2–0 Barcelona (Sp)	0
22/07	Botafogo 1–0 Bonsucesso	0
29/07	Botafogo 0–0 Vasco	0
05/08	Botafogo 6–2 Social-MG	2
12/08	Botafogo 1–2 Fluminense	0
19/08	Botafogo 1–0 Portuguesa-RJ	0
26/08	Botafogo 2–0 Olaria	1

29/08	Botafogo 1–1 São Cristóvão	0
15/09	Botafogo 1–2 Bangu	0
23/09	Botafogo 4–0 Canto do Rio	1
29/09	Botafogo 5–0 Flamengo	0
06/10	Botafogo 0–1 América-RJ	0
13/10	Botafogo 2–1 Olaria	1
14/10	Botafogo 5–1 Olimpic-MG	1
21/10	Botafogo 2–0 Canto do Rio	0
28/10	Botafogo 4–0 Madureira	0
01/11	Botafogo 4–0 São Cristóvão	2
04/11	Botafogo 2–2 Pastoril-MG	0
10/11	Botafogo 4–3 América-RJ	0
18/11	Botafogo 4–1 Portuguesa-RJ	0
25/11	Botafogo 2–3 Vasco	0
02/12	Botafogo 0–2 Fluminense	0
08/12	Botafogo 2–0 Bonsucesso	0
16/12	Botafogo 1–0 Flamengo	0
30/12	Botafogo 0–1 Minas Gerais select	0

	1957	GOALS
06/01	Carioca select 0–0 Bahia	0
23/01	Botafogo 2–4 Honved (Hungary)	1
27/01	Botafogo 5–1 A.I.K. (Sweden)	1
02/02	Botafogo 1–2 Cruzeiro	0
03/02	Botafogo 3–1 Atlético-MG	0
07/02	Botafogo-Flamengo select 6–2 Honved (Hungary)	1
17/02	Botafogo 1–2 Valeriodoce-MG	0
21/02	Botafogo 2–2 Internacional-SP	0
23/02	Botafogo 4–2 América-SP	0
24/02	Botafogo 0–0 Catanduva-SP	0
21/03	Brazil 7–1 Ecuador	0
23/03	Brazil 9–0 Colombia	0
13/04	Brazil 1–1 Peru	0
21/04	Brazil 1–0 Peru	0
25/04	Botafogo 2–3 Vasco	0
27/04	Botafogo 2–0 Portuguesa-SP	0
28/04	Botafogo 4–1 Ituitaba-MG	0
01/05	Botafogo 2–2 Botafogo-SP	1
02/05	Botafogo 2–1 Uberaba-MG	0
03/05	Botafogo 2–2 Uberaba-MG	0
05/05	Botafogo 1–1 Corinthians	0
09/05	Botafogo 3–3 Fluminense	1
11/05	Botafogo 1–5 Santos	0
15/05	Botafogo 3–1 América-RJ	1
18/05	Botafogo 1–0 São Paulo	0
19/05	Botafogo 4–1 Ass. Olímpica-MG	1
22/05	Botafogo 1–4 Flamengo	0
24/05	Botafogo 3–3 Sport-MG	0
28/05	Botafogo 7–3 América Três Rios-RJ	1
01/06	Botafogo 2–2 Palmeiras	0

02/06	Botafogo 1–1 Londrina-PR	1
11/06	Brazil 2–1 Portugal	0
16/06	Brazil 3–0 Portugal	0
20/06	Botafogo 3–2 Náutico-PE	0
22/06	Botafogo 2–2 Ceará	1
23/06	Botafogo 2–0 Ferroviário-CE	1
25/06	Botafogo 4–0 Maranhense select	1
29/06	Botafogo 2–0 Sevilla (Sp)	0
04/07	Botafogo 0–3 Barcelona (Sp)	0
06/07	Botafogo 4–0 Nacional (Uruguay)	0
09/07	Botafogo 4–0 Sevilla (Sp)	2
14/07	Botafogo 2–2 Nacional (Uru)	0
18/07	Botafogo 2–2 Barcelona (Sp)	1
27/07	Botafogo 3–1 Bonsucesso	0
04/08	Botafogo 4–0 Canto do Rio	0
10/08	Botafogo 6–1 Madureira	1
18/08	Botafogo 2–0 Olaria	0
24/08	Botafogo 5–1 Portuguesa-RJ	1
01/09	Botafogo 3–3 Flamengo	0
07/09	Botafogo 2–0 São Cristóvão	0
14/09	Botafogo 3–1 América-RJ	0
22/09	Botafogo 2–2 Vasco	1
29/09	Botafogo 0–1 Fluminense	0
05/10	Botafogo 0–0 Bangu	0
13/10	Botafogo 5–0 São Cristóvão	1
20/10	Botafogo 1–0 Bangu	0
27/10	Botafogo 3–1 Bonsucesso	0
01/11	Botafogo 4–1 Olaria	0
10/11	Botafogo 0–3 Vasco	0
17/11	Botafogo 1–1 Flamengo	0
30/11	Botafogo 2–1 América-RJ	0
07/12	Botafogo 3–0 Canto do Rio	1
14/12	Botafogo 4–2 Madureira	0
22/12	Botafogo 6–2 Fluminense	1
29/12	Botafogo 0–3 Alajuela (Ecu)	0

	1958	GOALS
01/01	Botafogo 0–3 Huracán (Argentina)	0
05/01	Botafogo 2–1 Saprisa (Ecu)	0
12/01	Botafogo 2–1 Nacional (Col)	0
15/01	Botafogo 0–0 Deportivo (Col)	0
19/01	Botafogo 4–1 Curacao select	1
21/01	Botafogo 4–0 Curacao select	1
26/01	Botafogo 4–0 Fraquiteño (El Salvador)	3
30/01	Botafogo 3–1 Atletico Marte (El Salvador)	1
02/02	Botafogo 1–1 Independiente (Arg)	0
06/02	Botafogo 0–2 Guadalajara (Mexico)	0
09/02	Botafogo 4–3 Toluca (Mex)	2
16/02	Botafogo 3–1 Zacatepec (Mex)	1
20/02	Botafogo 1–1 River Plate (Arg)	0

27/02	Botafogo 3–2 Corinthians	0
02/03	Botafogo 2–2 Santos	0
08/03	Botafogo 1–2 Portuguesa-SP	0
12/03	Botafogo 7–3 América-RJ	1
16/03	Botafogo 1–1 Fluminense	0
20/03	Botafogo 0–4 Flamengo	0
23/03	Botafogo 5–4 Atlético-MG	1
26/03	Botafogo 2–4 Vasco	0
29/03	Botafogo 3–2 Palmeiras	0
30/03	Botafogo 5–5 Carlos Renaux -SC	0
01/04	Botafogo 5–1 Santa Catarina Select	1
06/04	Botafogo 2–5 São Paulo	0
18/05	Brazil 3–1 Bulgaria	0
21/05	Brazil 5–0 Corinthians	2
29/05	Brazil 4–0 Fiorentina (Italy)	1
15/06	Brazil 2–0 USSR	0
19/06	Brazil 1–0 Wales	0
24/06	Brazil 5–2 France	0
29/06	Brazil 5–2 Sweden	0
13/07	Botafogo 2–1 Fluminense	0
16/07	Botafogo 3–1 Uzina-CE	2
18/07	Botafogo 2–0 Maranhense select	1
20/07	Botafogo 2–2 River-PI	0
23/07	Botafogo 1–0 Bahia	1
26/07	Botafogo 1–2 São Cristóvão	0
02/08	Botafogo 6–0 Olaria	0
10/08	Botafogo 0–1 Bangu	0
15/08	Botafogo 3–1 Bonsucesso	1
17/08	Botafogo 3–0 Santo Antônio-ES	2
19/08	Botafogo 2–2 Uberaba	1
23/08	Botafogo 4–0 Portuguesa-RJ	0
30/08	Botafogo 2–2 Flamengo	1
05/09	Botafogo 3–3 América-RJ	1
10/09	Botafogo 2–1 River Plate (Arg)	1
14/09	Botafogo 3–1 Canto do Rio	0
16/09	Botafogo 0–0 Grêmio	0
21/09	Botafogo 2–1 Madureira	0
28/09	Botafogo 2–3 Vasco	1
05/10	Botafogo 2–0 Bonsucesso	0
12/10	Botafogo 3–0 Madureira	0
18/10	Botafogo 5–0 Olaria	2
25/10	Botafogo 1–0 Portuguesa-RJ	1
01/11	Botafogo 2–2 Canto do Rio	1
09/11	Botafogo 3–2 Flamengo	0
15/11	Botafogo 2–2 Bangu	1
22/11	Botafogo 2–0 Fluminense	0
30/11	Botafogo 2–4 América-RJ	1
07/12	Botafogo 2–0 Vasco	0
13/12	Botafogo 4–1 São Cristóvão	0
27/12	Botafogo 1–2 Flamengo	0

GARRINCHA

	1959	GOALS
03/01	Botafogo 1-0 Vasco	0
10/01	Botafogo 1-2 Vasco	0
14/01	Botafogo 2-2 Flamengo	0
25/01	Botafogo 6-0 Goiânia-GO	2
27/01	Botafogo 3-1 Atlético-MG	1
01/02	Botafogo 1-0 Bahia	0
04/02	Botafogo 4-0 CSA-AL	0
15/02	Botafogo 6-0 Tuna Luso-PA	1
18/02	Botafogo 2-1 Remo-PA	0
22/02	Botafogo 1-1 Paysandú-PA	0
24/02	Botafogo 2-3 Santa Cruz-PE	1
21/03	Brazil 4-2 Bolivia	0
26/03	Brazil 3-1 Uruguay	0
29/03	Brazil 4-1 Paraguay	0
04/04	Brazil 1-1 Argentina	0
09/04	Botafogo 2-4 Santos	0
12/04	Botafogo 3-0 Goiás	0
15/04	Botafogo 1-4 Palmeiras	1
19/04	Botafogo 3-1 São Paulo	0
21/04	Botafogo 4-4 Internacional-RS	1
25/04	Botafogo 3-1 América-RJ	2
30/04	Botafogo 0-2 Vasco	0
13/05	Brazil 2-0 England	
18/05	Botafogo 0-1 A.I.K. (Sweden)	0
22/05	Botafogo 3-1 Gimonas (Swe)	1
24/05	Botafogo 1-2 Staevnet (Denmark)	1
26/05	Botafogo 5-0 Gothenburg select (Swe)	0
28/05	Botafogo 3-1 Norkopping (Swe)	0
30/05	Botafogo 3-1 Liège (Belgium)	1
03/06	Botafogo 2-2 Austria	1
06/06	Botafogo 5-0 Anderlecht (Bel)	0
10/06	Botafogo 4-3 Fortuna 054 (Holland)	0
12/06	Botafogo 4-1 Willen (Hol)	1
14/06	Botafogo 4-0 Sarre select (Ger)	1
17/06	Botafogo 2-2 Milan (It)	0
21/06	Botafogo 1-4 Santos (in Spain)	0
24/06	Botafogo 6-4 Atlético Madrid (Sp)	0
25/06	Botafogo 1-3 Feyenoord (Hol)	0
29/06	Botafogo 2-1 Sevilla (Sp)	0
11/07	Botafogo 5-1 Madureira	1
18/07	Botafogo 2-0 Portuguesa-RJ	0
26/07	Botafogo 0-0 Bangu	0
01/08	Botafogo 6-0 Bonsucesso	2
04/08	Botafogo 6-0 Sport-PE	1
08/08	Botafogo 4-0 Madureira	0
16/08	Botafogo 3-1 América-RJ	0
29/08	Botafogo 1-0 Vasco	0
05/09	Botafogo 2-0 Canto do Rio	1
13/09	Botafogo 1-2 Fluminense	0

26/09	Botafogo 2-1 São Cristóvão	0
03/10	Botafogo 2-1 Flamengo	0
10/10	Botafogo 6-1 Portuguesa-RJ	0
17/10	Botafogo 4-0 Olaria	0
25/10	Botafogo 2-6 Flamengo	0
31/10	Botafogo 5-0 Madureira	1
07/11	Botafogo 3-0 Bonsucesso	0
15/11	Botafogo 2-4 Vasco	2
20/11	Botafogo 3-1 Canto do Rio	0
29/11	Botafogo 1-3 América-RJ	0
05/12	Botafogo 3-0 São Cristóvão	1
13/12	Botafogo 1-4 Bangu	0
16/12	Carioca select 6-1 River Plate (Arg)	2
20/12	Botafogo 3-3 Fluminense	1
26/12	Botafogo 4-1 Bangu	1
30/12	Botafogo 2-0 Bangu	0

	1960	GOALS
06/01	Botafogo 1-2 Liga Univ. (Ecu)	0
10/01	Botafogo 1-0 Milionários (Col)	0
17/01	Botafogo 4-2 Santa Fé (Col)	0
24/01	Botafogo 2-0 Austria	0
27/01	Botafogo 2-0 Deportivo Cali (Col)	2
31/01	Botafogo 2-2 Costa Rica	0
07/02	Botafogo 2-0 Communicaciones (Guyana)	0
14/02	Botafogo 3-2 Necaxa (Mex)	0
21/02	Botafogo 0-1 León (Mex)	0
24/02	Botafogo 3-1 Mexico	0
28/02	Botafogo 3-1 Mexico	0
05/03	Botafogo 3-0 Alianza (Peru)	2
09/03	Botafogo 3-0 Universitário (Peru)	0
17/03	Botafogo 0-0 América-RJ	0
20/03	Botafogo 1-1 Corinthians	0
24/03	Botafogo 1-3 Flamengo	0
27/03	Botafogo 2-2 Fluminense	0
02/04	Botafogo 3-2 São Paulo	0
07/04	Botafogo 1-1 Vasco	0
09/04	Botafogo 3-2 Portuguesa-SP	0
16/04	Botafogo 3-0 Santos	1
23/04	Botafogo 3-1 Palmeiras	0
29/04	Brazil 5-0 Egypt	1
01/05	Brazil 3-1 Egypt	0
05/05	Brazil 3-0 Egypt	1
08/05	Brazil 7-1 Malmoe (Swe)	0
10/05	Brazil 4-3 Denmark	0
12/05	Brazil 2-2 Internazionale (It)	0
16/05	Brazil 4-0 Sporting (Portugal)	1
22/05	Botafogo 0-2 Alianza (Peru)	0
26/05	Botafogo 1-1 Sp. Cristal (Peru)	0
29/05	Botafogo 6-2 Universitário (Peru)	0

Date	Match	Goals
10/06	Botafogo 1–0 Bahia	0
12/06	Botafogo 0–0 Bahia	0
16/06	Botafogo 0–1 Palmeiras	0
19/06	Botafogo 4–0 Comercial-MG	0
29/06	Brazil 4–0 Chile	0
24/07	Botafogo 0–1 Fluminense	0
31/07	Botafogo 4–1 Ferroviário-PR	0
03/08	Botafogo 3–0 Portuguesa-RJ	0
07/08	Botafogo 0–0 Flamengo	0
14/08	Botafogo 4–3 Olaria	0
20/08	Botafogo 2–0 Canto do Rio	0
27/08	Botafogo 0–2 Vasco	0
04/09	Botafogo 3–1 Madureira	1
07/09	Botafogo 7–1 Atlético-MG	0
18/09	Botafogo 2–2 América-RJ	0
22/09	Botafogo 4–1 Bonsucesso	0
25/09	Botafogo 3–2 Botafogo-PB	1
01/10	Botafogo 4–2 Bangu	0
08/10	Botafogo 6–0 Olaria	0
15/10	Botafogo 1–1 Bangu	0
20/10	Botafogo 5–0 Portuguesa-RJ	2
23/10	Botafogo 6–1 Uberlândia-MG	1
30/10	Botafogo 4–1 Flamengo	1
04/11	Botafogo 3–1 São Cristóvão	1
06/11	Botafogo 6–1 Machadense-MG	2
09/11	Botafogo 2–1 América-MG	0
12/11	Botafogo 4–0 Canto do Rio	1
15/11	Botafogo 0–1 Guarani-SP	0
17/11	Botafogo 3–2 Ferroviário-PR	1
27/11	Botafogo 1–1 Fluminense	0
04/12	Botafogo 2–1 Vasco	0
11/12	Botafogo 3–3 América-RJ	1
17/12	Botafogo 5–3 Bonsucesso	1

1961		GOALS
11/01	Botafogo 0–0 Municipal (Peru)	0
14/01	Botafogo 2–0 Universitário (Peru)	0
18/01	Botafogo 4–2 Sporting Boys (Peru)	2
20/01	Botafogo 4–2 Milionários (Col)	2
21/01	Botafogo 4–0 Alianza (Peru)	1
24/01	Botafogo 1–0 Municipal (Peru)	0
03/02	Botafogo 4–1 Alajuela (Ecu)	2
07/02	Botafogo 4–0 Herediano (Ecu)	1
12/02	Botafogo 5–0 Santa Fé (Bolivia)	2
15/02	Botafogo 3–1 Deportivo (Col)	1
19/02	Botafogo 5–0 Pichincha select (Ecu)	1
25/02	Botafogo 3–1 Colo-Colo (Chile)	1
01/03	Botafogo 3–1 Portuguesa-SP	1
04/03	Botafogo 1–0 Corinthians	0
09/03	Botafogo 4–3 Fluminense	0

Date	Match	Goals
15/03	Botafogo 1–3 América-RJ	0
18/03	Botafogo 5–1 Vasco	0
22/03	Botafogo 3–0 Flamengo	0
01/04	Botafogo 2–4 Santos	0
05/04	Botafogo 1–1 São Paulo	0
07/04	Botafogo 4–2 Uberaba-MG	1
09/04	Botafogo 4–2 Uberlândia-MG	2
13/04	Botafogo 1–0 Corinthians	0
19/04	Botafogo 0–0 Palmeiras	0
23/04	Botafogo 2–1 Santos	0
30/04	Brazil 2–0 Paraguay	0
03/05	Brazil 3–2 Paraguay	0
07/05	Brazil 2–1 Chile	1
11/05	Brazil 1–0 Chile	0
17/05	Botafogo 1–3 Austria	0
20/05	Botafogo 2–2 Red Star (Yugoslavia)	1
23/05	Botafogo 1–1 Ujpest (Hungary)	0
26/05	Botafogo 4–1 Bayern 1860 (Ger)	1
28/05	Botafogo 7–2 Antwerp select (Bel)	0
30/05	Botafogo 1–3 Anderlecht (Bel)	0
01/06	Botafogo 1–2 Standard (Bel)	0
07/06	Botafogo 2–2 Milan (It)	0
10/06	Botafogo 3–0 Angers (Fr)	0
14/06	Botafogo 7–1 Servette (Swe)	0
16/06	Botafogo 2–1 Zamaleck (Egypt)	0
21/06	Botafogo 3–1 Toulouse (Fr)	1
24/06	Botafogo 2–3 Valencia (Sp)	0
27/06	Botafogo 2–3 Barcelona (Sp)	1
23/07	Botafogo 1–0 Operário-SC	0
17/08	Botafogo 1–1 Vasco	0
20/08	Botafogo 4–0 São Cristóvão	1
27/08	Botafogo 2–0 América-RJ	0
30/08	Botafogo 8–1 Londrina-PR	3
02/09	Botafogo 3–0 Bonsucesso	0
07/09	Botafogo 6–2 Estela do Norte-ES	2
10/09	Botafogo 2–2 Flamengo	0
14/09	Botafogo 3–0 Canto do Rio	0
17/09	Botafogo 6–0 Guará-DF	1
20/09	Botafogo 1–1 América-MG	0
24/09	Botafogo 2–2 Fluminense	0
01/10	Botafogo 2–0 Bangu	0
05/10	Botafogo 4–1 São Cristóvão	0
08/10	Botafogo 1–0 Olaria	0
15/10	Botafogo 2–2 Fluminense	0
31/10	Botafogo 1–1 Colo-Colo (Chile)	0
04/11	Botafogo 1–1 Indep.-Rivadávia (Arg)	1
14/11	Botafogo 2–1 América-RJ	2
19/11	Botafogo 4–0 Vasco	0
26/11	Botafogo 1–1 Flamengo	0
03/12	Botafogo 3–1 Bangu	0

07/12	Botafogo 2–0 São Cristóvão	0
10/12	Botafogo 2–1 Olaria	1
14/12	Botafogo 1–0 Fluminense	1
17/12	Botafogo 1–2 América	1
22/12	Botafogo 2–1 Vasco	0
28/12	Botafogo 3–0 Flamengo	0

1962		GOALS
03/01	Botafogo 3–0 Santos	0
10/01	Botafogo 4–2 Ferencvaros (Cze)	0
13/01	Botafogo 3–2 Colo-Colo (Chile)	1
18/01	Botafogo 3–0 Toluca (Mex)	0
25/01	Botafogo 0–2 Atlanta (Mex)	0
01/02	Botafogo 4–2 Ujpest (Hungary)	1
04/02	Botafogo 2–1 America (Mex)	0
07/02	Botafogo 4–1 Municipal (Peru)	0
10/02	Botafogo 3–1 Alianza (Peru)	0
13/02	Botafogo 0–1 Palmeiras	0
18/02	Botafogo 1–0 Fluminense	0
21/02	Botafogo 4–1 Vasco	0
26/02	Botafogo 4–1 América-RJ	0
01/03	Botafogo 2–3 Flamengo	1
11/03	Botafogo 2–1 São Paulo	1
14/03	Botafogo 1–0 Flamengo	1
17/03	Botafogo 3–1 Palmeiras	0
21/04	Brazil 6–0 Paraguay	1
24/04	Brazil 4–0 Paraguay	0
06/05	Brazil 2–1 Portugal	0
09/05	Brazil 1–0 Portugal	0
12/05	Brazil 3–1 Wales	1
16/05	Brazil 3–1 Wales	0
30/05	Brazil 2–0 Mexico	0
02/06	Brazil 0–0 Czechoslovakia	0
06/06	Brazil 2–1 Spain	0
10/06	Brazil 3–1 England	2
13/06	Brazil 4–2 Chile	2
17/06	Brazil 3–1 Czechoslovakia	0
	Twice World Cup Winners	
28/06	Botafogo 1–0 Palmeiras	1
04/07	Botafogo 3–0 Atlético-MG	0
08/07	Botafogo 1–0 Bonsucesso	0
15/07	Botafogo 2–0 Portuguesa RJ	0
29/07	Botafogo 0–0 Bangu	0
04/08	Botafogo 0–1 Vasco	0
08/08	Botafogo 4–0 Madureira	0
15/08	Botafogo 3–1 Santa Fé (Bolivia)	1
19/08	Botafogo 6–5 Milionários (Col)	2
22/08	Botafogo 3–1 Deportivo (Col)	1
30/08	Botafogo 2–0 Canto do Rio	0
02/09	Botafogo 5–2 São Cristóvão	2

07/09	Botafogo 1–0 América-RJ	0
15/09	Botafogo 2–0 Fluminense	0
23/09	Botafogo 3–1 Flamengo	1
28/09	Botafogo 2–0 Campo Grande	1
03/10	Botafogo 6–1 Royal-RJ	0
06/10	Botafogo 4–1 Bonsucesso	1
20/10	Botafogo 2–0 Olaria	0
27/10	Botafogo 1–1 Bangu	0
04/11	Botafogo 1–1 Vasco	0
14/11	Botafogo 6–1 Madureira	0
18/11	Botafogo 2–1 Canto do Rio	0
21/11	Botafogo 2–2 Internacional-RS	0
25/11	Botafogo 0–0 São Cristóvão	0
28/11	Botafogo 2–2 Internacional-RS	0
30/11	Botafogo 2–0 Internacional-RS	0
05/12	Botafogo 3–1 América-RJ	1
08/12	Botafogo 1–0 Fluminense	0
15/12	Botafogo 3–0 Flamengo	2
19/12	Carioca select 6–4 São Paulo select	1

1963		GOALS
12/01	Botafogo 1–2 Peñarol (Uru)	0
16/01	Botafogo 5–0 Barcelona (Ecu)	2
20/01	Botafogo 2–0 América (Col)	1
24/01	Botafogo 1–0 Deportivo (Col)	0
27/01	Botafogo 0–0 Milionários (Col)	0
04/02	Botafogo 1–1 Sp. Cristal (Peru)	1
09/02	Botafogo 0–1 Peñarol (Uru)	0
31/03	Botafogo 3–1 Santos	0
02/04	Botafogo 0–5 Santos	0
25/05	Botafogo 2–3 Univ. Chile	0
31/05	Botafogo 2–2 Saarbrucken (Ger)	0
08/06	Botafogo 1–2 Palmeiras	0
11/06	Botafogo 1–0 Anderlecht (Bel)	0
13/06	Botafogo 3–2 Racing de Paris (Fr)	0
15/06	Botafogo 0–0 Vojvódna (Yugoslavia)	0
19/06	Botafogo 0–0 Karisruhe (Ger)	0
30/06	Botafogo 1–0 Alianza (Peru)	0
04/07	Botafogo 3–1 Sp. Cristal (Peru)	0
28/08	Botafogo 0–4 Santos	0
14/09	Botafogo 2–0 América-RJ	0
22/09	Botafogo 2–0 São Cristóvão	1
13/10	Botafogo 0–0 Flamengo	0

1964		GOALS
30/01	Botafogo 3–2 Atlético-MG	1
02/02	Botafogo 2–2 Corinthians	2
07/02	Botafogo 2–3 Corinthians	0
01/03	Botafogo 2–0 Banik Ostrawa (Cze)	0

05/03	Botafogo 2–1 Racing (Argentina)	0
12/03	Botafogo 2–0 The Strongest (Bolivia)	0
15/03	Botafogo 2–1 B. Juniors (Argentina)	0
18/03	Botafogo 5–2 Aurora (Bolivia)	1
11/04	Botafogo 2–1 Flamengo	1
15/04	Botafogo 0–1 Vasco	0
19/04	Botafogo 2–0 Fluminense	0
25/04	Botafogo 1–3 Santos	1
28/04	Botafogo 3–1 Corinthians	0
03/05	Botafogo 4–3 Palmeiras	0
09/05	Botafogo 5–0 Bangu	1
12/07	Botafogo 0–0 América-RJ	0
14/07	Botafogo 4–3 River Plate (Arg)	0
16/07	Botafogo 2–0 Barcelona (Sp)	0
22/07	Botafogo 1–3 Campo Grande	0
09/08	Botafogo 3–0 Madureira	0
06/09	Botafogo 2–0 Fluminense	0

	1965	GOALS
10/01	Botafogo 3–2 Santos	0
13/01	Botafogo 0–0 Universitário (Peru)	0
16/01	Botafogo 3–1 Alianza (Peru)	0
19/01	Botafogo 4–2 Sp. Cr.-Municipal (Peru)	2
22/01	Botafogo 2–1 Universitário (Peru)	0
24/01	Botafogo 6–2 Melgar (Peru)	0
02/02	Botafogo 2–2 América (Mex)	0
06/02	Botafogo 2–2 Oro (Mex)	0
25/04	Botafogo 2–2 Portuguesa-SP	0
02/05	Botafogo 0–2 Corinthians	0
08/05	Botafogo 1–0 Flamengo	0
12/05	Botafogo 2–7 Fluminense	0
15/05	Botafogo 5–0 São Paulo	0
20/05	Botafogo 0–1 Vasco	0
02/06	Brazil 5–0 Belgium	0
06/06	Brazil 2–0 Germany	0
09/06	Brazil 0–0 Argentina	0
17/06	Brazil 3–0 Algeria	0
24/06	Brazil 0–0 Portugal	0
04/07	Brazil 3–0 USSR	0
04/08	Botafogo 4–0 América-RJ	0
11/08	Botafogo 3–0 Vasco	1
15/08	Botafogo 4–0 Tupi-Tupinambás-MG	0
22/08	Botafogo 1–0 Flamengo	1
05/09	Botafogo 0–2 Vasco	0
07/09	Botafogo 8–1 Entrerriense-RJ	0
12/09	Botafogo 3–2 Minas Gerais select	0
15/09	Botafogo 2–1 Portuguesa-RJ	0

	1966	GOALS
02/03	Corinthians 0–3 Vasco	0
10/03	Corinthians 1–5 Botafogo	0
13/03	Corinthians 2–1 Cruzeiro	1
19/03	Corinthians 2–0 São Paulo	1
21/03	Corinthians 1–2 Palmeiras	0
24/03	Corinthians 3–1 Flamengo	0
27/03	Corinthians 0–0 Santos	0
01/05	Brazil 2–0 Rio Grande do Sul select	0
14/05	Brazil 3–1 Wales	1
19/05	Brazil 1–0 Chile	0
04/06	Brazil 4–0 Peru	0
08/06	Brazil 2–1 Poland	1
21/06	Brazil 5–0 Atlético Madrid (Sp)	0
27/06	Brazil 8–2 Atvidaberg (Swe)	0
30/06	Brazil 3–2 Sweden	0
04/07	Brazil 4–2 A.I.K. (Swe)	1
08/07	Brazil 3–1 Malmoe (Sweden)	0
12/07	Brazil 2–0 Bulgaria	1
15/07	Brazil 1–3 Hungary	0
03/09	Corinthians 1–1 Real Madrid (Sp)	0
05/09	Corinthians 0–2 Cadiz (Sp)	0
09/10	Corinthians 0–3 Santos	0

	1967	GOALS
	Friendlies with Portuguesa-RJ	

	1968	GOALS
30/11	Flamengo 0–2 Vasco	0

	1969	GOALS
19/01	Flamengo 2–2 América-RJ	1
26/01	Flamengo 3–1 Robin Hood-SUR	0
28/01	Flamengo 2–3 Transwall-SUR	1
30/01	Flamengo 4–0 Robin Hood-SUR	0
02/02	Flamengo 2–0 Fast-AM	1
04/02	Flamengo 0–0 Nacional-AM	0
06/02	Flamengo 3–0 Paysandú-PA	0
09/02	Flamengo 2–1 ABC-RN	1
11/02	Flamengo 3–0 América-RN	0
13/02	Flamengo 2–0 Fluminense-RN	0
09/03	Flamengo 2–0 São Cristóvão	0
02/04	Flamengo 1–1 Bangu	0
12/04	Flamengo 1–0 Campo Grande	0

GARRINCHA

1970–1971

Friendlies with teams in Italy

	1972	GOALS
23/02	Olaria 1–1 Flamengo	0
01/03	Olaria 1–2 Rio Branco-ES	0
04/03	Olaria 1–1 América-RJ	0
23/03	Olaria 2–2 Comercial-SP	1
25/03	Olaria 1–5 Flumínense	0
16/04	Olaria 1–0 Bangu	0
19/04	Olaria 2–0 Bonsucesso	0
21/05	Olaria 0–1 América-RJ	0
19/07	Olaria 1–1 Botafogo	0
23/08	Olaria 0–1 Botafogo	0

	1973	GOALS
19/12	Brazil select 2–1 Foreign select	0
	Gratitude Game	

	1974–1982	GOALS
	Various appearances for small clubs	

25/12/82	Londrina-DF 0–1 AGAP-DF	0
	Last game	

398

Index